GCE A

A2 Level for **OCR**

Travel & Tourism

Ann Rowe • John D. Smith • Rosemary Demaine

Sue Stewart • Fiona Warburton

www.heinemann.co.uk

✓ Free online support
✓ Useful weblinks
✓ 24 hour online ordering

01865 888058

Heinemann

Inspiring generations

Heinemann Educational Publishers
Halley Court, Jordan Hill, Oxford OX2 8EJ
Part of Harcourt Education

Heinemann is the registered trademark of Harcourt Education Limited

First published 2006

10 09 08 07 06
10 9 8 7 6 5 4 3 2 1

British Library Cataloguing in Publication Data is available
from the British Library on request.

10-digit ISBN: 0 435 463 55 1
13-digit ISBN: 978 0 435 463 55 1

Edited by Alistair Nunn
Typeset and illustrated by Tek-Art, Surrey
Original illustrations © Harcourt Education Limited, 2006
Cover design by Pete Stratton
Printed in the UK by Scotprint
Cover photo: © Alamy Images
Picture research by Chrissie Martin

Websites
Please note that the examples of websites suggested in this book were correct at the time of
writing. It is essential for tutors to preview each site before use, to ensure that the URL is still
accurate and the content is appropriate. We suggest that tutors bookmark useful sites and
consider enabling students to access them through the school or college intranet.

Contents

Acknowledgements

The publishers and authors wish to thank the following for their kind permission to reproduce material and photographs in this book.

Austrian Airlines – page 296
Barden Mill Shopping Centre – page 6
The Beatles Story Ltd – page 103
Bolton Arena – page 14
Brecon Group for Community and Tourism – page 12
The British Canoe Union – page 194
British Mountaineering Council – page 193
Coggeshall Parish Council – page 109
Department of Tourism and Commerce Marketing, Dubai – page 186
Destination Lancashire – page 243
Earthwatch Institute – page 126
easyJet – pages 240, 250, 310
Gloucester City Council – page 275
Investors in People – page 308
Kaikoura District Council – page 145
Keswick Indoor Climbing Wall – page 179
Lake District National Park Authority – page 184
MEDASSET – page 139
Mercury Direct – page 66
Natural History Museum – page 296
NetTours – page 86, 92, 93
Newlands Adventure Centre – page 181
Paul's Tours sro – page 88
Pleasure Beach Blackpool – page 66
Responsibletravel.com – page 139
Rookin House Farm – page 181
Survival – page 126
TUI UK – pages 134, 276, 295
WalktheTalk.hk – page 100
World Tourism Organisation – page 151
World Travel and Tourism Council – page 15
www.career.edu – page 294
www.expatsinchina.com – page 215
www.islandbreaks.co.uk – page 245
www.staruk.org.uk – page 230
www.traveljobsearch.com – page 294

Crown copyright material is reproduced with the permission of the controller of HMSO – page 113

Photo acknowledgements
Harcourt Education Ltd / Debbie Rowe – page 1
Alamy Images / Picture Contact – page 22
Getty Images / Photodisc – pages 30, 249
Alamy Images / Justin Kase – page 33
Harcourt Education Ltd / Devon Olugbena Shaw – page 35
Alamy Images / char abumansoor – page 45
Emphics – page 47
istockPhoto / Milan Radulovic – page 51
iStockPhoto / Ross Williamson – page 52
Harcourt Education Ltd / Mark Bassett – page 76
Alamy Images / Picture Contact – page 81
NetTours – pages 92, 93
John D. Smith – pages 96, 99, 110, 111, 161, 178, 182, 187
Alamy Images / Chris Fotoman Smith / Alamy – page 119
Alamy Images / Bill Lyons – page 130
Alamy Images / Craig Lovell / Eagle Visions Photography – page 131
Alamy Images / StockShot – page 133
Getty Images / Photodisc – page 135
Corbis – pages 136, 157, 237, 300
Alamy Images / Dennis Hallinan – page 136
Alamy Images / Gavin Hellier – page 203
Alamy Images / Patrick Ward – page 206
Alamy Images / Christian Kober – page 207
Alamy Images / ImageState – pages 214, 239, 286
Sarah Lee / ENO – page 216
Alamy Images / World Pictures Ltd – page 217
iStockPhoto / Graeme Purdy – page 227
iStockPhoto / Sue Colvil – page 252
Getty Images / News and Sport – page 262
Alamy Images / Jochem Wijnands – page 283
Alamy Images / Werner Dietrich – page 306

Introduction

As you will have realised from your study of travel and tourism at AS level, this industry is growing rapidly and developing continually, so there are plenty of employment opportunities open to you at many different levels of operation.

About the OCR qualification

Having achieved an AS level award in travel and tourism, whether a single award for three units or a double award for six units, you will now want to convert these into an A2 qualification, again either a single award by studying three units or a double award by studying six units. For the single award, you will need to study units 9 and 10, which are mandatory, and choose one of the optional units, 11–14. You will sit an external examination for unit 9 and produce portfolio evidence for the other two units. For the double award, you will need to study units 9, 10, 15 and 16, which are mandatory, and choose two from the optional units, 11–14. You will sit two examinations, for units 9 and 15, and produce portfolios for four units – 10, 16 and two optional units.

The A2 course should help you to:

* demonstrate your understanding of theory from the AS level and apply it at a higher level

* assess and analyse tourism development and how it affects communities and travel and tourism organisations in all ownership sectors, both globally and nationally

* gain experience and confidence in planning and running a travel and tourism event, which will involve working as a team member

* broaden your experience of marketing practices and principles when undertaking the event or studying this area in more depth for the A2 double award examination

* develop your understanding of human resource issues within the industry and how these are affected by changes in demand for products or services and also by national and international legislation

* present yourself for interview and gain confidence in personal presentation for an interview

* have an opportunity to specialise in tourism development issues, ecotourism and cultural tourism

* appreciate the significance of the values and attitudes of key stakeholders as well as evaluate your own values and attitudes in relation to travel and tourism issues

* use the skills of research, evaluation and problem solving to a higher level than at AS so that you are able to analyse issues effectively and to justify any recommended improvements or developments

* develop your communication, information technology and number skills through presentations, the production of materials for portfolios and the analysis of statistical information.

You will find that, to succeed at A2 level, you need to be able to select appropriate information which will then be analysed and evaluated, and more marks are awarded for this skill than at AS level. As this qualification is vocational, it is important that you participate in the industry and select appropriate examples from the industry for your studies. You may have undertaken work experience, have a part-time job in the industry, or have undertaken visits to travel and tourism organisations and destinations during your AS studies; this type of experience should be continued during your A2 studies in order to develop greater awareness of the issues relevant to the industry, so that you can use appropriate examples in your work.

Understanding the marking scheme

As for AS level, there are three mark bands for each Assessment Objective (AO). To reach the second mark band you must ensure you have addressed all the points in the first mark band. Use the specification to guide you as to content; guidance is also given throughout the book. The totals for each Assessment Objective are added together to give you a final mark for each unit. It is your total mark for the unit which will be used to decide your final grade for the whole qualification.

As an example of this scoring, consider the assessment evidence needed for unit 10, 'Event management'.

* AO1 relates to the preparation of a business plan for your intended group project and if your work does not contain explanation of some or all of the components of the business plan (such as aims, objectives, customers, marketing, resource needs, team roles, staffing, timescales, legal

requirements or any information regarding how the event will be financed), or it is not laid out logically, then you will not have reached mark band 2. Your marks would therefore fall within the mark band 1 range and perhaps receive only 3 marks.

✱ For AO2, you may have demonstrated that you can effectively contribute to the planning, preparation and running of the event and your record of contribution (log-book) shows how you have been involved with the team and worked well as a team member. You will also have shown how you dealt with any problems experienced during the preparation and management of the project, though this may not have been done very sympathetically or without full consideration of others in the group and their feelings. You will also have provided an observation statement from your tutor which gives details of how you contributed to the team project. This type of work would fall within mark band 2, and you may get 6 marks for this.

✱ Your work for AO3 may show that you have undertaken extensive research from a broad range of sources when assessing the feasibility of the project and during the preparation and management of the project, which are clearly indexed. These might have included primary and secondary research into the feasibility of the project, and all the research undertaken was relevant to the decisions about the viability of the project, the operation of the project to meet relevant legal and financial constraints and resource issues. You might have produced appropriate contingency plans to cover potential problems during the development and running of the project, and fed appropriate information to other members of the team. This level of work would come within mark band 3, and may receive 11 marks.

✱ If your evaluation for AO4 covers your own performance and that of the team, both during and after the project, and you make some recommendations for improvement which are realistic but do not show strong analysis or effective use of evaluative tools, your use of terminology is demonstrated in your presentation and your understanding of the principles of successful event management is conveyed, this level of work would fall within mark band 2 and may receive 9 marks.

Your marks for this unit would therefore be 3 + 6 + 11 + 9, making 29 out of a possible 50 marks.

About this book

This book has been prepared to help you understand the units of the OCR qualification. There is a chapter for each unit, which has been written by senior examiners and moderators who have been involved with the development of the qualification. Each chapter will give you the knowledge required for that unit, with activities and discussion points to help you develop this understanding and apply it to various situations, which may involve some analytical skills. There is also guidance as to what is required for the assessment of each unit.

Each unit links very closely to the OCR syllabus. The 'What you need to learn' section of the specification is closely mirrored in the presentation of the units, so it will be easy for you to ensure you have covered all the knowledge elements. It is advisable to work thoroughly through each unit you are currently studying, rather than 'dropping into' a section. In order to achieve higher marks in the assessment (whether through examination or portfolio evidence) you will need to demonstrate in your evidence to examiners or moderators not only a thorough understanding of that particular unit but also your ability to analyse and evaluate relevant features.

Special features of this book

* **Think it over** is designed to provoke discussion on issues arising as you study a topic.

* **Key terms** are flagged to help you with the terminology.

* **Activities** are suggested that will give you more background information and insight.

* **Case studies** will give you an insight into real events and people and provide opportunities for discussion in your class groups or for individual work.

* **Theory into practice** activities are opportunities to implement the knowledge you have gained.

* **Assessment guidance** tells you more specifically how you can meet the evidence requirements for the unit.

* **Knowledge check** is there to aid your revision, particularly for the examined units.

Keep up to date!

Travel and tourism is such a dynamic industry that even by the time this book is published there will have been changes – it could be within an organisation, regulations made by governments, companies being taken over or merged. It is therefore important to keep up to date with developments. All the information given in this book was current and relevant at the time of writing, but you still need to discuss issues with travel and tourism employers and to read relevant articles in the daily, weekend and trade press. You will need to be able to demonstrate in your written work that you are able to analyse and evaluate trends in the industry and use the most up-to-date information that is available to you.

Enjoy your studies!

Tourism development

This unit covers the following sections:

* Agents of tourism development
* Objectives of tourism development
* Impacts of tourism development
* Destination management

Introduction

As you have learned throughout your studies, tourism is continuing to grow and develop both domestically and internationally. According to the World Tourism Organization, there will be 1.6 billion tourist trips made per year by 2020. So what does this mean to the many tourist destinations around the world? Tourism must be managed effectively to ensure that long-term sustainability is achieved and that the benefits are gained by all concerned. The main benefits of tourism development are economic, such as increased income and the creation of jobs. Governments see tourism development as a way of contributing to economic prosperity while at the same time offering social, cultural and environmental benefits. If tourism is managed effectively, the potentially negative effects of tourism development may be reduced.

This unit builds on introductory work carried out in unit 1 ('Introducing travel and tourism') and also units 3 and 4 ('Travel destinations' and 'International travel'). You should also familiarise yourself with unit 12, as ecotourism is closely linked to tourism development. Further reading of that unit will give you a better understanding of the social and ethical issues surrounding tourism development, and a broader knowledge of the various stakeholders involved.

How you will be assessed

This is a mandatory unit and is externally assessed. The external examination will consist of three sections. The first will be based on tourism development in the UK. This may be a rural or an urban destination. The second section will be based on an overseas destination. The third section will be based on a topical and vocationally related case study – this will relate to either a UK or an overseas destination. To pass the external assessment you need to ensure that you have studied all aspects of tourism development, from local issues to global issues, and in a wide range of contexts, places and environments. At the end of this unit you will find a case study with some sample questions that are similar to those you may expect to find in the examination.

In the examination you will be expected to demonstrate the aims and objectives of the different sectors and organisations involved. You will need to demonstrate an ability to analyse and evaluate information from the case study and to relate it to other examples of tourism development.

The marks for the examination will awarded with grades A–E.

Agents of tourism development

This section considers the various kinds of organisation – commercial and non-commercial – that are involved in tourism development. First, though, it will be helpful to look at what we mean exactly by 'tourism development'.

What is tourism development?

Tourism development is, broadly, the establishment of a destination for tourists. It can take many forms, for example the building of a new theme park in the UK, or the marketing of a 'new' destination, such as the Lakshadweep Islands off the coast of India. Whatever form it takes, all tourism development projects can be characterised in the following terms:

* **Infrastructure**. Tourism development can take place only where infrastructure is already being built, or at least is planned. Infrastructure includes roads, airports, ports, power and communication supplies, water and sewage disposal.

* **Scale**. A project can be as small as a local village event attracting day visitors or as big as the redevelopment of New Orleans following Hurricane Katrina in 2005.

* **Rate**. Tourism development can take place very quickly, as happened in the Dominican Republic due to investment, cheaper long-haul air travel and changes in consumer taste. In other areas tourism develops slowly, as has been seen in the growth of ecotourism and 'green' tourism.

* **Worldwide destinations**. Tourism development can occur in less economically developed countries as well as in more economically developed ones. All countries now recognise the economic benefits that tourism can generate.

* **Environments**. Tourism development can occur in urban areas such as towns and cities (Manchester and Barcelona are good examples) or in rural and marine areas (New Zealand and the Sinai Peninsula offer good examples).

* **Impacts**. Tourism development can have both negative and positive effects on the host populations and their environment. These effects will be considered in some depth later in this unit.

> ### Key term
>
> **Development** is a process of economic improvement. This can be new economic activity within an area or the regeneration of a local economy that has gone into decline. It usually involves the cooperation of the various organisations operating within both the public and private sectors. Such bodies are themselves termed agents of tourism development.

The individuals and organisations that carry out tourism development are referred to as the agents of tourism development. They fall into three sectors:

* private sector
* public sector
* voluntary sector.

These commercial and non-commercial organisations (see Table 9.1), which operate on a national and an international scale, often work together in partnerships to develop and promote their individual destinations. They do this to gain economic, social and political benefits (e.g. to increase visitor numbers and generate more income at the destination). There is also, though, scope for conflicts of interest to arise, rather than partnerships. For example, the owner of some land in a potentially prime tourist area may wish to sell it to a property company that could use it for the development of a new hotel or visitor attraction, but a local community group may object to this, on the grounds perhaps that it would cause traffic congestion.

Public, private and voluntary sector organisations will have different aims and objectives. We will now examine each of the three sectors and their reasons for becoming involved in tourism development.

PRIVATE SECTOR ORGANISATIONS	PUBLIC SECTOR ORGANISATIONS	VOLUNTARY SECTOR ORGANISATIONS
Hotel developers Landowners Development companies Consultancies Sponsors Leisure organisations Retail organisations Entertainment organisations	Local authorities National governments National and regional tourist boards Tourist information centres UNESCO (United Nations Educational, Scientific and Cultural Organization)	Community groups Pressure groups Conservation organisations National Trust Tourism Concern WWF (World Wide Fund for Nature)

TABLE 9.1. *Who makes tourism happen? Examples of the agents of tourism development*

Private sector organisations

As you can see from Table 9.1, private sector organisations include a variety of types of commercial company; typically, it is commercial companies that run tourist attractions and provide catering, entertainment and transport. They may be companies in their own right, such as easyJet, or part of larger, perhaps multinational groups, such as the TUI Group and Thomas Cook. Many of the products and services supplied by this sector are available to the general public through sales by travel agents and direct-sell tour operators.

Private sector organisations are in business to maximise income and make a profit. They are reliant on sales of their products and services, so they must ensure that customer perception is wholly positive. This is why such organisations will often support social and environmental causes, and may even commit themselves to this within their mission statements.

Key term

A mission statement is a brief statement of the organisation's purpose that often incorporates an ethical position, the target market, the products or services offered, and an indication of funding or profitability.

Without income and profit, private sector organisations cannot survive and sometimes smaller organisations go out of business or are bought out by larger companies. This is often the case with small independent travel agencies. A public limited company (generally the larger organisations, such as British Airways) must make a profit in order to give a return to their shareholders who have invested in the company. Small private sector organisations such as souvenir shops, local cafés and bed-and-breakfast establishments are unlikely to have shareholders but similarly must make a profit to survive in business.

Private sector organisations can receive funds from several sources, including:

✳ savings (e.g. a small business may make use of its owner's personal savings)

✳ loans (e.g. from banks and building societies)

✳ government grants (the government may lend or even give money if it thinks the venture can contribute to the economic well-being of an area)

✳ sale of shares (e.g. a PLC can sell shares through the Stock Exchange).

Because the travel and tourism industry is such a growth area and involves many people, private companies are keen to be involved, as they see the industry giving them a good return on their investment. Some specific examples are considered below.

Hotel developers

The worldwide demand for hotel accommodation seems to have no end and it is sometimes difficult to keep up to date with hotel development. This is especially true in destinations such as Dubai, Shanghai and Hong Kong. In destinations where tourism development is taking place it is essential for all major hotel groups to keep up with the competition and build hotels in order to gain market share. Many hotel groups continually change ownership and name, but their objectives are the same – to attract and keep as many guests as possible. There are many reward schemes and partnership schemes that encourage guests to stay in partner hotels. This is a good method of ensuring that client satisfaction is monitored and that business is guaranteed.

The Sol Melia hotel group started out 20 years ago by building high-quality hotels in Spain. It now owns hotels and resorts throughout Spain, the Canaries, Mexico and Cuba. Many tourists will choose to stay at these hotels based on past experience. The Starwood Hotel and Resort Group now owns all the Sheraton, Westin, Le Meridien and Luxury Collection hotels. Many of these hotels are found in destinations that are continually developing tourism.

Landowners

Landowners often choose to use their land for tourism development purposes and also to generate income to preserve their assets for the future. Well-known examples include Longleat House and Safari Park, which is the residence of the 7th Marquess of Bath. His house and extensive land has been made famous by the television series *Animal Park*.

Many landowners act as guardians in the preservation and conservation of land. One such example is the Forest of Bowland, an Area of Outstanding Natural Beauty in the management of which landowners play an important part. Landowners often work in close partnership with others in the private and voluntary sectors.

Activity

Look at the 'Partners' page on the website for the Forest of Bowland, www.forestofbowland. co.uk/about_us/partners, and see if you can decide for each organisation listed whether it is a public, private or voluntary organisation.

Development companies

Development companies (or agencies, as they are sometimes called) are very much involved in tourism development in overseas locations. This is partly because these countries lack the knowledge and also the investment to develop new resorts and attractions themselves. Development companies are often responsible for the infrastructure of a region, such as new airport and transport terminals, as well as new hotels and resorts.

Theory into practice

Use the Internet to view the two new Palm Island development projects in Dubai.

See if you can identify the different private sector organisations, and in particular the development companies.

In the UK, development companies are private sector organisations; however, they work very closely with the public and private sector in planning strategies for new developments. This is very important, as new developments can often lead to conflict – such as opposition from a group of local residents – and a coordinated approach that tries to take account of all views is paramount to the success of any new project.

Consultancies

The role of the consultancies is similar to that of the development companies, in that they are private sector bodies that work closely with the public sector in the strategic planning of tourism development projects. Consultants bring specialised technical knowledge and experience. Their role is:

* to liaise with all interested parties in the planning and management of projects

* to deal with legal matters in relation to planning permission and local authority regulations

* to analyse consumer trends and market needs in the provision of new facilities and developments.

Sponsors

The role of the sponsors in tourism development is becoming increasing popular. Although sponsorship is often associated with the marketing and promotion of destinations, there is no doubt that successful sponsorship can help to attract visitors and increase income within a region. A well-known example is First Choice Holidays, a tour operator that sponsors the television programme *I'm a Celebrity: Get Me Out of Here!*

The benefits to the sponsor include:

* increased 'free' advertising
* improved image and company profile
* enhanced awareness and perception of product
* increased sales and income.

FIGURE 9.1. *Promotional leaflet for the Barden Mill shopping centre near Burnley. Many such centres are close to the motorway network, so that they can attract visitors from a wider area*

For the destination or event that is being sponsored the benefits can include:

* increased customer awareness

* financial backing

* improved profile of area or event

* donations from interested parties.

Retail

Shopping seems to have taken the world by storm. Shopping malls originally started in the USA but have spread worldwide. Destinations such as New York, Singapore, Hong Kong and Dubai are now almost as famous for their shops and shopping centres as they are for their leisure attractions. In the UK, designer shopping outlets and mill stores (Figure 9.1) have become significant within the tourism industry. Many of these outlets are promoted by local and regional tourist boards, as they bring visitors and income to an area, and other local attractions and service providers can benefit as a result.

Large purpose-built shopping malls, such as Bluewater in Kent and the Trafford Centre in Manchester, have won prestigious awards for their contribution to the tourism industry. They not only attract domestic visitors but also tourists from overseas, who visit the UK on shorts breaks to take advantage of the range of products on sale. McArthurGlen has 13 designer outlet centres across the UK, France, Austria, Holland and Italy; these draw over 40 million visitors each year.

Entertainment and leisure organisations

Entertainment and leisure are essential components of tourism development. Private sector companies provide a wide variety of entertainment and leisure amenities and facilities – such as theatres, nightclubs, amusement arcades, golf clubs and other sports venues, and attractions such as Sea-Life Centres. Entertainment and leisure centres are only as successful as the number of people they attract.

CASE STUDY

Two leisure developments

The construction of the Lowry Centre on Salford Quays in Manchester was funded from the following public sources: National Lottery Distributors; Arts Council of England; The Millennium Commission; Heritage Lottery Fund; European Regional Development Fund; English Partnerships; Salford City Council; Trafford Park Development Corporation; EDS. However, the ongoing running of the organisation is largely unsupported. Consequently it must fund itself and its growing activities through its earnings, sponsorship and donations. The founder partner sponsor of the Lowry is EDS. EDS, the UK's largest information technology services company, has a five year £2 million sponsorship deal with the Lowry Project. It is one of the UK's largest commercial sponsorships of the arts. EDS will provide IT infrastructure and services. The Digital World Centre is being built as a joint venture between The Lowry Centre Development Company Ltd and Charterhouse Property Group.

According to the website of the Welsh Development Agency (www.wda.co.uk) a £50 million integrated waterfront leisure development is planned for Swansea. This is expected to boost the city's international profile. Plans for the leisure quarter include a casino, a multiscreen cinema, bowling and a wide range of cafés, restaurants and bars. These facilities would be complemented by a 14-storey apartment tower and other accommodation. The proposals were put forward by Discovery Properties Ltd, which was selected by the Welsh Development Agency as the preferred developer. Discovery Properties is working in partnership with City Lofts Group. WDA Area Development Manager Steve Piper said the leisure quarter would provide a significant boost for the city.

For these two cases:

* **Identify the private sector organisations.**

* **Identify the sponsors.**

* **Identify the development companies.**

* **Explain roles and objectives of each of the private sector organisations.**

Sources: Adapted from www.thelowry.com and www.wda.co.uk

Public sector organisations

All public sector organisations, whether in the UK or overseas, are funded and directed by central government. In the case of tourism development in a region you will find that these funds can be accessed from sources such as national tourist offices and regional and local tourist boards.

Why does the public sector get involved in tourism development?

For any region, basic infrastructure, services and facilities are necessary to meet the needs of the host population and those of the visitors. Planning regulations are necessary to look after the public's interest both now and in the future, but an important objective of national and local government is also to increase earnings from tourist receipts. To achieve these objectives, policies are formulated to guide the management and development of tourism. Governments are influenced by market reports on changing attitudes, outlooks and political changes.

We can summarise reasons for public sector involvement in tourism development as follows:

* to improve the balance of payments in a country, region or locality

* to aid regional or local economic development

* to help diversify the economy

* to increase income in a country, region or locality

* to generate new employment opportunities

* to promote an area as being a politically acceptable place to visit

* to promote tourism development.

National governments

National governments' role in tourism policies varies from country to country. In some countries tourism development is heavily supported by the private sector (e.g. Dubai and Singapore). In the case of many developing countries central government plays an extensive role in tourism development by supporting hotel development and subsidising the state airlines.

Good examples are provided by African nations such as Botswana and Namibia.

In the UK, the government does not get directly involved in travel and tourism facilities; instead, it provides financial assistance through government agencies which make grants available to regional and local authorities. It does this through the Department of Culture, Media and Sport (DCMS). DCMS champions good quality and service for tourists, from the UK and overseas. It encourages and helps the tourism industry to improve what it has to offer for all visitors and to promote a positive image abroad. It is also responsible for the listing of historic buildings and scheduling of ancient monuments, as well as the management of the Government Art Collection and for the Royal Parks Agency. From this you can appreciate the importance of the role of the DCMS in the tourism development policy in the UK. The DCMS is also involved in devising the strategic aims for tourism within the European Union (EU), which are to ensure that:

* programmes developed in the EU further the UK's key priorities as far as possible

* EU regulations allow the tourism industry to flourish (specifically, working with the Commission and lead government departments to ensure that the potential impact on the tourism industry is taken into account in developing new legislation in policy areas that affect tourism).

National tourist boards

The roles of national tourist boards are primarily to market and promote their countries on a domestic and international level.

The UK has four tourist boards:

* VisitBritain (formerly the English Tourism Council and the British Tourist Authority, which have now been merged)

* VisitScotland (formerly the Scottish Tourist Board)

* the Northern Ireland Tourist Board

* the Wales Tourist Board.

Speaking at World Travel Market in London in November 2005, Mr Niko Bulic, Director of the Croatian National Tourist Board, confirmed that Croatia was well on target to achieve a total of 255,000 visitors from Great Britain by the end of 2005. He showed that during the first 10 months of the year 251,920 Brits had visited Croatia. This represented a 26% increase on 2004 and was greatly assisted by more tour operators and flights to Croatia. He commented, 'it is the UK tour operators and partners who have had the confidence to operate so many flights and for being prepared to take a risk in Croatia. We are all sharing in our country's success.' He continued to confirm that there are now over 100 tour operators offering Croatia and those new operators who introduced the destination for 2005 were mainly up-market specialists, including Cox & Kings, Bales Tours and Tapestry. After confirming that over £200 million pounds had been invested in Croatian tourism during 2005 (in hotels, resorts and campsites) Mr Bulic stated that the government was strictly controlling all new buildings by means of stringent planning conditions, both in size of building and the types of materials used. The ecological preservation of the sea comes into this category too and, despite sailing holidays being a huge growth area with 50 marinas and over 15,000 sea moorings, development here was now also strictly controlled.

* What sort of private sector bodies were involved in the promotion of Croatia as a tourist destination?

* Why might the Croatian National Tourist Board be concerned about planning regulations?

Source: Adapted from Theodore Koumelis, *Travel Daily News*, 24 November 2005

Local authorities

Tourism development is not a statutory responsibility for local authorities; however, tourism is recognised as a major contributor towards local economies. Therefore in the UK all of the county and district authorities as well as most of the local authorities have established tourism teams that focus their attention on developing tourism within the area.

VisitBritain is a public sector organisation that is funded by central government. Its aim is to market Britain domestically and internationally. It invests £12.9 million in persuading the British to enjoy England! It runs marketing campaigns and builds partnerships with other organisations which have a stake in British and English tourism. For overseas customers it promotes Britain overseas as a tourist destination. For domestic customers it encourages British residents to take additional and/or longer breaks in England. It helps the British tourism industry to address international and domestic markets more effectively. It provides advice to government and devolved administrations on matters affecting tourism, and contributes to wider government objectives. It also works in partnership with the devolved administrations and the national and regional tourist boards to build the British tourism industry. To achieve all goals it seeks to ensure that its staff are open, accessible, professional, accountable and responsive.

* What are the benefits of marketing Britain to the British?

* What are the differences between the roles of national governments and national tourist boards?

Regional tourist boards

The role of regional tourist boards is similar to that of national tourist boards – to promote their area through support and development – but on a much smaller scale. They often work closely with the private sector through the promotion of attractions, facilities and accommodation. Regional tourist boards seek to stimulate and manage the development of tourism to bring economic, social and environmental benefits to the people who live and work in the region.

Tourist information centres

In the UK, tourist information centres are all run independently, though most are subsidised by local authorities. Thus, they all rely heavily on generating income to ensure their financial viability. The role of the tourist information centres is to give information and advice to tourists. The link with the private sector is important, not only to generate income but also to promote the area. Tourist information centres are often located in key areas to attract maximum visitor numbers.

With the increase in low-cost travel to many European destinations, tourist information centres have become increasingly popular as the first port of call for many visitors (Figure 9.2).

English Heritage

English Heritage is the government's statutory adviser on the historic environment. Officially known as the Historic Buildings and Monuments Commission for England, it is an executive non-departmental public body sponsored by the DCMS (see above). English Heritage is funded in part by the government and in part from revenue earned from its historic properties. It works with central government departments, local authorities, voluntary bodies and the private sector:

* to conserve and enhance the historic environment

CASE STUDY
South West Tourism

South West Tourism is a regional tourist board and so represents the interests of tourism businesses operating in the south-west of England. It is an independent company limited by guarantee and operates as a not-for-profit organisation, with a mixture of commercial and public funding. South West Tourism has approximately 4,500 commercial members (representing over 7,000 tourism businesses) and forms the centre of a three-way partnership between private enterprise, local and central government. Its key aims are: to attract visitors to the region, to help businesses give tourists a rich and rewarding experience, and to provide support on both the practical and the strategic needs of its members and of the industry as a whole.

* **Would you classify South West Tourism as a private sector, public sector or voluntary sector body? Give reasons for your answer.**

Source: Adapted from www.swtourism.co.uk

FIGURE 9.2. *The tourist office in Rheims. Why do you think it is situated in the grounds of Rheims Cathedral?*

- to broaden public access to the heritage
- to increase people's understanding of the past.

UNESCO

For the explanation of the role of UNESCO you should refer to unit 12 ('Ecotourism') or visit www.unesco.org.

Theory into practice

The newspaper article shown in Figure 9.3 is the sort of thing that may appear in the external assessment examination.

- Working in groups, discuss the role of the public sector in UK tourism development.
- Write up your findings, giving a valid conclusion and recommendations.

GOVERNMENT WASTE ATTACKED BY TOURISM CHIEF

The British tourist industry – worth £74 billion – is funded through inefficient government bodies that need shaking up, according to Lord Marshall of Knightsbridge, who will report to Tony Blair tomorrow.

The former chief of British Airways, and now chair of VisitBritain, Lord Marshall will urge the Prime Minister to appoint a tourism 'tsar' during a breakfast meeting at 10 Downing Street.

Amongst the issues to be discussed at Tuesday's meeting are the opportunities offered by the 2012 Olympics, which pundits predict could provide an additional £2 billion boost to the industry.

Lord Marshall said: 'The funding that comes from government to the tourism sector could be and should be better directed and spent in a more effective way, At present, the funding for this sector comes through five or six silos. Many of these go about doing their own thing without any real coordination or cohesion and without any overall direction.'

With responsibility for marketing Britain to potential customers in 36 countries, VisitBritain promotes major attractions which include the London Eye, Tate Modern and the Eden Project in Cornwall.

Lord Marshall complained that there was no 'point for overall control' of the many tourism bodies.

He said: 'Tourism in Scotland is devolved to the Scottish Assembly; in Wales it is the Welsh Assembly. In Britain all overseas promotion and marketing is funded through the Department for Culture, Media and Sport.

'In England, the eight regional development agencies are under the Department of Trade and Industry. In London, VisitLondon is funded through the Greater London Authority and the London Development Agency. And the 560 tourist information centres in England are funded by local government,

I think you have to believe and accept that there is inefficiency. There has to be a more effective way for this government funding to be spent.'

Britain's tourist industry employs 2.1 million people – about 7.4 per cent of the total workforce – and is made up of 180,000 businesses.

£13 billion of the £74 billion spent annually by tourists comes in from foreign visitors. This makes them a bigger export earner for Britain than crude oil (£9.3 billion), food, drink and tobacco (£10.5 billion) or vehicles (£12.1 billion).

Of the £48.4 million 'grant-in-aid' which VisitBritain receives from the Department of Culture, Media and Sport, £35.5 million is earmarked to marketing Britain in 36 overseas countries. Over the past three years, VisitBritain calculates that this investment has generated an average return of £1.3 billion in overseas earnings.

Lord Marshall believes that the government would not necessarily have to pump more money into the industry.

When asked if Britain needed an overall tourism 'tsar', he said: 'We do, I believe. I am not laying any claim on that. I just feel very strongly that a better job can be done for the amount of money that is currently being invested in the sector for the Government.'

FIGURE 9.3. *Adapted from* The Daily Telegraph *14 November 2005*

Voluntary sector organisations

The voluntary sector is made up from not-for-profit organisations, such as registered charities, community groups and pressure groups. Their role is an important one in the travel and tourism industry: they promote special causes, issues and interests, both domestically and internationally. Without the voluntary sector, many worldwide destinations would suffer and many cultures and traditions would disappear after the onset of tourism development.

Most small organisations within the sector are run entirely by volunteers, whereas the larger organisations are generally able to have a professional, full-time staff in addition.

The main source of funding for voluntary sector organisations is as follows:

* donations
* grants
* membership fees
* admission fees
* sales (e.g. cards and gifts).

In the UK the National Lottery is a notable source of donations and grants, but there are many other bodies that give large and small sums to charities.

The revenue is always invested back into the running of the organisation (which is why no profit is made). Some volunteers deliver frontline services such as environmental conservation and others work in a support capacity, such as raising awareness, campaigning and administration.

Community groups

Community groups often work at local level to campaign for changes that will benefit and improve the life of the community. Local issues – such as opposition to the airport extensions in Stansted and Heathrow, which will have an impact on the environment – can be just as important to some people as the saving of endangered species in Borneo can to others. Opposition to the expansion of air travel will obviously have a bearing on the travel and tourism industry, but community groups also seek to have a more direct influence. Consider the quotation below from the website of the Brecon Group for Community and Tourism (www.pco.powys.org.uk/brecongroup):

> The Brecon Group is a community group in Brecon that was a founding partner of the Beacons Trust. We have been responsible for promoting a Town Festival during the summer of 1999 and 2000 and a Georgian Festival last winter in Brecon with a second Festival this year in November. We have taken a lead role in the formation of the BBNP Tourism and Economy Forum. We feel that as a small group we can influence greater decisions within the National Park Area and also provide a point of contact for local people to form a voice and promote ideas as a group. We have also networked with other organisations to promote action in the town in association with other groups....

Pressure groups

The role of pressure groups is generally to influence plans made by local or national governments. Such plans can of course involve tourism development, and indeed many pressure groups are concerned with the negative impact

---

CASE STUDY

Pressure group action

Western pressure groups mounted a campaign against oil palm plantations because they were encroaching on the habitat of the orang-utan. This involved urging food companies and supermarkets to check on the source of the oil palm they used in their products. Friends of the Earth, the environmental campaign group, said that oil palm plantations were the culprit in the destruction of orang-utan habitats and therefore were threatening the very existence of the primate.

* What is the link between this campaign and the travel and tourism industry?

* Find an example of a pressure group campaign that relates directly to the international travel industry.

that tourism can have on the environment. This can lead to conflict between pressure groups and developers in the private sector. For example, private developers often wish to use land to build new tourist facilities, while local people (and others) wish to enjoy the land its natural state.

Some pressure groups that you may be familiar with are:

* the Countryside Alliance
* the Royal Society for the Protection of Birds
* Greenpeace
* the Ramblers' Association
* Friends of the Earth.

Conservation organisations

Attractive environments are sought by holidaymakers, but at the same time large numbers of tourists can threaten that environment. There are therefore both close links and some tensions between the travel and tourism industry and the work of conservation organisations. There are many such organisations, which vary greatly in scale as well as the breadth and nature of their interests. Here we look at three examples.

National Trust

You will have studied the role of the National Trust in unit 1, but did you know that the National Trust:

* is the largest conservation organisation in Britain
* is a registered charity
* protects and opens to the public over 200 historic houses and gardens and 49 industrial monuments and mills
* holds and protects over 540 miles of coastline?

Tourism Concern

Tourism Concern works with local communities to reduce social and environmental problems connected to tourism. It issues news bulletins, sells resources such as books and T-shirts to raise funds, and raises awareness. You should familiarise yourself with the work of Tourism Concern by visiting its website, www.tourismconcern.org.uk.

World Wide Fund for Nature (WWF)

The WWF campaigns to protect habitats and wildlife around the world. Its website features a page on the tourism industry (www.wwf.org.uk/researcher/issues/Tourism). What do you make of the following quotation from that page?

> WWF believes that 'sustainable tourism' is currently an unachievable ideal, not least because of the significant contribution that air travel makes to climate change. It is therefore more useful to think about 'responsible tourism' within the context of a wider sustainable development strategy.

Partnerships

Key term

Public–private partnerships are projects where bodies from the two sectors work together. Typically, the public sector organisation will pay a private company to provide goods or services it would otherwise provide itself.

In the past there has always been a clear distinction between the role of the public and private sector in tourism. In recent years this has become less clear cut, and it has been recognised that a partnership between the sectors is the way forward. For example, out-of-town developments such as leisure, sport and retail parks (Figure 9.4) cannot succeed without the cooperation of all the sectors: the public sector (here, the local authority) must give planning permission and help to develop the infrastructure; private sector investment is needed to fund the necessary attractions and facilities. In many towns and cities in the UK there are regeneration projects taking place. These could not take place without cooperation and agreement between government, private developers and local pressure groups. Partnerships between the sectors are also an important part of tourism development overseas.

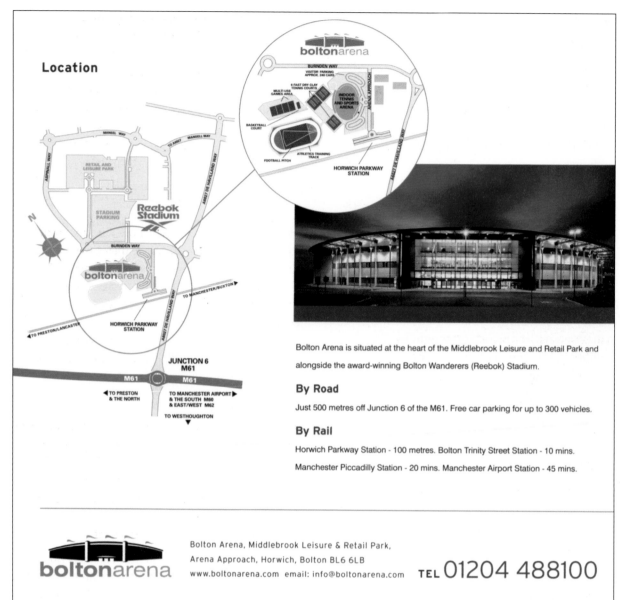

Location

Bolton Arena is situated at the heart of the Middlebrook Leisure and Retail Park and alongside the award-winning Bolton Wanderers (Reebok) Stadium.

By Road

Just 500 metres off Junction 6 of the M61. Free car parking for up to 300 vehicles.

By Rail

Horwich Parkway Station - 100 metres. Bolton Trinity Street Station - 10 mins.

Manchester Piccadilly Station - 20 mins. Manchester Airport Station - 45 mins.

Bolton Arena, Middlebrook Leisure & Retail Park,
Arena Approach, Horwich, Bolton BL6 6LB
www.boltonarena.com email: info@boltonarena.com   TEL 01204 488100

Registered Charity No. 1087039 Registered Company No. 4165498

FIGURE 9.4. *Bolton Arena is an out-of-town development that belongs to a charitable trust owned by a range of public, private and voluntary organisations. It has many indoor and outdoor facilities, which are also run by a mixture of organisations*

Objectives of tourism development

In this section you will learn why tourism is so important to the different organisations involved in tourism development. Each organisation has different objectives and these can be classified as follows:

* economic

* environmental

* socio-cultural

* political.

We will look at each of these in some detail because, in the external assessment, you will be expected to apply your knowledge and understanding of the objectives of tourism development to both UK and overseas case studies.

Economic objectives

Tourism is the world's largest industry and one of the main objectives of tourism development is economic gain. This is not a narrow matter of private sector providers of tourism services making profits.

Theory into practice

In economic terms, the travel and tourism industry is able to do three key things:

1 It gives vigour to economies.

2 It offers people jobs and career prospects.

3 It stimulates development.

It does this through:

* creating employment – direct and indirect

* increasing foreign currency earnings

* increasing visitor numbers and visitor spending within the local economy

* increasing income for commercial operators

* economic development and regeneration.

Tourism development is a truly global phenomenon. For less economically developed countries (LEDCs), tourism is often a vital source of income (and especially of foreign currency, which is often necessary for the purchase of goods and services on the international markets), and this income can be used for wider development purposes. Countries that are rich in physical resources – such as warm climate, beautiful beaches, scenery, rare ecosystems and abundant plant and animal life – are popular destinations for people from more economically developed country (MEDCs). However, MEDCs will also be keen to maximise their own income from tourism, and so they encourage their own tourism development. Examples of countries that are classed as LEDCs include Brazil, India, China, Mexico, Thailand and most African countries. MEDCs are countries that have already gained economic, social and political viability. Examples of these countries include the UK, the USA, Canada, Australia, New Zealand and most European countries.

Creating employment

Tourism is a service- and labour-oriented industry and therefore the opportunity for job prospects is relatively high, as indicated in Table 9.2. This is especially the case in LEDCs, where tourist developers rely on the local population to provide much of the workforce.

Job creation can be categorised as:

* direct, where employment is created within the industry, with jobs such as tour representatives, waiters, excursion providers, hotel receptionists

TRAVEL AND TOURISM ECONOMY RANKING	EMPLOYMENT	EMPLOYMENT FORECAST, 2004–13 (1,000s OF JOBS CREATED)
1	China	11,493
2	Indonesia	4,192
3	Mexico	3,914
4	India	3,845
5	CIS (former Soviet Union)	2,221
6	Brazil	1,854
7	USA	1,559

Source: World Travel and Tourism Council, *Blueprint for New Tourism* (2003)

TABLE 9.2. *Projected international job creation within the travel and tourism industry*

* indirect, where employment is created in other industries, with jobs such as gardeners, beach and pool maintenance, laundry and waste disposal.

In addition, many jobs will be created in the shorter term during the initial development phase, especially in the construction industry, as the building of infrastructure such as roads, airports and hotels all require local skilled workers.

Foreign currency earnings

Tourism is welcomed in many developing countries because it provides an inflow of foreign currency. Increasing these earnings is important as this in turn will increase gross domestic product (GDP) and improve the balance of payments.

Within the tourism industry, the UK now has a negative balance of payments. According to VisitBritain, despite the UK having record numbers of overseas visitors, they are taking shorter trips and more of them are now staying with friends and relatives. Although the annual number of overseas tourists coming to Britain more than doubled between 1979 and 2004, the amount they spent rose by only 40 per cent in real terms. For every £1 an overseas visitor spent in the UK in 2004, UK residents spent £2.32 while on trips abroad. In 1979, Britain recorded a tourism surplus of more than £2 billion, because the amount spent by visitors coming to the UK exceeded the sum spent by Britons while overseas. By 2004, that figure had been transformed into a deficit of more than £17 billion.

Overseas destinations in particular need foreign currency earnings to develop their tourist facilities further. In most countries that are developing tourism, the host population cannot afford to travel overseas. The result is that the balance of payments is generally positive, unless natural disasters (e.g. the Asian tsunami or bird flu) or political changes make travel to these destinations less desirable. This leads to a drastic fall in the economy of these countries that are reliant on visitor numbers and tourism income.

Increasing visitor numbers and visitor spending

All travel and tourism providers seek to maximise visitor spending through effective marketing and human resource management. Increased visitor spending can be encouraged by the provision of secondary services, such as catering and retail outlets at tourist attractions, tour operators and local travel agents selling car hire and excursions to tourists, hotels promoting special deals, short breaks, business and conference facilities and spa, leisure and health treatments.

There is a 'multiplier effect' in the money tourists spend on local facilities and services, in so far as the money stays within the local economy in the form of higher local wages being spent in local shops and so on. The multiplier effect is examined in more detail later in the unit; for now it is sufficient to say that it is important that the money brought into a region remains in that region. In this light, problems may occur in the case of 'all-inclusive' holidays, where money is paid in the tourists' country of origin and there is little benefit to the local providers at the destination. 'All-inclusive' hotels that provide all meals, entertainment and activities on site give tourists little incentive to venture outside to spend money at local bars and restaurants. Destinations should ensure that there is a good mix of accommodation providers, including self-catering, to ensure that the local economy thrives as a result of tourism.

Increasing income for commercial operators

You have learned from the previous section that commercial operators are from the private sector and are involved in the tourism business to increase income and make a profit. Commercial operators include:

* transport providers (air, sea and road travel, the last including car hire companies)

* accommodation providers (hoteliers, villa owners, self-catering establishments, but also cruise ships)

* tour operators and travel agents

* leisure and entertainment facilities.

In the UK and other MEDCs, commercial operators are well established and are reaping the gains of their investments. In regions that are actively developing tourism (e.g. Turkey, Dubai and the Red Sea Riviera), commercial operators are keen to get an early foothold in a competitive market and are actively involved in the provision of services and facilities.

Economic development and regeneration

Travel and tourism, as outlined above, is often the means of furthering economic development in LEDCs. However, tourism may also be the key to the regeneration of an area which has previously been in decline. This is often the case in regions of MEDCs that have experienced industrial decline. Regeneration can include the provision of jobs and training in the tourism industry. It also has many environmental benefits, including improving the appearance of an area and further improving the infrastructure around the area to be regenerated. Many examples occur in the UK, especially waterfront developments. The objectives for local authorities and tourism providers are to stimulate

CASE STUDY

Kaunos Tours, Dalyan, Turkey

Mehmet Cobanoglu started his travel business in 1993 by hiring cars and bicycles to tourists at the resort. His business steadily grew and now he offers a full range of excursions, outdoor adventure activities and accommodation in villas and hotels. He employs several staff, including guides, drivers, instructors and administrators. As a commercial provider of tourist services, his business is contributing to the multiplier effect of the resort. Mr Cobanoglu is a keen environmentalist. He offers advice and assistance to the mayor and local council on all tourism matters and on policies affecting the resort of Dalyan and the surrounding area.

* Indicate how small businesses such as Kaunos Tours contribute to the multiplier effect.

* Explain the importance of the relationship between commercial providers of tourist services and local government.

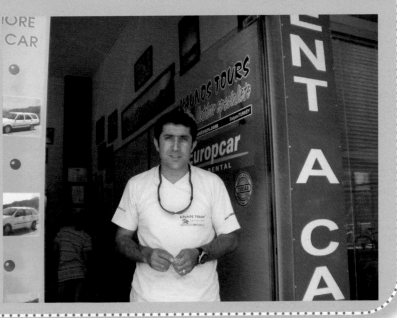

Canal restoration in Salford

A press release from the Northwest Regional Development Agency from October 2005 reported that work to build the first and most important section of the Manchester, Bolton & Bury Canal (MB&B) is under way in Salford. Funding for the £4.2 million restoration of the first phase, at Middlewood, had been granted from European Objective Two Funding, the Northwest Regional Development Agency (NWDA) and Salford City Council. The 500-metre stretch will reconnect the waterway with the River Irwell through the £600 million Middlewood Locks commercial development site, which will include housing, hotels, restaurants, bars and leisure facilities.

Campaigners see this as the first crucial step in the full restoration of the MB&B Canal. Mark Jackson, Project Manager at British Waterways, said: 'It's wonderful to finally be starting on site. This is the culmination of several years' hard work. The canal will form a centre-piece of a huge urban development project demonstrating how the public sector can work in partnership with the private sector to deliver significant economic benefits.'

Salford City Council lead member for planning, Councillor Derek Antrobus, added: 'Waterside regeneration is central to Salford's rejuvenation. The internationally renowned Salford Quays is the biggest success story to date, but the restored section of the Manchester, Bolton & Bury Canal at Middlewood, and the development that ensues, will undoubtedly become yet another powerful symbol of the new city.'

Maurice Gubbins, NWDA Area Manager for Greater Manchester, said: 'Reviving the region's waterways will not only provide unique recreational resources, but also deliver significant economic benefits, enhancing the environment and quality of life, increasing tourism, and creating areas where people want to live and work. This important project will be a powerful catalyst for further regeneration, improving the area's appeal as an investment location and creating new employment opportunities.'

Margaret Fletcher, Chairman of the Manchester, Bolton & Bury Canal Society, concluded: 'When the Middlewood section is complete, boats from the national waterway system will be able to cruise on the Manchester, Bolton & Bury Canal direct from the connected system for the first time for over 40 years. After many years of campaigning our aspirations are being realised.'

* **Why are canals so often at the centre of regeneration projects?**

* **What, here, is the connection between the provision of recreational resources and improving the area's appeal as an investment location?**

---

an awareness of a region or project, to increase visitor numbers and to increase the area's income. This benefits the local population as well as incoming visitors.

Environmental objectives

The saying 'tourism destroys tourism' is well known: protection of the environment is essential in areas that are subject to damage by tourist numbers. Thus, the main environmental objectives of tourism development are as follows:

* habitat preservation

* regeneration and conservation of the built and natural environment

* environmental education

* environmental improvements.

Pressure groups such as Tourism Concern and Friends of the Earth campaign for tourism development projects to be sensitive to the local environment. In the UK tourism development can lead to the improvement of derelict land and waterways and the conservation and restoration of some of our most important buildings. Natural land areas such as national parks and Areas of Outstanding Natural Beauty (AONBs) have environmental protection and education programmes to manage and inform visitors of the environment.

Habitat preservation

Natural habitats need to be preserved. This is often achieved by designating an area as a 'park' – such as the Great Barrier Reef Marine Park in Australia, safari parks in Kenya and national parks, both in the UK and overseas (there is more on this in unit 12, on ecotourism). The key objective is to preserve the area and to retain the biodiversity. Tourist activity is still threatening wildlife, but now people are working to reverse some of the effects of tourism. Moreover, in many instances income from tourists can be used within an area to help in its preservation; such revenue may come through admission charges, car parking fees and the sale of souvenirs, and so on.

What are the threats to wildlife?

In the last century, human activity has caused substantial losses and damage to flora and fauna. The main threats to habitats and wildlife are:

* direct habitat loss, for example through the building of new tourism development projects (e.g. hotels, marinas, golf courses)

* wear and tear due to vehicle use (especially in ecologically fragile environments, such as deserts)

* pollution (from an influx of visitors) putting stress on ecosystems and reducing the populations of particular species.

Regeneration and conservation of the built and natural environment

Tourism can help to regenerate or conserve the environment of destinations because tourists are attracted to areas that feature scenic beauty,

interesting wildlife and/or notable architecture. In order to meet the demands of tourists it is essential that destinations make conservation of the environment one of their primary objectives.

In the UK many steps are taken to protect rural areas, for example through their designation as AONBs or National Parks, and through the work of the National Trust. The Civic Society and English Heritage conserve certain parts of historic and industrial cities. Tourist spending in such places can provide the necessary funds to help conserve and improve the natural and built environment.

As indicated above, tourism development is often used as a means of regenerating run-down urban regions. In some areas it is similarly desirable to regenerate aspects of the natural environment where this has become degraded. The replanting of woodland areas is but one example.

Environmental education

Environmental education has come to the fore in recent years. Tour operators are keen to adopt a 'green' or 'responsible' policy to tourism matters. You can learn more about some of these by referring to unit 12, on ecotourism. Environmental education applies to both the host population and to the tourists. For the latter, methods include showing in-flight videos on aircraft, promotional material, signs, welcome meetings, information boards and leaflets included with travel documents. Many tour operators now include guidelines and information in their brochures about protecting the environment.

The voluntary sector is often associated with environmental education; examples include Tourism Concern and the Travel Foundation, which both clearly state their objectives of environmental protection. Their leaflets and brochures give tips and help to educate tourists.

Education about the environment is sometimes directed to the local populations as well as the visitors, as Figure 9.5 shows. Local populations can also be educated about the economic benefits they can derive from tourism if they learn how to preserve their natural environment.

FIGURE 9.5. *A poster issued by a local council in Turkey asking people to recycle their rubbish. It shows a turtle swimming through discarded plastic bottles and other rubbish*

This new fund could be used to carry out environmental improvements such as the provision of seating or fencing, verge improvements, tidying up eyesores, tree and shrub planting, nature conservation, and even painting murals.

Socio-cultural objectives

You need to be aware of and understand how tourism development can affect the lives of people who live in tourist destinations. Tourism brings

Environmental improvements

In the UK, environmental improvements can take place by the enforcement of local and national laws to protect the environment as well as by initiatives such as the introduction of 'Blue Flag' beaches, National Parks, the National Trust, AONBs and English Heritage. Similar initiatives have been taken around the world (e.g. national parks such as Yellowstone in the USA) and at international level there are schemes such as UNESCO heritage sites that aim to improve the environment.

It is important to appreciate that environmental improvement can be and should be implemented on a local level, in addition to such national and international initiatives. For example, Cambridge City Council has set up a new fund specifically for environmental improvement schemes. It has asked people to put forward ideas for improving their local environment. The projects should:

* have a direct, lasting and noticeable effect on the appearance or ease of use of an area or street

* be publicly visible and accessible

* benefit a large number of people

* have local support

* be small and easy to implement.

CASE STUDY
Blue Flag beaches and marinas

The Blue Flag campaign started in 1987 and today you can find the Blue Flag at beaches and marinas in 18 European countries. The Blue Flag campaign has aimed to improve the understanding and appreciation of the coastal environment, and to promote the incorporation of environmental concerns in decision making. The campaign is a private initiative under the Foundation for Environmental Education in Europe (FEEE) and is operated in each country by the member organisations. The Campaign gives an award – the Blue Flag – on the basis of criteria relating to: water quality; environmental education and information; environmental management (e.g. waste, nature protection, sewage treatment); and safety and other services.

* **How does the Blue Flag scheme improve the environment for wildlife?**

* **How does the Blue Flag scheme improve the environment for local populations?**

* **How does the Blue Flag scheme improve the environment for tourists?**

people of different countries together and we all need to increase our awareness and understanding of different cultures. Tourism can generate income to provide funds to keep traditional cultures alive and to improve the quality of life for the host population. The main socio-cultural objectives of tourism development are:

* to promote understanding of different cultures

* to improve quality of life for the local population

* to provide community facilities, as well as tourist facilities

* to develop a sense of pride in traditional culture and identity.

Promoting understanding of different cultures

When we travel as tourists, it is important that we realise that the destinations we are visiting are home to people of a different culture. Visitors often bring with them different religions, dress and values to those of the host population. This can have both positive and negative consequences (which are looked at below, under 'Traditional culture and identity'). As tourists we should educate ourselves about the culture and traditions of the people of the destination that we are visiting. Some countries that are easily accessible by package holidays from the UK, such as Morocco, Tunisia and Turkey, are Muslim countries, whose values and traditions differ greatly from those of the UK.

UNESCO states on its website (www.unesco.org) that it is its intention:

> to assist the 191 Member States in preparing their policies while reconsidering the relationship between tourism and cultural diversity, tourism and intercultural dialogue, and tourism and development. In this way, the Organisation proposes to contribute to the fight against poverty, protection of the environment and mutual appreciation of cultures.

Improving quality of life

Another socio-cultural objective of tourism development is to improve the quality of life of the local population. This can be done in many ways. For example, quality of life will be enhanced when the improvements to the natural and built environment considered above are implemented. The provision of many kinds of facility is another example, and this is looked at below.

The provision of community and tourist facilities

Quality of life will be further enhanced by the provision of various types of facilities. Generally speaking, facilities built for tourists will also be there for the local community to enjoy. These may not have been economically viable without the regular influx of visitors. Furthermore, improving facilities often leads to environmental enhancement, the creation of employment opportunities and further generation of income within the area.

In some rural areas in the UK, whole communities are dependent on the tourist trade. By improving facilities, tourists will be encouraged to visit the area and therefore the community can continue to benefit, not only from the facilities, but also from the income generated. The same applies also to many overseas destinations.

The facilities provided can be on any sort of scale, from a drinking fountain in a park to the

---

BLACKBURN – FIRST IN EUROPE FOR JAPANESE EXHIBITION

A groundbreaking and startling exhibition from the Fukuoka Asian Art Museum in Japan is to be shown for the first time in Europe as part of C21.

The exhibition, called 'Parallel Realities: Asian Art Now – work from the third Triennale' will be on display at Blackburn Museum and Art Gallery and Blackburn Rovers Football Club.

This contemporary exhibition includes work from 50 artists. For more information… watch this space!

FIGURE 9.6. *The C21 exhibition toured the UK in 2006. Its objective was to raise awareness of community arts and cultural events*

major regeneration of an urban site. Both will give benefits to local people, although the latter can offer solutions to larger local problems, such as unemployment.

CASE STUDY
London's Olympic Games, 2012

By hosting the Olympic Games in 2012, Londoners can expect to benefit from much more than the sporting spectacle. London will see improvements to its social, physical and economic landscape, in its poorest and most deprived areas. Furthermore, the greater interest in sport is expected to lead to an improvement in people's overall health. Alongside the world-class sports facilities that will be available after the Games, there will be a major new urban park – the biggest created in Europe in 150 years.

✳ **What facilities will the local community be able to enjoy as a result of hosting the 2012 London Olympics?**

✳ **List the socio-cultural objectives of the 2012 London Olympics.**

Many traditional socio-cultural events were on the verge of disappearing as tourist destinations were keen to adopt Western ways and habits. Fortunately, as a direct result of tourism, such events have been revived, and may now continue to be passed down from generation to generation. The negative aspect to preserving traditional cultures is 'staged authenticity'.

Key term

Staged authenticity occurs when 'special' cultural events are put on for the benefit of the tourists that in fact bear little resemblance to the original event or meaning. Examples include Greek evenings, Flamenco shows and tribal dances.

Tourism festivals are often supported by local and national governments, whose objectives are both to attract tourists and to preserve a traditional aspect of national or regional life. Bright and cheerful wine festivals have a long tradition in Germany and are popular with UK tourists. A wide variety of traditional cultural festivals appear the world over, but perhaps notably in India,

Traditional culture and identity

The mass tourism development of the kind seen in the 1970s and 1980s is no longer a priority for local and national governments. In line with consumer trends, today's tourists are more discerning in what they wish to see and participate in. As a result there has been a revival of traditional crafts, traditions, festivals and ceremonies to celebrate culture and diversity. The revival of these traditional activities has created a sense of pride in local people's own identity. Today's tourists will become more educated and aware of differing cultures and will find that local people in overseas destinations will also become more knowledgeable about Western cultures.

FIGURE 9.7. *La tomatina in Spain is a popular traditional festival for tourists*

A festival of Scottish music

It is not only the cultural value of Scotland's musical heritage that has gained recognition in recent years. A survey of folk festivals conducted by VisitScotland in 1990 estimated that such events generated around £10 million each year for the Scottish economy, much within small rural communities. An economic impact analysis of the 2002 Celtic Connections festival assessed the income boost for Glasgow from the event at £3 million, in just under three weeks.

The emergence of these kinds of figures prompted a joint investigation by the Scottish Arts Council (SAC) and VisitScotland into strategies for boosting traditional music's effectiveness as a cultural tourism attraction. The subsequent report pointed to 'large and unequivocal visitor demand for traditional music' and described such music as 'prime and unique assets in the competition for tourism income'. Long-term planning and continued investment in the sector, it confidently concluded, will 'produce twin benefits for economic prosperity and Scotland's unique and living cultural heritage'.

Folk music's effectiveness as a regenerative resource has been particularly apparent in some of Scotland's otherwise most marginal and fragile rural economies, such as that of Lewis, home to the Hebridean Celtic Festival. This four-day event, first staged in 1996, attracted a total attendance of 14,000 in 2004. (The population of Stornoway, by far the biggest town in Lewis, is only around 8,000.) This marked a 40 per cent increase on the previous year's attendance figures alone, with 2003's visitors reckoned to have contributed an extra £1.5 million to the local balance sheet. With dozens of folk festivals now taking place in Scotland each year, many communities are reaping similar benefits.

✳ **List the advantages of the revival of traditional music.**

✳ **What would be the implications for Lewis if the Hebridean Celtic Festival had to be cancelled one year?**

Source: Adapted from www.culturalprofiles.org.uk/scotland

Vietnam, China and Japan. They are attractive to all social classes and have been a part of people's lives for many centuries. Festivals are a place to enjoy and learn about the people's crafts and are occasions to remember national heroes. Festivals are also a place where different people can show their own customs and habits.

Political objectives

You have already learned about the role of the public sector in developing tourism as a means to create jobs and income within an area. Governments can have a influence on the patterns of travel not only directly, through their policies, but also indirectly, through their wider activities and the political climate that they promote. Changes in the political system in Eastern Europe, South Africa and the Far East (e.g. Cambodia and Vietnam) have led to greater freedom of movement for travellers. Investment by governments in the infrastructure of countries such as the United Arab Emirates has also led to an increase in visitor numbers and visitor spending.

Beyond the economic and environmental objectives considered above, political objectives can include the following:

✳ enhancing the image of an area

✳ creating a regional or national identity.

Enhancing the image of an area

This is particularly important for LEDCs (for which, as we have seen, tourism is vitally important), as many international tourists are put off visiting an area that has suffered a natural disaster, such as the Asian tsunami, or that has been involved in conflict of some sort.

In 1997, 62 foreign tourists were killed by terrorist groups at Luxor, Egypt. Egyptian tourism suffered very badly as a consequence. Since that time the government has worked tirelessly to enhance the image of the country. One element of this has been a marketing campaign that promotes Egypt as 'the Red Sea Riviera'. The objective of this campaign was to divert people away from the Luxor area and to enhance the image of the Sinai Peninsula on the Red Sea. The campaign has had outstanding results and tourism is flourishing in this area. However terrorists have also begun to target this region.

The same success has not been felt by the island of Bali, in Indonesia, which was subject to terrorist bombings in 2002 and again in 2005. The Indonesian economy is dependent on income from tourism, in particular that from Bali. There are potentially scores of such targets all over the globe and the impact will go well beyond Indonesia to damage the tourist trade of many other countries. It is up to the governments of such areas to promote their destinations, increase income and improve the lives of the local people.

Creating a regional or national identity

National and regional tourist boards are aware that many tourists seek destinations that have traditional cultures and identities. It is one of their objectives to establish their areas as a unique and desirable place to visit. In the UK, the regional tourist boards work closely with the private sector to promoting their area's specialities. This could be food, entertainment or attractions. Having a regional identity contributes to a feeling of well-being for the local population.

For many nations, the promotion of tourism helps to create an awareness of what that country has to offer. Such awareness is an intangible benefit, but it certainly works to improve a country's international relations and to attract foreign investors.

CASE STUDY

Piedmont's Winter Olympics

The Piedmont region in north-west Italy has seen numerous infrastructure developments for the Winter Olympics. Public funding worth US$18 billion was spent on construction work for the Games, and another US$1.2 billion was raised from sponsors and television rights for the actual organisation of the event. Alongside the new and improved sports facilities, were improved access and accommodation villages. Other programmes, included restoration of important historical buildings. All this should bring long-term tourism benefits to the whole region, long after the Games have finished. Even mountain villages and parts of Piedmont that were not directly involved in the Games will benefit. For instance, around US$219 million was spent on the skiing areas near Liguria and the coast. Funds also went to the castles and wine tourism routes in the Asti region, and US$29 million was spent on a spa designed by Japanese architect Kenzo Tange, to transform the spa town of Acqui. In the Olympic area, 5,600 new hotel rooms were added and there are now 93 hotels classified 4 or 5 star.

* **Explain how the Winter Olympics in Piedmont has enhanced the image of the area.**

Source: Adapted from *Travel Daily News*

Assessment guidance

The major objectives of tourism development are:

* to develop a tourism sector which, in all respects and at all levels, is of high quality, though not of high cost

* to encourage the use of tourism for both cultural and economic exchange

* to distribute the economic benefits of tourism (both direct and indirect) as widely and to as many of the host community as feasible

* to preserve cultural and natural resources, and to facilitate this through architectural and landscape design which reflects local traditions

* to appeal to a broad cross-section of international and domestic tourists

* to maximise foreign exchange earnings to ensure a sound balance of payments

* to attract the high spending of 'upmarket' tourists

* to increase employment opportunities.

Some of these objectives can be difficult to understand at first. For each one write a short paragraph with your own interpretation and understanding of the objectives of tourism development. Note that you need to synthesise information and to draw connections between different aspects of tourism development to achieve higher marks in the examination.

POSITIVE	NEGATIVE
Increased income	Increased living costs
Increased employment	Decline of traditional employment opportunities
Improved infrastructure	Seasonality of employment
Multiplier effect	Increased taxes
	Leakages

TABLE 9.3. *The main positive and negative economic effects of tourism*

Impacts of tourism development

You have now learned how tourism development can bring about major benefits to individuals, regions and countries all around the world. With tourism forecast to continue growing, there is little doubt that its ability to contribute towards economic growth and socio-cultural interaction will also continue to have an impact. The speed of its growth is giving cause for concern, however, and so host communities, governments and the travel industry itself have all begun to look at ways of maximising the positive and minimising the negative economic, environmental and socio-cultural impacts of tourism.

Economic impacts

We shall first consider the economic impacts that the travel and tourism industry has on a region or country. Table 9.3 summarises these.

Key term

Impact covers the effect that the travel and tourism industry may have on a country in economic, environmental and socio-cultural terms. It may be positive or negative.

Positive economic effects

Increased income

Tourism can:

* contribute to the balance of payments

* aid economic development

* increase income for commercial providers

* increase revenue from tax.

Increased income is especially important to LEDCs as it can bring in much-needed money to improve their economic stability. Tourism is the world's largest export earner and foreign currency receipts from tourism can bring in income to countries with a low GDP.

Increased employment

Income from tourism encourages small and medium-sized enterprises, thereby creating new job opportunities and promoting economic development. Direct and indirect employment opportunities arise as a direct result of increased visitor number.

Foreign exchange from tourism earns South Africa nearly US$3 billion per annum more than gold mining. Tourism's significant contribution to South Africa's GDP and employment is widely recognised. The industry has created more than 700,000 new South African jobs in the last 10 years.

Improved infrastructure

You have learned how tourism can stimulate the economy of a region or country and this leads to further developments of the infrastructure of an area. This can be relatively small in scale, such as the provision of car and coach parks in 'honey pot' areas such as the Lake District and small coastal towns. With a major new resort development such as the Sinai Peninsula in Egypt, where 3 billion Egyptian pounds was invested in the tourism sector in 2004–05, it can lead to major developmental infrastructure improvements such as:

* new transport facilities (principally airports and roads)

* construction of adequate water supplies and improvements to sewage systems

* provision of power and telecommunication systems

* new leisure and entertainments facilities

* redevelopment and improvement of existing tourist facilities.

Improved infrastructure is not only a benefit to the incoming tourist – it also enhances the lives of the host population. Previously run-down areas may get a 'new lease of life'. For example, in Manchester massive infrastructure developments took place following the success of the Commonwealth Games. Many areas surrounding new sporting arenas in the UK have undergone major infrastructure improvements in the form of transport links such as rail and metro connections. These benefit visitors and locals alike.

Multiplier effect

We came across the multiplier effect when considering the economic objectives of tourism developments. It occurs as a direct result of the

CASE STUDY

Zanzibar

Tourist arrivals in Zanzibar Island, off the coast of Tanzania, in 2005 were set to far outpace those of the previous four years. Visitors totalled 76,329 in 2001, 87,511 in 2002, 68,650 in 2003 and 92,161 in 2004. The tourism sector directly or indirectly employed nearly 45,000 of Zanzibar's one million people; it is hoped that the sector will surpass agriculture, which currently accounts for 35 per cent of GDP, as its leading revenue earner by 2015.

Political and economic changes over the past 20 years have encouraged tourism. Within the coastal zone, where there are several small fishing communities, there were no hotels in 1990. In 1997 there were along the same coast 80 hotels, which occupied and in practice controlled access to beaches and water, with the aim of securing privacy and leisure activities for tourists. The needs of tourism and tourists were prioritised while those of the local population were neglected.

The government of Zanzibar has recently focused on tourism as a main source of

foreign exchange and economic growth. Both local and foreign private companies, as well as individuals, are encouraged to invest in various kinds of tourist enterprise. This is perceived as one possible way to encourage economic activities which will eventually enrich the state through various systems of taxation, creating work opportunities, providing incentives for trading activities, and thus improved living conditions for people in general.

* How has tourism development affected the host population of Zanzibar?

* Explain what is meant by the fact that Zanzibar currently gains 35 per cent of its GDP from agriculture.

* Analyse the importance of tourism exceeding agriculture in economic terms.

* In what ways has tourism improved the infrastructure of Zanzibar?

* Summarise the positive economic effects of tourism on Zanzibar.

economic impact of tourism. Research has shown that the amount spent by visitors to an area is recirculated in the local economy. This happens when the wages that are earned by somebody working in the tourism sector is then spent in the local shops and on local attractions. When the money is retained in this way within the local economy, it is effectively worth more to an area than its face value, as it is spent and spent again (Figure 9.8).

The multiplier effect is more obvious in some places that are affected by seasonality. For example, in Newquay, Cornwall, many young people from the UK and overseas spend the summer working in the hotels, on the beaches and at visitor attractions. While they are there, the money that they earn is spent in the area, creating revenue for small business such as catering establishments and shops. The people who work in these businesses then spend their wages and so on, which is why the term 'multiplier' effect is used.

The actual value of the multiplier varies between destinations. As an example, if a couple book a short break to a hotel costing £200, this could be worth £200 × 1.4 (the hotel multiplier effect for that area), making a total of £280. The multiplier effect tends to be much larger in rural, seasonally popular areas than for major cities. For the UK overall, the multiplier effect is estimated at 1.7; that is, if a tourist spends £100 then the net benefit is estimated to be £170.

Negative economic effects

You have learned how tourism development has the potential to offer significant economic benefits to destinations. However it also has a number of associated negative economic impacts and you will need to know how these may affect people and destinations.

Increased living costs

An increase in the cost of living is often associated with tourism development. Prices rise simply because foreign visitors are wealthier and can afford to pay more for products and services. This is a particular problem in LEDCs, where the local population has a relatively low income. The prices of goods and services in tourist areas are sometimes increased in the peak holiday season in order to maximise tourism revenue. This is a disadvantage to local residents who may have to pay higher prices for food, entertainment, transport and other key services. It is not unusual for some destinations to operate a 'dual-band pricing', with one price for tourists and another for locals.

Local property and land prices can also increase after tourism development. Prime areas of land in developing tourist resorts often become valuable development land, making it too expensive for local buyers. House and property prices have increased not only in the UK but also overseas as more and more people buy property as a second or a holiday home. This has forced the prices of houses up and beyond the reach of many first-time local buyers. Moreover, there is little economic benefit to the host area or country if rental income from a holiday home is not locally retained.

Decline of traditional employment opportunities

When economic investment and activity shift from industries such as farming and fishing into tourism, traditional employment opportunities will decline, and with them traditional ways of life. The effects can be widespread: the migration of workers in countries such as Greece and Turkey

Income spent in a region is recirculated within the local economy

For example, seasonal work earnings will be spent locally and returned to the local economy

FIGURE 9.8. *The multiplier effect*

to the tourist 'hot spots' has led not only to shortage of workers in other sectors in the summer months but also to the breakdown of traditional family life, as many do not return home.

Seasonality of employment

The seasonality of the travel and tourism industry causes problems. As you have just learned, it is not unusual for workers in poorer countries to work for six months in the tourist resorts. They often work seven days a week, with very little time off. For the remainder of the year they may have to survive on the money they have saved over the summer season. This is a fragile arrangement. If a destination were affected by a political or natural disaster, say, that had a direct impact on the number of tourist arrivals, then many workers would be unable to care financially for their families.

Seasonal workers are usually paid minimum wages. It is not unusual for staff in LEDCs to be paid on average £1 a day. They rely heavily on tips to increase their income. Staff in 'all-inclusive' resorts suffer particularly badly in this respect.

Increased taxes

Because of the economic benefits of tourism, national and local governments alike are under some pressure to provide tourist facilities. These can range from the provision of car parks, toilet facilities, tourist information signs and promotional leaflets to the running of tourist information centres and leisure and entertainment complexes. Money is needed to provide such facilities and usually comes from taxes, local and national. These are more often used for the benefit of the tourist than for the local population, but it will be the latter who pay the tax.

In overseas destinations local councils must provide the services to keep resorts clean (e.g. street cleaners and beach cleaners). They must also provide street lighting and signposts in more rural areas, as well as road improvements and rubbish collection. The money to pay for these services is often raised by increasing taxes similar to our own community charge.

Leakages

Leakages occur when money leaves the economy of the country or region. These include taxes, savings, costs for imported goods from overseas, and profits made by multinational companies such as major hotel groups.

An example is imported 'brand' foods that can now be found in many supermarkets overseas. These have to be imported from the country of

---

CASE STUDY

Where does your pound go?

The Dominican Republic is the most popular tourist destination in the Caribbean, and has the largest 'all-inclusive' resort industry in the world, with 50,000 rooms. Although it had the highest economic growth in the Americas from 1996 to 2002, 90 per cent of its 8 million residents live below the poverty line. Of the money that we pay for our average all-inclusive holiday, 89 per cent stays in the UK – with the operator, the airline, insurance company, exchange broker and the travel agency. Of the remaining 11 per cent, the hotel gets just 3 per cent. You can imagine how much is left to pay the staff in the hotels.

Anna works as a chambermaid at a four-star hotel that all the major UK tour operators use. She works a nine-hour day and cleans 21 large rooms. If and when she takes a holiday she does not get paid, or for the lengthy overtime that she has to work. 'The conditions for the workers in the Dominican Republic are very poor,' she says. 'We live thinking every day what to eat and how to pay for electricity. We have to go to work thinking of this. We have to smile at tourists but it is not what we are feeling in our souls. We want to work and make your holiday happy, but it is difficult.'

* Explain how and why leakage has happened.

* Why are all-inclusive holiday packages particularly susceptible to leakage?

* What negative economic effects do all-inclusive holidays have in the Dominican Republic?

Source: Adapted from a Tourism Concern article

origin and as a consequence there is little profit to be made locally. Another example is the purchase of souvenirs that have been made in China and not the country in which they are sold; again, the money 'leaks' out of the local economy. These are examples on a very small scale, but what happens when leakage occurs on a much larger scale?

The World Bank estimates that, on average, 55 per cent of the income from international tourism leaves the country via foreign-owned airlines, hotels and tour operators, or payments for imported food, drink and supplies. Studies in individual countries show that there is great variability around this figure, which seems to be influenced by the size of the national economy: it was estimated at 75 per cent in the Caribbean but at as little as 25 per cent for India. A recent study by the World Resources Institute in the Annapurna region of Nepal found that only 10 per cent of the cost of visitors' holidays remained in the area. In 1996, a survey found that 57 per cent of Costa Rica's hotels and resorts were foreign-owned, despite laws prohibiting foreign-owned companies from owning coastal properties. In Indonesia, 90 per cent of four-star hotels were foreign-owned. A study of tourism 'leakage' in Thailand estimated that 70 per cent of all money spent by tourists ended up leaving Thailand (via foreign-owned tour operators, airlines, hotels, imported drinks and food, etc.).

All-inclusive resorts

All-inclusive resorts are still rapidly growing in number in the Caribbean, Far East and the Mediterranean, despite the concerns of many international organisations and governments. They are self-contained resorts offering package holidays on the understanding that the tourist pays a single fee which covers the cost of all activities, drinks, food and entertainment at the resort. This takes away custom from local facilities such as restaurants and bars.

Environmental impacts

The money and impetus which tourism brings to an area can help it to restore and maintain its environment, but the pressure that it brings is often detrimental to its development. We are now going to assess the positive and negative effects

that tourism can have on the natural and built environment. Table 9.4 summarises these.

POSITIVE	NEGATIVE
Improved assets	Traffic congestion
Landscaping	Erosion of natural resources
Conservation	Pollution of air and water; litter and noise
Regeneration	Panoramic view damage
Building regulations	Destruction of wildlife and breeding patterns

TABLE 9.4. *The positive and negative effects that tourism can have on the natural and built environment*

Positive environmental effects

Improved assets

> **Key term**
>
> Assets are the features that an area has to offer. These can be natural, for example the scenery and wildlife, or built, such as ancient monuments and historic buildings.

With access greatly improved, many people now have the opportunity to see wildlife and plants in their natural environment. This has led to the establishment of many schemes to protect the environment, as a direct result of people becoming more aware of its importance. People who enjoy the flora and fauna that the natural environment has to offer are more inclined to put pressure on local and national governments to protect the environment. Membership of the National Trust helps to provide funds for the protection of both the natural and built environment.

> **Key terms**
>
> Flora and fauna are the terms used broadly to describe, respectively, the plants and animals common to a particular area.

FIGURE 9.9. *Stonehenge is a well known historic monument*

Conservation

Tourism can also be a positive force in helping to conserve the environment of destinations. Tourists are attracted to areas of scenic beauty, regions of historical and architectural interest, and places offering abundant and interesting flora and fauna. Satisfying this demand is one of the motivations behind the move towards conservation of the environment. Tourist spending in conservation areas can provide the funds required to conserve and improve both the natural and the built environment.

Assets such as ancient monuments and historic buildings may benefit from tourism; if visitors are charged an admission fee or asked for a donation, the money can then be used for improvements and maintenance of the sites and buildings.

Landscaping

Any destination wishing to attract visitors must present itself as an attractive place, and for this reason tourism has played a large part in improving the appearance of the environment of many destinations. Residents as well as visitors benefit from the general landscaping and cleaning of buildings, rivers and trails. The most striking example of environmental enhancement and landscaping is where facelifts have been given to many of the derelict 19th-century riversides, which have been transformed in cities such as Sydney, New York, Bristol, Liverpool and Leeds. Tourism has been the catalyst for much of the landscaping that has taken place.

Landscaping can be carried out by using some of the following methods:

* planting trees and shrubs

* cleaning rivers and lakes

* sandblasting and improving the appearance of buildings

* repairing damaged fences, hedges and seats

* providing urban sculptures.

Regeneration

Regeneration, like conservation and preservation, is important to the tourism development process. Faced with the decline of traditional industries, many cities needed to develop new sources of employment and attract inward investment, to overcome dereliction and decay. Regeneration of cities can increase civic pride and attract local and national support. Birmingham is an excellent example of how a city can be regenerated – it is now one of the UK's leading cities for arts, entertainment, retail and conference events.

Building regulations

Few people understand the importance of environmental conservation. There is a widespread perception that those who want it are anti-development and anti-tourism. That perception is wrong. The way to provide for the growing needs of people (and for the increasing numbers of tourists) lies in sustainable development. The key to this is in forward-looking planning, which optimises the economic impact of tourism while protecting and enhancing the natural and built environment. Building regulations are an important element of such a planning framework. They can be used to ensure that any new development meets aesthetic, environmental and safety standards.

Governments have a responsibility to set guidelines and policies to enhance the development of sustainable tourism. Then, hand in hand with the private sector, they should implement and enforce them – using planning guidelines, building regulations and environmental auditing.

Negative environmental effects

Traffic congestion

In the UK, places such as national parks can receive over 100 million visits a year and come under particular pressure at weekends and in high season. Some parts of the Peak District and Lake District reach saturation point, with traffic jams for many miles. The large numbers of people who visit the countryside, especially by car, put pressure on the physical environment, resulting in pollution, and causing harm to the natural flora and fauna.

Most historic cities across Europe consist of narrow streets which were built long before cars, buses and coaches were invented. The influx of visitors at peak times has resulted in the closure of many centres to tourist traffic. This is to preserve the buildings from the effects of carbon monoxide pollution and also for the health and safety of locals and visitors to the area.

Traffic congestion can cause:

* inconvenience to local residents, who need to get to work and conduct their lives as normal
* local transport service disruption
* increased danger to pedestrians
* noise pollution.

CASE STUDY
Stansted Airport

English Heritage has expressed fears for the future of the historic environment of Essex as a result of the government's decision to go ahead with proposals for a new runway at Stansted Airport. It is feared that the proposals could result in the direct loss of nearly three square miles of historic Essex, including as many as 30 listed buildings and two nationally important ancient monuments. It could also have a serious impact on many adjacent properties and surrounding historic towns and villages. This view is supported by the 1984 planning inspector's report, which concluded: 'The development of an airport at Stansted with a capacity in excess of 25 million passengers per annum would constitute nothing less than a disaster in environmental terms.'

In contrast, English Heritage welcomed the government's intention to ensure that, over time, the price of air travel reflects its true environmental and social impacts and that an effort has been made to reduce the impact on the historic environment of the expansion of Heathrow and Birmingham International airports.

Simon Thurley, chief executive of English Heritage, said: 'As the government's statutory adviser on heritage issues, we have consistently argued that all the proposed major airport developments would have a significant negative impact on the historic environment. The expansion of Stansted will have a serious effect on local heritage. This will be directly through the loss of historic buildings and archaeology, but also indirectly and in the longer term through the loss of overall amenity of historic towns and villages. The damage will not just be caused by the new runway itself, but also by the associated infrastructure and development. We remain concerned about the apparent absence of systematic measures to manage demand for future air travel. We will continue to press for the maximum protection possible. Heritage is not just about visible buildings and scheduled monuments, but also the whole of the historic landscape and buried archaeology.'

* **Compare and contrast the possible positive and negative effects of the new runway at Stansted Airport.**

Source: Adapted from an English Heritage press release

Erosion of natural resources

Even in areas where tourists leave their cars and continue on foot, problems can arise. The prime one in rural areas is erosion – damage to grass, heather and soil. In the Lake District the paths that have been well trodden for years by fell walkers are visible from great distances. Sand dunes and peat bogs are particularly vulnerable. The pressure not only damages wildlife habitats but also disturbs and endangers wildlife. Many beach areas provide showers; these are not only to clean away salty water but to wash the sand off feet and sandals. Just imagine how much sand leaves a popular beach each summer!

Pollution of air and water; litter and noise

Air travel and road traffic inevitably pollute the air to some extent. They are also a prime source of noise pollution. Water is polluted by detergents and sewage. This is especially problematic in areas that had attracted tourists because of their pristine natural environment.

Solid waste and littering are a particular problem in areas with high concentrations of tourist activities and appealing natural attractions. Waste disposal is a serious problem and improper disposal is a major problem in the natural environment. Rivers, scenic areas and roadsides are all affected. For example, cruise ships in the Caribbean are estimated to produce more than 70,000 tons of waste each year, although some cruise lines are actively working to reduce waste-related impacts. Solid waste and littering can degrade the physical appearance of the water and shoreline and cause the death of marine animals.

In mountain areas, trekking tourists generate a great deal of waste, which is difficult to dispose of. Climbers sometimes leave oxygen cylinders and even their camping equipment. Such practices degrade the environment with all the rubbish typical of the developed world. Some trails in the Peruvian Andes and in Nepal frequently visited by tourists have been nicknamed the 'Coca-Cola trail' and 'Toilet paper trail'.

Panoramic view damage

Throughout this unit we have seen that there is pressure on destinations to develop facilities to entice tourists. These will include shops, toilets, car parks and entertainment venues, as well as hotels and other types of accommodation. Local building styles may be difficult and expensive to replicate, and there may be insufficient space to site buildings sympathetically or to screen them with trees or other suitable landscaping. Developments in a modern, efficient style can completely ruin the visual character of an old

---

CASE STUDY

Machu Picchu

More than 300,000 people a year visit the ancient Inca city of Machu Picchu, in Peru, to see the 500-year-old structures built from blocks of granite chiselled from the mountainside. As a result of the overwhelming interest, Machu Picchu may be at risk. Some geologists have warned that a massive landslide could send the stone ruins crashing into the Urubamba River below. The concern about landslides has bolstered arguments against a proposal to install a cable car that would replace the diesel-powered buses that carry tourists up to the mountaintop ruins. Conservation and cultural preservation organisations, including UNESCO, say a cable car would mar the natural vistas and increase tourist traffic to an unsupportable level of at least 400,000 visitors a year.

Similar concerns have arisen about protecting the Inca Trail. The number of people hiking along it rose from 6,000 in 1984 to 66,000 in 1998, according to UNESCO. Tea bags and water bottles litter the route, where campsites are scarce. In an effort to preserve the trail, Peru has restricted to 500 the number of people allowed on the trail each day and hikers must trek with a registered guide.

* **Do you think that the proposed cable car project should go ahead?**

* **List the positive and negative impacts this project could have on the area.**

Source: Adapted from an article for *National Geographic News*

village, town, or natural landscape. Ill-considered development can destroy what the tourists initially came to appreciate (Figure 9.10).

Destruction of natural wildlife systems and breeding patterns

'Wildlife tourism' can take the form of whale and dolphin watching, safaris and tiger trails. In today's environment very little is left to chance or opportunity. Often when an animal is spotted an exchange of mobile phone calls or radio messages soon leads to the arrival of tourist buses, cars, helicopters or boats. Such activities can have a negative impact on breeding patterns of the wildlife in an area. It has been known in certain parts of India that a single tiger is stalked day after day by tourists. This prevents the animal from

FIGURE 9.10. *Benidorm, in Spain, rapidly developed in the 1960s and 1970s with what is now known as a pencil development; viewed from the sea, the resort resembles a stack of upright pencils, and these totally obscure the natural landscape.*

CASE STUDY

Mediterranean under threat

About 150 million people live within 20 km of the Mediterranean, and each summer that population almost doubles with the arrival of tourists. But what they come to enjoy is slowly being destroyed. 'We must switch now to more responsible tourist practices … if we don't do this, the Mediterranean will become nothing more than a huge dead swimming pool,' said Paolo Guglielmi, of WWF. The Mediterranean supports a vast array of wildlife, but the boom in tourism over the past 50 years has placed this biodiversity under threat. The loss of natural habitats has led to more than 500 plant species in the Mediterranean being threatened with extinction, according to WWF. On top of that there is the damage caused by increases in waste and pollution: the Mediterranean receives about 10 billion tonnes of industrial and urban waste every year. Most endangered of all is the monk seal. Despite three decades of environmental awareness, less than 5 per cent of the Mediterranean coastline is protected. WWF is working with tour operators, local communities and governments to try to preserve habitats and manage the impact

of tourism in a sustainable way. One step forward has been the creation of a whale and dolphin sanctuary in the north-western Mediterranean. Covering 84,000 km^2 and the home to 18 different species of whales and dolphins, it is the first marine protected area in the northern hemisphere to include international waters. In the summer months, these are feeding grounds for up to 2,000 whales and more than 40,000 striped dolphins. Yet these waters are becoming increasingly polluted with untreated sewage and other waste from urban and industrial areas. Other threats include increased marine traffic from ferries, speed boats and whale-watching tourists. To regulate these activities the Italian, French and Monaco governments recently agreed a management plan for the sanctuary; the challenge now is to enforce it. Further marine protection areas are being opened in the eastern Mediterranean.

✳ Draw up a 10-point list of key planning and management actions that you think that the countries bordering the Mediterranean should take to resolve the various problems highlighted.

Source: Adapted from BBC News website, http://news.bbc.co.uk

Socio-cultural impacts

The money and impetus which tourism brings to an area can cause far more harm in socio-cultural respects than in environmental terms. This is because many of the environmental impacts can be resolved with the correct management and funding. The socio-cultural problems, however, can be far more deep-rooted and difficult to resolve. We are now going to assess the positive and negative socio-cultural impacts that tourism can have on an area (Table 9.5).

POSITIVE	NEGATIVE
Preservation of customs and crafts	Conflicts with host community
Provision of community facilities	Crime
Aiding of understanding	Loss of cultural identity
	Changes to family structure
	Social problems

TABLE 9.5. *The positive and negative socio-cultural impacts that tourism can have on an area*

Positive socio-cultural effects

Key term

Socio-cultural is a term which refers to people's lifestyles, values and traditions.

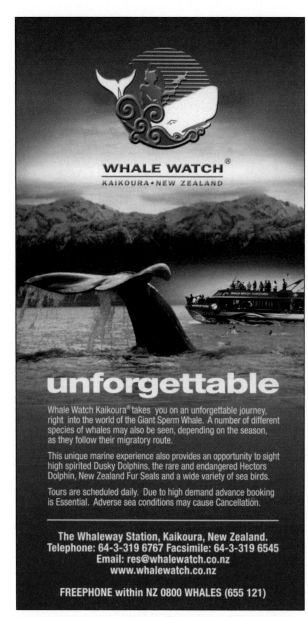

FIGURE 9.11. *An example of an environmental issue*

leading a normal existence. However, in LEDCs the revenue gained from tourists can take priority over any environmental concerns. In cases such as this it is usually international organisations that step in to put pressure on the local population to be more environmentally aware (see figure 9.11).

An issue of great concern is the disruption caused by tourism to the breeding patterns of turtles, many of which are endangered species. Both tourists and turtles seek sandy beaches. Even something as seemingly innocuous as the lights from a disco are said to disturb the egg laying of the turtles.

Preservation of customs and crafts
Examples of non-physical things that a community might want to preserve are values, respect, equality and language. Examples of physical things that a community might want to preserve are historic sites, architecture, cuisine, natural heritage, pristine forests, unpolluted waterways, flora and fauna. You will need to understand the importance of these issues.

Many tourists now seek the 'cultural product' offered by different regions; festivals, carnivals, food and drink, language or locally produced goods are high on the list. It is now possible in the UK to buy a selection of foods that are special to a region. This allows traditional methods of preparation to continue to be passed from generation to generation, in addition to providing employment. Likewise, in many European countries there is a return to traditional regional specialities as more and more people seek authenticity in their travels. Tourism provides the revenue to fund the preservation of ancient skills that would have died out without funding and interest. Traditional dances and music are essential elements of any long-haul holiday, as such things are what differentiate the destination from home. Tourism can help to foster local pride, revitalise traditions, reverse the drift of rural populations towards big cities in search of jobs, improve welfare and strengthen development of regions.

FIGURE 9.12. *Tourism can also help conserve crafts such as shoemaking, leatherwork, lace-making, engraving and pottery, all of which have a regional identity, and as a result of tourism will be preserved for future generations*

Provision of community facilities

Community and public facilities usually improve in tourist destinations. Transport, health services and leisure and recreation facilities may increase in quality as improved standards are necessary to

---

CASE STUDY

What do you know about the customs of Thailand?

The most distinctive Thai customs is the *wai*, which is similar to the Indian *namaste* gesture. It involves a prayer-like gesture with the hands and a bow of the head, and can indicate greeting, farewell or acknowledgment. In Thailand touching someone on the head may be considered rude, as may placing one's feet at a level above someone else's head, especially if that person is of higher social standing. This is because the Thai people consider the foot to be the dirtiest and lowest part of the body, and the head the most respected and highest part of the body. This also influences how Thais sit when on the ground: their

feet always point away from others, tucked to the side or behind them. Pointing at or touching something with the feet is also considered rude. It is also considered extremely rude to step on a Thai coin, because the king's head appears on the coin. When sitting in a temple, one is expected to point one's feet away from images of the Buddha. It is also customary to remove one's footwear before entering a home or a temple, and not to step on the threshold.

✱ **Do you think that tourists should familiarise themselves with local customs before visiting countries that have different customs and beliefs?**

meet the tourists' expectations. People's lives may become enriched by increased access to culture, entertainments and the opportunity to enjoy different parts of a country when there is better transportation. On a local level, people can choose to use their spare time more productively and enjoyably when there are more and better facilities.

Aiding of understanding

Cultural tourism has often been misunderstood and as a consequence some destinations look for the cultural resources that can be packaged and shown off to the visitor. Far too often this changes the character of the culture and creates a form of staged authenticity (see above).

A better approach to cultural tourism is to try to integrate the visitor into the local way of life and to aid understanding of the community as it is, by sharing stories, personal and community history, and values. Too often tourists eat separately from their hosts, while the hosts merely wait on them. This happens mainly in all-inclusive resorts or in enclave resorts where tourists do not need to venture outside of the resort.

Negative socio-cultural effects

Tourists and tourism are symbols of 'modern' Western values; perhaps because of the association with Western affluence, these values may be seen by some groups as being better then their own traditional values. There is also a 'demonstration effect', whereby local people wish to imitate tourists by wearing similar jewellery or clothes, or behaving similarly. In the West, personal achievement is sometimes seen as more important than personal relationships; if this view is adopted in other cultures it may have a range of negative impacts.

> #### Key term
>
> The demonstration effect is the tendency of a host population to imitate tourists, by aspiring to their values and material possessions.

Conflicts with the host community

Tourism can cause a great deal of inconvenience to both communities and individuals. People who live in popular tourist areas can have their day-to-day lives disrupted by the intrusive or antisocial behaviour of tourists. Imagine an old lady sitting in her garden in a Greek village making lace, as she has done for years. It is not uncommon for tourists to stand and stare and even wander into homes and gardens to look at local life. Inappropriately dressed tourists can often be seen wandering around churches with cameras and sun cream, with little regard for their surroundings. For many local people, life in the tourist season can be like living in a goldfish bowl. Consider what you would feel like if a tourist bus pulled up outside your house and tourists starting taking photos of you watching *Coronation Street* (a British custom)!

Crime

The relative wealth of the tourists also leads to conflict with the host community in the form of crime. Some European cities such as Barcelona are as renowned for their petty crime as they are for tourist attractions. Tourists are particularly vulnerable to crime as they carry with them things of value such as digital cameras, mobile phones, iPods, passports and money. Tourists are generally easy to identify by what they are wearing or what they are doing. All too often tourists do not realise or recognise the value of the money they have and as a consequence can easily be fooled into parting with their cash.

Loss of cultural identity

The arrival of a large number of outsiders in a small area (not only tourists but also seasonal workers, for example) results in a loss of local identity and in distrust, suspicion and conflict between 'us' and 'them'. This has a negative impact on the culture of a community. The situation is worsened if facilities and amenities are targeted to visitors and detract from the area's original features.

Wenceslas Square in Prague, in the Czech Republic, is famous for its historical events and architecture. Before the 1990s there were no shops in the square; however, following a tourism boom this famous landmark is now home to McDonald's, Benetton and Gap, among others. Prices in the city have escalated, petty thieves and beggars have appeared and the antisocial behaviour of visiting stag and hen parties is evident. Little remains of the cultural significance of the area.

Changes to family structure

Alongside the disintegration of traditional value systems we have looked at above, a breakdown in family and social structures is sometimes seen with the advent of tourism development. Agriculture, fishing and animal care are seen as being of lower status than service work in the tourism industry, and movement away from these brings about a dependency on the importing of basic goods. When the values and behaviours of the local community are threatened it can cause changes to the family structure, community relationships, collective traditional lifestyles and moral values. Tourism can scatter families by encouraging the migration of young people to tourist resorts. The associated transfer of economic power to the young people also undermines family structures.

Social problems

In some areas of tourism development, traditional social sanctions and controls have ceased to operate, and this has created social problems such as the prostitution of women and children, and drug addiction. In short, culture is on sale for profit without concern about its long-term impacts. Tourism particularly affects women who live in tourist destinations. Women do the extra work that becomes necessary when resources are diverted from indigenous people to tourists. In many parts of the developing world, women are left to raise families with limited resources. Prostitution becomes an easy way to make money and sadly is associated with many tourist destinations. Begging can also become a problem where wealthy tourists are in abundance.

Think it over...

Some 13–19 million children are working in the tourism sector worldwide. More than 1 million children are sexually abused by tourists every year.

Destination management

Tourism is generally not the sole industry or economic activity in an area and you have learned how tourism must integrate with other social and environmental activities in a destination to avoid negative impacts. Some of the impacts of tourism development are planned while others are unplanned. You should understand that these impacts need not 'just happen' but can be managed by tourism professionals for the long-term benefit of the destination and local community, as well as the travel and tourism industry.

Destinations do have to change with the times and various models and management strategies have been used to illustrate this point. You may be familiar with Butler's model of resort development, sometimes known as the destination life cycle, shown in Figure 9.13.

Destination management differs for UK and overseas destinations. In the UK the management role usually belongs to local authorities (public sector) in partnership with local or national businesses (private sector). Some seaside resorts are in decline for various reasons while others are still able to attract large numbers of visitors. Decline is generally due to a failure to take

Theory into practice

* Give two positive economic impacts of tourism development.

* Give two negative economic impacts of tourism development.

* Identify a tourist area in the UK that you are familiar with and assess the negative and positive impact that tourism development has had on the environment.

* Using the Internet and/or a selection of long-haul holiday brochures, select a destination that you were previously unfamiliar with. Use a simple table of two columns to list the positive and negative economic, environmental, and socio-cultural impacts of tourism to the destination. How do the values and traditions of the destination compare with those of the UK?

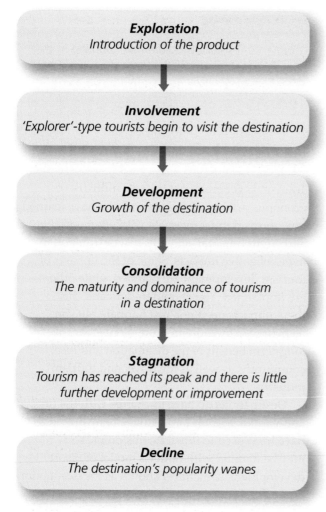

Exploration
Introduction of the product

Involvement
'Explorer'-type tourists begin to visit the destination

Development
Growth of the destination

Consolidation
The maturity and dominance of tourism in a destination

Stagnation
Tourism has reached its peak and there is little further development or improvement

Decline
The destination's popularity wanes

FIGURE 9.13. *Butler's model of resort development, sometimes known as the destination life cycle*

appropriate action at the critical time. The type of action that should be taken includes the following:

* good traffic management (e.g. car parks, coach parks, park-and-ride facilities, traffic-calming measures and pedestrian areas)

* the provision and maintenance of facilities such as toilets, signage, litter collection and tourist guides (Blue Badge, Guide Friday)

* the provision of information through marketing and promotional activities, tourist information centres and tourist signs

* reducing seasonality by encouraging overnight and short breaks throughout the year

* community consultation through public meetings to ensure that all developments meet

with and conform to local and government plans

* environmental impact assessment.

We are now going to look at some of the principles of successful destination management. There are two sides to this: maximising the positive impacts of tourism development, and minimising the negative impacts.

Maximising the positive impacts

Retention of visitor spending

The agents of tourism development are keen to ensure that visiting tourists spend their money at their destination rather than elsewhere. This clearly benefits the whole area by increasing tourism revenue and employment within the area – remember the 'multiplier effect'? One way to achieve this is to ensure that a wide range of amenities and facilities are provided. In resorts such as Center Parcs and Disneyland it is relatively easy to retain visitor spending in the resort, as a wide range of shops, catering, entertainment and leisure facilities have been provided to meet all customers' needs. However, in some LEDCs resorts and hotels are dependent on imported goods to satisfy customer needs. This then leads to leakage – as you have learned earlier in this unit.

Nepal attracts many international visitors who wish to take a trekking holiday in the foothills of the Himalayas. One of the problems observed

> **Think it over...**
>
> Sirubari is a village in Nepal which has followed an approach different from other villages along the major trekking trails in Nepal. It is not on the major trekking trails but is easily accessible by vehicle. Quality tourism is emphasised and there are no lodges charging only $1 a day (as there are along the major trekking trails) – a typical package costs US$80 for three nights. There is less leakage and 50 per cent of the tourist spending is estimated to remain in the village. There has been little adverse cultural impact in the area due to tourism, according to some experts.
>
> Do you think there should be more Sirubari-type village tourism in the future?

by the national government has been inadequate retention of tourism spending, partly because there is a high import content in the products consumed by tourists and partly because it is largely foreign-based tour operators that offer trekking holidays. As a result the economic gains have been limited, despite the growing number of tourists.

Investing tourism income

One way to maximise the positive impacts of tourism is to use at least part of the revenue generated to invest in projects that benefit the community. This can help to sustain the growth of tourism in the area, while improving the infrastructure and preserving cultural heritage. Destinations should manage their tourist activities with the involvement and consent of local communities. Local people should participate in planning and managing the provision of facilities to ensure that a fair share of profits goes back to the local community (perhaps in the form of health care, schools, etc.).

Sometimes it is necessary for the investment to come before the tourism, however. For example Manchester received a large amount of funding for it to be able to host the Commonwealth Games in 2002. The new infrastructure made it a more appealing place to visit. The Games themselves left a host of facilities for use by the local community, such as the Velodrome and the new City of Manchester Football Stadium.

Theory into practice

Community tourism (sometimes called community-based tourism) is a form of tourism which aims to include and benefit local communities, particularly indigenous peoples and villagers in the developing world. For instance, villagers might host tourists in their village, managing the scheme communally and sharing the profits. There are many types of community tourism project; in some, the local community works with a commercial tour operator, but all community tourism projects should give local people a fair share of the benefits and profits, as well as a say in deciding how tourism is managed.

Widening access to facilities and assets

Accessibility refers to:

* physical access to a facility

* the availability of products and services.

Access to natural and built attractions may be difficult or impossible for people who have a physical disability, such as wheelchair users. In the UK, though, the Disability Discrimination Act 1995 requires service providers (whether they charge for that service or not) to make 'reasonable adjustments' to any barriers that may prevent a disabled person using or accessing their service. Service providers include hotels, restaurants and holiday accommodation. They cannot refuse to meet the needs of a disabled person, or provide a lower standard of service because of a disability, unless it can be justified.

It is not only physical disability, though, that can restrict access to leisure facilities: a lack of money can be a real barrier. In the UK and in most overseas destinations in MEDCs, access to facilities for people on low income is generally very good. Discounts and concessionary rates for students, children and senior citizens are commonplace, and these help to widen access.

Staff training and development

By investing in staff training and development, tourist organisations can better meet the needs of their customers. There are many training courses and qualifications available within the industry, both in the UK and overseas. They cover areas such as customer service, tourism management, health and safety, food hygiene, travel service provider skills in computerised reservations, and countryside management and environmental skills. The benefits of training are threefold:

* For the organisation it enables a high-quality customer service to be provided, as in the case of luxury hotels. This in turn increases revenue and enhances the image and reputation of the organisation.

* For the staff involved it creates greater job satisfaction, by giving them increased job security and financial rewards.

* For the visitor, there will be good customer service.

Training and employment of local people

There are many job opportunities in the travel and tourism industry, but the local population may need training to enable them to work in these roles. Responsible tourism development should lead to increased employment and economic opportunities for the host population.

For some communities, the decline of traditional industries and the breakdown of family structures as a result of tourism have led to unemployment and poverty. By offering training and support to the local population, organisations involved in tourism development can help to build up the workforce and improve the community's chances for further employment. In some LEDCs governments sponsor training schemes and seek to increase the participation of ethnic groups in recognised tourist activities so that they can participate in the growing tourism industry.

Employment 'changes' for the local providers in the Gambia

A DFID Tourism Challenge Fund project worked with local people in the Gambia to achieve change and increase informal sector incomes. At Kotu beach, fruit sellers and juice pressers adopted a code of conduct to reduce the hassling of tourists and established stalls so that they no longer needed to hawk for business on the beaches. Guides and craft workers took similar initiatives, and hoteliers invited craft workers to sell within the hotels on a rota basis. Hotel guests benefited from a less hassled environment and made more use of the beaches. Fruit sellers' incomes increased by 50 per cent; juice pressers' by 120 per cent; guides' by a third; and craft workers in the market reported a doubling of their incomes and 43 new jobs. The Gambia now has a Responsible Tourism Policy supported by all stakeholders and a Responsible Tourism Partnership that is seeking to develop these initiatives and spread their impact.

Source: adapted from the International Development magazine

Tourism education

Attempts are being made to inform and to educate tourists so that they not only help protect and maintain the environment they are visiting but also take a greater interest in it, and thus enjoy their stay more. This is not just a matter for international tourism: in the UK, the countryside code encourages visitors to 'enjoy the countryside and respect its life and work'. This is presented to tourists on posters, leaflets and brochures.

For those who do travel more widely, many charitable organisations, such as the Travel Foundation (www.thetravelfoundation.org.uk), issue guidelines for travellers on what to do before they go and while they are there. These seek to educate and inform tourists on a range of social, cultural and environmental issues. As a student who is interested in travel and tourism, you should be familiar with such organisations' websites (see also unit 12, on ecotourism). Another example is Tourism Concern (www.tourismconcern.org.uk). It has produced a video, *Looking Beyond the Brochure*, and lots of resource materials for education providers (e.g. schools and universities). The organisation also provides talks and lectures, runs workshops and mounts exhibitions. It works to link sustainable tourism development into tourism courses, which is essential if future policy makers and practitioners are to understand ethical tourism.

Minimising the negative impacts

Planning control

You have learned in previous sections how unplanned tourism development has caused unsightly and disorganised resort development. Fortunately, many tourism developers have learnt from the mistakes made in the past and now enforce strict planning controls. There are of course some exceptions, such as the phenomenal growth of Dubai and Shanghai as tourist destinations. It is hoped that these destinations will be able to fill the thousands of hotel rooms that are currently being built.

Using the principles of sustainable tourism

Concern about the negative impacts of tourism on a destination has led to the development of the concept of sustainable tourism. Associated with this has been the growth of green, eco, responsible, alternative and low-impact tourism. In many parts of the world, sustainable tourism is being developed in line with Agenda 21, the international action plan devised in 1992 at the Earth Summit.

Key term

Sustainable in the context of development means that the needs of the present are met without the ability of future generations to meet their own needs being compromised.

Sustainable tourism identifies the maximum carrying capacity of a destination and ensures that this is not exceeded. If it is exceeded, there is likely to be an unacceptable change in the physical environment and a decline in the quality of the tourist experience. The carrying capacity is determined by three key factors:

* **Physical considerations** – how many amenities are there within the destinations i.e. beds, restaurants, bars etc. This will determine how many tourists the destination can comfortably accommodate.

* **Environmental constraints** – what the natural environment can comfortably absorb e.g. beaches, footpaths, disruption to wildlife etc.

* **Number of visitors** – there needs to be a consideration of the saturation point. At what stage will tourists consider the destination too crowded and therefore spoilt for tourism purposes? Tourists wish to see destinations as close to their original state as possible. Once a destination becomes overcrowded it becomes unattractive as a tourist destinatiton.

Think it over...

At what stage will tourists consider the destination too crowded and therefore spoilt for tourism purposes? Tourists wish to see destinations as close to their original state as possible. Once a destination becomes overcrowded it becomes unattractive as a tourist destination.

Theory into practice

Green Globe 21 (see www.greenglobe21.com) is the global benchmarking, certification and improvement system for sustainable travel and tourism. It is based on Agenda 21, and provides companies, communities and consumers with a path to sustainable travel and tourism. There are now four Green Globe 21 Standards: Company; Community; International ecotourism; and Design and construct. For example, the Green Globe 21 Company Standard requires: an environmental and social sustainability policy; compliance with the prevailing legislative framework; above-baseline environmental and social sustainability performance (assessed through the benchmarking process); an operating environmental management system; and continual consultation and communication with public and clients. By achieving a Green Globe 21 Global Standard, an organisation or a destination shows it is addressing its wider responsibilities. The Green Globe Standards are a powerful marketing tool for attracting environmentally concerned travellers and organisations that have adopted Green Globe 21 have seen an increase in profits.

Sustainable tourism in the south-west of England

The Local Sustainability Group for the South West (LSGSW) in 2000 produced a discussion paper as a reminder of what sustainable tourism actually entails, for a range of regional agencies, statutory and voluntary bodies, trade organisations and local authorities. Ten key points emerged, which were formed into a project checklist for the sustainability of a tourism development:

1   *Local opinion*. Have local people likely to be affected and interest groups been consulted and, if so, are they generally supportive of the proposals?

2   *Costs*. Have measures been proposed to remove or minimise the environmental costs to the community (e.g. traffic, air, noise, light pollution)?

3   *Benefits*. Will the economic benefits of the scheme spread into the local community beyond just employment (e.g. using local goods, services and suppliers)?

4   *Transport*. Will visitors be able to travel to the site easily without a car, and, if so, will they be encouraged to do so?

5   *Access*. Can people with disabilities access and use the site and facilities easily?

6   *Resource use*. Have measures been proposed to minimise use of fossil fuels, electricity, water and land in the development?

7   *Waste*. Have measures been proposed to minimise waste and to provide for recycling and reuse of materials?

8   *Local environment*. Do the proposals safeguard the local built and natural environment, including local character?

9   *Wildlife*. Will wildlife interests be safeguarded and/or enhanced?

10 *Quality*. Will the quality of the visit be given greater priority than visitor numbers?

✳ **Consider your local area or an area that you have studied and answer the above 10 points.**

Source: Adapted from www.oursouthwest.com/RegiSus/tourism

Visitor and traffic management

Many tourist destinations can become 'honeypots' in the peak season. This means that they become problematic in terms of traffic control. Large coaches carrying tour groups, day-tippers by car and public transport, may cause congestion on roads and in car parks. Small villages and historic towns, both in the UK and overseas are especially at risk from traffic pollution as their narrow streets and limited parking areas were not designed to cope with 21st century visitors' numbers and accompanying traffic.

Methods used to minimise traffic congestion include:

✳ **Park and ride schemes** – many towns now provide these to enable visitors to leave their cars and travel into the town/village by buses provided by the local authorities

✳ **Pedestrianisation schemes** – town and city centres are often closed to all traffic during peak times to allow pedestrians to enjoy the sights and attractions safely

✳ **One-way systems and traffic calming measures** – these are used to enable traffic to follow a route around the bus areas in order to alleviate congestion.

Assessing environmental impact

Public, private and voluntary organisations are responsible for maintaining the environment that is affected by tourist numbers. This is sometimes known as EIA (environmental impact assessment) or environmental auditing.

Assessing the impact allows the organisations concerned to have a clear idea of which areas are at risk. If damage has occurred, then plans can be made to reduce activity in an area. Measures can then be taken to repair any damage caused.

Examples of methods used to assess environmental impact include:

* National park and countryside rangers looking for footpath erosion

* The monitoring of exhaust fumes (carbon monoxide) levels in an area that is heavily congested by traffic at peak times

* Beach cleaners checking for plastic, oil and litter pollution on popular tourist beaches

* Historic houses being regularly checked for damage caused by tourists to floors and furnishings.

Knowledge check

1 Explain the role of development companies in tourism development.

2 How does the government provide support for travel and tourism?

3 How does the voluntary sector obtain funding?

4 How does the public sector work to promote tourism development?

5 How do the private sector bodies such as travel agents and tour operators help to promote tourism in overseas destinations?

6 What are the main aims of VisitBritain?

7 Why is the role of Tourism Concern so important to tourism development in developing countries?

8 How can pressure groups influence tourism development?

9 Give three advantages of a partnership between the sectors?

10 List five organisations from each sector and briefly outline their roles.

11 Explain 3 economic objectives of tourism development.

12 Explain the difference between an LEDC and a MEDC.

13 Why is tourism development so important for countries that are LEDCs?

14 Describe how the 'multiplier effect' occurs in areas of tourism development.

15 Investigate an area where you think 'leakage' has occurred; explain how and why it has happened.

16 Explain the meaning of the following terms; demonstration effect and staged authentication.

17 Describe two negative impacts of tourism on the marine environment.

18 Describe two positive impacts of tourism development for countries with a distinct cultural identity.

19 State the two key factors that determine whether or not tourism development is sustainable in a destination.

20 Describe two ways in which environmental auditing may be carried out at a tourist destination.

References and further reading

Websites

www.forestbowland.co.uk
www.namibiatourism.com
www.dcms.gov.org.uk
www.visitbritain.com
www.peopleandplanet.net
www.chinabroadcasst.cn
www.stb.com
www.english-heritage.org.uk
www.nationaltrust.org.uk
www.environment-agency.gov.uk

Tour operators

British Airways
Easyjet
Sol Melia Hotels
First Choice Holidays
TUI Group
Kaunos Tours
Thomas Cook Group

International Organisations

www.unesco.org
www.wttc.org
www.tourismconcern.org.uk
www.wwf.org
The Travel Foundation
Human Development report
Foreign and Commonwealth Office

Publications

TTG
Travel Weekly
Daily Telegraph
Travel Daily News
Cooper et al 1996
National Geographic
UNEP Magazine

Event management

This unit covers the following sections:
* Feasibility of the project
* Teamwork
* Marketing the event
* Financing the event
* Occasion management
* Carrying out the project
* Evaluation of the project

During your course you have studied different AS and A2 units and this mandatory unit is designed to bring together learning from these plus new learning from this unit. It requires you to undertake a travel and tourism project or event. You will work as part of a team to plan, manage, participate in and evaluate a real travel and tourism project, using essential industry skills such as team working, marketing, customer service, fulfilling legal responsibilities associated with events, maintaining appropriate records and monitoring finance.

You must be involved in all aspects of the event, from initial discussion about possible events to taking part in the final event. You may be given a specific team role or function, but you will need to participate in group discussions, developing your problem-solving and communication skills. You will later need to identify weaknesses and strengths in your own performance throughout the project, as well as those of the team, within your concluding evaluation of the project – and to analyse what went well and what could have worked better.

How you will be assessed

This unit is assessed as a portfolio for external moderation. It must be produced individually, though some documents will relate to group activities (e.g. minutes of meetings, marketing materials, correspondence). Your evidence will include:

✳ Preparing your own business plan (for Assessment Objective 1).

✳ Keeping a log-book or other record of your contribution throughout the entire project, including dealing with problems (Assessment Objective 2).

✳ Details of your investigative research for the feasibility study and additional research during the management of the project (Assessment Objective 3).

✳ All this will inform your evaluation of your performance and the team's performance, so that you can make recommendations for organisational and personal improvement (for Assessment Objective 4).

Assessment is explained in more detail at relevant points later in this unit.

Feasibility of the project

Before you can make a decision on the project you will undertake for this unit you must ascertain that your ideas are feasible. This means that you will need to think carefully about what type of project you and the rest of your team can undertake. If you do not have clear goals and reasons, or if you have not considered all the issues, there is a strong likelihood that it will not work well. Any group organising an event must take account of all the relevant factors in order to produce a comprehensive business plan, as required for this unit.

Obviously, you are not going to arrange anything as complicated as the Olympic Games, which will be coming to London in 2012, but in order to win this coveted event Lord Sebastian Coe and his team had to consider many issues to prepare their submission to the International Olympic Committee. They had to consider venues, location and construction of these in the time available, transport routes for participants and visitors, equipment and materials needed to staff the Games, benefits to and support of the community and the country as a whole, legal issues, security and safety, financial aspects such as funding this major construction project, schedules to ensure everything is completed on time, and contingency plans should any venue not be available. These all formed the feasibility study which then led to the creation of the business plan.

There must be a team of people organising the event to demonstrate your ability to work as a team member. The size of the team may depend on the number of students in your class – if you are part of a large class, then it would be advisable for that to be divided into smaller working teams.

Culture Secretary Tessa Jowell and Lord Sebastian Coe

If the team is too large, there will always be someone who lets the others do the work, so an ideal size would be between five and eight people in each team. Each group of students can run their own event according to their preferences; the teacher can ensure that the dates chosen by each group do not conflict and that each team works independently of the other teams.

Alternatively, it may be possible to arrange a larger event for your class to undertake, with sub-teams responsible for different parts of the event, as in the case study.

CASE STUDY

Promotional evening for Tenerife

A class of 20 students had visited Tenerife on a residential trip, during which they had videoed accommodation, attractions and excursions. One group edited this video into a promotional video for the location and played it during the Tenerife evening. Another team organised a fashion show as part of the event, after negotiations with a local shop which agreed to provide the clothing, using students as models. Another team contacted local businesses, such as travel agencies, wine merchants and food retailers, and invited them to have a display at the event. Yet another group produced typical snacks from Tenerife to offer to those who attended the event. All were involved in meetings to select the venue, market the event, arrange and manage finance and sponsorship, and to discuss issues and contingency plans, as well as evaluation methods.

* **Make a list of the points the students needed to consider in a feasibility study for this event.**

* **Compare your list with others in the group and discuss similarities or differences between your list and the group's lists.**

As part of the feasibility study for your project, there are some questions you will need to ask yourself and your team before you can prepare the business plan:

* What is the size of your group and do any of you have particular skills?

* What type of event or project might sufficiently stimulate your group?

* How will you find out if customers are going to be interested in your event?

* How will you inform people about this event?

* How much money is likely to be needed to stage this event and where will it come from? Might you need sponsorship or donations of prizes from organisations outside the centre?

* How much are participants likely to be prepared to pay for the event you are considering?

* Will your income match your expenditure, or, if the event is for charity, will it make a profit?

* Are you hard working and determined to make a success of this event?

* Can you meet tight deadlines and organise yourself to ensure the event takes place?

* How much time have you got to arrange this event?

* What are the legal or regulatory constraints that might affect the operation of the event (such as permissions from parents, head teacher, local authority regulations, health and safety issues)?

Your business plan will be for the event you finally decide to organise; beforehand, it is necessary to look at various alternative ideas for the event through a feasibility study to ascertain what can be achieved in the time allowed.

Seasonality, tangibility and perishability

Your feasibility study will need to consider the seasonality, tangibility and perishability of the proposed event.

* **Seasonality**. Someone might suggest organising a visit to a major attraction for other students in the school or college. But if you are organising your event during the winter months you will need to know whether that attraction is open. This is an example of seasonality.

* **Tangibility**. Anyone who is being encouraged to take part in your event is expecting to receive the goods or services you are providing, and if your marketing is not successful you will not achieve tangibility, or if it is misleading you will not be meeting their intangible expectations.

* **Perishability**. If you have booked a certain number of rooms for a residential trip for specific dates, but fail to attract enough customers or people drop out at the last moment, you may still have to pay for rooms booked, as the accommodation provider may not be able to re-let those rooms.

All these features are important when deciding on and planning your event.

SWOT analysis

Having undertaken this initial investigation, the group now needs to decide what event they will undertake for more detailed investigation to finalise information for the business plan. One interesting way often used to make final decisions on the event is to undertake a SWOT analysis (SWOT stands for Strengths, Weaknesses, Opportunities, Threats) and there are two ways of doing this. You could just put each heading on a different sheet of paper and identify ideas under each heading. Another way is to use a template such as the one illustrated in Figure 10.1.

This technique is often used during planning stages of marketing campaigns. If you are doing the A2 double award, you will study marketing in much more detail in unit 15, but those doing the A2 single award will nonetheless need to appreciate the benefits of this exercise. You may wish to refer briefly to unit 15 to ensure you really understand the purposes of SWOT analysis (see page 244), and focus your mind on what can be gained from undertaking the event and what difficulties you may have to overcome.

(see page 244)

Theory into practice

In your working group, discuss possible events to organise. What are your aims and objectives? What research do you need to undertake to decide whether an event is feasible in the time allowed, and whether it is likely to attract participants? Use the questions above as a guide. You need to undertake research relatively quickly so that you leave sufficient time to plan and organise the event you decide on, as a group, after the feasibility study. You could allocate different members of your group to investigate one idea each so that you have some information on which to base your final decision, including possible costs, initial market research into support or interest and what customers would be prepared to pay. You may need to contact outside organisations such as transport providers or attractions to obtain data.

Even if your teacher has guided you as to a possible event, you will still need to undertake a feasibility study to see if the idea is manageable and workable.

Keep all the records of your feasibility study for your portfolio evidence.

FIGURE 10.1. *Template for a SWOT analysis*

Produce a SWOT analysis for your chosen event. Consider the benefits and drawbacks of working in a group, the skills and abilities of those in your group, your mission statement and the purpose of the event. You will need to consider all four aspects of the analysis, though hopefully 'Threats' will not have too many entries!

Mission statement

You may decide to prepare a mission statement, which (if you remember from unit 2, 'Customer service') is a succinct statement of what you intend to do and perhaps why. One example of a mission statement produced by a group of students was:

Our company's mission statement is to take 16 disaffected children on a day trip to Jersey.

The example below was written by a group of students who organised a residential trip to Calais for year 7 students at their school:

Our mission is to further develop, strengthen and improve the students' knowledge of the French way of life, creating a less formal, stress-free and relaxed atmosphere for the students and staff by organising an exciting educational and entertaining visit to Calais.

Mission statements focus your mind on your group's intentions, so you can draw up your aims and objectives appropriately.

Aims and objectives of the project

✳ Now you have decided on an event you need to state your aims and objectives, which should naturally follow from the mission statement. What are your group's aims and objectives? Are they just to meet the criteria for the unit, or do you have other aims?

Some aims and objectives will be internal to the group, such as enhancing planning and communication skills, whereas others will be more relevant to the outside community, such as raising the profile of the school or college, creating funds for specific charities or providing benefits to the community.

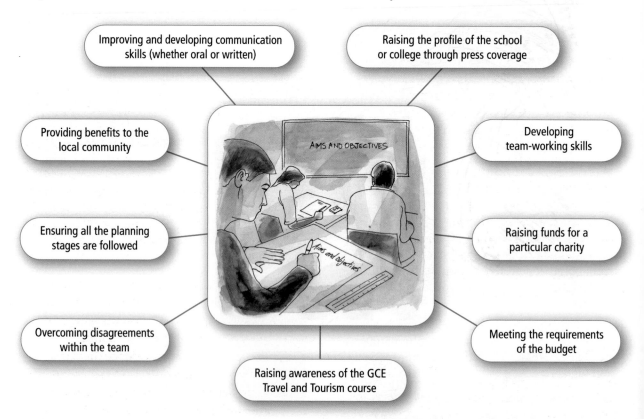

FIGURE 10.2. *Your group's aims and objectives for the event could include any of the above*

The aims and objectives you record should be comprehensive but also be realistic and achievable. To help you ensure this you can use the framework of the 'SMART' criteria, which will also assist your final evaluation. SMART criteria are those which are:

* **S**pecific – they apply to the chosen event

* **M**easurable – they can be assessed for effectiveness

* **A**chievable – the event can be staged within the deadlines set

* **R**ealistic – organised within financial boundaries to meet the objectives

* **T**ime–framed – deadlines are set for completion of the event and all the necessary steps leading up to it.

Who are your customers?

Who is the target market for your event – your potential customers? For instance, if you decided to stage a fashion show to raise money for a local charity, are the clothes being shown for male and female customers, young or older people, or anyone? In other words, you need to know who your potential customers are and what they might want before you can consider how to meet their needs. To return to the example, they may want to purchase the items after the fashion show, so what extra facilities might your team provide? They may want refreshments before or after the show, so is catering included in admission fees or charged at the time of purchase?

A student fashion show

How will the event be marketed and what methods will you use?

Marketing methods and strategies are discussed later in this chapter, but you will need to decide how you are going to attract customers to your event. You may have to undertake sufficient market research to provide evidence that your chosen event is viable. You must identify your potential market and demand for your project. Some basic market research would involve you giving out questionnaires to potential customers, to establish what they may be prepared to pay and how many are likely to be interested in taking part in the event. Remember the following points when designing questionnaires:

* keep the questions simple

* offer yes/no responses or multiple-choice alternatives

* ensure questions are relevant

* encourage high response rates by keeping the questionnaire brief

* cover as many potential customers as possible to give more reliable data.

If you have planned your questionnaire well, it should be fairly easy to analyse the findings in order to establish potential customer demand for your event. It is better to have too many people wanting to participate in your event than none at all. If the event has restricted numbers, then waiting lists could be advisable to compensate for any cancellations.

Having established that there will be a reasonable level of demand, you need to consider how you are going to inform potential customers. If the event is for a client group within your school or college, you may decide to use posters that give basic information, followed by circulars to tutor groups. If you are trying to attract outside customers, how will you inform them of the event? You may want to consider press advertisements (though these are likely to be expensive), larger posters for display at suitable venues or locations and press releases to local newspapers (the press may follow these up with some coverage in the paper or photographs).

Physical resource needs

All events will require some physical resources such as equipment, venues or premises and materials.

Equipment

If your event was a fête to raise funds for a local charity, you would need tables for the various stalls, chairs for stallholders and participants, some form of shelter for refreshment areas and power supply to this area if hot drinks are being provided. Different types of events will need different physical resources, so itemise what is required and from where it can be obtained, plus costs. A conference may require laptop and screen with suitable power supply, flip-chart pads and appropriate pens, overhead projector for transparencies. You may also need to consider back-up supplies should equipment fail during the conference.

Venues

Venues vary according to the type of event. If you were holding a conference for other schools in the area, you could use your own college or school, but you may prefer to arrange something at an external venue, such as a hotel. When carrying out your feasibility study you will need to ask the following questions:

* Can your chosen venue accommodate the number of likely participants?

* Is there a restriction on numbers that can be admitted?

* What are the comparative costs involved of internal and external venues?

The Armadillo conference centre in Glasgow

* Is your proposed venue suitable for your specific event?

* Can it cater for the event's needs?

You will also have to consider availability, as this may determine your choice of venue or the date of your event. Other considerations may be car parking or access for participants with limited mobility. Residential events would involve accommodation venues, so again availability and type of rooms offered would need to be investigated, as well as prices.

Materials

The types of materials required again vary considerably according to the chosen event, but include everything from paper (to produce questionnaires, publicity, correspondence, team minutes, etc.) and other stationery (such as pens / pencils, stamps, paper clips, tape) to catering requirements (drinks, snacks, china or paper cups, covers for the tables, cutlery, etc.).

The more material items you can realistically identify for your chosen event, the better prepared you will appear, and the less likely it will be that crises develop or that unexpected costs are incurred.

Financial aspects of the project

An important aspect of the feasibility study and your business plan is the management of the financial aspects of your project. Normally, a project will have a budget – this may be an amount of money allocated to the total project which must not be exceeded, or it could be how much income you will need to run the project to set the admission costs or make a profit. The timing for receipts of income and payments of expenses must be clarified. The timing of these is also important, as you will have to ensure that you always have sufficient income over the course of the project to pay any expenses as they occur.

Financial management is explained in more detail later in this chapter, but your feasibility study will need to identify:

* start-up costs

* basic running costs for the project

* how income is to be raised

* how payments will be handled.

In many institutions students are not allowed to handle cash, but as finance should be monitored throughout, it will be necessary to ensure records are as current as possible through negotiation with the finance officer of your institution.

You will also need to decide whether participants for a residential visit are to pay deposits, then regular payments, or make a firm commitment to the project by full payment initially.

One of the more common reasons why events fail is that the organisers have not considered how finance will be controlled, and then find that they do not have sufficient funds to provide what participants are expecting. Some students have undertaken smaller projects to raise money for the major event, or obtained sponsorship from outside organisations. Others have been provided with a basic fund or loan to start the project, but had to ensure that money raised during the project financed the event and repaid the loan.

Think it over...

Consider your suggested event or project and try to list all possible expenditures it might involve. Then consider how these expenditures might be funded to avoid making a financial loss. Compare your list with others in your team to compile a consolidated list of expenditure items. Then consider how income will be raised to meet these expenditures.

Staffing for the event

Skills and abilities of the members of your team

As part of your feasibility study you will need to identify the skills and abilities of the different members of your team, to ensure that everyone is allocated an appropriate role and that all roles are covered. Skills and abilities and how individuals operate within teams is discussed in more detail below, in the section on teamwork, to help you to select the 'right person for the job', but your business plan will need to identify the roles and functions of the various team members. These roles will probably include a chairperson or team leader, someone who is fairly numerate (to manage the financial aspects), another member in charge of marketing, possibly another for health and safety and legal issues, and someone to record team meetings. The last role may be rotated round members of the team, but records of team discussions and meetings are required for your portfolio.

Additional staffing requirements

Your team members may be the only people required to stage the event, but many events require some additional staffing, whether teachers or other people from outside your immediate team. If you are organising an educational visit, local authorities have strict regulations as to how many teachers must accompany a group, and ratios of male: female coverage. If you do need help from others outside your group, will these 'volunteers' be rewarded (financially or in other ways)? This may be an especially important consideration if you are organising a fund-raising event for a charity.

Activity

Investigate the roles of conference organisers, event managers, catering managers and facilities managers. Identify the skills and abilities each role requires. You might arrange a visit to a local conference venue to meet employees undertaking these roles.

Think it over...

Think about the various roles your event requires and then consider who might be the best person to undertake that role and why.

Administration systems

Any event or business will need a formalised administrative system – which may be paper based, computerised, or a combination of both – to monitor progress and store records. Details of administration management should be considered during your feasibility study and final recommendations should be given in your business plan.

Paper-based systems include documents such as business letters, minutes of meetings, invoices to suppliers, parental consent letters, passport applications and pro formas to be completed. Even if much of your life revolves around technology, you still need these paper-based records, so you will need to decide where and how they are going to be stored, and by whom. As some form legal contracts, there is a security issue here regarding their safe-keeping. You may decide to have a group file for this type of administration, which is kept in a secure place, so all members of the team have access to it during their planning and operating stage. It is generally not advisable to have one student keep all the records, as he or she may be absent on one of your planning days when you need vital information. It is recommended that this file is kept somewhere safe and accessible within the school or college.

Electronic administration systems may also be used. You may send email or faxes to certain individuals or institutions – but copies must be maintained to demonstrate communication skills as well as to record vital information. Various software packages may be used – you may want to set up a database for your event (for contact details, etc.), a spreadsheet (for financial records) as well as word processing packages.

You will need to consider the Data Protection Act when recording personal information. This applies to both paper-based and electronic records. It would be advisable to have a secure area for your project's electronic information, with a password to access the information known only to the team and the teacher in charge, to safeguard data which can be accessed only by the team members.

Another aspect of administrative procedures to consider is how complaints or comments will be processed. You may receive complaints from providers, participants and others and the group will need to formalise a complaints procedure to be followed should these arise. Complaints should be recorded and responded to as speedily as possible so that customers feel confident in the service you provide and you may want to refer back to the unit 2 (Customer service) to review the best methods of dealing with complaints.

Think it over...

* What type of administration records will you need to keep?

* What will be the best method of storing this information?

* Where should you store this information?

* Are you going to design your own business letterhead for your project, to give it a clear identity?

* What software packages will you use to ensure you have relevant records?

* How can you ensure that you will be able to access information whenever it is needed?

Project timescales

You will of course have to set a date for the staging of your event. This will then determine the period of time you will have for planning

and preparation, and it is important to set out a project time plan. This is often prepared using a spreadsheet, with a column for either each day of the week or for each week, with interim deadlines for completion of certain activities. It is a good idea also to identify who should complete these activities and by when, although this is not essential in the initial planning stage.

Theory into practice

Consider your event and the timescale you have to work within. What are the main features to be organised or arranged? Giving some thought to these, try to work out a possible schedule to ensure everything is covered. You could use a similar template to that shown in Figure 10.3, but obviously your column and side headings will depend on the type of event.

Legal aspects of the project

There are three legal aspects of a project proposal that will influence how and whether it will work:

* health and safety

* security

* insurance.

PROJECT TIMESCALES												
TASK / Week ending:	05-Dec	12-Dec	19-Dec	02-Jan	09-Jan	16-Jan	23-Jan	05-Feb	12-Feb	19-Feb	28-Feb	05-Mar
Feasibility Study and research	■	■										
Preparation of Bus plan			■									
Marketing				■	■	■						
Bookings provisional						■						
Risk assessment							■					
Legal documents								■				
Confirm bookings										■		
Collect deposits						■	■					
Parental consents							■					
Additional marketing								■	■			
Arrange rota for day										■	■	
Prepare evaluations										■		
Day of event											■	
Evaluate event												■

FIGURE 10.3. *Example of a project time plan*

Health and safety

During your AS-level studies you will have considered health and safety issues for internal and external customers in unit 2, on customer service, as well as other units within the AS programme. Now you need to relate this earlier learning to your own event. You will have to identify specific health and safety aspects of your event and find out what formal documents have to be completed for your school or college records.

It is advisable to undertake a risk assessment (see below) in order to highlight any possible health and safety issues, which will help focus your mind on potential problems and how these may be solved or minimised. Certain venues have limits on the number of people allowed in a specific area. They may undertake their own health and safety checks but you still need to ensure that these are adequate for your event; this might be investigated by a specific team member.

If you are using transport you may need to consider the facilities on that transport, such as seatbelts, toilets and bins for waste such as food. You may have to write a set of rules for participants to ensure their health and safety throughout the journey. Lists of passengers will be required to check that all are on board at each stopping point. It may also be necessary to restrict the size of baggage taken, to prevent blockages to exits or aisles, and so on.

For some events you may need to establish whether anyone has special needs (dietary, access, medical) so that arrangements can be made to cater for these in your planning. There may be other aspects of health and safety relating to your specific event which should be identified and checked to ensure you have covered most eventualities.

You will also need to make participants aware of action to be taken in case of fire or accident and ensure your team know all the procedures thoroughly so they can act as leaders for evacuation of premises. First aid training could be a useful skill to note when allocating roles to team members. You may also need to provide a first aid box at your event.

Security

The security of your documentation and records has been discussed earlier. You also should ensure the security of belongings of participants at your event. What arrangements do you need to put in place for storage of expensive equipment for example, or for documents such as group passports, admission or transport tickets?

Your school or college may also have regulations regarding security that need to be addressed when formulating your business plan. Check this with the bursar to ensure you have met all the institution's requirements.

Many of you have mobile phones. A useful recommendation is to enter 'I C E' ('In Case of Emergency') as a name in the contacts list on your phone, and alongside that the number of the person who should be contacted by emergency services if needed.

Insurance

Is your event going to be covered by the school or college's insurance policy, or will you need to arrange specific cover for your event? If you are arranging a residential trip with a tour operator, you may take out the group insurance provided, but ensure you include this charge in costs to participants.

If you are holding your event at a venue outside your school or college, what insurance cover does the venue have? Does it meet your needs or do you need additional insurance cover? Any equipment used should be fully covered under this type of policy, especially if you are holding a conference or exhibition where outside parties are providing their own. Does this equipment need to be checked by a third party before it can be operated?

These are all important issues for discussion and allowance must be made for any additional costs incurred.

Risk assessment and contingency plans

When undertaking a risk assessment you will need to consider, as a group, all the component parts of the chosen event and identify how great

Risk Assessment	Activity/Environment/Venue Time and Date of Activity People involved		Day trip to Jersey Wednesday 9 April 2003 8 disaffected children (7–10 yrs), 8 students, 3 adults (age 16+)	
1. Hazards List significant hazards that may result in serious harm or affect several people	2. Level of Risk High/ Medium/ Low	3. Who might be harmed? List groups of people who are especially at risk from the significant hazard identified	4. Is the risk adequately controlled? List existing controls or note where the information may be found (e.g. information, instruction, training, systems or procedures)	5. What further action is needed to control the risk? List the risks that are not adequately controlled and propose action where it is reasonably practicable to do so
Coach travel and journey	Low	All group	Use of reputable ferry and coach company. Brief students on ferry and coach crossing	Head count on and off every transport. Carry spare clothing for 1 male & 1 female in case of illness or accidents. Give information on location of toilets and 2 adults & 1 child when child needs the toilet
Kits (e.g. trips, falls, bumps, sick, abduction, run over)	Medium	As above	Briefing for all parents & children at college on Wed 26 March	Nominated person at college to hold list of children contacts and allergies who will be available on phone for duration of trip. Mobile phones are available and funds for local phones. First aid box on hand and all staff trained in first aid. Carry sun block and water for sunburn and dehydration problems.
Bad weather conditions before departure	Medium	As above	Alternative programme given to parents	Use back-up plans of going bowling.
Problems at Zoo visit	Medium	As above	Two groups consisting of adult, 4 students and 4 children.	All to meet at DoDo Café
Living Legend visit	Medium	As above	As above	Meet at The Jersey Kitchen
If return boat cancelled due to adverse weather	Low	As above	On programme given to parents	Structured contingency plan in place
Child protection	Low	As above	All 8 students and 3 teachers have been police checked	

FIGURE 10.4. *Example of a completed risk assessment pro forma. Adapted from work for candidate Kelly Ingreville at Guernsey College of FE*

Key terms

Risk assessment is a requirement of all local authorities and institutions and must be carried out thoroughly. It must cover all aspects of the event and for each identify the level of risk, the people at risk, how that risk will be controlled and any further actions needed.

Contingency plans cover 'what if?' scenarios. They detail what you would do if one of a range of possible problems occurs.

a risk each part is and to whom, and then identify the action to be taken if the danger materialises. A completed risk assessment form will need to be prepared for your centre management team. It is possible that your centre will have a pro forma for this, which should be completed, or you could use one similar to the example shown in Figure 10.4.

Whatever form it takes, you will need to present evidence of risk analysis being undertaken for your portfolio.

The first step in contingency planning is to try to think of all the possible problems that could arise in relation to your event (these will be the ones beyond your control – those under your control you should have dealt with!). You then need to decide what actions you could take to overcome these difficulties. The contingency plans will form part of the overall business plan.

How will the project be reviewed and evaluated?

You will need to gather information on the success or otherwise of your event in order to address the Assessment Objective 4 criteria, so you should decide *before* the project begins how this information could be obtained (Figure 10.5) and

Contingency plans for a trip to Calais

A group of students had organised a day trip to Calais. They had made the ferry bookings for a specific date, organised entry to certain attractions and prepared documentation for the visit. However, on the day of the proposed visit there were blizzards – roads were blocked, ferries were cancelled due to adverse weather and there was no way the students could reach the ferry port. They had to consider possible alternatives to this visit at very short notice. They had included a similar possibility in their contingency plans but had graded it only as 'low risk'.

However, with the changed circumstances it became a higher risk and alternative arrangements had to be made to occupy the students for that day.

✳ **What contingency plans should have been made for the following circumstances?**

- **One of the organising students does not turn up on the day.**

- **The coach breaks down between the college and the ferry.**

✳ **What other 'what if?' scenarios might occur and what contingency plans would need to be made?**

from whom. Obviously, the participants can give important feedback, even if you do not get 100 per cent return, but how will you get this? Would you use a simple questionnaire for each participant to complete? Or would you consider oral feedback? The value of questionnaires is that there is

information to analyse at a later stage. Verbal feedback may be positive, but people may just be polite and not want to upset the organisers.

Are you also going to obtain feedback from teachers or other adults who were observing you undertaking the event? This can provide valuable

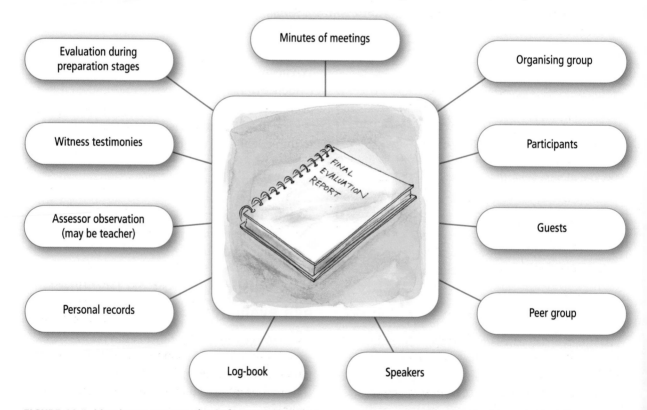

FIGURE 10.5. *You must ensure the information you draw upon in your final evaluation covers all areas*

data on your own individual performance as seen by someone who understands the requirements of the specification, and would probably be quite honest and forthright, giving you more information when considering skills you need to develop or the operation of the group as a whole. This should be in written format, too, so that you can refer to it in detail when preparing your concluding evaluation.

What about other members of your team? Might they have some valuable feedback to give, especially on your personal contribution to the group effort? This could be in the form of a questionnaire, but a group discussion or debriefing session could be videoed, though the opinions of others may not be as frank as in a written statement. You should also have records of group discussions from team minutes and your own log-book, which will also provide useful supporting information for your analysis. Questions could include:

✳ How well did the team work together?

✳ How did you solve problems/conflicts?

✳ Were arrangements satisfactory and had you given participants all the information they needed?

✳ What did you do well?

✳ If you organised another event in the future what would you change?

✳ Did you meet your aims and objectives?

What criteria are you going to use to evaluate and review your event? For participants, you need to know, for example:

✳ whether they enjoyed the event

✳ how they heard about it

✳ whether they were given all the information they needed before the event

✳ whether it was well organised

✳ what the good and bad points were of the event.

Obviously the questions asked will need to relate to your chosen event but these are some ideas you might consider.

You also need to review progress on an ongoing basis to check that all the team are undertaking assigned duties to schedule. You will need to refer to your overall time plan to check whether, as a group, you are meeting the deadlines set. Remedial action may have to be taken quickly to overcome any difficulties and keep the project on track.

The business plan

Now we have addressed all the relevant items for a feasibility study, you are almost ready to prepare your business plan. But there are still some important decisions to be made and you will need to study the next sections of this unit.

Activity

Contact one of the local major banks to see if they have leaflets or materials which may help you formulate your own business plan for your event. (HSBC, for example, have a pack of information and a disk which provides an outline business plan – though this is designed for people setting up their own new business.)

How can you find out more about the structure of business plans? What are the features of a business plan?

Teamwork

So what constitutes a team? One definition quoted by Needham and Dransfield (1993) is:

A team is a small group of people who have developed to the stage where they are able to perform effectively, each member adopting the role necessary to work with others, using complementary skills.

The success of your event will depend on the ability of the group to work as a team. Many aspects of the travel and tourism industry involve working in groups – whether on reception, in the catering section, or as representatives at an overseas destination. You may or may not know the other members of your group well, but by the end of the project you should have overcome any differences and have gelled as a cohesive team. You will be interdependent on each other – no one member should be left to do all the work!

What is the purpose of your team?

The primary purpose of your team is of course to organise an event, but there are also other reasons for working in a team. One is to improve your communication and cooperation skills. Another is to share the workload when organising an event – it would be too much for one person and often other people in the group can offer good ideas or suggestions to aid decision making.

Team structure

Though your team will generally work together informally, there will be times when a more formal structure will be needed. Both when planning and when staging the event, you will probably need to hold meetings as a group, where the views of others are heard and discussed. At meetings, specific tasks or functions can be allocated to individuals to complete before the next meeting.

How often you hold formal meetings will depend on the timescale allowed for your project, but as a minimum they should be weekly, when each team member will feed back progress reports to the rest of the team. These formal meetings should be recorded by producing minutes of the meeting, so that everyone has written proof of what has been decided, particularly if someone in the team was absent from the actual meeting. Also of course, these records are needed for your portfolio.

Whether you follow the standard format of formal minutes is largely a matter for the team to decide, but you do need to record the following:

* the date (and time) of the meeting

* those present and any absentees

* approval (or otherwise!) of the minutes of the last meeting

* specific agenda items discussed (these could be feedback on venues, costs, legal issues, progress to date)

* whether there are any issues which need to be followed up – usually noted as 'Matters arising'

* the date agreed for the next meeting.

More informal or *ad hoc* discussions may well take place among the group between one formal meeting and the next. Nevertheless, you will need to log *all* your actions, discussions and decisions for your portfolio evidence, as well as copies of the minutes of formal team meetings. Referring to the case study 'Promotional evening' (on page 48), each subgroup held meetings to discuss matters relating to their specific function as a subcommittee of the whole group. This enabled them to focus on their identified responsibilities but reports were made to the formal group regularly.

Roles and responsibilities of team members

Different team members may be expected to carry out specific functions and we now need to consider what types of role a team event requires. These could include a marketing manager, a group leader and a finance officer. Each event will have different requirements for roles within the team, but what is most important is that you choose the right person for each particular role or responsibility. It is also recommended that you consider the nine roles identified by Belbin as crucial to teamwork (see Belbin, 2004, and also www.belbin.info):

1 **Chairperson/coordinator** – coordinates team efforts and leads the group, but may seem bossy or delegate tasks which should be done by him – or herself.

2 **Shaper** – a potential chairperson, able to motivate the group to complete the task successfully and thrives on pressure.

3 **Plant** – describes a creator or inventor who may have good ideas and suggestions but may be rather shy or lacking in confidence, or is so preoccupied that she or he could annoy others in the team.

4 **Monitor/evaluator** – checks the progress of the group and can analyse situations and suggest better ways of making progress, but lacks drive and the ability to inspire others.

5 **Resource investigator** – a good mixer with others in the group, can suggest new ideas or

contacts to the team; often an extrovert with a short attention span or who loses interest quickly.

6 **Specialist** – can break down tasks into manageable units and is usually a very hard worker who thrives on pressure and is zealous in efforts to get things going.

7 **Team worker** – supports the team and encourages others to work together but may talk too much or be indecisive.

8 **Implementer** – turns concepts and ideas into practice, carrying out ideas systematically and efficiently.

9 **Finisher** – watches deadlines closely and checks for unfinished business to ensure deadlines are met and tasks completed.

CASE STUDY
Assigning team roles

✳ Tom has a rather laid-back attitude to work and is a bit of a joker, but his sense of humour can encourage team members to work together, and can put effort in when pressed.

✳ Susan is conscientious and hard working and is possibly a prefect at school as well as being leader in a local youth group. She can be a bit dominating and overpowering at times.

✳ Sanjiv has shown he can meet tight deadlines, but is rather quiet, though does have some bright ideas.

✳ Zara is rather serious but hard working and very keen to help others out, though she is very quiet and unassuming. She has some good ideas and will share them with others.

✳ **Consider Belbin's nine team roles and identify which student best fits which description.**

✳ **If you had to suggest a team of three who could meet deadlines and work well together, which students would make a successful team?**

Team building and interaction

In smaller teams (and yours is likely to be a small one) members may take on more than one role, and one interesting way of analysing the skills of its members is to undertake a team-building exercise such as the one suggested below.

Give your team some newspapers and a tennis ball. As a team, you have to build a tower 1 metre high which will support the tennis ball. While undertaking this task try to analyse your group and identify which of Belbin's team roles they play. Can you fit a Belbin type to all the members of your team?

To undertake the analysis you might have one person act as an observer of the others and taking notes:

* Who had the ideas and suggestions?

* Who got the group started on the task?

* Who helped and supported others in the group?

* Who in the group was reliable?

* Did anyone block progress or interrupt others?

* Who listened carefully to ideas and supported the others?

* Was anyone negative or outspoken in such a way as to undermine the confidence of the team?

If this observer then gives feedback to the group, the information can be used to illustrate group dynamics and interaction. This could help the selection of suitable members to specific roles.

During your work on unit 2 (Customer service), you may have done some exercises to improve your listening skills and undertaken some practical activity where you had to ask questions in order to extract some required information. In some of your other activities you might have encouraged others to join in a discussion. Now you will need to show development of this learning by using these interpersonal skills as an effective team member. You will want to receive feedback from others on your team as to your performance, but it may also include learning something about yourself from others that you do not particularly like. Nevertheless, you must avoid resentment, as it will destroy the team dynamics, leading to awkward situations and problems.

Sometimes a heated discussion can appear negative to an observer, but it could also lead to more tolerance within the group and better team development. Arguments may develop but what is more important is how they are solved in order to meet the aims and objectives of the project as a whole.

Factors affecting team roles, such as skills and abilities

Belbin's model identifies certain skills and abilities for particular types of team member. You will need to consider each team member's skills and abilities in order to identify who is most suitable for specific roles within your team. So, for example, if you needed someone to look at the marketing for your project, what skills and abilities should they have? They should probably be innovative and creative, and fit the description of 'plant' in Belbin's theory. The person who looks after the finance may be a 'specialist' or even an 'implementer'.

If you saw how your group worked at the team-building task, did it affect how roles were allocated within the members of your team? Did the exercise change your opinion from your first thoughts during the feasibility study? Did it help identify your own personal strengths and weaknesses? Are there any aspects of your personality you need to control while organising the event to ensure that you achieve the aims and objectives of the task?

It is important to try to allocate suitable roles to each member of the team – if you have too many 'coordinators' in your team, there could well be conflict and clashes of interest, but if you have too many 'monitor-evaluators' they will keep waiting for someone else to do the work. It is vital that the team 'clicks' together in order to work well to manage the event successfully, leading to the team functioning with synergy (working together).

Factors influencing the working of the team

Communication

We have considered the skills and abilities of team members and how these affect the structure and operation of the team. But one of the main factors which influence the working of the team is their ability to communicate effectively with each other, not only in meetings but also during less formal discussions. Again, thinking of the communication section within unit 2:

* How well do you listen to others in the group?

* What body language are you displaying?

* Does your actual use and tone of language affect others?

You will need to be aware of your own communication skills and also those of the others in the team. No one should be expected to read your mind, so you must be able to explain your feelings and views if you are to be valued as a team member.

Leadership

Another aspect affecting team operation is the style of leadership being shown by the coordinator. There are three traditional styles of leadership:

* The **autocratic** leader tends to direct from the top, with little involvement or discussion with those in the lower ranks of the organisation. This is a 'Do as you are told' approach.

* A **democratic** leader gives consideration to the views of all members of the team in order to reach a consensus, to meet the aims and objectives.

* The **laissez-faire** approach is more 'You do what you think is best – I'll not interfere.'

Though these descriptions are very simplistic, it can be seen that the democratic approach will

probably serve your team best. It could happen, however, that the person chosen to be leader starts off being democratic but – when the going gets tough and deadlines are approaching with little having been achieved – becomes rather autocratic in order to get the schedule back on track. However, this could lead to mutiny within the team!

It has been known during projects like this that the original chairperson or coordinator has been 'deposed' in the planning or preparation stages and another person elected to take the role, because of leadership style or personality clashes within the team. This is not too great a problem if dealt with sensitively and democratically.

You should all have the same aims and objectives within this project, so the team needs to work together as well as possible. Katzenbach and Smith (1993) suggest that before a 'group' becomes a 'team' they must pass a certain threshold. Their definition of a team is:

A small number of people with complementary skills who are committed to a common purpose, performance goals, and an approach for which they hold themselves mutually accountable.

Figure 10.6 shows a simple framework for the development of teams, in which there are five stages:

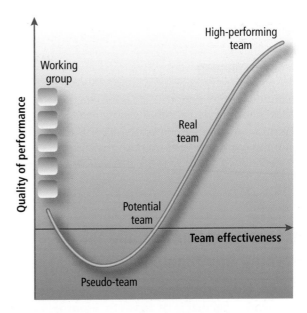

FIGURE 10.6. *Team performance curve*

1 **The working group**. The members of the group are simply a collection of individuals, who do not see the need to become a team, but each member produces something which helps complete the task. There is no cohesion and each could just as well be working on his or her own.

2 **The pseudo-team**. Here the individuals are 'pretending' to be a team. There is no benefit of being within that team, as individual performance would be better if they were working alone; the team is goal-less, unfocused and has no common sense of purpose. Each member is confused as to tasks set and becomes frustrated or antagonistic to others, so that the group crumbles quickly.

3 **The potential team**. This collection of people has a clear performance need and want to have some input to the group, but lacks the discipline needed for a common approach. They may also not have established final aims and objectives (mutual accountability) but there is a chance for the team to work after guidance.

4 **The real team**. This is the one which matches the definition of a team given above.

5 **The high-performance team**. Here the team exceeds the definition for a real team because they are deeply committed to the goals and are mutually accountable. Each carries equal weight in their efforts and wants to work with the others to exceed their aims and objectives.

Think it over...

Consider a high-performance team (such as Manchester United Football Club, or the Red Arrows) and consider why they are so successful. Are there any examples you can think of for a pseudo-team? If so, why are they not achieving – what is going wrong?

Access to resources and the working environment

Another factor which influences how well your team works together is its access to resources – do you have the materials you need when you want

them? If you are timetabled in a classroom but need access to computers to produce materials, this will surely affect your performance and hinder your progress. You may need to identify the best location for your planning and preparation to ensure you have the equipment and materials for the job in hand.

Also, if your classroom has two or three different groups working on their own events at the same time, you may be distracted and delayed by the activities of others. Difficulties such as these need to be discussed with your tutor so that you can operate in a conducive environment that enables effective communication. It is possible there is another smaller room with the equipment and facilities you need where you could work better. Access is needed to all the team's documents when you are working – if someone is absent and he or she has the information required for planning, this will delay your progress and affect your time schedules.

Assessment guidance

For Assessment Objective 2, do not forget to keep a record of all your discussions and feelings in your log-book while you are making decisions about team roles. Note that if your performance as part of the team is minimal and only just sufficient to show participation in planning and performance, you will achieve only mark band 1.

Marketing the event

Marketing mix

Reference has already been made to marketing in this unit (you should have included marketing strategies in your business plan). You may also wish to refer to unit 15, where marketing is covered thoroughly. Even if you are not undertaking the A2 double award (for which unit 15 is mandatory), you still need to be aware of certain marketing terms, particularly the marketing mix. This is used to define what are often referred to as the four 'P's of marketing – product, place, price and promotion.

Product

Your event will be the product in this case, and you need to establish that you are offering the right product to the right customers. Initial market research identifies possible demand for your chosen product. You may, for example, if you are thinking of organising an educational visit, offer three possible destinations to see which attracts the most potential customers.

Place

As far as place is concerned, this is *where* you will market your product and what *channels of distribution* you will offer. If you are selling tickets for your event, how are they going to be made available? Can people purchase them only from the team or also from other outlets?

You may also want to consider where the event is going to be held – this is another aspect of place. Is your event likely to face competition from other local events at a similar time? If, for example, you decided to organise an event to raise money for Children in Need or Comic Relief, are there other events in the area which sound more attractive or are more accessible to customers than yours?

The placing of your product in the marketplace is very important and should be given full consideration during the feasibility study. You may need to convince potential sponsors that you have investigated this aspect of the marketing mix.

Key term

Channels of distribution is a term used to describe how and where potential customers can find out about an event or be notified of an event or attraction. Distribution may be through the post, by personal callers, at tourist information centres, by direct mail or flyers, or other contact points such as hotel receptions. Flyers and leaflets will usually give a telephone number, web page, fax number and address. A large event may also use advertising in the media, such as television, radio or press, but this is usually regarded as a marketing technique rather than marketing materials.

Price

Price is obviously an important aspect for any travel and tourism organisation, and this is especially so for an event. Various types of pricing policy are used by organisations. If you look at the admission costs for Alton Towers, for example, you will see that the price varies according to the season and the age of the customer; in addition special rates are given to groups. Travel agencies also consider price and you may have seen advertisements such as 'We won't be beaten on price' as a way of attracting customers to a specific travel agency. Another method used to attract customers is price discounting for late deals, such as advertisements on Teletext or in travel agency windows. Hotels may also offer discounts for weekend breaks to attract additional business at a quieter time of the year.

For your event you will need to consider what price people will be prepared to pay for the product or service you are offering. Some information on this may be obtained through your market research. It would be disappointing if you decided to organise a residential trip to New York only to find that the cost was beyond the means of your potential customers.

Promotion

The final aspect of the four 'P's is promotion, which is how travel and tourism organisations raise awareness of the products and services they offer. There are two main strategies used for promotion: marketing materials and marketing techniques.

Marketing materials

During your studies so far you will have studied many examples of marketing materials from organisations in the travel and tourism industry. These would include flyers or leaflets promoting a particular tourist attraction or facility, obtained from various locations. Posters typically display less information than flyers; they will use colour to catch the eye and give only basic information about the venue or attraction. Travel agencies often offer late deals in window displays to attract passing customers to their products. Some hoteliers in Blackpool use Christmas cards as marketing material, sending them to past customers along with a tariff sheet for the coming year to attract repeat business.

Many organisations use some form of advertising to raise awareness of their products or services and increase sales. The cost of the various methods must be weighed up against the potential extra earnings from the media chosen, and market research may assist an organisation in choosing an appropriate type of marketing communication.

These are all examples of marketing materials used by organisations – but why do they use them? Obviously, the main aim is to raise awareness, appeal to customers and stimulate their interest in the product or service being offered, to gain more business.

The marketing materials have to be appropriate for the purpose. This means that the choice of materials must be suitable for the type of event or function being marketed. Marketing materials for an attraction aimed at children would need to appeal to that audience, so the wording and illustration should match their needs: that is, they must be simple, clear and eye-catching. These children and their parents would be your target market.

Key term

The target market is the people who would be most interested in using your product or service.

Relevant information about the event must also be displayed on the marketing materials,

CASE STUDY
Marketing materials

Figure 10.7 shows examples of marketing communications used by well known organisations. For each:

* **Identify the product or service being offered and the target market for this type of promotion.**

* **How has the layout and use of colour influenced your potential interest in these products or services?**

* **Identify how each of the 'four P's' has been illustrated on these materials.**

* **Why might these organisations consider this type of marketing material to stimulate business?**

FIGURE 10.7.

such as the name of the event, date, time, location and contact details. Some attractions would also include locational maps on leaflets or flyers – potential customers need to know where to go or how to reach the attraction by road or rail and so on.

Finally, marketing materials produced must be in an accurate and appropriate format. Producing colourful flyers is expensive, and if your costs have to be kept to a minimum it would be as well to consider which presentation materials suit the purpose intended. Again, you should look at unit 15 for a more complete consideration of marketing communications, to increase your awareness of the range.

Marketing strategies

Having identified various types of materials you might use to promote your event, it is then necessary to consider how these can best be presented to the potential audience, that is, the marketing media to be used and the expected response. It would be of little value if a small bed-and-breakfast establishment in Cumbria advertised on national television, but it may pay to put a small advertisement in specific newspapers or have an entry on the Cumbria Tourist Board's website. One of the main restrictions on strategy is the cost in relation to expected return and when you come to organising your event you will need to consider how much you wish to spend on marketing and what strategies would best suit your event.

Examples of strategies used by travel and tourism organisations include such features as discounting (e.g. two for the price of one, and buy one, get one free – BOGOF), special rates (free child places, family rooms, group discounts), loyalty incentives (e.g. Hilton Honors programme, or reduced entrance fees for National Trust members). Another technique, which may be suitable for your event, and which is virtually free, is the use of a press release. This is a statement sent to local or regional newspapers informing them of a forthcoming event, its aims and any features which makes it interesting or unique. The press may express interest by investigating this further, attending the event and taking photographs for use in an article.

You will need to identify the types of marketing materials in your business plan and portfolio with an explanation or reasons for your choice of strategy.

Financing the event

As mentioned briefly in the opening section of this unit, you have to consider the financing of your event. It is important to monitor the financial aspects of your event closely, and the way in which this is done is by establishing your budget. Close monitoring of funds should be undertaken from the start of the programme to ensure that money does not run out before the event takes place.

Key term

A budget is a statement giving *anticipated* expenditure and income.

Budget

Your budget should comprise the following elements:

* the initial sources of finance and the total sums available to you at start-up
* anticipated items of expenditure over the period of planning and development
* clear allocation of funds to specific components of the event
* contingency funds to cover you for the unexpected
* the anticipated profit or loss for the event.

Sources of finance

These could be from a loan (which may be from a bank, parents or friends, etc.), from sponsorship (where a particular organisation gives a grant to support a project, such as National Lottery, Sport for All, local business), from cash reserves already held in an organisation (so they are using past profits to support a new venture), or from shares sold to investors in the new company or project.

Anticipated items of expenditure over the period of planning and development

These items include any costs which may be incurred before the main sales of the product, such as start-up costs, initial market research materials and analysis, as well as postage costs for correspondence and other administration (e.g. photocopying), printing costs for documents and marketing materials produced, any materials which have to be purchased during the planning process, deposits for venues, tickets or accommodation bookings and insurance. This information should have been gathered during the feasibility study and is used when devising a budget.

Allocation of funds

If an event has various components, like the promotional evening from the case study earlier in this unit, there needs to be a clear allocation of funds to specific components of the event. This is so that expenditure on each component can be closely monitored. It may be that one component does not cost as much as has been allocated but another component has been underestimated. You need to ensure that there are sufficient funds

to cover both possibilities. If both components exceeded the budget allowed, where is the funding to come from to cover these extra costs?

Contingency funds

Contingency funds should be allocated within your budget in order to cover any unexpected expenditure. Look again at the case study of the group who organised the ferry crossing to Calais which had to be cancelled due to adverse weather: payment had been made for ferry tickets but they could not travel to the ferry. They had to arrange an alternative activity, but where did the money come from to pay for this? If there were contingency funds allowed in the overall budget, these could have been used to cover interim or emergency costs. Something usually occurs which has not been foreseen, even with the best plans, and a budget should identify a sum of money for contingencies.

Anticipated profit or loss

The final aspect of the budget is the anticipated profit or loss for the event. Even if you plan to spend just as much as your income, there is always the possibility that some extra cost will be incurred which changes your anticipated profit to a loss. It is often better to slightly overcharge customers initially and then give them a refund if the event is planned to just break even (where costs = expenditure and there is no profit or loss). If you were hoping to raise funds for a charity, then you aim to keep expenditure to a minimum to make the maximum income or profit.

An example of a simple budget for a hypothetical event is given in Table 10.1.

Theory into practice

Set out the budget shown in Table 10.1 on a spreadsheet, using Excel or similar and appropriate formulae to calculate sub-totals, final totals and also anticipated income from people reserving places. Now adjust the rate per booking for car-booters to see what difference this makes to your profit or loss. Consider any other adjustments you might be able to make to the figures to increase your profit.

There is no amount set aside for contingency funds, which has been recommended. What would happen if it turned out to be so wet three days before the event that you could not use the field because it was flooded? If the owner of the field kept a £25 deposit and you moved the event to a car park for which you were charged £100, what would be the effect on your budget?

Item	Expenditure (£)	Income (£)
Loan from school for start-up		100
Income from car boot bookings (30 @ £10 each)		300
Income from refreshment sales		150
		550
Payment for use of field	50	
Payment for portable toilets	100	
Marketing costs	100	
Purchase of refreshment materials	100	
Stationery costs	20	
Repayment of loan	100	
	470	
PROFIT		80

TABLE 10.1. *Budget for car boot sale*

Cash flow forecast

Key term

A cash flow forecast identifies when receipts and payments will be made, usually on a monthly basis.

The budget anticipates that sales reach their target and everyone will pay money in at the same time. But some expenditures will be made at different times and it is essential to ensure there is sufficient capital in the funds to pay for these interim expenses. A cash flow forecast helps to identify when specific expenditures will need to be made to ensure there is capital to cover them.

Look again at the example of the car boot sale used for Table 10.1, and say there is a period of three months from project set-up to the actual date of the sale. A cash flow forecast for the event might look something like that shown in Table 10.2. This again could be set out on a spreadsheet using formulae to calculate sub-totals and data carried forward from one month to another. Your formulae might look similar to those shown in Table 10.3.

The cash flow forecasting statement is used to monitor and control expenditure, to ensure there is always sufficient income to pay accounts. Many organisations will record financial transactions in spreadsheet packages. These can provide all sorts of management data, such as occupancy rates and availability of flights or hotel rooms. The document would record all income and all expenditure (including salaries and wages, which are not included in the example) so that the effects of seasonality and perishability can be monitored, with action taken to increase income where appropriate. It is strongly advised that you consider using a cash flow forecast for your event, so that as a group you can control the finances and anticipate possible losses or gains.

Theory into practice

Having set up your spreadsheet for the care boot sale, you could now use the figures from the last Theory into practice section to see the effects on the cash flow. When you come to plan the cash flow forecast for your own event, you could use a similar spreadsheet so that you can check the movements of cash during the process.

Income and expenditure account

If you also maintain an income and expenditure account you can relate this to your cash flow statement to check that the amounts coming in are sufficient to cover your expenses. If we take the example of the car boot sale, the income and

	January	February	March
RECEIPTS	£	£	£
Start-up loan	100		
Cash in hand	0	50	5
Advance bookings (£10 per car)	0	50	250
Receipts from refreshment sales			150
TOTAL RECEIPTS	100	100	405
PAYMENTS			
Market research	10		
Advertising	20	50	
Posters and signs		10	10
Deposit for field	10		
Deposit for toilets		25	
Stationery costs	10	10	
Balance for field			40
Balance for toilets			75
Purchase of refreshments			100
Repayment of loan			100
TOTAL PAYMENTS	50	95	325
Balance carried forward	50	5	80

TABLE 10.2. *Cash flow forecast for a car boot sale*

	January	February	March
RECEIPTS			
Start-up loan	100		
Cash in hand	0	=SUM(B8–B21)	=SUM(C8–C21)
Advance bookings (£10 per car)	0	50	250
Receipts from refreshment sales			150
TOTAL RECEIPTS	=SUM(B4:B7)	=SUM(C4:C7)	=SUM(D4:D7)
PAYMENTS			
Market research	10		
Advertising	20	50	
Posters and signs		10	10
Deposit for field	10		
Deposit for toilets		25	
Stationery costs	10	10	
Balance for field			40
Balance for toilets			75
Purchase of refreshments			100
Repayment of loan			100
TOTAL PAYMENTS	=SUM(B11:B19)	=SUM(C11:C19)	=SUM(D11:D20)
Balance carried forward	=B8–B21	=C8–C21	=D8–D21

TABLE 10.3. *Spreadsheet formulae used in the cash flow forecast for a car boot sale*

expenditure monthly account might look like the one shown in Table 10.4 (note that these are 'actual' figures and will not necessarily match those in your cash flow forecast, as shown in Table 10.2). The balances are shown monthly in the table, but some events may require more frequent balancing, such as weekly, in order to allow expenditure to be monitored more closely.

Profit and loss statement

From the income and expenditure record, it is possible to prepare a final profit and loss statement for the event, which will summarise the accounts and show the final profit or loss. As the car boot sale does not have any fixed assets (things such as equipment and buildings owned by the business) or current assets (raw materials and stocks of finished goods, debtors or cash reserves at the bank), the balance sheet for the event could look very similar to the budget but (as with the income and expenditure account and the cash flow forecast) it will give actual figures rather than those forecast when planning the event.

Date	INCOME	£	Date	EXPENDITURE	£
15.01	Cash from school	100.00	17.01	Photocopying for market research	10.00
			26.01	Deposit for field booking	10.00
			28.01	Advert in local press	15.00
			28.01	Posters	10.00
			31.01	Cash in hand	55.00
	Total January	100.00		Total February	100.00
1.02	Balance brought down	55.00			
			4.02	Deposit for toilet booking	25.00
			5.02	Advertising in local press	10.00
12.02	Advance booking Jones	10.00			
13.02	Advance booking Smith	10.00			
14.02	Advance booking Green	10.00	16.02	Posters and signs	7.50
			28.02	Stationery & postage	7.00
			28.02	Cash in hand	35.50
	Total February	85.00		Total February	85.00
1.03	Balance brought down	35.50			
			6.03	Signs and posters	10.00
6.03	10 Advance bookings	100.00			
8.03	5 Advance bookings	50.00			
9.03	2 Advance bookings	20.00	9.03	Tea, coffee, paper cups, stirrers	76.00
10.03	5 advance bookings	50.00	11.03	Balance on toilet hire	75.00
11.03	1 advance booking	10.00	11.03	Balance on field booking	40.00
12.03	2 bookings	20.00	12.03	Milk and food	27.00
13.03	Receipts from refreshments	130.00	16.03	Repayment of loan	100.00
			16.03	Cash balance	87.50
	Total March	415.50		Total March	415.50

TABLE 10.4. *Income and expenditure account for the car boot sale*

Did the car boot attract 30 stalls? Did the team spend the marketing budget fully, or did they overspend on any item? The only way to get a true picture of the final outcome of the day is to refer to the budget and insert final data, as shown in Table 10.5. The profit and loss statement will show the sales (income) less the cost of these (such as refreshment materials) to give the gross profit. From this figure there are deductions for expenses to give the net profit.

Balance sheet

A business would normally produce a balance sheet at the end of its financial year. It would give a full statement of its financial performance during that year. There are certain terms used on a balance sheet of which you need to be aware, though it may not be necessary to produce a balance sheet for your chosen event.

An example of a balance sheet for a sole trader is given in Table 10.6. The balance sheet has an assets section and a liabilities section. The assets section is broken down into two parts. *Fixed assets* are essential to the running of the business, and include items such as land and buildings, machinery, vehicles. These are possible sources of cash but would take some time to sell. Then there are the *current assets*, which are items that are easier to release for cash, such as stocks of goods, people who owe the company money (debtors), money in the bank and cash available for immediate expenses.

From the total for assets are deducted *current liabilities*, which are debts the business needs to repay within a short period. Current liabilities include *creditors* (suppliers of goods on credit to the business for which the business still has to

pay) and *bank overdraft* (short-term loan repayable on demand from the bank). In our example of the car boot sale, because the advance bookings are payments made by potential car-booters in anticipation of the event, they could be repayable if the event did not take place (if they were sold as refundable payments). These would be called 'creditors' on a balance sheet, as they are a liability until the event takes place.

Other current liabilities could include any taxes owed and any other short-term loans, such as the loan from school to start the event. The total of the fixed assets and current assets less the current liabilities gives the *working capital*.

From the figure for working capital, the business needs to make some deductions in order to establish the value of the business. So, from the working capital it is necessary to deduct any *long-term liabilities*. This figure could be made up from a mortgage taken out to buy the business or a bank loan used to finance the business – these are often referred to as deferred liabilities, as repayment is not due until some time in the future, usually longer than one year.

The figure reached at this stage must be balanced with the figure showing how the business has been financed. This is called *capital* and would usually be the amount of money provided by the owner(s) of the business to start, as it is owed to the owner(s) by the business. Added to this figure would be any *net profit* earned during the year, less *drawings* (which is the term used for income taken from the business for the owner's personal use). The total from these calculations must match that for the value of the business.

Documents used in financial transactions

If we refer back to the car boot example, there are certain documents you would need to produce

	Expenditure (£)	Income (£)
Sales (bookings & refreshments)		410.00
Less cost of sales (refreshment materials)	103.00	
Gross profit		307.00
Add other income:		
Loan from school		100.00
		407.00
Less expenses:		
Stationery	17.00	
Advertising & posters	52.50	
Hire of field	50.00	
Hire of toilets	100.00	
Loan repayment	100.00	319.50
Net profit		87.50

TABLE 10.5. *The profit and loss statement*

	£	£
Fixed assets		
Land and buildings		80,000
Equipment		13,200
Motor vehicles		8,700
		101,900
Current assets		
Stocks	9,700	
Debtors	3,750	
Bank	2,100	
Cash	970	
	16,520	
Less current liabilities		
Creditors	9,000	
WORKING CAPITAL		7,520
		109,420
Less long-term liabilities		
Bank loan	9,000	
Mortgage	30,000	39,000
		70,420
Financed by:		
Capital		70,000
Add net profit		5,286
		75,286
Less drawings		4,866
		70,420

TABLE 10.6. *Balance sheet for A. Jones (sole trader) at 31 August 2006*

in order to support your evidence and which are commonly used by businesses to record:

* **order forms**, orders for services to be provided

* **invoices** from suppliers, sent to the person ordering the goods

* **receipts**, to record payments received.

You may have considered giving your group a trading name and logo, which should be displayed on all orders and invoices.

An order form is sent from one company to another. It will state the type and quantity of product and the price quoted, plus notes of any discounts or credit terms. For the car boot event, there would therefore need to be an order form sent to book the field and another to book the toilets. These would have your business name as a letterhead, with the name and address of the supplier typed on. Most businesses number order forms so that they can record expenditure and keep more accurate records. You may also have completed an order form with the refreshment requirements, or these may have been paid for in cash from a local supermarket or wholesaler, but you would need to obtain a receipt as a record of that expenditure.

Invoices are sent from the supplier to the person ordering the goods. You may receive an invoice from the person who lets the field and also one for the hire of the toilets. These are always numbered, which makes them easier to refer to when checking payments made against invoices.

Receipts are issued to those who make payments to the business. In the case of the car boot sale, each person making an advance booking should receive a receipt as a record of payment made, which would be recorded in the income and expenditure account, along with details of orders and other invoices.

You will need to decide within your team what types of documents must be prepared to record payments and receipts for your own event and give details in your business plan of how you will record financial transactions.

Occasion management

With the business plan in place, which includes a projected time-management plan, you can now make final decisions as to what happens and by when to monitor progress closely. This is occasion management. Most people achieve more when working to deadlines, but all team members must understand their importance for success in the venture.

However, circumstances may alter during the development of the event, and amendments may need to be made to team structure or roles, timescales adjusted to take account of any changes made either during meetings or *ad hoc*, which should be recorded on the time plan. All team members must be aware of any difficulties or any amendments to procedures.

Decisions must be finalised regarding venues, equipment and materials and the necessary bookings made as early as possible to ensure availability. Deposits may be required, so consideration must be given to the capital available. The team will need to formalise the risk assessment and consider all relevant aspects of health, safety, insurance and security.

Hospitality issues should also be clarified. What type of catering is needed? Are there any problems in terms of accessibility? What support materials will have to be purchased? Other features of hospitality and customer service should also be finalised, such as name badges or labels to identify team members, or uniforms for staff. Are handouts or programme information going to be needed on the day?

The processes of evaluation will have been identified on the business plan and it is important that the time plan identifies dates for interim evaluation to take place to monitor progress and decide on any remedial actions.

Carrying out the project

Preliminary decisions have now been made and preparation for the event begins in earnest. During this period it is essential that you maintain your log-book, recording all your activities, including handling of complaints and problems, and those of the team, as they occur.

Completing the tasks you have been allocated

In your team, you may well have been given specific tasks to complete at various stages of the process. These could be initial investigations into facilities or project ideas, obtaining quotations from suppliers, assisting with preparation of the time plan and risk assessment, or maintaining records of team meetings. You will need to refer to the time plan for task completion dates, and to records of decisions made during team meetings, in order to work effectively as part of the team and not delay the planning and preparation processes. If you fail to carry out your tasks, it could affect others in the team which in turn is likely to cause friction.

CASE STUDY
Managing a one-day conference

A group of students organise a day conference for travel and tourism students in institutions in the area and invite a number of guest speakers. They have booked a room in a hotel with conference provision, and have requested morning coffee, afternoon tea and buffet lunch for the 40 delegates, and the room to be arranged in cabaret style.

Referring to your earlier investigation into job roles and the responsibilities of a conference organiser:

* **Identify the responsibilities of a hotel's conference organiser in relation to this type of event.**

* **Identify the information the students would need to provide to enable the conference organiser to meet their requirements.**

Dealing politely with customers, members of your team and others

You should be using the skills you developed in the unit 2 (Customer service) to support 'internal customers' (your team members) as well as any external customers you contact. You need to communicate effectively, listen carefully and respond to complaints and solve problems. Your teacher will be observing you undertaking these roles and will note any issues in feedback to you.

If you are rude or aggressive, this can lead to conflict and a decline in personal relationships, which in turn will disrupt the working of the project. Even if you do not fully agree with decisions made, if these have been agreed by a consensus then you must comply with the wishes of the majority. You cannot 'do your own thing' – you will have to cooperate fully with others while working on the project.

Supporting other team members while the project is being carried out

One of the essential components of this unit is demonstrating your team-working skills. A team spirit and a sense of purpose should develop. This will increase your job satisfaction while undertaking the project. All members of the team need to work towards the same aims and objectives, supporting each other.

Some team members may need more encouragement than others, and your role as a team member will include giving support and helping others throughout the project. Problems could arise which may or may not have been covered within the contingency plan, and you all need to work together to solve any difficulties. If you were part of a hockey team, for example, and refused to pass the ball to others, this would lead to confusion and ill-feeling among the other team members. You need to develop the ability to work effectively with the team and respond to situations. Your ability to read body language to ease problematical situations will be of benefit here.

If the team does not work well together, this could lead to failure through bad management, reflecting not only on your performance but that of the other students. It is important that all members collaborate with each other.

Reacting quickly and confidently to any problems that may arise

The ability to respond appropriately to unforeseen problems is crucial for the effective operation of the event. It is not good practice to let others shoulder any problems, as you will need to demonstrate your own personal problem-solving skills at all times. Very often, problems will have been discussed with the team, and suitable courses of action decided by consensus, but it could happen that a problem arises within your own area of responsibility. It is how well you react to the situation, while maintaining the progress of the overall project, which will demonstrate your ability to think clearly and make appropriate decisions.

Good teamwork will be key to carrying out your project

You must understand the needs of the project fully to deal with any problems confidently and satisfactorily.

Keeping to deadlines

We have already discussed the need for an overall project plan and regular progress review. The time plan for the overall project acts as a prompt for actions to be undertaken, but to meet targets all members of the team must meet deadlines. If you are the type of person who reacts only at the last minute this will frustrate other members of the team and could lead to friction, whereas if you plan your approaches methodically and perform the set tasks to time, you will not only achieve the satisfaction of meeting deadlines but you will also gain the respect of the team. All members of the team will need to collaborate well to meet the agreed schedule or adjustments made to those schedules.

Knowing when to get help and advice from others

If you are a very independent individual, you may find it difficult to seek assistance. However, members of an effective team will seek help when needed. Advice may be requested from other members of the team, staff or outside organisations, which should be sought at an early stage, rather than later, and considered carefully. If you let the problem fester, hoping it will go away, this is likely only to lead to difficulties in communication, which will cause friction and dissension between team members, and the success of the event may be put in jeopardy.

This is a valuable learning exercise for the future – most employees have to work as part of a team, so skills developed during the planning and preparation of the event are invaluable.

Assessment guidance

To meet Assessment Objective 2, you will need to demonstrate your ability to contribute effectively to the planning, preparation and running of the event, working as an effective team member, cooperating with others to meet aims and objectives, as well as work under pressure. You will need to demonstrate communication and interpersonal skills developed in other units of the qualification, such as customer service, hospitality, and marketing.

You must keep an ongoing diary or log-book throughout the whole process of planning, preparation and running the event, in which you record not only what you personally have done on each day, or week, but what the team members have done and how this has affected your role and your dealings with others. This log-book should record positive as well as negative aspects of the team's operation, and will be a valuable reference record when undertaking the evaluation work for Assessment Objective 4.

During the planning and feasibility stages of your project, you will have undertaken a wide range of research on all the issues for the business plan. This will relate to possible events, market research, locations or venues, staffing, finance and legal issues. Research will also feature in your ongoing evaluation, and in preparing for the event and in managing it. All of this research should be recorded, possibly in your log-book, but relevant documents should be kept as evidence for your portfolio to support findings. For Assessment Objective 3 you will need to produce evidence of this research. It should have drawn on a wide range of sources (individuals, organisations, primary and secondary, supervisors and team members as well as participants). All this evidence should be kept and indexed (which may be in the form of appendices in your portfolio), with references made to its relevance to the running of the project with contingency plans included.

Evaluation of the project

Project evaluation should have begun at the earliest stages. In your business plan you will have identified various methods to judge the effectiveness of your project's management and teamwork, and your time plan may well have highlighted target completion dates. In your business plan you will have suggested how you are going to assess the success of the event. You may have considered questionnaires for participants or customers, where feedback on issues such as facilities, services, success of marketing, reactions to the event and so on are obtained. These would give valuable information, which can be analysed numerically when preparing your final evaluation report.

Interim evaluation

It is important that evaluations are ongoing, not done just at the end: all projects should have interim evaluation points. These may be official meetings where updates are given on progress by various team members, and decisions made as to necessary remedial action to be undertaken and by whom. These interim evaluations should cover the following questions and more:

* Are we keeping to our deadlines?
* Are we likely to meet our targets?
* What issues do we need to address or reconsider?
* Is our marketing appropriate?
* Is the team working effectively together?

This will enable you to monitor your progress during the development of the event, and highlight any potential problems within the team, perhaps in meeting targets or in meeting deadlines. If you failed to meet a target, you may have to consider alternative forms of marketing, for example. If issues such as these are discussed at regular intervals, it enables all members of the group to assess the situation and come to a consolidated decision on remedial action. This is all part of developing good teamwork and communicating effectively as a team member.

Final evaluation and report

You may have received feedback through correspondence from facility or venue providers (or, in the case of the car boot sale, from those who made bookings for selling space at the sale). It could provide useful information about how the event could be better managed in future, which should form part of your evaluation. An example of a feedback form is shown in Figure 10.8.

Your tutor may also have prepared an observation report on your individual performance, identifying areas of good or weak performance, your contribution to the group work and your ability to respond to difficulties or solve problems.

Many groups also undertake team evaluations, where other members of the team provide feedback on each individual's performance as they

OCR Training: Delegate Feedback Form

OCR
RECOGNISING ACHIEVEMENT

Please complete this form and hand it to one of your course trainers. Your comments will provide valuable feedback that will help us to improve our training provision.

Training course title: ____________________

Date attended: ____________ Venue: ____________

Your name: ____________ Job Title: ____________

Centre name: ____________________

Contact e-mail: ____________________

(Please note, completion of your email address indicates you agree to receive further information from OCR Training or Mill Wharf Training).

TODAY'S COURSE:

Please rate the following by entering the appropriate number in the boxes below:

1 – Excellent   2 – Good   3 – Satisfactory   4 – Poor

1. Overall quality of this course ☐
2. Clarity and achievement of aims and objectives ☐
3. Suitability of course structure ☐
4. Effectiveness of delivery style(s) of trainer(s) ☐
5. Handling of delegates' questions and comments ☐
6. Relevance of information provided by trainer(s) ☐
7. Quality of information in the delegate pack ☐
8. Quality of presentation of the delegate pack ☐

OCR TRAINING ADMINISTRATION AND TODAY'S VENUE:

9. Overall effectiveness of OCR Training administration ☐

*(Please consider **pre-course administration** such as the speed of booking confirmation and the quality of OCR Training correspondence)*

10. Accessibility of venue and clarity of directions ☐
11. Quality of the service at the venue ☐
12. Effectiveness of room layout and equipment ☐
13. Standard of catering ☐

Please turn over....

FIGURE 10.8. *The OCR training delegate feedback form*

see it. These can be quite revealing in relation to your interpersonal skills and ability to cooperate, and can be used to inform your overall evaluation. You may have certain personality characteristics you were not aware of, and the highlighting of these can inform your personal development and affect your own values and attitudes. Another good method of team-based evaluation is a debriefing meeting after the event, at which you discuss any improvements that could have been made to the event itself, what areas could have been more successfully managed, how well the team worked together, and so on.

When you have the data to undertake the evaluation, you should consider the structure of your report. A formal report style, with numbered sections and sub-headings, is recommended. References should be made to items in the appendices and cross-references given to other sections. Remember that the majority of marks for the unit are given for this evaluation report.

The report should cover the following points:

* Did we meet our objectives?
* Were key deadlines met and if not what were the consequences?
* Did our planning promote effective performances?
* Was the project effective/successful in meeting customer needs?
* Were the promotional techniques and materials used satisfactory in meeting target audiences?
* What went well and what went less well for me individually?
* How well did the team work as a whole throughout the project?
* How did working as part of a team help or hinder me or change my values and attitudes?
* How effective have my evaluation techniques been?

Assessment guidance

For Assessment Objective 4, you need to demonstrate your ability to evaluate your own performance and the performance of the team, throughout all the stages of the project, using information gathered during your research as well as from your log-book and records. You may choose your own presentation style, but the end result must relate to the issues and be logically presented (possibly in a report format with use of appendices). To reach mark band 3, your final piece of work will show good use of technical language and accurately convey your findings.

Knowledge check

1 What issues must be considered in a feasibility study?

2 How does a mission statement and list of aims and objectives help to focus ideas?

3 Identify the purposes of market research.

4 Explain the benefits and usefulness of team-building exercises.

5 Complete a risk assessment form suitable for a half-day visit to a local attraction for a group of AS Travel and Tourism students.

6 Devise a feedback questionnaire, which can be easily analysed, suitable for participants on this type of visit to complete.

7 Identify the standard items used in records of formal meetings.

8 How do Belbin's team roles help allocate suitable group members to specific roles?

9 Explain the differences between marketing materials and marketing strategies.

10 Complete a budget statement using the following data:

hire of hall £200; marketing costs £50; printing costs and stationery £40; sponsorship £60; loan £50; expected income £500.

References and further reading

Books, journals, magazines

Belbin, M. (2004) *Management Teams – Why They Succeed or Fail* (2nd edn). Oxford: Butterworth/Heinemann.

Katzenbach, J. and Smith, D. (1993) *The Wisdom of Teams: Creating the High-Performance Organization*. Boston: Harvard Business School Press.

Needham, D. and Dransfield, R. (1993) *GNVQ Business: Advanced*. Oxford: Heinemann.

General

Guidance from banks on preparation of business plans

Visits to events to consider features of their planning and preparation

Visits to conference or event venues to discuss roles of organisers

The guided tour

This unit covers the following sections:

* Different purposes and types of guided tour

* Merits and deficiencies of different types of guided tour

* Devising and delivering a guided tour

Introduction

Many people are attracted to the idea of tour guiding – that is, accompanying a group of visitors around a particular site, giving information on the history or geography of that area, pointing out items of interest and generally being responsible for conducting the group efficiently. It can undoubtedly be a rewarding experience, but those who do this as a full-time or even a part-time occupation do a large amount of research beforehand. Many people have heard of the term 'Blue Badge Guide'. Such guides hold the well established and internationally recognised Blue Badge Guide qualification. This is obtained after being trained and passing both a written examination and a practical test – on foot, on site and on coach – throughout the whole of the region in which the guide intends to operate. Such individuals will be recognised as an official Blue Badge Guide in each regional tourist board area in which they have qualified.

How you will be assessed

This unit is assessed through your portfolio work. You will investigate the range of guided tours; you will also devise and deliver a guided tour. Your evidence will include:

* an account of the range of guided tours available and the plan of your guided tour (Assessment Objective 1)

* evidence of your delivery of your guided tour, with any supporting participants' documents (Assessment Objective 2)

* relevant research and analysis into your investigation of the range of guided tours and also your guided tour (Assessment Objective 3)

* an evaluation of the success of your guided tour, including your recommendations for improvement (Assessment Objective 4).

Assessment is explained in more detail towards the end of this unit.

Different purposes and types of guided tour

The tourist guide's main role is to escort groups or individual visitors (who may be from abroad or from the guide's own country) around the monuments, sites and museums of a city or region, and to interpret, inspiringly and entertainingly, in the visitor's own language, the cultural and natural heritage and environment. In addition to these traditional sorts of guided tour, in which a group is guided by a person, there are also written forms of guided tour, audio guided tours, and even virtual tours, based upon computer presentations of various kinds. Some guided tours

Activity

To help you understand and appreciate that there is a wide variety of guided tours available to leisure travellers, research examples to complete Table 11.1.

use a combination of these methods. The variety and the purposes of different kinds of tour are looked at in more detail in the next section.

Purposes of a tour

It is important that you appreciate that guided tours can have both an *explicit* and an *implicit*

TYPE OF TOUR	EXAMPLE SELECTED	PURPOSE: TOPIC/THEME	TARGET MARKET	TIME(S)	PRICE(S)
Tours guided by a person					
Walking tour					
Coach tour					
Tour based on other vehicle					
Written forms of guided tour					
Written tour using a map					
Written tour using a leaflet					
Written tour using a book					
Audio guided tours					
Audio tour at one site					
Audio tour of more than one site					
Virtual tour					
Tour using a variety of methods					

TABLE 11.1. *Types of guided tour: research and complete the examples*

purpose. The explicit purpose will usually be to give visitors information about a particular place or facility. However, the individual or organisation providing the guided tour may have other, implicit purposes, such as:

* encouraging the visitor's interest
* disseminating the organisation's aims and objectives
* raising the visitor's awareness of cultural and ethical issues.

The explicit purpose of the guided tour of a city, say, is essentially general sightseeing and to get an introductory feel for the destination. Such tours are primarily aimed at the casual leisure visitor and last a relatively short time. Most visitors will want to take photographs of landmarks, pause at selected stops and perhaps explore a museum. (Of course, guided tours

are likely to be available within the museum itself, or perhaps even only specific parts of it if it is a larger museum.) For orientation and familiarisation purposes, such tours introduce visitors to the variety of attractions available in the destination. The tour guide will point out important features during the tour and individuals will commonly return to locations that interest them later in their stay. The guide's commentary will follow a generalised pattern and visitors with a specific interest may not have their needs or interests fully met.

Look at the case study below and at Figure 11.1, which shows a group of visitors being taken on a tour of the $3 billion Emirates Palace Hotel in Abu Dhabi in the United Arab Emirates (UAE). What do you think are the purposes of such these tours?

CASE STUDY

A walking guided tour of the Emirates Palace Hotel

Spring 2005 saw the opening of what is probably the world's most expensive hotel development. Guests in the hotel's 394 bedrooms, where nightly rates range from $600 to $12,000, get a handheld computer to interact with the television, stereo and 30 separate lights in each room. The $2,500 Linux-based AMX handheld, with an 8-inch colour screen, can also arrange a wake-up call, download a movie, record a television show or call for maid service. The hotel is government-owned but managed and run by Kempinski Hotels & Resorts. It has a separate floor reserved for Gulf Arab royalty.

The Emirates Palace is one of the most luxurious venues in the world. It boasts, for example: 114 domes, of which the largest – the Grand Atrium – is higher than the dome of St Peter's Basilica in Rome; 1,002 Swarovski crystal chandeliers, including some of the world's largest; over 1,000,000 square feet of marble, imported from Italy, Spain, China and India; 200 fountains amid exotic park grounds, home to over 8,000 trees; and a heliport. It has an unbroken bubble of wireless Internet access on its 250-acre (100-hectare) grounds, which even works next to the two swimming pools and on the private beach.

The hotel's conference centre is also highly luxurious and technologically advanced. Its facilities include an auditorium with seating for 1,200 guests and a main ballroom that can accommodate up to 2,800 persons. There are 48 meeting rooms, including a media centre and business centre. State-of-the-art technology is present in all meeting and function rooms.

The hotel complex has a series of touch-screen information points positioned throughout the various public areas to keep residents and visiting guests alike fully up to date about the property's various events and facilities.

The whole development is aimed at both the domestic and international business and leisure markets. However, as it is a newly opened property, it will take time to establish itself and build up a sustainable client base. It is for this reason that guest services staff conduct privately arranged tours of the property.

It is possible to take a guided walking tour around the hotel, but this is not available to the general public without prior contact with the hotel's guest services department and is offered at fixed times. However, prospective leisure and business users could not fail to be impressed by the range of facilities available and both types of visitor would clearly have their needs met during the 60-minute show-around. The person conducting the tour is a hotel employee and can thus supply or will have access to all appropriate additional information about the hotel's products and services.

* **Explain how this tour would meet the needs of both leisure and business visitors. In what ways might their needs differ?**

In this case the *explicit* purpose of the guided tour is to give visitors, who may be potential customers, information about the property and its range of services. The tour, however, is clearly serving a series of *implicit* purposes for the hotel and the managing company (Kempinski), in that the guided tours are designed:

* to encourage the visitor's interest in staying as a guest

* to allow visitors to see various facilities at first hand and thus raise awareness among potential customers

* to be an opportunity to counter any adverse press comments that might be made and to allow individuals to reach their own conclusions about the property.

CASE STUDY
Net Tours in Dubai

FIGURE 11.1. *Net Tours promotional leaflet*

The Net Group has 175 personnel and five well-equipped desert campsites in Dubai. Figure 11.1 shows an example of the company's promotional material. The company's operation includes the following divisions:

* Net Tours, as the largest private tour operator in Dubai, arranges hotel reservations, visa processing, 'meet and assist' services and transfers to hotels. It offers the whole spectrum of tailor-made tours, covering the cultural, historical and modern attractions of Dubai, Abu Dhabi and other emirate states. Local services range from desert safaris to cruises on a dhow (the traditional Arab boat), city tours, mountain tours, sand skiing, camel treks and customised round trips.

* Net Cruises caters to the cruise-ship industry.

* Netco Transport is the logistics arm of Net Group. It primarily facilitates intra-Group transportation. The company's impressive fleet of four-wheel-drive vehicles and luxury coaches, as well as its private garages and dhow, are a definite advantage in ensuring efficient service to customers.

Net Tours offers its clients an extensive range of options. Many visitors to Dubai will have a Dubai City tour, which takes four hours and costs 100 dirhams. The company offers a range of additional tours, run along similar lines, such as:

* Cultural Dubai Tour (four hours, morning or afternoon, 100 dirhams)

* Modern Dubai Tour (four hours, morning or afternoon, 100 dirhams)

* Abu Dhabi City Tour (seven hours, 230 dirhams)

* East Coast Tour (nine hours, 230 dirhams).

The longer tours are popular with those who wish to learn something about the history and culture of this part of the Middle East.

The company's website posts some customer comments, which include the following:

'We are back home in England now, so we thought we would write to you and thank you for the most exciting experience we had while on your jeep safari. We cannot thank you enough for the good time we had, not to mention all the history & culture we learned from

you. You are the best. We have told all our friends about you. So you might meet them on one of your safaris. We cannot wait to return to Dubai, and do it again.'

'We would like to thank you and your team for making our cruise an enjoyable one. Special thanks go out to Mr. Sarath Wijesekara, Dhow Cruise In-Charge for his excellent coordination in making the cruise a great success.'

'Last week we had a wonderful time jeeping on the sand dunes with your organisation. I want to say my special thanks to our driver, Saidhali, who was able to drive in an excellent way, always controlling the jeep and other cars, letting passengers have a lot of time, explaining and describing the desert life and answering all our questions. He is an outstanding professional! If I'll have the opportunity to be in Dubai City again, I'll call you for another ride.'

'To begin with the whole group is over the moon with Dubai and I am sure they will return individually for a holiday. I would like to thank you for the Dhow Cruise dinner, excellent driving and hospitality, the transfers, always punctual and with a smile. The guide for his great spirit and guidance. Last but not least you for the great organisation. I hope that we will be able to have more groups, this time bigger, which would please me very much to work hand in hand again with such a great company.'

It is clear that these customers were impressed with the overall product supplied to them by Net Tours but there are some significant differences. Let us look at each of the comments in turn.

The comments from the first customers indicate the following:

* they undertook a desert safari using jeeps

* cultural and historical information was available, so they may well have visited Hatta

* the driver may well have provided additional information

* the tour clearly exceeded the customers' expectations.

The third customer comment emphasises the role of the driver in delivering a tour guide function. However, the second and fourth sets of comments appear not to be from private individuals but rather from members of corporate groups. Net Tours thus provides different variations of their standard products to meet individual client needs. This high degree of customer satisfaction strongly suggests that the company is meeting its *explicit* aim of providing quality tours. Furthermore, the fourth customer's comments suggests that Net Tours is achieving some *implicit* aims, such as obtaining repeat custom and effectively using its tour operations to showcase related products and services. There is clear evidence from the four quotations that Net Tours is actively servicing both leisure and business travel customers.

* **List some implicit purposes of these guided tours.**

* **List some explicit purposes.**

* **How many different types of tour are offered by the company?**

Merits and deficiencies of different types of guided tour

Not all tours will meet the expectations of their different customers. It is important that you are able to identify the advantages and disadvantages of each type of tour and come to a conclusion about how well it meets the needs of different types of customer. The aspects you should consider include:

* the purpose of the guided tour
* the type of tour it is
* the availability of the guided tour
* the time the tour takes
* its cost
* the extent to which the tour meets the interests of its targeted customers
* how well it meets the needs of different types of customer

CASE STUDY

Walking tour of Prague

Figure 11.2 shows details of an easy 3- to 4-hour walking tour of Prague operated by Paul's Tours. The company's main city tour is known as the 'Real Tour of Prague', an all-encompassing walking tour of the major sites which aims to give the history of the city over the last 1,000 years. Visitors joining the tour have pick-up points from two of the main hostels as well as a centrally located meeting point. An important attraction for many visitors will be the fact that the tour includes a stop for lunch in a traditional Czech pub.

* **Identify five famous city landmarks to be visited during the tour.**

* **Explain three ways in which the tour will appeal to young adults.**

* **Explain two advantages for customers of the tour starting outside Muzeum Metro.**

* **Research details of another Prague walking tour and compare it with this one.**

FIGURE 11.2. *The promotional leaflet provided by Paul's Tours for the guided walking tour of Prague*

The REAL TOUR of Prague

- An enjoyable and informative way of experiencing one of Europe's most beautiful cities.
- Excellent guides, owned by a British expatriate and graduate of European History.
- The tour takes you into the Castle complex, the St. Vitus Cathedral, the Jewish Quarter and the Old Town Square. You will also see the Charles Bridge, the Astronomical Clock, the Executioner's Pub and much more!
- 1000 years of history from the first Slavic dynasty to communism, the floods and now the European Union.
- We stop for lunch in a traditional Czech pub.
- Hear about the best bars, clubs and latest cultural events.
- No additional charges (apart from during the break).

Main Meeting Point at 12.30 pm

Outside Muzeum Metro
On line A and C. We meet in front of the horse statue, at the top of Wenceslas Square. Tickets available from guide holding up The REAL TOUR of Prague sign.

Pick-up Points at 12.00 noon

Hostel Clown and Bard	**The Travellers' Hostel**
Bořivojova 102, Praha 3.	Dlouhá 33, Praha 1.
(www.clownandbard.com)	(www.travellers.cz)

(Tickets from their receptions)

Tour Details	Days
Sept - May	Mon, Wed, Thurs, Sat
June - Aug	Mon - Sat
(No tours 20th Oct - 31st Oct and 1st Jan - 10th Jan)	

Reservations are not necessary

Only 300 Kč

For more info and comments

Paul's TOURS s.r.o.

Tel.: +420 602 459 481
www.walkingtoursprague.com

* whether there are any procedures in place to identify and solve problems which arise during the tour's operation.

We can now start to look at some examples of the different types of guided tour and in each case we shall try to assess their relative merits and deficiencies.

Tours guided by a person

Walking tours

Many destinations stage a variety of guided walking tours, and in your earlier research you may have come across many of these. The case study presents a typical example.

To look at the merits and deficiencies of walking tours, let us examine a specific example. Since 1991, Big Onion Walking Tours has led locals and visitors alike on innovative and exciting walking tours through New York's neighbourhoods, exploring particular aspects of the city's history. The company has won numerous awards, including Best Walking Tour in New York City from *New York* magazine. Some of the tours are listed in Table 11.2.

Advantages and disadvantages

All Big Onion Tours are available for private bookings. Private tours can be arranged for a weekday or weekend, day or evening. The company can accommodate 1 or 300 walkers

TOUR THEME	ITINERARY USUALLY FOLLOWED
Chinatown	New York hosts the largest 'Chinatown' in the western hemisphere. This neighbourhood has been settled by people from many provinces of mainland China, as well as Taiwan, Vietnam, Thailand and Malaysia. Visitors learn about Chinese immigration as the tour stops at the Chinese Consolidated Benevolent Association, the Church of the Transfiguration, the Lee Family Association, Hip Sing Tong and the Lin Zeju and Confucius statues
The 'Official' Gangs of New York Tour	This tour explores the legends of Five Points and Herbert Asbury's 1928 classic *The Gangs of New York* – the inspiration for Martin Scorsese's film. Stops include: Paradise Square, 'Murderers Alley', the African Burial Ground, the lost intersection of Five Points, and sites associated with Bill 'The Butcher' Poole, William M. Tweed, Master Juba, and the 1857 Police and 1863 Draft Riots
A Gay and Lesbian History Tour	Discover the many facets of lesbian and gay history as we trace the development of Greenwich Village. Stops include: the Stonewall Inn, the Duplex, and sites associated with Bayard Rustin, Willa Cather, Eleanor Roosevelt and Audre Lorde
Historic Harlem	As the centre of African-American history and culture, Harlem is one of New York's most significant neighbourhoods, featuring an array of historic churches, theatres, clubs and homes. Stops include: Abyssinian Baptist Church, Striver's Row, Hamilton Heights and sites associated with the 'Harlem renaissance'
Immigrant New York	A walking tour through the multi-ethnic Lower East Side to see the historic and architectural landmarks associated with African, Chinese, German, Irish, Italian, Jewish and Latino immigrants. Stops include: the 'Tweed' Courthouse, Five Points, the African Burial Ground and sites associated with Dr Sun Yat Sen, Jacob Riis, Abraham Cahan, Pierre Toussaint, Emma Goldman and many others

TABLE 11.2. *A selection of Big Onion's New York walking tours*

and for the larger groups provides multiple in-house trained guides. The company works closely with each client to customise its walks if and as required, and this approach has resulted in a variety of customer types making use of the products and services available.

Educational groups can be catered for:

✳ Big Onion tours are appropriate for all ages, from primary school to university level.

✳ The company can assist in integrating their tours into an educational establishment's academic curriculum.

✳ The guides use a selection of visual aids to help bring the history of New York alive.

Private individuals, community groups and even government agencies can also be catered for. The tours appeal to both domestic and international

FIGURE 11.3. *The promotional leaflet for the tour of Ibn Battuta shopping mall*

visitors. The tours can provide a valuable insight into the local community and are an excellent introduction to the diverse social fabric of the city.

A variety of business customers can make use of the facts that:

* The walks are perfect local neighbourhood orientation events that a company might wish to send its associates and employees on for information purposes.
* Walking tours are great for team building, special events and entertaining clients.

However, the tours run only at certain times and special requests need to be pre-booked with the company.

Many destinations stage a variety of guided walking tours and we now end our consideration of this type of tour with a look at a specialised example from the Middle East. Only in Dubai will you find a guided tour of a shopping mall (Figure 11.3), as illustrated in the following case study.

CASE STUDY
The Voyages of Ibn Battuta Learning Adventure Tour (of a shopping mall)

The management of Ibn Battuta Mall have introduced storytelling tours at the mall, providing an opportunity for the visiting public to better understand the historic value of the architecture as well as the life of Ibn Battuta. This famous Arab traveller and explorer was born in Tangiers, Morocco, in 1304. He studied law as a young man. As part of an educated elite and it seemed only natural that Ibn Battuta would leave his home in order to increase his understanding of the world; over 30 years he travelled some 75,000 miles across the eastern hemisphere.

The mall has been constructed and designed to trace the route that had the most impact on his life. The Andalusia, Tunisia, Persia, Egypt, India and China courts within the mall are representative of each region that Ibn Battuta visited. In addition to the breathtaking architecture, the mall uses the six courts to allow retail zoning, easy access for visitor convenience and the placement of 'edutainment' features.

The tours begin with a brief introduction from the tour guides ('scribes' – in the role of the author of a contemporary book about Ibn Battuta), who are dressed in traditional 14th-century attire. In each court, the scribes will pause and provide a detailed history as to the experiences faced by Ibn Battuta on his travels in that country. The stories narrated cover all aspects of Ibn Battuta's travels, from the watermelons he tasted to the magnificent mosques he came across. The stories are both entertaining and educational, as visitors are taken on a journey in the footsteps of the Arabian hero. The tour guides also offer an insight into the forthcoming 'inventions' to be installed at the mall over the coming months. The inventions already installed, the elephant clock and the Chinese junk, are also discussed in terms of their importance and significance to Ibn Battuta.

Advantages and disadvantages
Bookings for tours, which are in both English and Arabic, can be made at the customer service desks located in the Tunisia and China courts. Several tours are conducted during the day; they start at the Persia court and last around 45 minutes. Visitors can refer to two information leaflets that are available at the information points. The response to the storytellers has been extremely positive and visitors have been enthusiastic about learning

of the importance of Ibn Battuta, who he was and the great impact he had on history. The public have also expressed a great deal of interest in all aspects of the mall tour, ranging from the architecture, inventions and even the wardrobe of the tour guides.

* **What conflicts are there in having guided tours within the confines of a busy retail and leisure facility?**

* **Will the tour be more suited to children or adults?**

Theory into practice

To help you generate additional information to support Assessment Objectives 1 and 3, compare the relative merits and deficiencies of *two* contrasting guided walking tours with which you are familiar.

Non-walking tours

Walking tours with a guide are ideal for indoor exhibits of various kinds and for relatively small areas outdoors, but to cover a large town or city, for example, some sort of non-walking tour becomes necessary. Open-top buses and coaches are typical, but boat tours are a popular alternative in many locations. Can you think of other kinds of transport that would lend themselves to a guided tour? The following case study, which looks again at Net Tours in Dubai, will perhaps suggest a few more.

CASE STUDY
Tours with a guide in Dubai

Figure 11.4 shows an image that is frequently associated with holiday guided tours. Net Tours offers its clients an extensive range of options. Many of the sites that are visited during these tours are featured on the company's promotional leaflet, shown as Figure 11.5.

Many visitors to Dubai will have a Dubai City tour, which reveals the main contrasts between the cultural and the modern aspects of the city's development. The tour begins at Jumeirah Mosque and proceeds toward Bastakia. Next stop is the Dubai Museum. Further attractions included on this tour are the textile market and a ride across Dubai Creek using the local *abra* (water taxi). This brings visitors to the spice market and the dazzling Gold Souk, with its impressive array of international jewellery designs in nearly 350 shops.

FIGURE 11.4. *Tour bus in Dubai*

FIGURE 11.5. *Net Tours excursions leaflet*

Many of the company's tour products involve trips into the desert. Coach transport is thus inappropriate and Net Tours maintains a fleet of Toyota Landcruiser four-wheel-drive vehicles to service their various desert safaris and related trips.

A camel trek (at 300 dirhams, or just under £50 at 2005 exchange rates) is a fun way to experience the desert. While riding the 'ship of the desert' on a camel caravan, the adventurous visitor can catch a glimpse of some strange insects crawling on the

FIGURE 11.6. *Desert sunset on trek*

FIGURE 11.7. *Dune bashing*

sands, see the amazing desert vegetation and admire the scenery. An hour-long trek allows visitors the chance to view the desert sunset (Figure 11.6). The trek ends with a brief drive to the Bedouin camp maintained by the company. Net Tours offers a variation of this tour as an overnight safari.

Half-day and full-day desert safaris by off-road vehicles are also available. The full-day desert safari offers a splendid chance to live the desert experience. A typical Arabian welcome awaits you at the company's Bedouin campsite followed by camel ride. Then you go 'dune bashing' – a thrilling four-wheel-drive bash against sand dunes as shown in Figure 11.7.

A very popular tour is the Hatta Trek, which takes you into the heart of the desert and offers a glimpse of Dubai's heritage as well. A short ride across sandy dunes takes you to the company's enjoyable Bedouin campsite in the region of Hatta. The tour provides the opportunity to go camel riding, relax on the mountains and swim in the Hatta Pools, drive through a wadi and then visit the Hatta Heritage Village.

In order to assess the merits and deficiencies of the tours provided by the company, a variety of indicators can be used. All Net Tours products are made available subject to the following policies:

* All prices are per person unless stated otherwise.

* Safaris involve off-road driving through rugged country. Therefore they are unable to accept passengers younger than 3 years, those over 65 years and expectant mothers.

* Food and non-alcoholic beverages are included in all safaris. Half-day tours are without meals.

* Net Tours safari vehicles are all fitted with air conditioning, short-wave radios and seatbelts. They are licensed to carry seven passengers, excluding the driver. Passengers are required to wear seatbelts during the tour.

* Photography of military and some government installations is not permitted. It is advisable to ask for permission before taking the pictures of Arab men; Arab women must not be photographed.

* Net Tours reserves the right to cancel or change any part of the programme without prior notice.

* All tours and excursion are subject to confirmation.

* **Drawing on the list above, complete a list of disadvantages of the tours offered.**

Think it over...

There is much competition between suppliers of guided tours in Dubai, but tour operators and guides can operate in Dubai only if they meet the various requirements stated by the government of Dubai's Department of Tourism and Commerce Marketing (DTCM). For example, a tour guide working in Dubai must have passed 'the tour guide program that prepares participants to work as guides in the emirates' and it is the DTCM that will 'grant nationals and others who have successfully completed the training program the relevant certificates of the course'. Failure to comply could result in a 20,000 dirham fine (around £3,250) and the cancellation of a licence to operate. Thus, the authorities exert a significant basic quality control over all guided tour operations.

* What regulation is there of tour operators in the UK?

* What are the implications of regulation for the merits and deficiencies of the tours in Dubai?

Written forms of guided tour

Visitor leaflets

Many tourist and visitor attractions provide detailed leaflets so that visitors are able to guide themselves around the site. Kentwell Hall and Gardens in Suffolk (see Figure 11.8) is one such attraction. Kentwell Hall is one of England's finest moated Tudor houses. It was described by *Country Life* magazine as 'The epitome of many people's image of an Elizabethan house.' Built and enhanced by successive members of the Clopton family in the first half of the 16th century on riches accrued from the wool trade, the exterior of the buildings has remained mainly unchanged since.

Kentwell is not a stately home stuffed with museum pieces – it is a lived-in house full of interest and vitality, which exudes a strong sense of history. It has been the home of the Phillips family since 1971. The owners were keen to show how the house might have been lived in and sustained a community in its heyday in the 16th century. They wanted to bring the period to life for visitors, young and old, who might otherwise have only had a sketchy knowledge of the 16th century. To this end they devised their Re-creations of Everyday Tudor Life, the first of which

FIGURE 11.8. *Kentwell Hall and Gardens in Suffolk*

took place in 1979. The novelty of this approach was that it concentrated upon everyday domestic life rather than battles, which most living history at the time featured. Visitors who come to see the house and the Tudor Re-creations on selected dates are able to use various written guides to help them explore the property. During an outing to Kentwell Hall the following information sources can be used:

* an information leaflet, issued at the time of entry

* a promotional flyer, which is available from local information centres

* the guidebook, which is available from the Hall's on-site shop.

Visitors are given a suggested itinerary to follow:

* the house itself, where there is a variety of additional printed information about the content and features of particular rooms – furthermore, on Re-creation days, some 200 Tudor men, women and children are available to provide additional clarification as required

* next, to behind the house, to the 15th-century moat house and the camera obscura

* next, to the gardens, both into and around the outside of the walled garden

* finally, the stable yard and farm.

Throughout the property, additional written information is provided about the various features on public view to help visitors understand the significance of the various displays.

Theory into practice

Kentwell has been a leader in educational school visits and receives some 600–700 school parties a year. To help you generate evidence for AO1 and AO3, undertake research on Kentwell Hall and then compare the extent to which a tour would appeal to adults and to children on a school visit. Assess the merits and deficiencies of the tour for both types of visitor.

Guidebooks

Hundreds of tourist guidebooks are regularly published, mainly by giant international companies. Throughout the year they are constantly checking with the attractions to which they refer and updating their information. However, many guidebooks are also produced on a more localised basis and many individual attractions will have a shop selling such publications to boost their revenues. Most locations that attract visitors – such as heritage sites, but also the countryside and urban or rural built attractions – benefit from effective interpretation. Obvious benefits include enhanced public understanding and appreciation, better visitor management, and increased return visits and referrals. It is for such reasons that tourist guidebooks are made available for use in many locations.

Written guided tours are intended not only for those visiting a particular tourist facility – they can cover routes of all types. For example, a guest staying at Abu Dhabi's Emirates Palace may be interested in exploring the UAE and Gulf region more widely. There are many guidebooks to help such travellers and *Off-Road in the Emirates* by Dariush Zandi is one such example, written for enthusiasts of four-wheel drive vehicles. The book features some 15 specially chosen routes, which vary in terms of both their duration and landscape.

Think it over...

Try to provide an example of each of the following tourist and visitor attractions and consider how the visitor experience might be enhanced by following a written guide.

* country parks
* national parks
* forests
* farms
* gardens
* botanical gardens
* landscape geology
* wildlife
* nature trails
* nature reserves
* bird reserves
* environmentally sensitive sites (SSSIs) (e.g. wetlands)
* long-distance footpaths

* canals and towpaths
* lakes
* piers and promenades
* ancient monuments
* historic houses
* castles
* battlefields
* churches, chapels, abbeys, cathedrals
* villages, towns and cities
* city walls
* industrial sites
* archaeological sites
* racecourses
* museums
* galleries
* wildlife parks
* zoos.

CASE STUDY

Written guide to Buraimi Oasis

Buraimi Oasis is a huge green depression in the desert that straddles the border between the Eastern Province of Abu Dhabi and the Sultanate of Oman. It is surrounded by Oman's Hajar Mountains to the east, an isolated mountain named Jebel Hafit to the south, and the endless dunes of the Rub' Al-Khali, or Empty Quarter, to the west. All of the settlements in the UAE section of the oasis are districts in the modern city of Al-Ain, and all in the Omani section are parts of the town of Buraimi. So 'Buraimi Oasis' is the name of the depression, and Buraimi is the name of the town in the Omani section of it.

In the days before the oil boom, the oasis was a five-day overland journey by camel from Abu Dhabi. Today the trip takes about two hours on a tree-lined freeway. Driving enthusiasts following Zandi's Route 8 will leave Buraimi and complete a 98 km round trip to Khatwa village. On this particular excursion you can visit:

* two forts at Buraimi

* Fossil Valley

* hanging gardens and vertical cliffs of Jebel Qatar

* the oasis of Mahda – an authentic Omani village

* Khatwa village, with its oasis, date plantations, fruit gardens, and mud and stone buildings with palm roofs.

A feature of the 2002 second edition of Zandi's book is the use of Global Positioning System (GPS) coordinates to identify the precise location of the attractions itemised along the various routes. This makes these written guided tours particularly useful for off-road enthusiasts and adventurous motorists alike. Furthermore, detailed maps for each route are included and it is little wonder that over 25,000 copies of the book have now been sold.

For tours such as this, written for a particular type of tourist, advantages will far outweigh disadvantages. Let us briefly analyse the effectiveness of the above tour from the driver's point of view.

Advantages and disadvantages

First, the purpose of the tour is clear, in that the driver will have selected it from the list of possible tours because of some interest or attraction. In the scenario mentioned above, the eventual destination is easily accessible from Abu Dhabi within a day, via the main highway to Al Ain. However, do not forget that the weather can still be a hazard, even in the desert. The sites to be seen are described in some detail and so the driver knows in advance whether a particular place is likely to be of interest. In any case, it is always possible to ignore some points. For example, not all will have an interest in looking for fossils. A major disadvantage that might arise is if any aspects of the tour have changed since the time of publication of the guidebook. However, this will always be the case with printed sources and the user should make allowance for this possibility.

* **What advantages and disadvantages would there be to this tour being led by a guide, rather than the driver using the guidebook?**

Information sheets

Information sheets are one of the ways in which tourist and visitor attractions can communicate with their customers. They are cheap enough to produce for them to be given away free and so can be widely distributed (for example, left at tourist information offices for people to pick up).

Interpretation of the location is central to how visitors experience a particular destination, regardless of whether it is historic, cultural or environmental. Good site interpretation will have an influence on visitors and leave them feeling engaged, stimulated and inspired. It may provoke their curiosity, stimulate their imagination, or encourage them to think or behave in specific ways. They are also likely to enjoy themselves more and thus be more likely to return or tell their friends. Therefore, information sheets can help the individual attraction with a marketing function as well.

CASE STUDY
Information sheet for a parish church

FIGURE 11.9. *The church in Messing*

Figure 11.9 shows the parish church in the Essex village of Messing. Visitors are able to follow a walk around the church and grounds using a written guide. The church dates back to 1194 but many visitors will be equally interested in the fact that the ancestors of George Bush, the President of the United States of America, came from Messing. During the 17th century, approximately 7 per cent of Essex's population emigrated to the New World and most of them settled down to form part of the Massachusetts Bay Colony. One such emigrant was Reynold Bush, a farmer, whose family had ties with the Messing area going back to the 14th century.

The tour of the church draws the visitor's attention to the following:

* the 19th-century fount
* the nave
* the pulpit window
* the large medieval chest
* the organ and choir stalls
* the royal arms, dated 1634
* the east window
* the chancel
* the communion stalls
* the US flag presented to the church in 1989.

Additional detail is provided about each of the items and the visitor can reflect about the many changes that have taken place since Messing was the Anglo-Saxon Maesa's settlement.

* **Investigate the range of leaflets and promotional flyers available at your local tourist information centre.**
* **How many can be used for undertaking a guided tour on your own?**
* **Which are the most useful and why?**

Audio guided tours

Audio tours by their very nature tend to be impersonal. Whereas a personally guided tour around a facility will allow participants to ask questions, it is not really possible to interact with a recording in the same way. It is thus likely to be very difficult for visitors using an audio guided tour to have immediate needs or problems addressed.

There are, however, a variety of circumstances in which tourists can make good use of audio guided tours, such as the foreign-language options on city bus tours and at larger international visitor attractions. Walking tours have traditionally been based on an audio cassette tape and player that were rented to the tourist to listen to while following a set itinerary. More recently various types of handset have become available. We will consider here some of the most recent technological developments in the field.

Audio walking tours using mobile phones

A recent development in audio guides has taken place in Hong Kong. These audio guides, called 'Walk the Talk', have received very positive reviews in *Time* magazine, the *Asian Wall Street Journal*, the *South China Morning Post* and *Business Traveller Magazine*. Very simply, they involve the use of a mobile phone connecting to a local phone number for personal use, a map and a complimentary phone card with two hours' prepaid airtime. These are walking tours and they work just like audio guides found in museums and popular heritage sites, except that you listen using your own mobile phone. By simply dialling one phone number, you can walk around Hong Kong and be entertained with rarely told (but true) stories of the history, architecture, movies and people that have made the city great. You can start your self-guided tour anywhere. You just dial the number listed on the easy-to-read maps and follow the walking route. You can pause, fast-forward, rewind, as well as hang up and rejoin the walk later. After the first time you dial in, you are prompted to enter a secret code and you then have three days of unlimited access.

Walk the Talk has two tours to choose from:

* Central: 'Barren Rock to World City'. This walk is a tour of Hong Kong's Central District and it starts by the famous Star Ferry terminal. It provides an exploration into how the city came into being. What brought all the people to an island that less than 200 years ago was just a barren rock? Visitors hear about how the city was founded by opium taipans, marvel at the stunning glamour of buildings, hear harrowing tales of the Japanese occupation and get some insider tips on Asia's premier party-zone, Lan Kwai Fong!

* Tsim Sha Tsui: 'Buccaneer's Den to Neon Mecca'. This tour takes the visitor on an adventure through Tsim Sha Tsui, the district of immigrants, starting at the Star Ferry by the harbour. The tour traces Tsim Sha Tsui's transformation from buccaneers' den to tourist mecca. The commentary tells the visitor about the entrepreneurs from every corner of the world who made it all happen. The tour goes on to explore the living sets of Hong Kong cinema as it introduces Bruce Lee, Jackie Chan and Wong Kar-wai in their own back yard.

The significance of this innovation in the international leisure visitor marketplace may be judged by the comments posted on the Walk the Talk website. Examples include:

I've visited Hong Kong many, many times over the last 30 years. I just took your Central walk at 5 this morning (a bit jet-lagged!) and learned facts about history, culture and social issues of Hong Kong with a depth I've never picked up from any other source. I wish you the best of luck in your venture – bravo!
(David from London)

I took your walk of Central today. Your information about all the skyscrapers was very interesting (please add more) and the mix of history with anecdotes and analysis was funny and a really new thing for me. You guys should come do this in Istanbul. (Armagan from Istanbul)

For an outsider that was totally uninitiated, your TST walk was fantastic! Your mix of information and entertainment was perfect and I thought it was great how you chose to tell me these stories of Hong Kong in a dialogue format (you could work on Rudyard Kipling's accent a bit – there's a hint of Aussie there mate…). (Aisha from Bristol)

Dear Stefan and Dave, Walking 'with you' in Tsim Sha Tsui a few days ago, I had lots of fun learning new stuff about Hong Kong. Seeing HK through your eyes and walking in your footsteps was much more satisfying than reading about it or taking a group tour on a bus! Thanks! When are you gonna do a KL walk?!

(Sharon from Kuala Lumpur)

Closer to home, HandHeld History offers several mobile phone walking tours around London and other significant historic sites. The actors Stephen Fry and Joanna Lumley, in partnership with English Heritage, take you back in time. In 2005, HandHeld History had seven walks available around London, with each lasting about 30 minutes. HandHeld History charged £1.50 for each of its walks. It was also possible to become a member and enjoy less expensive access charges for all of their content. The £1.50 price excluded mobile phone airtime charges but allowed for unlimited access during a 48-hour period. In addition, HandHeld History also provided information via WAP and SMS. Overseas visitors had free access to the walks if they rented a mobile phone from Vodaphone.

Activity

Research Walk the Talk, HandHeld History or a similar 'wireless walk'. Assess the suitability of using mobile phones for the delivery of an audio guided tour.

Audio walking tours using personal CD players

Also commercially available in the UK are guided tours that you can play on your personal CD player while taking the walk around a number of famous and historic locations. In one example, a series entitled 'A Stroll Back in Time', short dramatised plays are used to bring the points of interest to life. The audio CD comes with an easy-to-follow map to guide the visitor to 'stroll' to points. Those available include:

* *Royal Westminster Guided Stroll*, visiting Westminster Bridge, the Houses of Parliament, the statue of Oliver Cromwell, Westminster Hall, the Jewel Tower, the statue of George V, St Margaret's Church, Westminster Abbey, the Cenotaph, Downing Street, King Charles Street, Horse Guards Parade, the Banqueting Hall, Trafalgar Square and Buckingham Palace.

* *City of Bath Guided Stroll*, visiting Royal Crescent, the Circus, Assembly Rooms and Museum of Costume, the Saracen's Head, New Bond Street Place, Royal Mineral Hospital, Trim Street, New Theatre Royal, Cross Bath, King's and Queen's Roman Baths, Bath Abbey Churchyard, Sally Lunn's House, Nelson House – Pierrepont Street, Pierrepont Place, Old Orchard Street and Pulteney Bridge.

* *York City Heritage Guided Stroll*, visiting York Minster, the statue of Emperor Constantine, Minster Yard / College Street, the Treasurer's House, Merchant Taylor's Hall / Bedern, Black Swan Inn, Whip-Ma-Whop-Ma-Gate, the Shambles, the Pavement, Coppergate, Roman Bath Inn and Eboracum Legion Bathouse, the Mansion House, the Guildhall, Stonegate, Barleyhall and Guy Fawkes' House.

Audio guided tours for drivers

A similar idea has been adapted for driving tours and an innovative, award-winning product is available for visitors in Herefordshire to use in their own cars. Called 'Herefordshire's Hidden Extras', it is a series of five circular audio car tours on CD or tape – each designed to offer a full day out. The series is aimed at people who have arrived in Herefordshire by car and who would like to know more about the area, but who are not in a position to hire a private guide. The information you hear on the audio track combines the knowledge of local tour guides and local specialists, and aims to help visitors get off the beaten track. Clear and detailed directions are given on the tape/CD. In addition, each tour pack comes with a map of the route, as well as an information sheet giving details of nearby facilities and attractions. Marches Tours & Talks – a small association of tour guides – has produced them, with funding from Tourism Enterprise and facilities support from BBC Hereford & Worcester. Table 11.3 provides further details of the five tours.

Theory into practice

Using the information provided so far, together with your own research, assess the appeal of the different types of audio tours to different types of user. Your views will generate additional evidence to support your work for Assessment Objectives 1 and 3.

TITLE OF TOUR	DETAILS OF ITINERARY
The Golden Valley and Beyond	This was the first in the series of Herefordshire's Hidden Extras audio car tours. It takes the visitor through 45 miles of the beautiful Golden Valley and out to the very edge of the Black Mountains, near the Offa's Dyke long-distance footpath. It suggests visiting Longtown Castle and then the little border town of Hay-on-Wye, where visitors can browse in some of the 40 bookshops.
The Black and White Villages	This tour follows the well known Black and White Trail through north Herefordshire. The 45-mile route will take you through several of the county's picturesque, half-timbered villages, as well as directing you to see the unique Romanesque fount at Eardisley, the little border market town of Kington, and Leominster.
Mortimer Country	This 45-mile circular route begins and ends in Ludlow and also takes in the Welsh border town of Presteigne, with its famous Judge's Lodging Museum. The tour takes you to villages such as Wigmore, with its castle ruins, Leintwardine on Watling Street and to Shobdon, with its Strawberry Hill Gothic church and the Romanesque Shobdon Arches. Listeners are introduced to current residents as well as some of the historical characters who played an important part in shaping the area. For instance, Lady Brilliana Harley, who defended Brampton Bryan against the Royalists in the 17th century, is just one of the people you will hear from.
Ledbury and Bromyard	'Booze and views' is the unofficial title for the fourth audio car tour in the Herefordshire's Hidden Extras series, designed to lead independent visitors and locals alike through the delights of east Herefordshire. The circular tour, of just over 50 miles, covers such topics as cider and wine production and divulges curious facts about hops as it guides you through some spectacular scenery.
Ross-on-Wye and Beyond	This is the final audio car tour in the series. The circular route takes you for 47 miles through the stunning scenery of the Lower Wye and Monnow Valleys. You are guided to Goodrich Castle, then up to Symonds Yat East to Yat Rock, where you can look down the River Wye running through its deep gorge. From there you can discover the delights of the edge of the Forest of Dean and look down at Monmouth from the Kymin. The route takes in the ruins of Skenfrith Castle, the remote church at Garway with its Templar foundations, and Ross-on-Wye, where you can look down from the Prospect at the famous horseshoe bend in the river.

TABLE 11.3. *Herefordshire's Hidden Extras*

Audio guided tours used in visitor attractions

There are many reasons why a visitor attraction may decide to develop an audio guide. A principal one is that the guide will offer a consistently high level of interpretative information. Also, it will be a service that does not need to be booked in advance and is available all the time. Furthermore, for blind and partially-sighted people, for example, there are access considerations: at its best an audio guide can offer an independent visit for such clients, in which they are not reliant on members of staff or other people for assistance.

There may, though, be instances when an audio guide is not the most appropriate type of visitor guide – where exhibitions change frequently or the venue has a complex or changing layout.

Antenna Audio has been a leader for over 15 years in supplying operating systems to museums, historic sites and other types of visitor attraction all over the world. Over 70 million people visiting over 800 tourist and visitor attractions have now experienced an Antenna Audio tour. Major attractions using their technologies include:

* the Metropolitan Museum of Art in New York
* London's National Gallery
* the Louvre in Paris
* Edinburgh Castle
* the Alcatraz Cellhouse
* the Tower of London.

The case study below looks at an example of where an Antenna Audio system is in use – the Beatles Story in Liverpool.

CASE STUDY

Beatles Story audio tour

The Beatles Story in Liverpool's Albert Dock was established in 1990. The attraction is divided into 18 separate features and charts the success of the group from their early days in Hamburg right through to the eventual break-up of the band and their subsequent solo careers.

The exhibition faithfully recreates scenes and places to illustrate the career of the Beatles. Among many other features – such as George Harrison's first guitar, valued at over £1 million, John Lennon's orange-tinted glasses (also valued at over £1 million!) and the Cavern ('where it all began') – a 'Living History' audio tour has recently been introduced. This is narrated by Julia, John Lennon's sister. It gives visitors a personal and exclusive insight into the personal lives and feelings by those who really knew John, Paul, George and Ringo. Particularly special is the inclusion of some taped conversations between Julia and Paul McCartney, plus the voice of Brian Epstein taped shortly before his tragic death, a tape that has been held privately by the Epstein family for over 30 years. Other contributors include Sir George Martin, Alan Williams, Sid Bernstein and Cynthia Lennon.

The 'Living History' is now available in Japanese, French and Spanish and further translations are due to be produced. The audio system allows visitors to

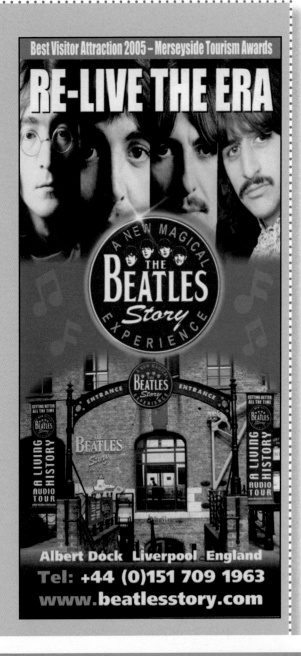

access different commentaries to help them appreciate the full significance of the material on display in each of the attraction's sections. The focus of the whole exhibition has been broadened from concentrating mainly on the group's public appearances and achievements. The new input from those with first-hand experience will allow visitors to gain an insight into the personal lives and feelings of the group. The digital soundtrack and video-clips all combine to transport the visitor back to the era.

All of these developments are taking place at the right time because in 2008 Liverpool will take on the mantle of European Capital of Culture. The improvements made at the Beatles Story will allow the attraction to offer a warm and respectful international welcome, which means multi-language signage, literature and commentary. Initial visitor reaction to these improvements is positive and there has been a particular increase in Japanese interest.

* **Suggest reasons why this audio tour is attractive to many visitors.**

* **What evidence is there that the attraction had explicit reasons for the new 'Living History' audio tour and other new features?**

* **What implicit reasons might there have been for the changes?**

Virtual/computer-based guided tours

Several of the examples considered above illustrate the ways in which applications of communications technology can be made use of for the provision of guided tours. We now consider some further applications that are influencing the ways in which visitor information can be made available to the travelling public.

Have you ever dreamed of being a guide – of being able to share and involve unlimited groups of curious tourists about some aspect of your city or your area? Until very recently, to be such a guide not only did you need a great deal of knowledge on the things you had to describe but you also had to be physically present at the location. That meant that you did not often find Korean guides to the Vatican in Rome, a Thai-speaking one at the Metropolitan Museum of Art in New York City or Arabic guides in Rio de Janeiro. However, things may be about to be changed in some fascinating ways.

For instance, thanks to the new low-cost media and recording technologies available today and to the relative ease and minimal cost with which these can be distributed, anyone anywhere could become a virtual guide for their fellow nationals. By utilising simple audio tools on a computer, it is easy for anyone to record a dedicated audio tour inside a gallery or museum, by either going once on-site with a small portable audio recorder or by following a well-planned remote tour of the place with the help of maps, photographs, notes and printed guides collected by you or others at that place. The recorded material could then be distributed and made available by means of 'podcasting', the Web and its associated technology. By posting such recordings in digital format on your site, you will make it very easy for anyone with an Internet connection to download your 'virtual guide' to their preferred location.

We have already seen how mobile phones are being used for visitor tours. The next stage of development is very likely to involve iPod and MP3 players playing selected tour guide files downloaded directly from the Internet. This is the future and it is worthwhile reflecting on the fact that we already live in the age of the virtual tourist. From the comfort of sitting in front of a computer screen at home, school, college or work, we can visit destinations and take virtual tours of visitor attractions with a click of the mouse! However, such systems do present problems and there are issues relating to the following:

* What guarantee is there over the guide's accuracy?

* Who would vet the content?

* What arrangements would there be to avoid mischief-making?

* How useful would such a system really be?

We cannot predict the future but we can review some of the more significant ways in which virtual tours are being used. Many of the examples used thus far in this unit have had some virtual/computer-based content. Many providers of guided tours have information on their websites and this allows you to assess the likelihood of any one of the providers being able to satisfy your particular needs and wants. This applies to the examples of tours guided by a person (e.g. Paul's Tours, Big Onion Walking Tours and Emirates Palace in Abu Dhabi). Furthermore, mention was made of the various ways in which Emirates Palace deploys extensive communications technology. The hotel uses modern technology in the same way as some visitor attractions to give interactive tours. This is always a help when the property covers a large area and even shopping malls are following suit to help shoppers accurately locate their store requirements. Indeed, it is now common to find tour providers' websites offering sample clips to inform customer choice. Furthermore, Walk the Talk actually makes its tour of Macau freely available!

Activity

Investigate a selection of websites and note the variety of customer-friendly options that they provide. This will help you generate evidence to support Assessment Objectives 1 and 3.

CASE STUDY

White Scar Cave

White Scar Cave in the Yorkshire Dales National Park is the longest cave on show in Britain. The guided tour begins near the original entrance, which was found in 1923. The path visitors take winds its way past cascading waterfalls, between massive banks of flowstone, and through galleries decorated with cream- and carrot-coloured stalactites and stalagmites. Beneath the steel-grid walkways visitors can see an underground stream rushing and foaming on its way. The highlight of the tour is the 200,000-year-old Battlefield Cavern. Over 100 metres long, with its roof soaring in places to 30 metres high, this is one of the largest caverns in Britain. It contains thousands of stalactites, which hang from the roof in great clusters.

Visitors to the cave's website, www.whitescarcave.co.uk, are immediately given the option in the centre of the home page to take the virtual tour. This tour has animation with sound. The way the tour is presented makes it very visitor-friendly. Log on to the Cave's website and investigate the following.

* What is the purpose of the first interactive screen shot?

* What does the tour indicate about health and safety in the caves?

* What is interesting about the tour?

* What visitor target group is the tour aimed at?

* How does the web page 'The History' enhance the virtual tour?

* How does the 'Rocks & Water' web page enhance the virtual tour?

* How does the Geological Clock interaction (www.whitescarcave.co.uk/geolo.htm) enhance the virtual tour?

* Why is there a page for schools and groups?

* How helpful is the 'Visiting Us' web page?

* Can you identify explicit and implicit purposes of this virtual tour?

* Would you like to visit the attraction? Explain your answer.

Consider the merits and deficiencies of virtual/computer-based guided tours. You should comment on:

* their purpose

* the various types available

* their availability

* the time they take

* their possible cost

* the extent to which they can meet the interests of their targeted customers

* how well they can meet the needs of different customer types

* whether there are any procedures that can identify or solve problems which may arise.

Now select a specific virtual tour of your choice and analyse it in terms of these points and also state its merits and deficiencies. This information will help you to supply further evidence for Assessment Objectives 1 and 3.

Devising and delivering a guided tour

It was highlighted in the introduction that tourist guides should be qualified to deliver a guided tour. In the UK, the Association of Professional Tourist Guides (APTG) states that tourist guides should have a 'wide general knowledge with specific reference to the history, geography, art and architecture, economics, politics, religion and sociology of the area of qualification'. As a student, you are not expected to be qualified of course, but you are expected to devise and deliver a guided tour in a professional manner. The Travel Services NVQ (Commentaries and Interpretation for Tourism) level 3 qualification highlights the following as being appropriate vocational skills and you now have the opportunity to demonstrate your capabilities:

* researching and planning interpretations and presentations on areas

* developing positive working relationships with customers

* enhancing your own performance at work

* creating, developing and maintaining effective working relationships

* contributing to maintaining the quality of services and operations

* resolving on-site emergencies and problems

* delivering and evaluating interpretations and presentations on areas

* leading groups of people

* preparing and providing practical information, advice and assistance to visitors

* agreeing tours and guided walks.

You need to produce a report which demonstrates your planning, the tour itself and your evaluation of it. Let us now look at what will be involved in producing a report that addresses each of these aspects.

Planning

Any activity requires careful preparation if it is to run smoothly and the delivery of a guided tour is no exception. You must follow a logical planning process.

First, you will have to decide on the purpose of the tour and its objectives. It is likely that your group will contain people under the age of 18 years and that you will be participating in the activity to help you generate evidence to meet the assessment requirements of this unit. Whatever you do decide on, the tour themes that you initially consider will need to be assessed in terms of their fitness for purpose.

At this planning stage you should consider:

* identifying a location for the tour

* making sure that it is suitable for the chosen tour

* the form of transport, if appropriate

* the budget and funding arrangements

* undertaking a risk assessment

* undertaking an exploratory visit.

In the light of the above you should then give additional consideration to:

* risk assessment and hazard control measures

* emergency procedures and student home contact

* transport arrangements

* insurance arrangements

* costs

* staffing details, including their qualifications and experience

* contingency plans for bad weather and so on.

Any outdoor education trip is a learning adventure which develops personal values and concepts, generates skills for lifelong learning, encourages group cooperation, and enhances knowledge of and appreciation for the environment. Good planning will ensure a successful experience for all concerned. If the tour is being developed as a group activity, the participants, under the careful guidance and direction of their teacher/tutor, should determine the goals and objectives of the tour and identify ways to accomplish them. They will thus become committed from the outset to making the trip a success.

Among the factors to be considered in deciding on the type of tour to be undertaken are the following:

* characteristics of customers (such as age, special needs and special skills)

* purpose for which the tour is being undertaken

* length of time the tour will last (including travelling time)

* distance to be travelled, transportation and destination

* activities to be undertaken while on the tour

* season of the year

* support tasks to be performed.

Information sources

Once you have identified a location for your tour and decided on its theme, you then need to consider what information will be made available. Furthermore, you will be expected to provide evidence of your research. There are many sources of information available to help you plan the content of your chosen tour:

* industry professionals

* gazetteers

* brochures

* maps

* guidebooks

* press

* trade journals

* promotional leaflets

* websites.

A good starting point will be a visit to the local tourist information centre. These carry a wide range of promotional leaflets, brochures, guide-books and other material relating to the local region. Furthermore, they are frequently used as an outlet for the booking of local guided tours and they will provide information about local Blue Badge Guides.

Activity

Indeed, information and advice about how to devise, deliver and evaluate a guided tour could be obtained from the individuals who actually provide them throughout the year. Ask your tourist information centre whether any local guides might talk to your group.

Once you have collected some printed materials you can extend your search by using the Internet. You can easily find out more information by visiting any websites that appear on the printed materials that were available at the tourist information centre. The Internet allows you to research quite widely. Newspaper articles will often be stored on the paper's website and these are an excellent source of additional information.

Depending on the type of tour you select, further research could be undertaken at your local library, town hall or museum. These are locations that carry information for the local population as well as visitors and details of anything with local interest are likely to be available there.

Action plan

You need to be able to provide answers to questions such as the following if your guided tour is going to work well:

* Does the tour under consideration require any specialised material or resources?
* If so, who will provide them and at what cost?
* Is the tour affordable?
* Are materials included in the price?
* Where will the tour actually take place?
* How do you get there?
* Is transport provided?
* Is the tour suitable for all members of the group?
* Are there physical ability and fitness constraints?
* Is the size and gender composition of the tour group an issue?
* If you are planning to guide a school group, are there particular health and safety or child protection issues?

In addition, there are a couple of questions you need to ask of yourself:

* Have you the expertise to deliver what you propose?
* Will you need supervision?

Furthermore, you need to understand that a good tour meets the interests and needs of its customers. On the basis of your research you need to select an itinerary and provide information that is fully appropriate for your target audience. To see how this might work in real life, let us consider an actual example: a guided tour of Coggeshall in Essex.

A guided tour of Coggeshall

Let us now look at just one way in which all of the above could be put into practice. You will be able to base your own tour on the following structure, regardless of where it takes place and how it is done exactly.

The historic village of Coggeshall, with a population approaching 5,000, is situated in north Essex on the old Roman military road between Colchester and St Albans. The village was mentioned in the Domesday survey and during the 15th, 16th and 17th centuries Coggeshall was one of the most industrialised places in the area, ranking alongside Colchester in importance in the wool trade. Coggeshall has over 200 listed buildings, which include two important National Trust properties – Grange Barn and Paycocke House. The remains of a 12th-century Cistercian abbey lie on the outskirts of the village and on Church Green stands the church of St Peter-ad-Vincula, an Essex 'wool' church.

The village's museum, run entirely by volunteers, attracts around 4,000 visitors a year and is open from April to October on Sundays and bank holidays. It gives an insight into Coggeshall's long and interesting history and guided walks around the town can be arranged for groups. The museum also operates a tourist information point on behalf of the parish council, and the volunteer curator answers queries by letter, telephone and email about Coggeshall and its history. The two National Trust properties are open from April to October.

The village can easily be used as the context for devising and delivering a short guided tour. However, there would not be much point in attempting to copy something that already exists. An individual with convenient access to

Coggeshall might consider designing a tour with a theme, just as Big Onion have done in New York, that complements but does *not* replicate the ideas contained in Figure 11.10.

The actual site of the abbey and its remains tend to be neglected. Therefore the idea of a guided walk from the centre of Coggeshall to the abbey's site would be an addition to the walks that already exist. Such a tour could be delivered either in person or in written form, as a tourist leaflet (or indeed as an audio guided tour or even a virtual tour, although this is likely to be overly ambitious for a student project). The tour would be of some interest to existing types visitor but could easily be customised to meet the needs of groups such as:

* Key Stage 3 history and/or geography pupils

* Key Stage 4 leisure and tourism students

* post-16 travel and tourism students

* students visiting the area

* a group of family and friends

* a group of leisure visitors.

Sources of information to help support the tour's content include:

* Coggeshall Museum

* Coggeshall Library

* existing printed materials such as those shown in Figure 11.10

* the Internet (e.g. the website of the parish council www.coggeshall-pc.gov.uk)

* the local history group.

FIGURE 11.10. *The promotional leaflets for three existing guided tours of Coggeshall*

Once you are satisfied that there is sufficient material available to support the content of the guided tour, a feasibility study should be planned to make sure that the proposed itinerary will actually work.

A suitable starting point for the tour would be the car park, which is less than 1 km away from the abbey ruins. If young people are undertaking this guided tour then health and safety will be very important. There is ample free parking for cars and minibuses and the enclosed space ensures that the participants can be safely monitored by their supervising adult. The car park is also adjacent to the museum and library and it would be possible to visit both, subject to arrangements.

The tour would then move along Stoneham Street passing the Victorian clock tower shown in Figure 11.11 and turn right and cross over into Bridge Street. The tour then passes Rood House and crosses the River Blackwater. After the bridge, the tour takes the first turning on the left which is Abbey Lane and this marks the start of a conservation walk along an official public footpath. The route is described on the website (http://countrywalks.defra.gov.uk) of the Department for Environment, Food and Rural Affairs (DEFRA) as follows:

> The permissive bridle path allows horse riding through Abby Farm, linking the B1024 to Abbey Lane. An attractive area of open access alongside the River Blackwater can be accessed via the public footpath at Abbey Bridge. You will see pasture, hay meadow and restored grassland protecting the remains of a 12th century Cistercian monastery and several 16th and 17th century buildings.

After 350 metres the tour will reach the site of St Nicholas Chapel, shown in Figure 11.12, and the tour then moves on following the official

FIGURE 11.11. *Coggeshall's Victorian clock tower*

route. After another 150 metres the remains of Coggeshall Abbey are reached and the two buildings of interest are shown in Figure 11.13 and Figure 11.14. The tour finishes at the Abbey Bridge, a further 100 metres away, and this location represents the most obvious hazard on the tour. Figure 11.15 shows that a risk assessment is needed because:

FIGURE 11.12. *St Nicholas Chapel*

* the horses have helped to create a muddy, slippery surface and so proper footwear will be needed in wet weather
* walking on the wall is unsafe
* overhanging branches add to the difficulty
* there is open water here.

There are no other hazards on the tour and participants will be expected to follow the country code and young people will be under the control and direction of their supervising adult. The topic of risk assessment is treated in some depth in unit 13, Adventure tourism.

The content provided on this walk relates to the key locations that are passed by. Supplementary information sheets could be produced as required. Below is what might be produced for our guided tour of Coggeshall taking in the abbey (this has been adapted from an account given online at http://www.british-history.ac.uk/report.asp?compid=39835):

Coggeshall Abbey, founded by King Stephen and Queen Maud, was one of the 13 English houses of the order of Savigny, the whole of which joined the Cistercians in 1147. Savigny itself was situated within the county of Mortain, and to this connection with Stephen, as count of Mortain, the selection of the order of the new abbey was no doubt due. The choice of the site, on the other hand, came from the queen, Coggeshall being one of the manors held by her father, Count Eustace of Boulogne.

In her foundation charter she granted the manor to the monks to hold as fully as she and her father had held it, and the grant was confirmed by charters of Stephen and their son William, Count of Boulogne.

FIGURE 11.13. *Abbey remains still showing outline of former medieval doorway arch*

FIGURE 11.14. *Abbey remains – former abbot's lodging house*

FIGURE 11.15. *A risk assessment is needed at Abbey Bridge*

The date of the foundation is given in different annals in years from 1137 to 1142, but the most probable seems to be 1140, as given by the historian Ralph, the sixth abbot, who states that the convent assembled on 3 August. He is certain to have had good evidence, and moreover correctly records an eclipse in the same year. This date is consistent with the evidence of the Queen's foundation charter. Ralph tells us that the high altar was dedicated to St Mary and St John the Baptist on 15 August 1167, by Gilbert Foliot, Bishop of London, who on the same day solemnly celebrated mass at that altar, Simon de Toni being the abbot.

Henry II, by a charter dated at Rouen early in his reign, granted protection and liberties to the abbey, and confirmed several grants made to it; and this charter was confirmed by Edward I in 1290. Richard I on 15 September, 1189, granted a charter of liberties; John on 1 January, 1204, granted licence for the abbot and convent to enclose their wood in their manor of Coggeshall; and Henry III on 2 April, 1257, granted licence for them to enclose woods in Tolleshunt Major, Tolleshunt Tregoz, Inworth, Childerditch and Little Warley, with various detailed provisions.

During the Peasants' Revolt in 1381 some of the insurgents entered the Abbey and carried away goods and charters, writings and other things, a fact which appears to indicate its unpopularity at the time.

The rents from the possessions of the Abbey in Coggeshall are given in great detail in the account of the bailiff for the year ending Michaelmas, 1531. In this the gross income of the abbey amounts to £298 0s 8d; and deductions of £12 6s for rents, £8 0s 8d for pensions, £20 13s 4d for fees, including those to John, Earl of Oxford, and Henry, Earl of Essex, as chief stewards, and £5 18s 8d for alms on three anniversaries. The outgoings reduced the net income to £251 2s. The Abbey was thus rich enough to escape the first dissolution in 1536. Henry More, appointed 1536, was the last abbot.

The Abbey itself and all its possessions were granted in fee to Sir Thomas Seymour on 23 March 1538, at a rent of £25 2s 2½d yearly. Part, including the site, was sold back by him to the crown on 12 May 1541. In a survey taken preparatory to this in April it is noted that the church is prostrate and defaced, but that the lodgings and cloister yet remain untouched. The charges on lands included pensions of £5 and upwards to the three last abbots, John Sampford, William Love and Henry More, and four other monks, Thomas Brykelsey, John Roydon, George Cokenell and Thomas Bysshom.

The seal attached to the deed of surrender is of white wax, measuring about 2 inches across. The Virgin crowned is seated in a canopied niche, with the infant Jesus on her knee; and in a smaller canopied niche on each side is a group of six kneeling monks. In the base, under an arch, is a shield of arms, France and England quartered.

It is possible to download a map from the DEFRA website that actually shows the entire route already described (Figure 11.16). It would therefore be perfectly possible to produce a customised map for the tour's route which shows the location of various places of interest. Depending on your level of skill with information technology, such a map might be further customised with text relating to the main buildings and locations actually seen. In our example, the following could be added:

The Clock Tower
A Coggeshall landmark, it was heightened and refurbished in 1887 to commemorate Queen Victoria's Golden Jubilee.

The Rood House
The house is thought to be the site of a Holy Rood or great cross that marked the entrance to the Abbey's lands. It was pulled down and burnt by Robert Gardner in 1532. The house was birthplace of Dr John Gardner (1804–80), co-founder of the General Apothecaries Company and the Royal College of Chemistry.

Long Bridge
Also known as Stephen's Bridge after the king during whose reign Coggeshall Abbey was founded. The bridge arches contain some of the oldest post-Roman bricks in Britain, dating from the 12th century. It was built when 1.5 miles of the river was diverted by the monks to provide a head of water to drive the mill.

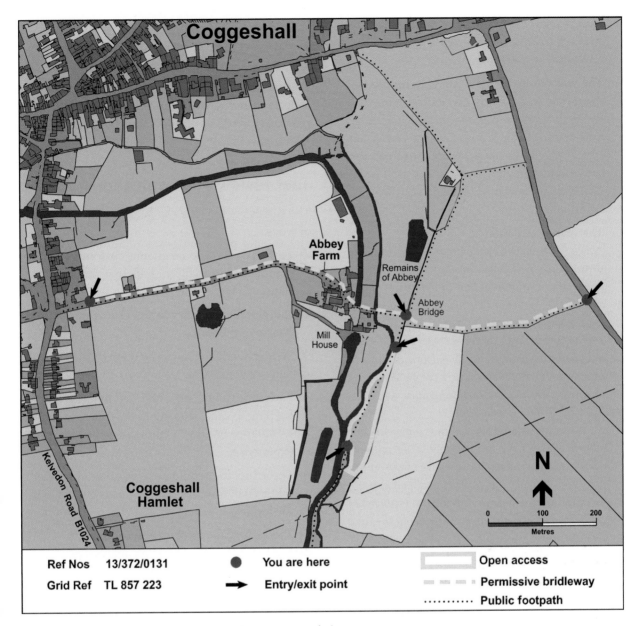

FIGURE 11.16. *Map downloaded from the DEFRA website*

St Nicholas Chapel

The only remaining whole building of the abbey complex is the former Gate House, now the St Nicholas Chapel. When the abbey was suppressed in 1538, Thomas Cromwell's agents auctioned off the lead roof of the largest abbey building, St Mary's Church (the lead or copper in their roofs was then the most valuable part of the abbey buildings). The church was probably pulled down; if it hadn't been its flint rubble would have disintegrated away because the roof was gone – this is what happened to most of the abbeys. All you can now see of

St Mary's Church is the faint outline of its walls on the ground. What is now the St Nicholas Chapel was converted to a horse-barn, with a pig-sty attached. In 1860 the chapel was sold to the vicar of Coggeshall, and, after restoration, is still used for Anglican services.

The Abbey Lands

This area is an ideal site for a Cistercian abbey. The order always tended to base its communities in quiet valleys and by a river for fishing and by which to build mills to grind the corn they grew on the fertile agricultural soil. The sheep farming undertaken by the monks gave a great boost to the woollen and cloth trade, which was eventually to make Coggeshall so prosperous.

The work done by the Cistercian monks

Apart from being farmers the monks were also millers, brewers, tanners and, most significantly, brick-makers. Bricks had not been made in Britain since Roman times and so the bricks and tiles which can be seen in the Abbey remains and at St Nicholas Chapel today are some of the oldest post-Roman bricks in the country.

The Abbey remains

Abbey Farm, owned by the Brew family (Charlotte Brew was the first female to ride in the Grand National), has buildings that contain parts of the old Abbey. The front of the main dwelling-house is more modern, of late Tudor design. However, the rear has several walls of the old Abbey buildings, with pointed Gothic arches, and doorways leading into the long ambulatory, where the monks warmed themselves with hot air carried by flues, an inheritance from Roman times.

Above the ambulatory, which is now used for the storage of farm tools, were the monks' dormitories. The domestic water supply was piped from springs across on the other side of the River Blackwater. The so-called Monk House at Abbey Farm is almost as complete as the chapel, and was probably the Abbot's own dwelling.

Folklore

A local ghost story mentions a pallid wrinkled monk walking silently around the Abbey with a lit taper, before leaving and making his way along the old lanes towards the River Blackwater.

This forms the basic content of the guided tour and the information can be provided either by the guide or by a customised map/leaflet. Indeed, it would in any case be good practice to provide a tour information sheet. Furthermore, such a sheet could draw visitors' attention to places of interest not featured on the tour itself such as:

* Paycockes
* Grange Barn

* St Peter's Church.

The tour itinerary is now flexible enough to focus on history, geography or more general interest. The guide's spoken delivery can expand on key aspects as and where appropriate. This is how the particular guided tour will meet the needs of those taking part in it.

Tour review and evaluation

The success of the tour can be judged in a number of ways:

* Participants could be given a customer comment card to fill in, such that shown in Figure 11.17.

* Individuals will offer feedback during the course of the tour.

* Written feedback might be offered, such as a letter of complaint.

* Each tour can be self-evaluated in terms of keeping to time, sticking to the itinerary and whether or not the visitors seemed to enjoy the experience.

* The actual tour could be compared with other Coggeshall tours, or similar ones conducted in the locality.

On the basis of the information collected, a detailed SWOT analysis (i.e. an analysis of strengths, weaknesses, opportunities and threats) can be performed and a table created to highlight areas for further development. Figure 11.19 illustrates how this might look for the Coggeshall guided tour.

PARTICIPANT FEEDBACK QUESTIONNAIRE

Name: ....

Group: ....

Date of tour: ....

Please give some feedback based on your experience of this tour. Circle the most appropriate number on the scale below where 10 is best.

Quality of tour as a learning experience

1   2   3   4   5   6   7   8   9   10

Relevance of tour to your needs

1   2   3   4   5   6   7   8   9   10

How would you summarise your experience of the tour?

....

....

....

What was most effective?

....

....

....

What was least effective?

....

....

....

What would have made it better?

....

....

....

Any other comments or suggestions?

....

....

....

....

Thank you!

FIGURE 11.17. *Sample customer comment card for the Coggeshall tour*

THE GUIDED TOUR WITNESS STATEMENT

Name of candidate: ....

Type of tour: ....

Location of tour: ....

Date of tour: ....Group size:...........

Individual's contribution to the tour:

....

....

....

Demonstration of communication skills:

....

....

....

Interaction with others:

....

....

....

Presentation skills:

....

....

....

Initiative shown/problem solving:

....

....

....

....

Signed: ....Date:.................

Name and status: ....

....

....

....

FIGURE 11.18. *Guided tour witness statement*

Strengths	Weaknesses
◯ Unique selling point is focus on the Abbey	◯ Might be too short
◯ Tour is short and accessible to all	◯ Not a lot to see, therefore limited appeal
◯ Can be tailored to meet individual requirements	◯ Museum rarely open
◯ Few, if any, health and safety issues	◯ Special arrangements need to be made
Opportunities	**Threats**
◯ Limited competition	◯ There are other local destinations with better attractions
◯ Could be combined with other local visits	◯ Competition from others
◯ Could serve the educational market	◯ Over-use will have negative effects
◯ Development is possible (e.g. new content)	◯ Complaints and objections

FIGURE 11.19. *Coggeshall Abbey Tour SWOT analysis*

Assessment guidance

We now have the opportunity to consider the extent to which the Coggeshall guided tour meets the requirements of Unit 11's assessment evidence grid.

Assessment Objective 1 asks you to give an account of the range of guided tours available and the plan of your guided tour. In terms of the requirements of Assessment Objective 1's mark band 3, assess the extent to which the guided tour has the following:

✳ a comprehensive plan

✳ the ability to run smoothly and successfully

✳ procedures to be followed in dealing with problems

✳ thorough knowledge and understanding.

For Assessment Objective 1 you should produce a *comprehensive* plan of your guided tour. It can be argued that an action plan would have helped to clarify the circumstances in which the proposed tour would operate. What was the definition of a short tour, why was Coggeshall a suitable destination and has enough explanation been given about the itinerary being followed? Furthermore, the images selected to illustrate the sites covered by the tour could have

been used in some detail to emphasise the suitability for stops at these precise locations. For example, by the bridge and Rood House the pavement is very narrow and this may not be the best of locations to halt with a group of young people. After all, part of the purpose for undertaking an inspection visit is to identify potential strengths and weaknesses. It is very important to provide evidence of the procedures to be followed in dealing with problems and to show that you have a thorough knowledge and understanding of all the issues.

Assessment Objective 2 asks you to show evidence of your delivery of your guided tour, with any supporting participants' documents. In terms of the requirements of Assessment Objective 2's mark band 3, assess the extent to which the guided tour is:

✳ well structured

✳ well delivered, detailed and contains no omissions

✳ clearly explained in terms of its purpose

✳ of an appropriate type (i.e. fit for purpose)

✳ providing extensive evidence of good-quality, appropriate and informative support materials, in a form suitable for participants

* using materials which show full application of knowledge and understanding

* using materials which are logically presented, with appropriate terminology, whose meaning is clear and conveyed accurately.

The tour's purpose needs to be clearly explained for Assessment Objective 2. The account does this but not in as much detail as it might. For example, how does the tour actually meet the needs of particular types of potential client? This requires some specific comment and exemplification. The details supplied give the history well, and this could easily meet the needs of a student or adult interested in local history. However, for the purposes of the higher mark band these details should be not only provided but be explained in terms of their fitness for purpose. It should be clearly pointed out, for example, how the tour has been planned and how various sources have been researched to allow the production of good-quality appropriate and informative support materials for participants.

Assessment Objective 3 requires you to do relevant research and analysis for your investigation into the range of guided tours and also for your own guided tour. In terms of the requirements of Assessment Objective 3's mark band 3, assess the extent to which the guided tour of Coggeshall has:

* provided evidence of independent and comprehensive research

* used a range of sources

* used relevant research findings to inform its content.

Here you will want to show that your research is relevant and that you have used your findings to support the tour's operation in appropriate ways. This aspect would allow you to comment on the relative importance of the different sources you have used. In the Coggeshall example, no reference has been made to people as information sources, tourist boards and other organisations. The features of the museum and library have not been given in much detail and the strengths and weaknesses of existing publications could be commented on. For example, a technique such as the AIDA (attention, interest, desire and action) model, which you study as part of marketing in unit 15, could be very appropriately used to criticise the leaflets shown in Figure 11.10. Then the model could be applied to the written materials produced to support the tour and particular comments made about using the same criteria of attention, interest, desire and action.

To meet the mark band 3 requirements of Assessment Objective 4, your guided tour has to have a critical and comprehensive evaluation, and you must make recommendations for improvement. AO4 does need to be approached quite carefully and it should be noted that to obtain the highest marks the evaluation must be based on at least *three* methods. Therefore something along the lines of the evaluation tools shown in Figures 11.17 and 11.18 will be very important, for a number of reasons. The structure of the participant feedback questionnaire (Figure 11.17) allows you to undertake both a quantitative and a qualitative analysis of participant opinion. Let us briefly look at some of the more important aspects.

* The 'group' entry will show the type of client attracted and therefore allows you to match comments made as being evidence for fitness for purpose.

* The quality and relevance ratings will allow you to quote precise figures to illustrate your evaluation analysis.

* The effectiveness entries will give you customer feedback which informs your future planning of a subsequent tour.

This information will certainly give you a lot of ideas to help you complete a SWOT analysis of your tour. The points listed in the SWOT analysis (Figure 11.19) might easily have been extended if participant feedback questionnaires had actually been completed.

A witness statement (Figure 11.18) would provide evidence to help you evaluate your own performance during the tour. This would help you to focus on your own self-evaluation. For this unit you need to include at least one detailed witness statement from an independent observer or tour participant as supporting evidence. Figure 11.18 indicates the type of information that will be of use. Remember that you have to evaluate *both* the tour *and* your performance in it. In this way you can make fully justified recommendations for future improvements.

The Coggeshall tour has all the makings of a top-mark performance but there is still quite a way to go before it satisfies all the higher assessment evidence criteria. If you follow the various pieces of advice provided in this final section you should be able to obtain a very good mark for your portfolio work. Good luck!

Knowledge check

1 Identify *three* advantages and *three* disadvantages of each of the following types of guided tour: a city-centre sightseeing coach tour; a walking tour around a town or city using a guide book; an audio tour of a major visitor attraction.

2 Explain the advantages of taking a tour delivered by a Blue Badge Guide.

3 Describe the circumstances in which interactive touch-screens will be of use to visitors taking a guided tour.

4 Outline why many organisations have virtual guided tours as part of their website.

5 Suggest why some guided tours provide printed information for their customers.

6 Give *two* examples of the way in which a guided tour can be used to serve both explicit and implicit purposes and explain each of your choices.

7 Why should guided tours undertake a risk assessment before operation?

8 Identify and explain the key steps to be followed in planning a guided tour.

9 Outline the ways in which the success of a guided tour can be evaluated.

10 What are the essential personal skills and qualities that a tour guide should possess?

References and further reading

Websites

Tours in Dubai

www.arabian-adventures.com
www.bigbustours.com
www.halatours.net
www.northtours.net
www.wonderbusdubai.com
www.planet-travel-tours.com
www.mmidubai.com
www.orienttours.ae
www.altayer-travel.com
www.snttadubai.com
www.nettoursdubai.com

Other sites

www.walkingtoursprague.com
www.bigonion.com
www.emiratespalace.com
www.kentwell.co.uk
www.ibnbattutamall.com
www.walkthetalk.hk
www.marchestourstalks.co.uk
www.tourmate.com
www.antennaaudio.com
www.beatlesstory.com
en.wikipedia.org/wiki/Podcasting
www.whitescarcave.co.uk
www.coggeshall-pc.gov.uk
www.british-history.ac.uk/report.
   asp?compid=39835

Books, journals, magazines

Zandi, D. (2002) *Off-Road in the Emirates* (2nd edition), Dubai: Motivate Publishing.

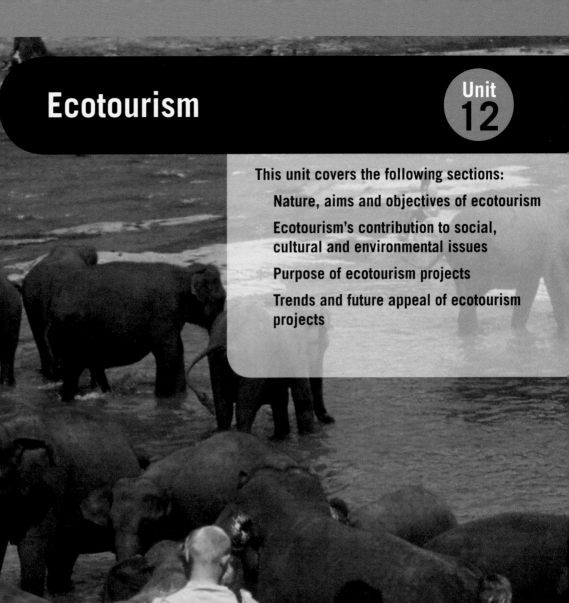

Ecotourism

This unit covers the following sections:

Nature, aims and objectives of ecotourism

Ecotourism's contribution to social, cultural and environmental issues

Purpose of ecotourism projects

Trends and future appeal of ecotourism projects

Introduction

This unit explores the attitudes of tourists and host countries to the issues surrounding recreational and tourism activity in natural surroundings. The travel and tourism industry has a responsibility to ensure that travel to, and tourism in, natural areas respects both their culture and their ecology. This unit also explores the economic opportunities and benefits for local people in the conservation of natural resources.

Until recently, few travellers would even dream of visiting a rainforest, but now many tourists are looking for new locations to visit. They are leaving traditional beach locations to visit remote, unspoiled areas all over the world. These tourists want to avoid the fast pace and congestion of typical tourist destinations, and choose instead to holiday in locations that offer more adventure, stimulation and learning. This growing trend has come to be known as ecotourism. Tour operators and travel agents need to be aware of it, and to provide products and services that meet the needs of tomorrow's travellers, while also meeting and respecting the needs of the host population.

This unit is strongly linked to unit 9 (Tourism development), which is externally assessed. Many of the principles learned in tourism development may be applied in a practical manner to this unit. If you enjoy learning about the preservation and conservation of the natural environment and the differing cultures on our planet, then you will enjoy working through this unit.

How you will be assessed

This unit will be assessed through your portfolio work. You will need to produce an in-depth written and illustrated account of your investigations into an ecotourism destination. This may be on anywhere in the world. You will have to evaluate the evidence you have researched and provide substantiated conclusions about the future trends in ecotourism, as well as about the management of your chosen destination. You will be expected to express your own values and opinions clearly within your work. The areas your report will be assessed on are:

* knowledge and understanding of the aims and objectives of ecotourism and the role of ecotourism in relation to your project (Assessment Objective 1)

* application of your knowledge and understanding of ecotourism contribution to environmental, social and cultural issues (Assessment Objective 2)

* your research and analysis when investigating an ecotourism project, in terms of environmental, social and cultural issues (Assessment Objective 3)

* an evaluation of the future trends and appeal of worldwide ecotourism principles and projects which relate to your chosen project destination (Assessment Objective 4).

Assessment is explained in more detail at relevant points later in this unit.

Nature, aims and objectives of ecotourism

Tourism has become a major world industry. We are travelling further and in far greater numbers than ever before. We journey into the heart of the rainforests and up the highest mountains, soak up the sun on tropical beaches and dive in coral reefs. We stand and gaze in wonder at the ruins of ancient civilisations and venture close to the most amazing wildlife on earth. According to the WTTC (World Travel and Tourism Council; see www.wttc.org) there are nearly 700 million international travellers a year, and this figure is expected to double by 2020. But while this tremendous growth of tourism has expanded our holiday options and boosted jobs and income in developing countries, it has also become a cause for concern. The economic benefits that tourism brings to these destinations can be cancelled out by its impact on the environment and local communities. Fragile coastal ecosystems, in particular, are suffering from the development of massive hotel complexes, local water supplies are drying up through excess demand and ancient cultural sites are under threat from the ever increasing need for more land for tourism development. All of this means that the type of holiday we choose is becoming increasingly important. We must ensure that the very places we love to visit are safeguarded.

What is ecotourism?

There are many definitions of ecotourism – also called 'green' or 'responsible' tourism – but the most common use of the word is to describe any

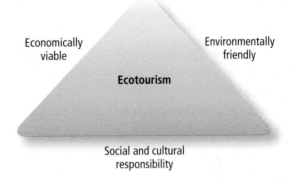

FIGURE 12.1. *What is ecotourism?*

recreational activity in natural surroundings. The International Ecotourism Society (see www.ecotourism.org) takes this definition one step further and adds social responsibility, in defining ecotourism as: 'responsible travel to natural areas that conserves the environment and improves the well-being of local people'. This means that those who implement and participate in ecotourism activities should adhere to the following principles:

* minimize impact

* build environmental and cultural awareness and respect

* provide positive experiences for both visitors and hosts

* provide direct financial benefits for conservation

* provide financial benefits and empowerment for local people

MASS TOURISM	ECOTOURISM
No zoning or seasonal beach activity	Seasonal beach activity and beach environment assessments conducted
Active diving activities without coral replacements and marine life assessments	Coral replacements and close watch on coral preservation. Coral regrowth through donation
Non-guided tours in nature parks and no monitoring of tourist activities by park rangers	Guided tours in the parks and frequent monitoring by rangers
No information or education given to the host community or tourists on environmental practices	Briefing campaigns and education for the host community and tourists on good environmental practices
Tours without stressing the importance of the environment	Tours with a local guide who will be educating and briefing responsible travellers
Economic benefits not equally distributed, especially to the locals, and lack of cultural preservation	Tourism gains used to preserve cultural heritage and distributed equally to the host community
No briefing on customs or beliefs of natives at a particular destination	Information given on customs and beliefs of natives at the destination
No efforts to conserve the national identity of locals	Efforts made to enhance and conserve the identity of the locals

TABLE 12.1. *Mass tourism and ecotourism compared and contrasted*

* raise sensitivity to host countries' political, environmental, and social climate

* support international human rights and labor agreements.

Global tourism is one of the largest industries in the world and ecotourism is a new force, which could shape the future of the industry. Table 12.1 contrasts ecotourism with mass tourism, to help you appreciate what is distinctive about ecotourism and how it may be defined.

Now that we understand what the general idea of ecotourism is, we can look at some of the objectives.

The aims and objectives of ecotourism

Ecotourism should be transforming the way modern, conventional tourism is conducted. There is a great potential to make it the dominant way in which we travel, if we can create the necessary public awareness and public understanding of how the travel industry operates. Ecotourism can play its most important role by educating tourists at first hand about the conservation of endangered ecosystems and the development needs of local people. There are three aspects to this: research, education and conservation.

Research

The importance of research is fundamental in the preservation and conservation of the world's natural resources. Finding out what needs to be done is mainly carried out by voluntary organisations such as the Earthwatch Institute, which supports the fieldwork of research scientists worldwide. Such fieldwork involves, for example, collecting baseline information, which is essential for making decisions for sustainable tourism management. UNESCO's research – much of it in the form of trends and statistics – is used worldwide for monitoring cultural practices and visitors to heritage sites. Ongoing research is a valuable method of monitoring worldwide trends and can highlight the need for education.

Education

For ecotourism destinations to be successful, both the host community and the traveller need to be educated. Only by educating and inspiring the next generation of leaders in education, business and the general public, both at home and overseas, will the destinations visited be able to remain close to their original state. Furthermore, education of the local community can have a lasting positive social and economic effect on an area.

Conservation

The protection of natural or man-made resources, including landscapes, buildings and their contents, are the primary objective of conservation. Turning research and education into real and lasting improvements for a destination can benefit conservation projects. Conservation International's mission is to protect the earth's most threatened biodiversity; the organisation currently works in more than 30 countries on four continents. Conservation International believes that carefully planned and implemented tourism development can play an important role in conservation, and so works to ensure that local people benefit from it. Those communities receive training and support to establish and manage sustainable ecotourism businesses.

The roles of organisations involved in raising awareness of ecotourism

It is important to understand the roles of the different types of organisations in raising people's awareness of ecotourism. Such organisations are found in the private, public and voluntary sectors. Each sector has different objectives and methods of generating or receiving income. They are sometimes referred to as commercial or non-commercial organisations. You will have studied the general roles of these organisations in other

TYPE OF ORGANISATION	CHARACTERISTICS
Private sector	The travel and tourism industry is dominated by private sector organisations. These are in private or shareholder ownership and are profit making. Many are PLCs (public limited companies owned by shareholders). Their main aim is to make a profit
Public sector	Public sector organisations receive funding through local or national government. Their main aims and objectives are to provide a service to the public and be concerned with wider issues such as overall numbers of tourists, quality and environmental issues
Voluntary sector	Voluntary sector organisations often have charitable status. Some larger ones have paid staff to manage the operation and voluntary staff, while smaller ones will typically be run by volunteers. Many of these are pressure groups, such as Greenpeace and Tourism Concern
Commercial organisations	Can be large companies or small businesses but their main aim is to make a profit
Non-commercial organisations	Non-profit making (see voluntary sector)

TABLE 12.2. *Types of organisation involved in ecotourism*

units; however, Table 12.2 provides a summary to remind you.

We are now going to study the role of organisations in raising awareness of and responding to ecotourism issues; examples are taken from each of the above sectors.

Private sector

British Airways

The annual British Airways 'Tourism for Tomorrow Awards' recognise any organisation in the tourism industry that has made a positive contribution to its local environment or heritage. An independent panel of representatives from the United Nations Environment Programme, the Smithsonian Institution and commercial television organisations judges the entries.

An example of a winning entry for was the Ecotaj Environmental Initiative entered by the Taj Group of India. Their achievements included energy and water conservation, the installation of

waste-water treatment plants, water recycling for gardens and cooling towers, materials recycling, and the introduction of solar power and chlorine-free treatment systems for swimming pools.

British Airways Holidays advertises its support for a number of voluntary organisations and the assistance it gives to conservation projects in its holiday brochures. It does this to raise the awareness of and focus attention on a number of social and environmental issues; additionally, of course, it will generate good publicity for the airline and the other organisations concerned.

In 2004 the Tourism for Tomorrow Awards were managed by the WTTC. British Airways and the WTTC have been working together to move the awards to a new stage of development. In 2005 the winners of the Tourism for Tomorrow Awards were:

* Destination Award – Jurassic Coast, UK

* Conservation Award – Damaraland Camp, Namibia

Winner in 2005 of the Conservation Award: Damaraland Camp, Namibia

The Damaraland Camp is part of the Wilderness Safaris groups of lodges in southern Africa. It was among the first in Namibia to link together tourism, community partnership and conservation. The result was an 180,000-hectare protected area established and managed by the local communities who directly benefit economically through tourism as partners in Damaraland Camp. In the 10 years of the project, wildlife populations in the nature conservancy area have doubled and the model of private sector–community partnership, successfully pioneered by Damaraland Camp, has spread to other areas of Namibia and southern Africa. This has not only helped to conserve vitally important natural areas, but also promoted the economic development of the local communities.

* **Use the Internet to research the winners of the Tourism for Tomorrow awards and find out why they were voted winners.**

* Investor in People Award – Haciendas del Mundo Maya, Mexico

* Global Tourism Business Award – Casuarina Beach Club, Barbados.

Key term

The World Travel and Tourism Council (WTTC) is the global business leaders' forum for travel and tourism. Its members are the chairs, chief executives and presidents of the world's most prominent travel and tourism organisations. It is the only body that represents the private sector in all parts of the travel and tourism industry worldwide. For more information, visit www.wttc.org.

Voluntary sector

Earthwatch

Earthwatch is a worldwide charity that organises and funds educational projects on how to solve environmental problems. Their approach is positive, long term and constructive. Its methods include research, education and conservation. Earthwatch can offer help with every aspect of the environment – animals and birds, seas and forests, communities and cultures. Over the last 25 years Earthwatch has helped to create 12 national parks in 11 countries and has organised and funded over 1,800 research projects in 150 countries.

For people who intend to work in the travel and tourism industry it is important to know the trends in the market and the demands of

PROJECT	WHAT IS INVOLVED	COST
Kenya's Black Rhino	Making a black rhino sanctuary work to its best potential	£1,500
Music and Folklore of Russian Villages	Can modern Russian culture coexist with traditional folk music traditions? Help find out how	£1,050
Spanish Dolphins	Testing the efficiency of managing ecosystems in a conservation area	From £995
Ancient Civilisation on the Mississippi	Discover the environmental impact of North America's prehistoric 'city of the Sun'	£850

TABLE 12.3. *Examples of Earthwatch expeditions*

FIGURE 12.2. *Earthwatch web page advertising one of its many expeditions*

travellers. Members of Earthwatch can apply for discounted prices on all-inclusive trips to help with projects. There is a demand for such trips – from the type of traveller who chooses to pay for a holiday that involves working on a local project in a number of worldwide destinations. Earthwatch advertises these working holidays in its brochure and online (see Figure 12.2 and www.earthwatch. org). Table 12.3 gives some examples.

Survival

Survival is an international charity that has supporters in over 75 countries. Its main role is to support tribal people. It does this in three complementary ways: campaigns, education and funding. The campaigns are directed at a range of public and private sector organisations to help raise awareness; Survival gives tribal people a platform to put their case to the world. If we ignore tribal people through the lack of education they could disappear. Survival is supported by British Airways.

Public sector

UNESCO (World Heritage Sites)

Heritage is our legacy from the past, what we live with today and what we pass on to future generations. Our cultural heritage and natural heritage are irreplaceable. Places as unique and diverse as the wilds of East Africa's Serengeti, the Pyramids of Egypt, the Great Barrier Reef in Australia and the cathedrals of Latin America make up our world's heritage. World Heritage Sites belong to all the peoples of the world, irrespective of the territory on which they are located. UNESCO seeks to encourage the identification, protection and preservation of cultural and natural outstanding heritage around the world.

According to its website (http://whc.unesco.org/en/about/), UNESCO's World Heritage mission is:

✳ to encourage countries to sign the World Heritage Convention and to ensure the protection of their natural and cultural heritage

✳ to encourage States Parties to the Convention to nominate sites within their national territory for inclusion on the World Heritage List

✳ to encourage States Parties to establish management plans and set up reporting systems on the state of conservation of their World Heritage Sites

✳ to help States Parties safeguard World Heritage properties by providing technical assistance and professional training

✳ to provide emergency assistance for World Heritage Sites in immediate danger

✳ to support States Parties' public awareness-building activities for World Heritage conservation

✳ to encourage participation of the local population in the preservation of their cultural and natural heritage

✳ to encourage international cooperation in the conservation of our world's cultural and natural heritage.

Activity

Access the Earthwatch website (www.earthwatch.org) and study the range of projects that are available. Consider some of the ideas for your own ecotourism research project.

Other useful organisations you may wish to investigate are:

✳ Friends of Conservation

✳ Green Globe 21

✳ World Tourism Organization

Study the ways in which these organisations have worked closely with travel service providers to raise awareness and focus attention on their initiatives.

Ecotourism's contribution to social, cultural and environmental issues

The relationship between culture, heritage, the environment and tourism has received a great deal of attention throughout the world. Yet rarely have individuals or organisations representing these interests worked together on a local, regional or national basis to discover ways in which they can develop a strong and mutually beneficial working relationship that conserves natural and cultural resources. With the ease of travel to the far-flung corners of the world, it is not often distance but rather culture and heritage that separate people. It is important to create stronger links between the indigenous people of the host community, their historic sites and monuments and the tourists who are seeking a high-quality ecotourism experience.

Ecotourism's contribution to social and cultural issues

The effect of tourism on the social lives and cultures of a destination may be both positive and negative. On the one hand, a select group of ecotourists can often focus attention on the culture of a destination and help to preserve its original presentation and beliefs. This is possible because relatively small numbers will have a low impact. Mass tourism, on the other hand, generally causes 'original' tourism to disappear and 'staged authenticity' to occur.

Although the tourism industry wears an eco-friendly face, and pays lip service to environmental concerns and good practice, it has also served the cause of environmental destruction, particularly in the developing world.

* In Hawaii, traditional burial grounds have been razed to make way for new resorts.

* In Bali, devout Hindus are horrified that their temples are overshadowed by monstrous ugly marinas and large hotel developments.

* In Goa, farmers and fishermen have been forced off their lands, forced to seek new livelihoods for which they are ill-equipped.

* In Costa Rica and Belize, coral reefs have been blasted to allow for care-free water sports.

* In Phuket, Thailand, the yacht club has been constructed over a public road, effectively denying local people access to their homes beyond.

* Golf courses are being developed all over the world, but they take land away from local communities, consume enormous amounts of scarce freshwater and leave in their wake hazardous chemical effluents that damage the biodiversity of the land.

* It is estimated that the water needed to supply a single new golf course can supply a village of 5,000 people.

Is tourism in conflict with nature and the human habitat?

Staged authenticity refers to how a local culture can become degraded and stylised to suit tourism-related entertainment, where the host population provides experiences for tourists that are not actually authentic but are staged to look more real than the real thing.

There is therefore a balance to achieve in having the right numbers of tourists, and in having tourists of the right type. What types of tourist do you think are likely to participate in an ecotourism experience? Cohen (1974) has provided a useful classification of tourists according to their different roles, and these roles can be studied in relation to tourist goals or holiday choice activities. Have a look at Table 12.4.

For each of the tourist types in Cohen's classification (Table 12.4), discuss the range of holidays that are currently on offer to meet the needs of each group. Consider which types may be classified as ecotourists.

Remember that commercial and non-commercial organisations alike must decide on the objectives of the destination, be those objectives education, conservation, social, environmental or leisure. Only once the objectives have been decided will it be possible to attract the right type of tourist.

In some regions, like Cameroon in Africa, the promotion of ecotourism would need little effort, as the area is quite well known as a cultural destination. It would still be necessary, nonetheless, to take steps like limiting the number of visitors (probably by making the tours more expensive). But what if the number of people was still beyond the capacity of the locals to handle them (both service-wise and psychologically)? In addition, the length and frequency of contact between tourists and locals might eventually make the local culture evolve into a purely tourism-based one, thereby diminishing its authenticity. Before destinations promote cultural tourism, they should first make sure that they can handle the visitors.

Ecotourists visit other cultures to witness authenticity. A negative impact of new tourist arrivals may sometimes lead to authentic ritual materials and heirlooms being sold and lost forever, along with some dignity and self-respect on the part of the host population.

TYPE OF TOURIST	CHARACTERISTICS OF TOURIST	TYPE OF TOURISM	DEGREE OF FAMILIARITY SOUGHT ON HOLIDAY
The organised mass tourist	Low on adventure he/she is anxious to maintain his/her 'environmental bubble' on the trip. Typically purchasing a ready-made package tour off the shelf. He/she is guided through the destination having little contact with local culture or people	*Institutionalised tourism.* Dealt with routinely by the tourism industry – tour operators, travel agents, hoteliers and transport operators	High familiarity
The individual mass tourist	Similar to the above but more flexibility and scope for personal choice built in. However, the tour is still organised by the tourism industry and the environmental bubble shields him/her from the real experience of the destination	As above	Familiarity
The explorer	The trip is organised independently and the tourist is looking to get off the beaten track. However, comfortable accommodation and reliable transportation are sought and, while the environmental bubble is abandoned on occasion, it is there to step into if things get tough	*Non-institutionalised tourism.* The individual travels, shunning contact with the tourism industry except where absolutely necessary	Novelty
The drifter	All connections with the tourism industry are spurned and the trip attempts to get as far from home and familiarity as possible. With no fixed itinerary, the drifter lives with the local people, paying his/her way and immersing him/herself in their culture	As above	High novelty

TABLE 12.4. *A classification of tourists (adapted from Cohen, 1974)*

In the remainder of this section, we consider the effects, positive and negative, tourism may have on various aspects of the indigenous culture and beliefs, before we go on to look separately at the effects of ecotourism on environmental issues.

Handicrafts

Tourists have collected souvenirs and handicrafts throughout history. (Many stately homes and country houses in England bear testimony to this very fact – for example, Castle Howard in Yorkshire houses a vast array of artefacts collected by the 4th Earl of Carlisle on his travels through Europe.) Many worldwide destinations produce handicrafts that are diverse and exciting to see. The preservation of these many crafts is important to the national identity of local peoples. Ecotourists wish to see authentic crafts and value the traditions and workmanship involved.

A good example of preservation of traditional crafts is the Middle Eastern country of Jordan. Jordan is quickly developing and many old

FIGURE 12.3. *Jordanian pottery*

customs and traditions are on the verge of
extinction. Traditional handicrafts in Jordan
have been passed down over many generations.
Jordanian crafts include beautiful handmade glass,
earthenware vessels (Figure 12.3), skilful basket
and carpet weaving, and exquisite embroidery.
Crafts produced on a smaller scale include
artistically decorated sand bottles, finely chiselled
sculptures and crafted silver jewellery.

The Queen of Jordan has been encouraging
the development of high-quality artisan centres
in Jordan's ancient villages to integrate socio-
economic development with sustainable tourism.
The Noor Al Hussein Foundation (NHF)
has renovated two farmhouses and plans to
transform these into a handicrafts village that
will preserve the cultural heritage of the region.
This will help to enhance the tourist appeal and
increase the economic benefit to the community
at the same time as preserving their handicrafts
and heritage.

Unfortunately, there can also be a negative
side to the sale of traditional crafts, especially
in the case of those that have been derived from
animal and other organic materials. The sale of
products derived from the killing of protected
animal species – such as sea turtles, reptiles, wild
birds (for their feathers) and mammals (e.g. for
their furs) – and rare plants such as orchids should
always be avoided. As a responsible tourist, you
should avoid all animal products.

Language

The ability to communicate effectively with
tourists and with the host population is
fundamental in ensuring that there is a successful
tourism experience. Ecotourists do not expect all
tourism providers to be able to speak English,
German, French or any other tourism-generating
country's language. Many of today's tourists
automatically expect the English language to
be understood without any consideration of
the training and general hospitality of the host
involved.

Religion

In some tourist regions, religion has become an
attraction. Religious buildings and events have

become 'something to view' and many visitors may not possess the beliefs of that particular religion. Many of the most visited sites in the world – such as Mecca, Lourdes and Jerusalem – have religious connections. On occasion, conflict may arise when local worshippers are disturbed by tourists during traditional ceremonies such as weddings and funerals. In St Lucia, they have even built a new resort hotel on a sacred site! Ecotourists should be sensitive to local cultures and religions. Conduct that is acceptable in certain western countries is not appropriate in many parts of the world. For example, nude sunbathing in Muslim countries such as Turkey and Dubai would cause great offence.

Visitors to churches, temples and shrines, whose primary purpose is as a house of worship for local residents, should be quiet and respectful.

Dress

Traditional dress is very much part of the culture of a region. The best way to appreciate the diversity of traditional dress and costumes is to look at photographs, videos and travel brochures from traditional destinations.

Perhaps the most colourfully costumed people in the Americas are the Highland Maya of Guatemala. While traditional native dress has disappeared in many parts of the world, Guatemala remains a place where a high percentage of the indigenous people still proudly wear their traditional dress, called *traje*. Figure 12.4 shows an example of traditional dress in Guatemala.

Think it over...

What positive effects might tourists have on local religion? What negative effects might they have?

FIGURE 12.4. *Traditional dress of Guatemala*

CASE STUDY

Traditional dress in West Papua, New Guinea

Tourism in Papua is an expanding industry but it brings with it the potential to exploit indigenous West Papuans, both culturally and economically. Virtually all tourists who come to West Papua travel to the Baliem Valley in the highlands. The main town, Wamena, draws tourists who are interested in trekking and in the culture of the local Dani tribes. Unfortunately, that interest in the culture is often exploitative, and the Indonesian administration of the tourism industry is mostly concerned with economic return.

The indigenous people are often treated as objects of curiosity. Although the Indonesian administration has previously tried to force them to wear clothes and live a more 'civilised' lifestyle, today they are happy if they go naked because it is good for tourism. Nowadays, when villagers can afford it, the custom is to sport modern dress – cotton shorts, T-shirts and dresses. Government policy, the missionaries and now tourism have taught the locals to see traditional dress as backward, something to be ashamed of. In the village of Manda, for example, clothed villagers are barred from the village while near-naked tribes people, well rehearsed and divided into two 12-member teams, cook and dance in the traditional way for camera-carrying tourists. The tourists pay for the food, the dancing, the photos, some handicrafts and a night's accommodation. The next day, after the tourists have left, the villagers climb into their clothes again (clothes bought using the profits of tourism).

Tourism can, however, provide opportunities for indigenous people to obtain cash and develop their livelihood, while respecting their tradition. The village of Dukun, for example, manages its own cooperative venture, formed to profit from tourism, yet helps them feel pride in their culture. Here, self-determination helps to sidestep the culture shock. Tourists can stay in a village, completely built by the cooperative to house visitors, for $2 a night. The villagers will dress traditionally, dance and have a feast for paying tourists. Tourism can be in keeping with the dignity of indigenous people and can help them to feel pride in their traditions.

Source: Australia West Papua Association, Sydney (www.cs.utexas.edu/users/cline/papua/letter.htm)

* Are the tourists visiting Manda preserving or demeaning local culture?

* How do you feel that the use of dress has contributed to the culture and social and economic benefits to the wider region?

Architecture

Hotels and restaurants serving tourists are being built at astonishingly rapid rates around the world. Unfortunately, many of these buildings do not fit in with the surrounding environment and local architecture. Instead they stand out and become more of an eye-sore than a place that people would want to visit and stay in.

Many countries are now adopting more rigorous planning laws. Spain and Turkey are examples of countries that are restricting the building of high-rise developments, opting instead for buildings of only two storeys. This protects the view of the natural environment and is more in keeping with the overall topography of an area. If you look in any of the brochures of the mass-market tour operators you will notice that the many traditional European holiday resorts such as Benidorm, Salou, Magaluf, Palma Nova, Playa de las Americas and Puerto de la Cruz will all have pictures of high-rise hotels. These were mainly built in the 1970s and 1980s. Compare these pictures with more recent resort development such as destinations in the Greek

Islands, Cyprus, Turkey and further afield in the Caribbean and Far East. You will see that newer developments are much more in keeping with the natural environment. One exception to this rule is the development of Dubai in the United Arab Emirates. Here development appears to be unrestrained, with hundreds of new sky-high hotels being built. Again, look at pictures of hotels in many island destinations, such as the Maldives and the Seychelles. Here you will find that hotel development is in harmony with the environment and many new buildings are of small, bungalow-style design. This type of accommodation can be easily replaced and will leave little damage to the environment.

Traditions

Traditions can take many forms, most of which are considered separately in this section, such as dress and music, but also others such as dance, arts and

food. The majority of worldwide destinations that wish to develop tourism – eco or otherwise – have an important role to play in the preservation of local traditions.

Arts and music

Music always contributes to a sense of local identity and is of interest to many tourists. In Britain alone, think of the regional significance of, say, the bagpipe, the male voice choir and the brass band. Art comes in many forms, from the decoration of buildings and ancient sites such as the tomb paintings in the Valley of the Kings in Egypt to the Neolithic cave paintings in France. Whatever form it takes, it should remain in its original state so that it may be viewed and celebrated for future generations.

Contribution of ecotourism to environmental issues

Ecotourism demands education for both the host communities and the travellers. Well before departure, those tour operators that have a responsible tourism policy will supply travellers with reading material about the country, the environment and local customs. This information is there to prepare travellers and to help them learn about the environment and people that they are about to visit. The International Ecotourism Society's guidelines state that tourists should 'minimize their negative impacts whilst visiting environments and culture'. Essential to good ecotourism are well-trained guides with skills in natural and cultural history, environmental concerns, ethical principles and effective communication skills.

Protection of the physical environment cannot be solely the concern of the ecotourism specialist part of the industry. The following is the 'Sustainable Travel Policy' of the giant TUI Group of tour operators (see www.tui-group.com):

The TUI Group and all Group companies and their employees are characterised by their long-term dedication for the responsible sustainable use of the environment and natural resources.

For the TUI Group the sustainable use of nature and ecosystems is of the utmost significance. This safeguards the capacity of natural resources to regenerate and the long-term future of the Group.

Each Group company and every employee bears environmental responsibility. The compatibility of the products, services and processes with the environment is a constituent part of the TUI quality standard. We support the development and widespread use of environmentally friendly technologies.

Beyond compliance with statutory environmental regulations, the TUI Group endeavours to continuously improve its environmental performance.

At home and abroad the TUI Group has a good reputation with respect to the sustainable management and use of nature and the environment.

The credibility of TUI's environmental seriousness as a corporate value represents an ongoing commitment and challenge. Management and employees are called upon to take an active role and contribute ideas for further developments.

Source: TUI Group

The importance of the environment as a tourism resource can be seen in the following statement by Dr Michael Frenzel, chairman of the executive board of the TUI Group:

An intact environment is the pre-requisite for each fascinating holiday experience, and therefore an essential aspect of tourism. No other globally active economic sector is as strongly dependent as tourism on clear water, natural beaches, clean air and an intact environment.

Nonetheless, ecotourism does have a particular role in focusing attention on, and contributing to, the management of the following aspects of the physical environment:

* ancient and historical sites
* the marine and coastal environment
* inland environment and habitats
* biodiversity and endangered species
* energy systems
* water supplies
* waste disposal.

We shall therefore look at each of these in turn.

Ancient and historical sites

Many ancient built sites, such as the Taj Mahal in India, are fortunate to be classified as 'World Heritage Sites' and thereby under the protection of UNESCO. There are currently 812 sites worldwide that are so classified, and more are continually being added. (The full list of these is available on the UNESCO website, www.unesco.org.) Many of these sites have recently been damaged, such as sacred sites in the mountains of Afghanistan, damaged by the Taliban, and many ancient and biblical sites in Iraq, damaged in the second Gulf war.

Ecotourism can contribute to the protection of these sites through the education of visitors and promotion of the issues faced by the host population. Through the economic benefits of tourism the need for environmental impact assessments and environmental auditing becomes obvious, and long-term protection and planning can be implemented.

Marine and coastal environment

The increasing popularity of the world's most visited marine and coastal environments can be both a blessing and a curse. In the positive sense this popularity may directly lead to the establishment of conservation and preservation schemes. On the negative side, there may be a threat posed to the integrity and composition of the natural marine environment. The plight of whales and dolphins affected by tourist activities such as oil pollution from tourist boats and disruption of breeding patterns caused by tourist boats sailing close to breeding grounds is a cause for concern. Through your studies you will have already appreciated the complexity of the issues involved and how the problems may begin to be solved when destinations adopt ecotourism policies. The following case study provides an illustration.

The Taj Mahal – a UNESCO-protected World Heritage Site

CASE STUDY

Sharm el-Sheikh: a fragile marine environment

The recently developed Egyptian resort of Sharm el-Sheikh is one of the most accessible and developed tourist communities on the Sinai Peninsula. Running parallel to the beaches in the area is a stretch of reef which is one of the richest (and most famous) in the world. The concentration of marine life exceeds all expectations and is comparable to that on the Great Barrier Reef in Australia. For centuries the coastline was devoid of human settlement, but then, as in many developing countries, the immense economic potential of recreational activities such as snorkelling and scuba diving was recognised. Luckily, the Egyptian government realised the damaging potential of this tourism boom and in 1983 declared the area of the reef as the Ras Mohammed National Park.

When you dive or snorkel it is important not to touch the coral, as it may die as a result. When viewing areas of the reef from the cliff tops you can see areas of dull grey rocks: these are not rocks but dead coral where tourists have walked out to sea to touch, photograph and view the coral. The Egyptian government set up a project to establish a long-term monitoring programme to investigate the effects of trampling on the reefs. The project aims to establish the carrying capacity of the reef and to search for solutions to help mitigate the damage caused to the coral.

* **What other negative effects of the local tourist industry might there be?**

* **What positive effects might it have?**

* **Do you think it would be better if tourists stopped going to Ras Mohammed National Park altogether?**

Inland environment and habitats

The inland environment and habitats are classified as follows:

* bush
* river
* forest
* mountain
* wetland
* lake
* island
* semi-desert
* desert
* saltpan.

You need to consider the ways in which the natural habitats of flora and fauna are protected. It is perhaps more easy to understand the threat of pollution on marine life and the wear and tear on ancient sites, but what about the thousands of acres of land that are inhabited by wildlife? Many of these areas come under the protection of a national park. The first national park in the UK – the Peak District – was established in 1949, and this was closely followed by the Lake District. Today there are 12 such parks in the UK. Their main purposes are:

* to conserve and enhance the natural beauty, wildlife and cultural heritage of the park
* to promote opportunities for public understanding and enjoyment of the special qualities of the park.

The same principles apply to national parks in other worldwide destinations. Some of the most well known include Yellowstone National Park in the USA, Mount Fuji National Park in Japan and the famous wildlife parks of Southern Africa (the Serengeti, Kruger and the Masai Mara). South Africa alone has dedicated over 3 million hectares of its total landmass to the conservation of its natural heritage. This 'world in one country' has a stupendous variety of habitats and wildlife.

Activity

Visit the following website www.ecoafrica.com/saparks/ to investigate the range and diversity of South Africa's national parks.

Africa's wild species and habitats are important economic resources for national economic development, as there is considerable scope for increasing revenues from tourism. The revenues can go to further conservation but can also be used for socio-economic development more widely. Authorities and managers of national parks and protected areas are beginning to look outwards and to develop linkages with local communities around tourism and other aspects of their work. For this to be achieved there needs to be a strong conservation framework in place in national parks and other conserved and protected areas. Furthermore, the development and management of natural resources that cross national boundaries have become a central conservation issue in Africa, in recognition of the need to maintain ecological integrity and the free movement of wildlife across such artificial frontiers.

Namibia's national reserves and game parks (Table 12.5) are owned by the government and managed by the Ministry of the Environment and Tourism. Since the country gained its independence from South Africa in 1990, there has been an increase in the number and size of private conservation areas. This may cause problems in the future as there is limited control and monitoring of privately owned projects.

The most popular form of accommodation for ecotourists in Africa's national parks is the eco-lodge. Eco-lodge accommodation is environmentally friendly, that is, it can easily be removed, without trace or damage to the environment. Visitors to many national parks prefer this type of accommodation as they feel that they are part of the natural environment and are not causing any disturbance to the wildlife or using any valuable local resources.

PARK	AREA (KM²)	DESCRIPTION
Mamili National Park	320	Largest wetland area with conservation status in Namibia
Caprivi Game Park	5,715	Extends for about 180 km from the Okavango River to the Kwando River
Mudumu National Park	1,010	Expanse of dense savannah and mopane woodlands, with the Kwando River as its western border
Etosha National Park	22,270	One of the largest game reserves in Africa
Waterberg Plateau Park	405	Some 200 m above a surrounding sea of bush and savannah, the park is home to some 25 game and 200 bird species
Namib-Naukluft Park	50,000	A vast wilderness
Von Bach Game Reserve	43	A popular venue for aquatic sports, south of Okahandja

TABLE 12.5. *Examples of national parks and game reserves in Namibia*

Eco-travellers are often attracted to visiting national parks

The following is taken from the online travel agency responsibletravel.com, www. responsibletravel.com:

Ten ways to tell if your eco-lodge is really an eco-lodge (rather than just 'greenwashing')

1. Ask the lodge owners if they have a written policy regarding the environment and local people. If it's not written down ('yeah, yeah we do all that stuff ') then it probably means they are not taking it seriously.

2. Ask them to describe the single contribution to conservation or local people that they are most proud of.

3. Ask them how they measure their contribution to conservation and local communities.

4. Ask the lodge owner how many local people they employ, what percentage this is of the total, and whether any are in management positions.

5. Ask them what they have specifically done to help protect the environment and support conservation, and which local charities they work with.

6. Ask them what percentage of produce and services are sourced from within 25 km of the lodge.

7. Ask them how they treat waste water (coral and other wildlife is being destroyed by Caribbean hotels pumping effluent out to sea), and how they heat their building (solar is better than firewood, which can cause deforestation).

8. Ask them what information and advice is provided to tourists on local cultures and customs.

9. Ask them if they employ guides from the local community (local guides not only provide unmatched insights into local cultures, but are also aware of areas/ behaviour that might cause offence among local people).

10. Ask them for ideas on how you might get involved with local people and conservation in a worthwhile and rewarding way for you and the destination.

CASE STUDY

Zakynthos National Marine Park (ZNMP), Greece

In the summer months at Zakynthos, every day hundreds of tourists dig out the clay from the rock face of the cliff to use for 'spa' treatments. These cliffs are on the protected beach of Gerakas, which is used by loggerhead turtles for nesting.

As a consequence, the cliff face has collapsed three times, with rocks the size of cars ending up on the beach.

The following account is taken from the website of MEDASSET, the Mediterranean Association to Save the Sea Turtles (www.medasset.gr). The account outlines some of the issues faced by areas that have been designated as 'protected'. In this instance there is conflict between the public and private sectors.

Backed into a corner, the Greek government has been forced to clean up its act before the European Commission's October deadline, or face the European Court of Justice (ECJ) and the imposition of a multi-million euro fine for neglecting its commitments to the turtle nesting beaches of Laganas Bay (Zakynthos).

With less than two months to go before the deadline, as the bulk of tourists left the island having disrupted yet another crucial nesting season for the endangered loggerhead sea turtles, Mrs Amalia Karagounis, the recently government-appointed President of the ZNMP, started to show her mettle.

With unprecedented government support for her position and just enough money to pay part of the wages owing to guards and ZNMP staff since 2003, she used her considerable skill to enforce almost all of the ECJ ruling's demands throughout the bay (excluding the 'strictly protected' Daphne beach): daytime guards were posted on a number of beaches; information signs, kiosks and barriers preventing vehicle access were restored; illegal businesses were closed down; a port police post was established with regular patrols of the bay and a boat was brought in to patrol the sea; buoys delineating restricted areas were replaced; and on some beaches excess furniture was removed, although much mysteriously found its way back!

The President has now turned her attention to the illegal buildings and tourist infrastructure on Daphne beach. Since the beginning of September, a bitter debate has raged between Mrs Karagounis and the head of the Local Zakynthos Administration (Prefect). Eleven years after the Greek government ordered the buildings pulled down, and despite having signed the demolition order himself, the Prefect claims that it is not his job to do so, and that the responsibility lies with the government. His role is 'not one of destruction', he said, but to protect the local inhabitants and foster the development and promotion of Zakynthos. He has suggested that to solve the problem the state should compensate those affected by conservation measures. 'We are here to protect interests of local people in Daphne and those of the Greek state,' he said, apparently forgetting that it was the law of the Greek state that he was being asked to enforce! The President of the Park responded, saying: 'Compensation to landowners should not be confused with demolition'. Meanwhile, at the Greek Constitutional Court (07–09–05), Daphne landowners lost an appeal to remove restrictions (imposed by the Presidential Decree establishing the ZNMP) on private property development within the boundaries of the Park.

The ZNMP President is optimistic of receiving the 60,000 euros which has been owed to the Park since 2003 by the Mayor of Laganas and the Prefect of Zakynthos, for their share of a LIFE/ Nature EC project. She also hopes to take funds, as of next summer, for beach furniture rental tenders, and with this money run a self-financing Park. But is this possible? In January 2005 300,000 euros was needed to cover the Park's debts (a figure which will have increased considerably since then). Since March 2004 funds have been promised repeatedly by the Ministry of Environment, in the press and in Parliament, but until now only 190,000 euros has been paid, barely covering back taxes and wage bills.

* **What measures would you undertake to ensure the long-term protection of the loggerhead sea turtles of Laganas Bay, Zakynthos?**

* **Identify at least _three_ representatives from the public sector and state what their motives are for their interest in the island.**

* **What actions would you take to prevent the clay for 'spa' treatments being removed from the cliff?**

* **Discuss the importance of the actions of Mrs Karagounis, the President of the Zakynthos National Marine Park (ZNMP).**

* **Discuss the advantages of the principles of ecotourism to the park, against the possible disadvantages to the host population of Zakynthos.**

Biodiversity and endangered species

There are places where special measures need to be taken to protect natural resources. The 1972 United Nations Convention Concerning the Protection of the World Cultural and Natural Heritage, in common with the 1992 United Nations Convention on Biological Diversity, contributed towards the development of a worldwide system of protected areas. Conservation of the biodiversity within these areas is essential for sustaining viable populations of species. Such conservation will also directly and indirectly support indigenous and local communities' lives and livelihoods.

We can look at the case of New Zealand to see three examples of how the biodiversity of the country is being affected. Many native plants, animals and their habitats in New Zealand's land and freshwater ecosystems are under threat from human activities and encroachment, and unwanted introduced organisms such as possums and deer. The government funds the New Zealand Biodiversity Strategy as part of its attempts to halt the loss of biodiversity and to protect land.

Possum fur souvenirs are to be found in every tourist shop and outlet in New Zealand. Possums were introduced to New Zealand in 1837. They were initially bred for their fur, but now there are over 70 million of them in New Zealand, eating their way through all the natural vegetation. Through education in schools and through information leaflets distributed to tourists and local communities via the public and voluntary sectors, it is hoped that the continuing population growth of possums can be halted. This will enable the natural fauna to start to grow again.

The second example is the case of the New Zealand parrot, called the kea. Keas are a protected species and are found in the South Island's high country. Although keas are seen in reasonable numbers, the exact size of the wild population is unknown – it is estimated at between 1,000 and 5,000 birds. In past decades there has been increasing human activity in alpine environments. Associated with this activity are the food scraps that people leave. For kea, our food sources have become a welcome high-energy food source and groups of kea frequent public sites around Fiordland car parks and at Milford Sound. In view of this, many signs have been placed around public car parks asking people to resist the temptation to feed the kea. One reason why it is important not to feed keas is that a kea's natural food is mainly plant material, such as berries, roots, shoots and insect larvae. Eating human food is as bad for keas as living on a daily diet of junk food would be for humans. Feeding young kea also discourages them from looking for and learning about natural foods. They can become dependent on human scraps.

Keas are often found in car parks in New Zealand, as they are fed by tourists

Ecotourists are sensitive to the environment and the biodiversity of the regions in which they visit. If you were to be an ecotourist you would read the signs and be educated about the threats to species such as the kea.

A final example in New Zealand is the decline of the tree fern. Many gardening enthusiasts, particularly in the UK, are buying tree ferns.

These species have been made popular by the many television programmes featuring garden make-overs. The tree fern makes an instant impression in any modern garden. Sadly, this species grows only in a stable climate and tree ferns rarely survive a second season in the UK. Should a species such as this be removed from its natural environment?

CASE STUDY

Galápagos Islands

The Galápagos Islands are home to many rare species. Recent tourist activity has led to an increase in invasive species and the threat caused by the amount of waste generated by the many tourist visitors. Fortunately, the Islands, with the help of UNESCO, have developed a management programme to harness and control tourism activity.

1. *Raising awareness*
In the Galápagos Islands World Heritage status contributes to raising national awareness of the islands' importance for conservation.

> *In effect it reaffirms to Ecuadorians that the site represents something unique. World Heritage designation also acts to engender a sense of pride and responsibility among the population of Ecuador as they realise that they are the guardians of an irreplaceable heritage of humanity. The local community also has great pride and is willing to protect its heritage.* (Scott Henderson, Conservation International)

Recently, the local awareness was evidenced by very well attended civic marches in favour of shark conservation.

> *The visitors are aware and informed of World Heritage status via our unique guide system, which means that every visitor has close contact with a naturalist guide licensed by the Galápagos National Park Service (GNPS). Also, the GNPS visitor's pack includes information about*

WH status and at the same time asks the cooperation from every one to preserve this unique treasure for future generations. (Felipe Cruz, Charles Darwin Research Station)

2. *Increasing protection*
Recently, attempts were made to modify tourism regulations in a way that would have undermined the participatory management system and reduced the authority of the Ministry of the Environment in Galápagos. A letter from the World Heritage Committee played an important role in stopping this potentially damaging alteration. The government of Ecuador has also been encouraged, by the World Heritage Committee and others, to protect the islands further, through enactment of the Special Law for Galápagos which includes:

* stricter controls on immigration to the site

* the creation of a quarantine system to combat alien species

* the creation of a much larger marine reserve around the islands, with improved legal protection

* limitations on property rights and economic activities to make these consistent with the goal of conservation

* increased national funding for the site.

3. *Enhancing funding*
It is virtually certain that without World Heritage status the Galápagos would still

receive significant external contributions. As such, the impact of World Heritage in increasing funding for this exceptional site may be less than in other protected areas on the World Heritage List. Nevertheless, in the opinion of managers closely involved with the islands, World Heritage status helps to focus attention on the site, which results in the appropriation of more funds. The fact that this site has World Heritage status probably plays a more significant role in increasing funding opportunities than it does for other high-profile sites.

> *World Heritage designation, in the case of most protected areas, increases the associated funding potential of the site. Although this is not an official eligibility criteria for Global Environmental Facility (GEF) funds, the designation does increase the chances of securing GEF resources.* (Gonzalo Castro, Biodiversity Team Leader, GEF Secretariat)

4. *Improving management*
Through the World Heritage Centre opportunities have been provided for Galápagos managers to receive more training. Asked whether increased networking and exchange between sites would improve management further, all consulted managers replied emphatically that it would. In the words of one:

> *It will be a useful tool that will improve the management of other sites tremendously, as well as being a help to Galápagos managers. A network of managers to share problems and work together for solutions with the support of the World Heritage Centre would be the most effective mechanism to increase our capacity and that of managers of other sites.* (Felipe Cruz, Charles Darwin Research Station)

5. *Harnessing tourism*
In the Galápagos Islands tourism is a major consideration. Alongside the entrance fee, the Galápagos National Park also charges fees to the tour operators and other services and clients.

> *While this fee is not related to the fact that the Galápagos Islands are a World Heritage site, it is clear that the status helps in justifying the fee to the visitors and users.* (Felipe Cruz)

For the Galápagos Islands the threats from its associated tourist industry are considerable. Two of the most significant are: the threat to local fauna caused by the year-round tourist presence, which leads to local population growth, increased invasive species and degradation of more land for urbanisation and agriculture; and the threat caused by the waste generated by the large number of visitors to the park.

In the Galápagos particularly, the increased introduction of alien species destroys the local biodiversity and natural habitat. In light of this, the World Heritage Committee recommended that quarantine measures be introduced and that programmes be initiated to eliminate goats and other feral animals. The government of Ecuador responded by introducing an inspection and quarantine system and by exterminating goats on a number of islands.

According to managers questioned on the subject, overall, since the site became a World Heritage it has benefited significantly, especially in extending the site to include the Marine Reserve, and the Ecuadorian governmental passage of the Special Law for Galápagos.

Source: adapted from www.unesco.org

* **UNESCO's web page http://whc.unesco.org/en/list/ categorises World Heritage Sites by as 'Cultural', 'Mixed' and 'Natural'. Select a 'Natural' site to investigate further.**

Energy systems

The Scottish Tourist Board runs a Green Tourism Business Scheme (GTBS) that encourages tourism businesses to be environmentally friendly, whether they be hotels or guest houses, bed-and-breakfasts, self-catering accommodation or attractions. The GTBS has over 400 members, all of whom are rigorously assessed and given a bronze, silver or gold award, depending on the level of energy efficiency they achieve. They are encouraged to introduce measures as diverse as using low-energy light bulbs, recycling paper products to make fire briquettes, using local produce on menus, and promoting wildlife walks and cycle hire in their area. All these measures would reduce energy or fuel usage and therefore have an effect on climate change.

More immediate effects of energy usage on the environment are often apparent in more remote locations. For example, as a general rule, it is usually the smaller (and more expensive) lodges and camps that do more for the local environment in the way of energy systems. Such properties also find it easier (and cheaper) to replace their wood-burning stoves with solar and wind power, and to employ more responsible sewage and waste disposal methods. As areas such as the Masai Mara park, in Kenya, come under increasing environmental pressure, many camps are banning the use of firewood outright, while others have installed their own constructed wetlands for recycling their waste water naturally.

Reductions in energy consumption can have wider benefits for the environment and for tourists. The small town of Dalyan in the province of Mugla, Turkey, on the south-western Mediterranean is set in the centre of a broad delta, an area of outstanding natural beauty and historic interest. The river is home to many species of bird, fish and turtle. However, at the height of the season hundreds of diesel-powered boats travel up and down the river, causing heavy pollution of the reed beds and river. Dalyan is one of the first Turkish resorts to have tested a new solar powered boat. The main aim of this project is to preserve the waterways of the Dalyan Delta from diesel pollution, to give the fauna and flora a healthy and safe living environment. Because tourist trips are inclined to cost more on solar powered boats than diesel

FIGURE 12.5. *Kardak Tourism Banner on the Dalyan River, advertising their solar powered boat*

powered, the village of Dalyan in partnership with Kardak tourism promoted the new service by displaying banners by the riverside (Figure 12.5).

The scale of energy usage in western societies, and by their tourists, has been illustrated in Kaikoura, South Island, New Zealand. In August 2002, Kaikoura became the first community in New Zealand to become 'Green Globe 21' benchmarked. As part of the benchmarking process, the effect of each person in Kaikoura, including tourists, on the environment was estimated. Table 12.6 shows the results based on the year from July 2003 to June 2004, for each person in Kaikoura (4,745, which included an average of 1,262 tourists per night).

WHAT USED	AMOUNT USED	EQUIVALENT TO....
Energy	103 gigajoules	Enough to light thirty-two 100-watt light bulbs for one year
		To offset the carbon dioxide emissions produced by this energy needs each person to plant 467 trees (that's 5.51 tonnes of CO_2 each person is producing)
Vehicles	278,528 kg of nitrogen oxides	
	26,624 kg sulphur dioxides	
	169,984 kg of particulates	
Drinking water	1,969 kilolitres	Enough to fill 38 average-size swimming pools
		Even omitting rural irrigation from the calculation, it's still enough to fill 7 average swimming pools (384 kilolitres)
Waste	380 kg of solid waste	20 black rubbish bags of waste to landfill (Kaikoura was actually rather good in this respect, as New Zealanders average 900 kg of solid waste a year)

TABLE 12.6. *Energy usage per person in Kaikoura, South Island, New Zealand*

Information taken from www.kaikoura.co.nz/main/GreenGlobe

Theory into practice

In Kenya many hotels and lodges, away from the cities, are now investing in alternative energy sources. Solar power, in particular, is the preferred alternative, and most responsible properties today use some kind of solar system for their electricity and water heating. Wind power is not yet as widespread. One area in which Kenya has made impressive gains is in the recycling of organic waste to provide an alternative source of fuel for water heating and cooking. With the growing bans on fuel wood – particularly in the national parks – fuel briquettes are being made from an increasing variety of waste materials. In Nairobi, a briquette machine producer, the Millennium Fuel Project, is encouraging women's groups to produce their own briquettes and to sell the surplus to safari camps and lodges in the Masai Mara park. Such practices will help to save the remaining forests in the country's main reserve, which have been ravaged by tree-felling and charcoal burning.

Think it over...

Study Table 12.6 and then try to imagine the impact that tourist activities have on major holiday destinations.

Water supplies

Water is a very scarce commodity in many parts of the world, and increasingly a source of conflict between people and wildlife. Eco-lodges are crucial conduits of water conservation awareness and practice, particularly in remote rural areas. As well as simple initiatives – such as encouraging guests to reuse towels and minimise their water use – many eco-lodges are introducing firmer water conservation measures, for example restricting water pumping to certain times of the day, installing low-pressure showers, and promoting the use of both recycled water and rainwater. Although these measures do not always make for optimum comfort, the eco-lodges usually would urge guests to appreciate how such measures help them to coexist with water-starved communities, livestock and wildlife. Many lodges and camps are also growing trees and encouraging local communities to plant woodlots, both as a sustainable source of firewood and for the protection of water catchment areas. Tourists are encouraged to find out from their chosen lodge whether they have any water-saving initiatives and support them during their visit.

Waste disposal

Hotels and lodges generate large volumes of solid and liquid waste and, because many of them are in remote areas where local council services are not available, they have to find ways of preventing their sewage from contaminating the environment. Initiatives to manage solid waste range from responsible purchasing to waste separation and recycling. As well as composting 'green waste' and using it in their vegetable gardens, most eco-lodges and camps are now returning their non-degradable waste (tins, glass, paper, batteries, etc.) to larger towns and centres where it is recycled. The management of liquid waste is more challenging in remote areas, although interest is growing quickly in the use of constructed wetlands for recycling waste water for return to the environment. Peer pressure – and increasing pressure from discerning guests – is also forcing many camps and lodges to use biodegradable 'green detergents' to improve the quality of their grey water.

CASE STUDY

Horizontes Nature Tours in Costa Rica, Central America

Horizontes Nature Tours is a full-service land operator specialising in nature, culture and educational travel. The company is in its 18th year of operation and enjoys an enviable reputation for excellence throughout the travel industry. It aims to provide ecotourism agencies worldwide with ways to implement practices that help to ensure cultural and environmental well-being.

The company employs 25 naturalist guides. In its programmes the company tries to show the real face of Costa Rica: environment, natural challenges, culture and people. The company wants to show visitors the people, the cuisine and the positive and negative sides of conservation of nature and culture.

Costa Rica is a researcher's paradise – professional scientists (especially biologists) and many students come to study its natural resources. The company decided to take the opportunity to share the experiences of the research teams and create an internationally recognised nature destination. International tourists can now enjoy national parks, private reserves, butterfly farms and marine parks.

After 20 years in Costa Rica the ecotourism industry has influenced the whole country.

Many businesses in Costa Rica are striving for international certification of standards. Ecotourism has become the main industry and the main source of foreign currency.

Source: adapted from the International Ecotourism Society (www.ecoclub.com)

✳ Consider how the objectives of research, education and conservation have benefited Horizontes Nature Tours.

✳ Give two reasons why travel agencies may recommend Horizontes Nature Tours.

✳ Ecotourism projects have led to both social and environmental improvements in Costa Rica. Select one other destination which you have studied or are familiar with and discuss the objectives of an ecotourism project.

Think it over...

The ASTA's 10 commandments on ecotourism

The American Society of Travel Agents (ASTA; see www.astanet.com/about/environmentalawards.asp) has drawn up the following.

Whether you are travelling on business, pleasure, or a bit of both, all the citizens of the world, present and future, would be grateful if you would respect the 10 commandments of world travel:

1 Respect the frailty of the earth.

2 Leave only footprints. Take only pictures.

3 To make your travels more meaningful, educate yourself about the geography, customs, manners, and cultures of the region you visit.

4 Respect the privacy and dignity of others.

5 Do not buy products made from endangered plants or animals.

6 Always follow designated trails.

7 Learn about and support conservation-oriented programmes and organisations working to preserve the environment.

8 Whenever possible, walk or utilise environmentally sound methods of transportation.

9 Patronise those members of the travel industry who advance energy and environmental conservation; water and air quality; recycling; safe management of waste and toxic materials; noise abatement; community involvement; and which provide experienced, well trained staff dedicated to strong principles of conservation.

10 Ask your ASTA travel agent to identify those organisations which subscribe to ASTA environmental guidelines for air, land, and sea travel.

Assessment guidance

For the Assessment Objective 2 you need to apply your knowledge and understanding of ecotourism's contribution to environmental, social and cultural issues in relation to your chosen project destination. To achieve the higher marks you must give a detailed and comprehensive explanation of the influences of ecotourism principles upon environmental, social and cultural issues as they relate to your project destination. You should provide detailed examples from a range of sources and present your work logically, and your meaning should be clear and accurately conveyed.

Purpose of ecotourism projects

Now that you have learned most of the theoretical aspects of ecotourism and seen how ecotourism has had an influence on a variety of worldwide destinations, it is time for you to prepare for the practical studies required for this unit.

Ecotourism projects are appearing in a diverse range of environments. Many of them attract worldwide recognition due to their impact on indigenous cultures or their better advertised environmental impacts. It seems that any tourist destination can adopt an eco-friendly policy to attract a new wave of international traveller and to sustain tourism in the destination.

Sustainable tourism is one of the most important objectives of ecotourism projects and it can take many forms in its quest to conserve the destination.

Aims and objectives of the project

All ecotourism projects must set out their aims and objectives, not only to attract volunteers and visitors but also to attract funding. The three general aims of any ecotourism project are:

* **environmental sustainability**, to reduce environmental impacts and conserve biodiversity

* **social sustainability**, to reduce social impacts and provide sustainable livelihoods

* **commercial sustainability**, to ensure their own survival (at minimum, projects must be self-financing to cover recurring costs).

When researching ecotourism destinations you will need to justify what is needed for ecotourism projects to be commercially sustainable. Is there:

* sufficient market demand

* good management

* controlled costs?

Many projects market and promote themselves, on an international basis, through the use of mission statements and overall visions, to achieve credibility and support. Examples of such mission statements and visions might be:

* **Mission**. To enable communities to balance ecosystem protection and economic development by pioneering a model for sustainable conservation.

* **Vision**. To help protect and conserve the diminishing biodiversity of the destination and to make the local and international community aware of its endangered status.

All individual ecotourism projects also set out their own specific aims and objectives and this should be something you can find for your chosen project destination.

Consider, for example, the Locus ecotourism project in Aberfeldy, Highland Perthshire, Scotland, and how it set out its aims and achieved its objective. The Locus project was developed from an original initiative by local business people and professionals to encourage tourism in the area and thereby support sustainable local economic activity. An infrastructure of genuinely local economic and community initiatives was prepared over many years. Agricultural, leisure, commercial, media and other initiatives were in place before the 'visible' end-products and projects could be established. A further aim of the project was to foster both a local development company and a major green tourism initiative in which visitors are guided from an introductory exhibition in the tourist information centre to a series of trails. Information present on the trails emphasises present-day activities and people working in the scenic Perthshire Highlands. The objectives of the project were achieved and the project won a 'Dynamic Places' award from the Scottish Enterprise Body.

Features of the project

Each ecotourism project has its own features and these will give the destination its unique appeal. The key features may be environmental, cultural, built attractions, marine life or other wildlife, for example. When researching your project you should ensure that the destination's key features are identified and the reasons for their appeal given. Table 12.7 gives a series of examples of key features and their attractions of types of ecotourism offered in Kenya.

TYPE OF ECOTOURISM	KEY FEATURES	APPEAL
Nature tourism	Tourism primarily supported by natural attractions – wildlife, flora and fauna, landscape, geographical features among others	This type of tourism characterises Kenya's tourism industry. Safaris are popular and people will also enjoy the scenery
Rural tourism	Visits to places perceived to be not influenced by urbanisation and its impacts. Such places would be characterised by low industrialisation, low population density, subsistence and primary economic activities and unsophisticated community lifestyles	Tourists visit such places to experience and participate in rural lifestyles, that is, to stay in rustic accommodation such as farmhouses and inns, among other activities. Adventure tourist such as backpackers and specialist tourists favour this type of tourism. In Kenya, the Kisii highlands have rich potential for this sort of tourism
Agricultural tourism	Visits to agriculture-based attractions such as plantations, farms, and estates	Tourists to these places enjoy the climatic conditions of the destination, and learn agricultural practices. Examples of the agricultural tourism include Kericho and tea-growing regions of the Rift Valley
Cultural tourism	Visits to local communities perceived to maintain their ancestral traditions	Visitors to these destinations are attracted by the people's lifestyles, their cultural practices (such as rites of passage and ceremonies) and their economic activities, among other aspects of community living. Activities undertaken here include participation in dance and music, festivals, buying souvenirs and artefacts, and photography. In this regard the Masai and Samburu peoples are important to Kenya's cultural tourism

TABLE 12.7. *Types of ecotourism offered by communities in Kenya, Africa*

Organisations involved in the management of the project

For ecotourism projects to become successful and sustainable they are dependent on a number of factors, and one of the key factors is the involvement of organisations in the management of the project. As mentioned previously, organisations may be in the private (commercial), public (non-commercial) or voluntary sector.

In many ecotourism projects the sectors often work together to promote success and long-term sustainability.

The following organisations have all been recognised for their work with ecotourism projects. Although you may recognise the names of some of these, you should also be aware that many smaller, less well known organisations are frequently involved in local projects. These examples are given here to illustrate the range of organisations and their roles that may be involved in the management of the project you choose. Finding out which organisations manage your chosen destination will require thorough research on your part.

Voluntary sector

Tourism Concern

Tourism Concern, through its volunteer programmes, promotes awareness of the effects of tourism on people and their environments and campaigns for just and sustainable tourism.

World Wide Fund for Nature (WWF)

The WWF operates in more than 100 countries. It funds a wide range of conservation projects.

Sri Lanka Wildlife Conservation Society

The Sri Lanka Wildlife Conservation Society (see www.slwcs.org) was the first organisation to be established outside Sri Lanka for the sole purpose of helping to conserve and preserve the dwindling biodiversity of Sri Lanka. The society is a non-profit, tax-exempt organisation based in the USA. The following are some of the projects that the organisation arranges and helps to fund:

* a leopard survey

* 'Saving Elephants by Helping People'

* mapping of tsunami-affected protected areas.

Independent volunteers have joined this organisation since 2003 to help initiate and sustain various projects aimed at helping them to achieve their long-term mission and vision.

Public sector

United Nations Environment Programme

The body promotes environmental issues generally, not specifically in relation to tourism.

World Tourism Organization

The World Tourism Organization is a specialised agency of the United Nations. It is the leading international organisation in the field of tourism, and serves as a global forum for tourism policy issues and a practical source of tourism know-how.

Private sector

World Travel and Tourism Council

The Council is a forum for global business leaders. It is the only body that represents the private sector in all parts of the travel and tourism industry worldwide.

Tribes Travel

Tribes Travel was a 2002 winner of the British Airways Tourism for Tomorrow award. It works in cooperation with local communities to offer locally owned and locally run services such as hotels. It tries to ensure that the local people are happy to receive tourists in their home region, and are informed of the possible impact.

Effectiveness of the project in environmental, social and cultural terms

Many countries such as the African nations and countries in the Far East are more interested in attracting tourism investment than in attempting to measure the environmental and cultural impacts that increased tourism brings.

Significance of planning and education to sustain the future management of the project

Throughout this unit you have seen how the principles of ecotourism need to involve the host population. It is no good promoting 'eco', 'green' or 'responsible' tours unless the host population can benefit. The benefits can be economic – through employment and an increase in income (at the national level, with the receipt of foreign currency earnings).

There is a need to plan for future projects to ensure their success and sustainability. Education is important, not only of the tourist, but also of the host population. For example, it is unlikely that local people will be suitably trained or experienced to handle the range of jobs required. If they are trained in specific areas such as accommodation, transport, guiding services and customer services, then the benefits of direct and indirect employment will be felt.

Analysis of the effectiveness of the project, in terms of visitor numbers and local, national or international involvement

The effectiveness of any ecotourism project is dependent on local, national and international involvement by a number of organisations. Its effectiveness will be both determined by and depend upon the number of visitors the destination can generate. This represents something of a dilemma: if visitor numbers continue to grow, how can ecotourism projects and principles survive?

Think it over...

Low volume almost always means high costs, and high volume will lower costs. But can ecotourism ever be a high-volume part of the industry?

Tourism research confirms that as tourists become increasingly better educated and more affluent, they expect their ecotourism experience to be both educational and enjoyable. More and more tourists are saying that an important factor in their choice of travel destination is the desire for an authentic experience through interaction with the local culture in its natural context. Decisions must be made to determine the maximum number of visitors a destination can manage in order to uphold the principles of ecotourism, while at the same time providing economic benefits for the host population.

Assessment guidance

For Assessment Objective 3 you need to research and analyse an ecotourism project in a destination of your choice, in terms of environmental, social and cultural issues. You need to use a range of appropriate research techniques to obtain information. This information must be up to date and accurate, as the travel industry is continually changing and updating resources, awards and funding. For higher marks you must use a broad range of sources and give many examples.

Trends and future appeal of ecotourism projects

From Figure 12.6 it can be seen that, according to the World Tourism Organization, overseas travel is set to continue its growth. In the summer of 2005, 57 per cent of all overseas holidays taken from the UK were package holidays (source ABTA website,

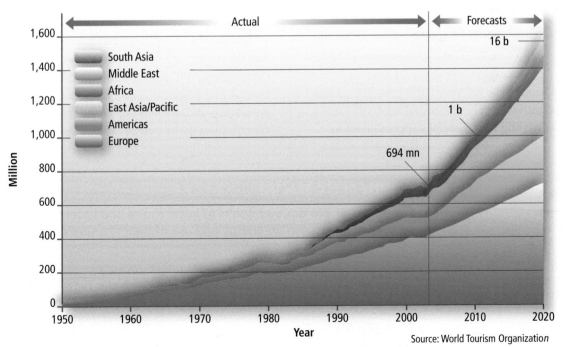

FIGURE 12.6. *Long-term prospects for tourist numbers, projected to 2020*

(www.abta.com); this means that the other 43 per cent were arranged independently.

It is necessary when evaluating the future trends and appeal of any ecotourism project that the following issues are taken into account and considered:

* seasonality
* transportation and access
* political and economic stability at the destination
* competition
* match between target market and facility, the site and the tour operator?
* willingness to pay (ecotourism projects are typically low volume and high cost)
* what support is required from local and national government and other local, national and international organisations.

Activity

Access the website of the World Tourism Organization (www.world-tourism.org) and also that of the Association of British Travel Agents (www.abta.com). In the statistics section, look for the visitor numbers to the top tourist destinations.

* What are the trends?
* Which are the most popular destinations?
* Do ecotourism destinations attract high or low visitor numbers?

In relation to the last point, the growing appeal of ecotourism can be measured relatively easily by calculating the financial support given to such projects by local, national and international organisations, such as the ones in Table 12.2, and other stakeholders.

Development of specialised, proactive and volunteer holidays

The development of specialised holidays to ecotourism destinations is becoming widespread, as many big-name operators such as TUI wish to be linked with 'responsible' and 'green' tourism. Many operators offer 'educational' holidays that feature eco-practices. These are often promoted through the public sector (e.g. tourist boards) as well as the private sector (e.g. accommodation providers, airlines and travel agents – see Table 12.8).

Many tour operators offer ecotourism holidays that feature social/cultural and environmental activities (see Figure 12.7). For example, some ecotourism holiday companies offer travellers the opportunity to work with animals. One such example is 21st Century Tiger. This is a unique wild tiger conservation partnership between the Zoological Society of London and Global Tiger Patrol. All of the funds raised through contributions and volunteer 'holidays' go directly to wild tiger projects. The partnership works closely with in-country counterparts in order to develop the capacity within the country to sustain conservation work. All the projects are comprehensively vetted to ensure that they have sound practical conservation and scientific credibility, and are making a fundamental contribution to the conservation of wild tigers.

TYPE OF ORGANISATION	EXAMPLE OF ECO-PRACTICE
Hotels	Placement of eco dos and don'ts in hotel rooms and hotel literature, such as cutting down on energy and use of water to save natural resources
Airlines	Video presentations on board aircraft to inform passengers of eco-practices and to appreciate ecotourism principles before landing at the destination
Travel agents/tour operators	Issue passengers with eco-practice information leaflets before departure

TABLE 12.8. *How the private sector is incorporating eco-practices into its operations*

Volunteer Abroad for 1-3 Weeks on Community Development Programs

Where You Can Serve
Volunteer Abroad
Volunteer in the USA

What You Can Do
Join a Service Program
Volunteer as a Group
Sponsor A Child
Support A Program

Who We Are
The Organization
Program FAQs
Volunteering Model

How to Join Us
Online Application
Information Form
Volunteer Center

Site Map

We have a Place for You!

This is service at its best. Lend your heart and hands to local people who are improving lives across the globe. Choose by region of the world, or by service project. You learn first-hand about your host community's culture and history while serving as a valuable resource to children and adults. At the same time, you wage peace and gain new perspectives of the world in one, two or three weeks.

Service projects: Child Care, Tutoring, Teaching English, Conservation Work, Health Care, Construction/Repair, and more. No specialized skills needed!

In special consultative status with the United Nations.

FIGURE 12.7. *How do you think a volunteering holiday fits with ecotourism principles?*

Think it over...

Check out the websites of the following eco-operators and see the range of holidays that you can participate in. If you could choose a holiday, which would it be?

* Ecovolunteer (www.ecovolunteer.org)

* Ecotourism at Conservation International (www.ecotour.org)

* British Trust for Conservation Volunteers (www.btcv.org).

Provision of marketing and promotional techniques

It has been suggested, through research conducted by travel organisers, that the majority of travellers who book or arrange ecotourism holidays may be classified as follows:

* between 35 and 55 years of age
* college graduates taking a 'year out'
* 'lifelong learners'.

Good ecotourism projects have strong marketing links and relationships with travel agents and tour operators. This enables them to promote their products effectively and to attract their target market. Consider this article which appeared in *The Times* newspaper (27 August 2005):

> Most 'responsible travel' is booked by women. Tom Chesshyre charts the rise of the eco-babe

Men are from Mars and women care for planet Earth – that's the message from eco-travel companies, who say that women now account for three-quarters of bookings. About 75 per cent of sales on one of the UK's leading on-line sustainable tourism agents – www.responsibletravel.com – are to women, even though the founder of the site had never realised this before Times Travel asked him to break down his bookings. Justin Francis, of Responsible Travel: 'I had no idea the trend was so strong. But there it is: women seem to care more when they go on holiday.' Most are in their twenties, thirties and forties – a youthful lot indeed.

Travel agents and tour operators are facing uncertain times because consumer tastes and trends are changing. The Internet is allowing people to make their own travel arrangements and ecotourism destinations will need to maximise their exposure to attract the type of client to whom ecotourism appeals. They will need to provide marketing materials in the form of easy-to-read literature which is sensitive to the host country but still attracts visitors.

As well as individual operators marketing their own products and services (see Theory into practice), the whole notion of ecotourism, responsible and culturally aware travel is promoted by the activities of third parties, such as the Association of Independent Tour Operators (AITO), which represents about 150 independently owned tour operators, provides its own responsible tourism guidelines. This has formed part of its membership criteria and operators have been given two or three stars for their performance in responsible tourism. Through this method of promotion, tourists can feel safe in the knowledge that 'what they see is what they get'. The Foreign and Commonwealth Office runs a 'Know before you go' campaign that encourages holidaymakers to familiarise themselves with the customs and culture of holiday destinations. Finally, you should check the website of Tourism Concern, which offers a wealth of reliable information and resources on a range of destinations worldwide.

Coordination of health and safety requirements

Like all holiday destinations, consideration must be given to health and safety. This is especially important in relation to ecotourism, as many of the destinations are 'off the beaten track' (they often involve travelling long distances into natural environments). When researching your chosen destination you should bear this in mind.

Assessment guidance

To complete the Assessment Objective 4, you need to evaluate the future trends and appeal of ecotourism together with the principles that relate to your chosen project destination. World events, both natural and man-made, can have an impact on the popularity and appeal of destinations. For example, the bird flu outbreak in 2006 had affected the number of visitors to some countries in the Far East and Europe. Destinations that promote ecotourism are just as susceptible to changes in trends as are the more commercially popular destinations. When considering the appeal of destinations you should take recent world events into consideration. To gain the higher marks you must be able to draw valid and substantiated conclusions about how you see the future trends and appeal of ecotourism issues worldwide. You should refer to and use examples and clearly express your own values and opinions within your work.

Theory into practice

The website of the Travel Foundation (www.thetravelfoundation.org.uk) provides some excellent examples of the promotion and marketing of ecotourism. It begins with the statement 'The Travel Foundation is a UK charity that cares for places we love to visit' and invites readers to 'Check out how you can make a huge difference when you travel.' It also tells you where you can obtain its leaflets (e.g. Advantage Travel, Co-op Travel, Guerba and Rainbow Tours travel agents), which may be a useful addition to your portfolio for this unit.

1 Give a definition of ecotourism.

2 What is the difference between ecotourism and mass market tourism?

3 What do the following initials stand for?

* WWF

* WTTC

* AITO.

4 Suggest what the main objectives are of:

* social/cultural ecotourism

* environmental ecotourism.

5 What is meant by 'take only photographs, leave only footprints'.

6 List five regions that are popular ecotourism destinations.

7 Explain the term 'conservation'.

8 What is the source of funding for each of the following?

* private sector

* public sector

* voluntary sector.

9 Explain the importance of preservation of national identity.

10 What is the tour operator TUI's sustainable travel policy?

11 Identify three organisations concerned with the preservation of the natural environment.

12 Give three examples of accommodation used for eco-travellers.

13 Which organisation presents the 'Tourism for Tomorrow' award?

14 What is solar energy?

15 Identify two endangered marine species.

References and further reading

Books, journals, magazines

Cohen. E. (1974) 'Who is a tourist: a conceptual clarification'. *Sociological Review*, vol. 22, pp. 527–555.

Websites

www.fco.gov.uk/travel
www.greenglobe21.com
www.responsibletravel.com
www.tourismconcern.org.uk
www.tribes.co.uk
www.wttc.org
www.tourismfortomorrow.com
www.northsouthtravel.co.uk
www.roughguide-betterworld.com
www.fairtourismsa.org.za
www.ecoclub.com
www.unesco.com
www.wwf.org
www.conservation.org

Adventure tourism

This unit covers the following sections:

- Adventure tourism activities (ATAs)
- Development of ATAs
- Management of the impacts of adventure tourism
- Benefits of ATAs
- Choosing a feasible and safe ATA
- Role of national governing bodies and regulatory bodies in ATAs
- Effective planning and participation in your chosen ATA
- Evaluation your chosen ATA

Unit 13 Introduction

More and more people are taking part in adventure activities, both at home and abroad. In recent years there has been an increasing trend for adventure tourism activities to be developed in many locations and this global trend is illustrated by the advertisement shown in Figure 13.1. Emirates have chosen an adventure tourism activity to illustrate destination appeal in their new promotional leaflet for flights to New Zealand. Adventure tourism is also an important and dynamic element of the UK's domestic tourism market, particularly in Scotland and Wales. It is also becoming increasingly important in many English destinations, such as the Lake District, Peak District, Yorkshire, the South West and south coast.

Adventure tourism is currently experiencing strong growth as interest in more active and healthy lifestyles increases, and outdoor pursuits become more fashionable and mainstream. The facts and figures available indicate that:

* Adventure holidays now account for around 4 per cent of all domestic holidays taken in the UK.

* Overall, at least 10 per cent of UK-based holidays currently involve some form of participation in adventure activities, and the proportion is higher for both Scotland (15 per cent) and Wales (17 per cent).

* At least 11 million holidays in the UK each year include an adventure activity.

* Annual spending by UK holiday visitors who engage in adventure activities during their stay is at least £2 million.

The figures for UK adventure tourism are likely to be even higher if participation in hill walking, mountain biking and motorised land sports are taken into account, as well as adventure day visits.

How you will be assessed

This unit is assessed through your portfolio work. You will investigate adventure tourism activities (ATAs) through the use of examples at a local, national and international scale. You will also provide in a report evidence of your involvement, as part of a group, in the planning of and participation in an ATA. In particular, your report will focus on:

* the growth of ATAs in your local region, one other region of the UK and in an overseas destination of your choice (Assessment Objective 1)

* an assessment of the impacts and benefits of adventure tourism in your chosen areas and the ways in which these are managed (Assessment Objective 2))

* research and analysis into assessing the feasibility of, and planning of, one group ATA (Assessment Objective 3)

* an evaluation of your own performance and the group's performance in the planning of and participation in the ATA, including recommendations for improvement (Assessment Objective 3).

Assessment is explained in more detail at relevant points later in this unit.

Adventure tourism activities (ATAs)

Adventure tourism as we know it has evolved from 19th-century outdoor and wilderness recreational activities, such as hunting, shooting and fishing. In the 20th century, with the rise in popularity of rambling, hiking and camping, a much wider cross-section of the public started to experience the great outdoors. However, unlike other forms of outdoor recreation, where setting provides the primary attraction, adventure tourism offers individuals and groups the opportunity to become more experienced in particular outdoor pursuits. These activities can be pursued at increasing levels of difficulty or challenge. Thus, adventure travel is primarily associated with activities where the purpose of a trip is to be engaged in experiences through participation rather than in sightseeing at traditional tourist attractions or locations.

What distinguishes adventure travel from traditional outdoor recreation is the deliberate pursuit of risk and uncertainty of outcome – this is why it is 'adventure'. In such activities the individual will often face increasing levels of risk or personal threat and it is this that produces the 'white knuckle' experience, the 'adrenaline rush' that is sought by these tourists.

Table 13.1 shows the wide range of activities that can be classed as adventure tourism. It is clear that

FIGURE 13.1. *Promotional leaflet produced by Emirates airline, showing one sort of adventure holiday, in New Zealand*

most of these are outdoor leisure pursuits that will generally take place in unusual, exotic, remote or wilderness settings. They will often involve some

TYPE OF ACTIVITY	EXAMPLES
Climbing activities	Mountaineering, rock climbing, sport climbing, abseiling, bouldering, sea-level traversing and coasteering
Caving	Pot holing, mine exploration
Non-motorised water sports	Dinghy sailing, windsurfing, kite surfing, canoeing, kayaking, white-water rafting, surfing
Motorised water sports	Personal watercraft use, water-skiing, ribbing, wakeboarding, scuba diving
Motorised land sports	4×4 driving, enduro biking, motocross, rally driving and quad biking
Air sports	Hang gliding, paragliding, micro-lighting, gliding, parachuting
Mountain-based activities	Mountain biking (trail riding, downhill riding), hill walking/trekking
Other land-based activities	Orienteering, gorge walking/canyoning, skiing, snowboarding, land yachting, para-karting, cycle touring, bungee jumping, rope courses and participation in challenge events

TABLE 13.1. *Activities that may be classed as adventure tourism*

form of unconventional means of transportation and they tend to be associated with some physical activity – often at a high level. The activities undertaken may entail some element of risk.

Let us now have a look at a selection of ATAs and examine what each involves.

The main adventure tourism activities

Below is an alphabetical listing of the main ATAs. More information on these can be found in travel brochures, sports magazines and the Internet.

Think it over...

In the assessment guidance below you will be asked to give locations for the activities discussed here. Think it over as you work through. You may also have to do some research on this.

Bungee jumping

Bungee jumping is an activity in which you jump off a high place (generally several hundred feet up) with one end of an elastic cord attached to your body or ankles and the other end tied to the jumping-off point. When you jump, the cord will stretch to take up the energy of the fall; you then fly upwards as the cord snaps back. You oscillate up and down until the initial energy of the jump is dissipated.

The first modern bungee jump was made on 1 April 1979, from the 250-foot Clifton Suspension Bridge in Bristol, and was made by four members of the Dangerous Sports Club. The jumpers, led by David Kirke, were arrested shortly after, but continued with jumps in the US from the Golden Gate and Royal Gorge bridges, spreading the concept worldwide. The first operator of a commercial bungee jumping concern was a New Zealander, A. J. Hackett, who made his first jump from Auckland's Greenhithe Bridge in 1986.

Canyoning

Canyoning is a sport popular in several countries. It involves travelling down creeks or streams within a canyon by a variety of means, including walking, scrambling, climbing, abseiling, swimming and even using an inflatable air mattress (Lilo). It requires skills in navigation, rope work and climbing; it is also necessary to avoid hypothermia! Figure 13.2 shows a Lake District variation of this activity.

FIGURE 13.2. *Following a stream in the Lake District*

Caving

Caving, as shown in Figure 13.1, is the recreational exploration of caves. The challenges of the sport depend on the cave being visited, but often include the negotiation of pitches, squeezes and water. Climbing or crawling is often necessary, and ropes are used extensively.

Caving is often undertaken solely for the enjoyment of the activity or for physical exercise, but original exploration is an important goal for many cavers. It has recently come to be known as an 'extreme sport' and is a very popular activity in many UK regions, such as the Yorkshire Dales.

Dog sledding

Dog sledding involves being pulled by one or more dogs over ice and snow. Numerous types of sleds are used, depending on their function. Modern sleds usually feature drag or claw brakes, whereas older ones relied on hooks attached to the sled with a rope. The activity takes place in, for example, the Cairngorms, Norway and Alaska.

Hill walking

Hill walking may include some degree of climbing and scrambling.

Horse riding

Horse riding is a very suitable activity for those who are looking for an alternative to the mechanised excitement of motorbikes and mountain bikes. It is a source of both recreation and adventure and can be enjoyed in a variety of environments.

Hot air ballooning

Hot air ballooning originated in France in 1783. The first flight was made on 21 November 1783, in Paris, by Pilâtre de Rozier and the Marquis d'Arlandes. Since the balloon moves with the wind, there is no steering and the passengers lack the perception of movement, other than the shifting view.

Karting

Karts can be any sort of open, simple, small four-wheeled vehicle – kart, go-kart or gearbox/shifter kart, depending on the design. They are usually raced on scaled-down tracks but are sometimes driven as entertainment or as a hobby by non-professionals. UK Karting (www.karting.co.uk) provides comprehensive information on the sport in Britain. Karting is one of the fastest-growing forms of motor sport in the world; it offers speed, thrills and great competition.

Kayaking

Kayaking is the use of a kayak for sport or recreation. Kayaks are propelled by handheld paddles. White-water kayaking involves taking a kayak down rapids. Sea kayaking involves taking kayaks out on to the ocean and can be thought of as hiking or backpacking over water, with the similar goal of sightseeing and touring. At the end of 2005, three UK kayakers became the first Britons to complete the circumnavigation of South Georgia in the South Atlantic.

Kite surfing

Kite surfing, or kite boarding, involves using a power kite to pull a small surfboard (on water), a wheeled board on land or a snowboard over snow. The kite pulls the surfer up into a powerful planing motion similar to water-skiing. The activities are popular in the UK and across Europe, as well as in many more destinations around the world.

Mountain biking

Mountain biking is a form of cycling which uses very sturdy bicycles with (usually) straight handlebars and wide tyres. It is done off-road and encompasses both competitive racing and purely recreational cycling.

Mountaineering

Mountaineering concerns the ascent of mountains of various shapes and forms, using various types and amounts of mountaineering equipment. (See also 'Rock climbing'.)

Orienteering

Orienteering on foot is simply cross-country running or walking using a map and compass to find your way through a series of control points marked on the map. It originated in Scandinavia 100 years ago, but is now a popular competitive sport in all parts of the world. Orienteering can take place anywhere from remote forest and countryside to urban parks and school playgrounds. The most challenging orienteering takes place in remote areas with demanding terrain and fewer paths.

Paint-balling

Paint-balling is a game whose participants use gas-powered markers to launch at each other marble-sized pellets containing coloured liquid. Among the more common of the many variations is a version of 'capture the flag', in which two teams of players attempt to seize each other's banner without being struck by a pellet.

Paragliding and hang gliding

Paragliding was developed from parachuting – it is essentially gliding with a specially developed parachute canopy. Paragliders are more portable and a little easier to learn to fly than hang gliders; they are more hampered by strong winds but are easier to land in small fields.

Hang glider pilots, suspended from their gliders by a special harness, launch from hills facing into the wind, from winches on flat ground or by being towed aloft from an airfield behind a microlight aircraft.

Quad biking

Quad biking is the off-road use of four-wheeled motorbikes. The activity is now popular throughout the UK and has become a major attraction in the sand dunes of Dubai.

River rafting

River rafting is a recreational activity in a raft (powered only by paddle) to navigate a river or other body of water. In areas with fast-flowing water and rapids, the term white-water rafting is used.

FIGURE 13.3. *An unusual form of safari*

Rock climbing

Rock climbing is one of the activities associated with mountaineering. It is highly specialised and can present considerable risk. It is a very popular outdoor activity, as there are many suitable locations.

Safari

Safari (from a Swahili word meaning a long journey) is an overland journey made to observe (or hunt) wildlife. It is most commonly used to describe tours through African national parks. Specialised variations have been developed in certain destinations, such as the one shown in Figure 13.3.

Sailing

Sailing a small boat is both fun and challenging. You have to balance and shift the crew's weight with every turn, sometimes having to hike out over the water to prevent the boat from capsizing. In high winds many small boats can achieve high speeds by planing or rising on top of the water. It has been said that the skill of the sailor is inversely related to the size of the sailboat. Sailing can take place in a very wide range of locations, from small reservoirs to the open ocean.

Scuba diving

Scuba diving is the use of independent breathing equipment to stay under water for long periods for recreational diving and professional diving. Generally the diver swims under water, but walking and the use of propulsion vehicles are possible while breathing from scuba equipment. The word 'scuba' is an acronym for 'self-contained underwater breathing apparatus'.

Skiing

Skiing (both downhill and cross-country) is very popular and each year the sport attracts new followers, particularly from the younger age groups. However, the activity is tiring and technically demanding for the beginner.

Skydiving

Skydiving involves individuals jumping out of aircraft, usually from an altitude of around

4,000 metres (12,000 feet) and free-falling for a while before activating a parachute to slow the landing down to safe speeds.

Snow and ice climbing

Snow and ice climbing is a highly strenuous and skilled sport that combines hill walking and climbing expertise. It requires expensive specialised equipment and clothing, as shown in Figure 13.4, and usually occurs under the most extreme weather conditions.

Snowboarding

Snowboarding is a board sport on snow similar to skiing, except that participants strap a single composite board to their feet on which to slide. It is an increasingly common winter sport throughout the world. A snowboarder's equipment consists of: snowboard, boots, bindings and winter clothing. Snowboarding became a Winter Olympic Games sport in 1998.

Snow-kiting

Snow-kiting is an outdoor winter board sport that combines the airfoil and techniques used in

kite-surfing with the footgear and gliding surface used in snowboarding. Snow-kiting differs from other snow sports, in that it is possible for the snow-kiter to travel uphill with ease, if the wind is blowing in the right direction. Snow-kiting is becoming increasingly popular in places often associated with skiing and snowboarding, such as Switzerland, Austria, Scotland and the western United States.

Surfing

Surfing has a unique and often powerful appeal resulting from its outdoor beach lifestyle association with Hawaii, California and Australia. It is now very popular and Newquay has become the home of the sport in the UK.

> **Think it over...**
>
> Team-building activities are often promoted as being adventure activities. However, they tend to have a low risk and include such things as zip wires, 'Tyrolean traverses', 'Commando crawls', 'postman's walk', barrel and plank swings, night lines, raft building and rope traverses over water. Why do you think adventure-type pursuits lend themselves to team-building? Why do you think low-risk activities are used?

Wakeboarding

Wakeboarding is a relatively new board sport, created from a combination of water-skiing, snowboarding and surfing techniques. As in water-skiing, the rider is towed behind a boat, or a cable-skiing setup, but typically at slower speeds (18–24 mph). Instead of skis, the rider wears a single board with stationary non-release bindings for each foot, standing sideways as on a snowboard or skateboard. The boards are shorter in length than a snowboard (typically 130–147 cm) and wider (up to 45 cm), as well as being convex rather than concave like a snowboard.

Walking, hiking, rambling, trekking

Walking or hiking can be undertaken with the specific purpose of exploring and enjoying the scenery within particular destinations. It usually takes place on trails in areas of relatively unspoiled

FIGURE 13.4. *Snow and ice climbing*

WATER-BASED ATAS	LAND-BASED ATAS	AIR-BASED ATAS
Canyoning	Caving	Bungee jumping
Kayaking	Dog sledding	Hot air ballooning
River rafting	Karting	Kite surfing
Sailing	Horse riding	Paragliding
Surfing	Mountain biking	Scuba diving
Zorbing	Mountaineering	Skydiving
	Orienteering	Wakeboarding
	Paint-ballling	Windsurfing
	Quad biking	
	Rock climbing	
	Safari	
	Skiing	
	Hill walking	
	Snow and ice climbing	
	Snow-kiting	
	Snowboarding	
	Trekking	

TABLE 13.2. *Categorisation of adventure tourism activities*

Key terms

Rambling is generally considered to involve walking over low-level routes which are regarded as being non-arable, open terrain.

Trekking is applied to long-distance hiking in mountainous regions, especially those of Nepal and India.

wilderness. In the UK such walking is usually carried out on land above 300 metres and will involve rough and possibly hazardous ground. (See also 'Hill walking', above.)

Windsurfing

Windsurfing (also called boardsailing) is a sport involving travel over water on a small board (like a surfboard). The wind acts on the single sail, which is connected to the board via a flexible joint. The sport is a hybrid between sailing and surfing.

Zorbing

Adventure tourism lends itself to innovation. Zorbing is a recreational activity which emerged in the early 21st century. It involves rolling down an incline in an inflatable, usually transparent, sphere made from PVC. Zorbing originated in New

Zealand in 2000. The inside of a zorb contains several straps to keep the rider in place.

Theory into practice

All ATAs can be placed into one of three categories: those activities that are water-based; those that are land-based; and those that are air-based. Table 13.2 has placed the ATAs listed above into one of these categories but there are some mistakes. How many can you find? Are there any ATAs that could be correctly placed in more than one category?

Assessment guidance

Assessment Objective 3 requires you to undertake relevant research and for Assessment Objective 1 you have to produce a report that examines ATAs in your local region, in one other region of the UK and in one overseas destination. This will include identifying the ATAs that are present in these three chosen locations. To help you prepare for these requirements, complete Table 13.3 using the ATAs listed above. (Note that risk and hazard in ATAs, for the last column in the table, are discussed below – see page 192.)

ATA	LOCAL AREA LOCATION	OTHER UK LOCATION	INTERNATIONAL LOCATION	RISK OR HAZARD
Rock climbing	North Wales	Lake District	Swiss Alps	Blizzards

TABLE 13.3. *Important destinations for adventure tourism activities*

Development of ATAs

If you have completed the task based on Table 13.3 correctly, you will be able to see that certain forms of adventure tourism tend to take place in certain types of location. There are particular reasons for this and we will now look briefly at some of the more important of these. Whether and how adventure tourism develops in particular locations will be determined by:

* environmental factors
* historical factors
* accessibility factors
* social factors.

We shall then go on to look, by way of example, at the characteristics of the adventure tourism market within both the USA and the UK.

Environmental factors

The development of adventure tourism in some locations is very strongly linked to the prevailing environmental conditions. Ski resort development is a very good illustration of this relationship. Cold climatic conditions and mountainous relief can combine to produce the ideal ingredients for the development of a ski resort. Winter sports holidays are now very popular and they attract a wide cross-section of visitor types. Ski resort development has taken place throughout Europe, North America and Australasia and there are now many established destinations for skiing enthusiasts to visit.

Historical factors

Some adventure tourism destinations have evolved because they have had a long history of expeditions and exploration. The Victorians were fascinated with the idea of exploration – discovering new locations and experiencing different cultures. They were also given to challenge and it is common today to see trips and tours being marketed as following in the footsteps of famous explorers such as David Livingstone (Africa) and (from the Edwardian era) Ernest Shackleton (Antarctica). There are other key historical factors that have stimulated demand for adventure tourism in the UK.

In 1932 there was a mass trespass on Kinder Scout in the Peak District to highlight the lack of public access rights to the nation's open countryside. This was the stimulus that eventually saw the creation of National Parks in 1949, with the passing of the National Parks and Access to the Countryside Act in that year. The Act made it clear that the purposes of the Parks were to preserve and enhance natural beauty and to promote their enjoyment by the public. The Environment Act 1995 revised the purposes of National Parks, which are now stated to be as follows:

* to conserve and enhance the natural beauty, wildlife and cultural heritage of the National Parks
* to promote opportunities for the understanding and enjoyment of the special qualities of those areas by the public.

The Act also amended the 1949 Act to introduce a duty on public bodies to have regard to these purposes when carrying out their functions. A further boost was provided by the Countryside and Rights of Way Act (CRoW) 2000, which dramatically changed the opportunities for access to open country, not only in National Parks but across land throughout the UK. That Act also further protected designated Areas of Outstanding Natural Beauty (which were also created by the 1949 Act).

CASE STUDY

Ski resort

Villars-sur-Ollon is a traditional Swiss ski resort, set in the heart of the Vaudoise Alps, some 60 km from Lausanne and Lake Léman in the Canton de Vaud. Winter skiers have over 100 km of pistes to try out within the wider Villars region, and there are 45 ski lifts and 43 identified ski runs. The ski runs cover valley slopes ranging between 1,250 m and 2,200 m and this variation in altitude will mean that some skiing is possible early and late in the season, thus extending the resort's operational dates. The resort also gives access to 44 km of cross-country ski trails, and this further extends the choice of skiing, which in turn increases the resort's potential appeal.

In addition to this, casual walkers and serious hikers can enjoy seven trekking and discovery itineraries on snow shoes, and 12 winter walk itineraries, of which 3 km are suitable for prams (for benefit of families with very small children). Technically inclined hiking and/or snowshoe enthusiasts can access GPS mapped itineraries.

Within the wider Lake Geneva region, there is a varied choice of sporting activities. The lakes of Geneva, Neuchâtel and Joux offer sailing, swimming, water-skiing, canoeing, kayaking, diving by submarine and fishing. For extreme sports enthusiasts, there is windsurfing, paragliding, hot air ballooning, ski acrobatics, climbing, bungee jumping and river sports (rafting and canyoning).

* **How has the development of the wider Villars region for adventure tourism been strongly influenced by the prevailing environmental conditions?**

* **To help you examine the growth of ATAs in your chosen locations, as well as generating evidence for Assessment Objective 1, explain the extent to which another destination's climatic conditions have had an effect on the types of adventure tourism it can offer.**

Activity

Look at the website of the National Association for Areas of Outstanding Natural Beauty (www.aonb.org.uk) to research their history and status.

In 1965 the Pennine Way, the first official long-distance footpath, was declared open. This is a 267-mile walk from the Derbyshire Peak District to Scotland. The route takes walkers through contrasting environments and allows them to visit various locations of historical and cultural interest such as:

* the site of the Kinder Scout mass trespasses of the 1930s

* the Southern Pennines, a cradle of the Industrial Revolution

* Haworth, home of the Brontë sisters

* the Settle–Carlisle Railway

* Roman remains and Hadrian's Wall

* the Scottish Borders.

Accessibility factors

Ease of access has always been an important factor for the growth of any tourist destination. The development of many UK destinations went hand in hand with the expansion of the railway and road transport networks. The growth of the railways between 1832 and 1870 linked, for the first time in a fast and cheap way, the industrial cities to the coastal resorts and areas of countryside. The Lake District – now a prime UK destination for adventure tourism – started to receive day visitors in large numbers after 1847, when the railway reached Windermere.

Tourism in its present form is inconceivable without transport and for domestic tourism the car is of major significance. The increase in car ownership has given rise to major changes in leisure activities. Some three-quarters of the population of the UK live in or near large towns, and for many of these people the countryside has become an important recreational resource. An important step in the Lake District's continuing development was the extension of the M6 motorway northwards to Kendal and Keswick in the early 1970s. This made the destination more easily accessible to the car-owning general public.

Recent developments in air transport have resulted in many overseas locations becoming available to the adventure traveller for the first time. The easy availability of budget flights to destinations near the Alps means that some UK skiing enthusiasts can travel to Europe more quickly and cheaply than they can to the Highlands of Scotland.

> **Think it over...**
>
> Compare the costs involved in travelling from south-east England to both the Alps and the Cairngorms for a group of four adult skiers for a winter weekend break. Which destination appears the more accessible?

Social factors

The trend in the UK over the past 40 years or so has been towards a reduction in basic working hours and an increase in holiday entitlement. The average number of hours worked per week, including overtime, decreased from 45 in 1961 to less than 40 at present in many sectors of employment. In 1961, 97 per cent of full-time manual workers had a basic holiday entitlement of only two weeks a year. Today the majority of employees have between four and five weeks of paid annual leave. Both the reduction in hours worked per week and the longer holidays have enabled people to partake in more of a greater variety of leisure activities, including adventure tourism.

Furthermore, over the same period, the increases in the amount of leisure time people have available have been paralleled by increases in their disposable incomes. Consequently, we are all subject to high-profile advertising and other promotional activities of attractions, destinations and other leisure facilities. All these help to create a greater awareness of the many opportunities for leisure activities that are now available.

Since the 1970s, studies in travel and tourism marketing more generally have identified new and increasing challenges arising from social and demographic changes. Increased spending power per capita and greater leisure time are two key factors that have transformed the traditional leisure travel marketplace. A discerning public, with greater travel experience, is now able to benefit from more convenient and cheaper transportation. This, in turn, has resulted in substantial changes to levels of travel and leisure demand. There have been significant changes to the patterns of international travel since the 1980s and there has been dramatic growth in specific types of tourism, such as ecotourism, nature tourism and special interest tourism, including adventure tourism.

While travel costs still remain a significant determinant in making travel decisions, tourist satisfaction is increasing in importance. A good travel product must provide something besides value for money to attract the tourist for some deeply satisfying purpose. This has led to a remarkable shift towards new patterns in holiday choices, to accommodate the expanding range of interests and leisure travel activities and 'experience-oriented' visits and trips. Adventure travel has gained more popularity among today's sophisticated travellers, who want a holiday 'experience' rather than just spending their often limited leisure time sitting on a beach.

Social and market characteristics of adventure tourism in the USA and the UK

American adventure travellers tend to be young (aged 18–34 years) and affluent (approximately 25 per cent are from households with annual incomes of $75,000 or more). Some 8,000 US companies now offer adventure packages; these have generated an average of $7 billion per year over recent years. Adventure travel

FIGURE 13.5. *The entrance to Yosemite National Park in California*

generates around $15 billion of the approximately $100 billion annual industry revenues (and an estimated $2–4 billion of these revenues come from California adventure travellers alone).

In the USA, adventure travel is growing at least 10 per cent per year. More than 50 per cent of the US adult travelling population, or 147 million people, have taken an adventure trip in their lifetime; 98 million have done so in the past five years. (Figure 13.5 shows a popular destination in the USA for such trips.) Thirty-one million adults have engaged in 'hard' adventure activities like white-water rafting, scuba diving and mountain biking. An additional 25 million engaged in both 'hard' and 'soft' adventure activities. The activities most commonly participated in during adventure vacations are camping (85 per cent), hiking (74 per cent), skiing (51 per cent), snorkelling or scuba diving (30 per cent), sailing (26 per cent),

kayaking or white-water rafting (24 per cent) and biking trips (24 per cent).

In the UK, many people get their first taste for adventurous travel during their student days and it is now very common for young people to have a 'gap year'. This is one reason for the current increasing interest in experiencing 'active' holidays. This, in turn, has been matched by the rapid growth in equipment manufacturing and the extended capability of commercial operators, including outfitters and retailers, to deliver an ever increasing range of 'activity' travel products (Australia and North America have been leading the way in this respect). As a result, adventure travel is now one of the fastest-growing travel market segments and has broadened both its scope and its appeal within international travel and tourism. The variety and availability of adventure travel products for a wide range of interests and abilities appear to be limitless.

As in the USA, in the UK there has been a growing interest in outdoor activities on holiday, partly as a result of an increased concern about health and fitness, an ageing population that is becoming more active and the fact that outdoor

Think it over...

What is the difference between a 'hard' and a 'soft' ATA?

pursuits are more mainstream and fashionable than they used to be. Activities are also now seen as a way in which to relax and mentally unwind on a holiday. A large number of holidays include some form of outdoor activity, regardless of whether or not it was the main purpose of the trip. For example, in 2003, over 45 million trips included short walks, 25 million included long walks and 12 million included hiking, hill walking or rambling. Five million trips were made which involved cycling and three million included sailing, yachting, boating, canoeing or windsurfing. About 24 per cent of all visitors to the countryside took part in some type of outdoor activity on holiday.

Adventure tourism activities are usually undertaken by people during one of three types of visit:

* a holiday where the adventure activity is the main purpose of the trip, such as a skiing or diving trip

* during the course of a holiday at a particular destination but not as the main reason for travel

* day visits where participation in the activity is the main purpose of the trip, such as a day's climbing in the Peak District.

Although specific activity holidays appeal to a relatively small proportion of the population, they have been a stable market that has represented over 10 per cent of all domestic holidays and the sector is expected to grow by 3 per cent by 2007. Even with competition from overseas destinations that have better weather and cheaper options, about 75 per cent of activity holidays are still taken in the UK.

The organisations involved with the development of ATAs in the UK

The rapid expansion of the UK adventure tourism market has been influenced by a variety of organisations and it is important that you can appreciate the scale of their involvement. These organisations can belong to the private sector, the public sector or the voluntary sector. You should already be familiar with the concept of commercial and non-commercial organisations from your

TYPE OF ORGANISATION	UK EXAMPLE
Activity provider	
Adventure travel company	
Equipment/clothing manufacturer	
Film or television programme	
Specialist magazine	
Specialist website	
National tourist office	
Local authority	
National Park authority	
Forestry Commission site	
National governing body	
Youth group	
National Trust site	
Youth hostel	
Activity club	
Charity	

TABLE 13.4. *Types of organisations involved in the development of adventure tourism*

work on the structure of the travel and tourism industry in unit 1. It is important to remember the key characteristics of private, public and voluntary sector organisations, as there are often conflicts of interest between the organisations involved in tourism development in any location; this is usually because of different values and attitudes (see the case study on page 183 on values and attitudes). However, even private sector organisations will respond to prevailing public concerns and many companies emphasise the fact that they encourage sustainability and responsible tourism.

Private sector organisations

Major business organisations in the private sector operate for profit and for some of these organisations the key priority will be the maximisation of profit. Many businesses are in direct competition with each other and maintaining market share is another very important aim. Many adventure tourism providers are private sector operations. For many of these providers, maintaining a steady cash flow to meet fixed operating costs will also be important. Such concerns will affect all tourism providers regardless of whether they are sole traders, public limited companies, private limited companies

or working within a type of partnership. The following case study illustrates the dynamic nature of this sector.

Public sector and voluntary sector organisations

Public sector organisations tend to be funded by local and/or national government in order to provide a service to both visitors and people living in the local area. They are not profit driven as such, but operations are expected to keep within budget and offer value for money as well as returns on investments.

The voluntary sector contains many types of organisation that are not controlled by government and that are not solely operated for profit.

Public and voluntary sector organisations frequently work in partnership and we shall

Activity

To help you understand the many influences and organisations that are at work in the development of ATAs in particular destinations, make a copy of Table 13.4 and complete it by providing a named UK example of each category.

CASE STUDY

A private sector operation in adventure tourism

In 2005 Dragoman Overland was created by the merger of Dragoman and Encounter Overland. With over 40 years' experience of operating overland trips, the merged company launched five new styles of overlanding. Dragoman Overland now has a fleet of over 35 trucks around the world. Its routes across Central Asia are famous and it is the largest operator in South America.

The company has an extensive knowledge of the destinations visited and has created support teams in appropriate locations to service the overland tours. The organisation is also an innovative adventure company, having pioneered the original overland

routes and developed responsible tourism policies from an early stage.

The company currently offers trips in five different guises tailored to offer passengers different experiences: Escape, Discover, Encounter, Family and Ultimate Overland. The different types of trip vary from a comfortable 'see it all at your leisure' longer journeys to shorter 'see as much as you can' in two to three weeks. Further details can be found at www.dragoman.com/tripstyles.

* **Research Dragoman Overland's products and services.**
* **Where does the company advertise?**
* **What is the nature of its appeal?**

now briefly look at one such arrangement, which involves the Council for National Parks (CNP), which has implications for UK adventure tourism in a particular location.

The Council for National Parks (CNP)

The Council for National Parks (CNP) is a charity that works to protect and enhance the National Parks of England and Wales and areas that merit National Park status, and promote understanding and quiet enjoyment of them for the benefit of all. The CNP is the only national, voluntary sector organisation dedicated to National Parks. It is an umbrella organisation of over 40 environmental and amenity groups and aims to give the voluntary sector a shared vision and voice on all National Park issues. CNP works in partnership with the National Park Authorities, as well as many other bodies (see www.cnp.org.uk).

Key aims of CNP are:

* to protect and enhance National Parks by promoting good practice, fighting threats and influencing policy

* to promote sustainability within the National Parks that is compatible with their purposes, for the benefit of society as a whole

* to secure a new National Park for the South Downs and to research other areas as candidate National Parks

* to build support across all sections of the community for National Parks, and to improve the links between urban communities and National Parks.

Key issues for the future development of adventure tourism in the UK and in overseas destinations

* Ease of access needs to be ensured. The development of many adventure activity sites is currently constrained by limited access to suitable water, countryside and coastal sites.

* Adventure activities need to be managed effectively to ensure that they do not cause conflict or have other negative effects. This is vital if the development of adventure tourism is to be environmentally sustainable.

* There is a need to educate adventure tourists about safety.

* Many adventure activities require more and improved facilities to enable and support participation.

* Adventure sports can cause damage and disruption, so events need to be staged in locations that have the capacity to accommodate them.

* The adventure tourism industry has many small-scale independent operators, so booking and information services need to be made more user-friendly to encourage growth.

* There is a need for separate coverage of adventure activities in destination marketing, particularly for destinations with a strong adventure tourism product.

When you research your own destinations, consider the extent to which the above issues have been dealt with. What evidence can you provide about them and what is their relative importance?

Assessment guidance

For your report for Assessment Objective 1 and the research and analysis you do for Assessment Objective 3, you have to investigate the development of ATAs in two UK destinations and one overseas destination. You need to show that you appreciate the fact that the development of adventure tourism within the UK is influenced by a variety of organisations. When you are doing research about a particular destination you need to identify individual providers and to present information about the values and attitudes of the different organisations influencing the activities that you have identified. However, you need only to consider those organisations involved in the development of ATAs in your chosen destinations. Remember that for Assessment Objective 1 you must link organisations with the reasons for the growth and development of the ATAs.

Management of the impacts of adventure tourism

Many ATAs take place in fragile environments and among people whose culture and traditions are different from our own. In order for it to be sustainable, any tourism development should attempt to make a low impact on both the local environment and the local culture. Your previous research into Dragoman Overland's products and services will have provided good examples of the ways in which this can take place. However, many tourism developments help to generate income, increase local employment and aid the conservation of ecosystems. By doing this, the tourism developments taking place within particular destinations will be examples of responsible tourism, in that they are both ecologically and culturally sensitive. Furthermore, the destination as a whole is likely to be improved for both local people and visitors.

The positive and/or negative impacts caused by any tourism activity may be:

* economic
* environmental
* socio-cultural.

> ### Key term
>
> Sustainable tourism refers to operations that are managed for the long-term benefit of the environment and of the local people.

Economic impacts

Economic impacts vary and most of you will readily appreciate that local income and job opportunities will increase as tourism is developed. The local economy will gain from visitor spending and overseas visitors will bring valuable foreign currency, which will contribute to improvements in the nation's international trading position. Local and national government will benefit from increased tax revenues and this money will frequently be used to improve the local infrastructure. However, such positive economic impacts can be limited if the local economy is relying on tourism alone. Furthermore, overseas developers may take profits out of the country and many of the new jobs that are created may be only part time and may be low skill/low pay. Managerial positions may be reserved for qualified foreign staff and so the long-term benefits of tourism for the host destination may be quite limited.

Environmental impacts

Adventure tourism can bring important environmental improvements to particular destinations. Wildlife reserves clearly protect both the fauna and flora from visitor disturbance and help to preserve the natural landscape for future generations. However, new developments can spoil the landscape ('visual pollution') and increasing visitor numbers can generate congestion as well as placing increased demands on the local infrastructure. This is particularly significant for adventure tourism because activities usually take place in the more remote wilderness areas, which are often sensitive to change. All new developments in such areas must involve the loss of habitats, the removal of soil and vegetation and the generation of different types of pollution.

Socio-cultural impacts

Socio-cultural impacts are also variable. Contact with other cultures is good, provided that one does not dominate the other, which can happen all too easily with the 'demonstration effect'. Similarly, local customs and traditions can be ignored as the host population seeks to meet the needs and expectations of visitors for short-term economic gain.

> ### Key term
>
> The demonstration effect takes place in many tourist areas. It is when a traditional culture suffers because the younger members of that society adopt the values and attitudes that visitors have been demonstrating.

Sustainable development

It is important that destinations attempt to manage these impacts in a sustainable way. It will make sense to try to maximise the positive effects of tourism within particular locations but it will be equally important to try to minimise the negative effects. This can be a difficult balancing act, in that many of both the positive and the negative effects are likely to be proportional to tourist numbers. There will, however, be a limit on the number of tourists a particular destination can sustainably manage, and this is known as its carrying capacity.

Key term

Carrying capacity is the number of visitors that can be managed without causing significant negative impacts.

Destinations where ATAs are undertaken can be at different stages of economic development. These stages are also linked to the 'life cycle' of tourist destinations, and hence to the question of sustainability. For the following classifications of resorts, think whether or where they fit in the life cycle of an adventure tourism destination, and whether they have been or could be sustainably managed for this purpose:

* **High-density recreation areas** are where substantial development has taken place and the area now uses all available resources to provide recreational activities. Such areas will be characterised by having many resort hotels and facilities managed for maximum visitor usage. Examples are Disneyland and other purpose-built resort complexes.

* **General outdoor recreational areas** are those which similarly have undergone substantial development, but these areas offer a greater choice of activity and the resorts are some distance away from main population centres (e.g. ski resorts and sailing centres).

* **Natural environments or established wilderness areas** offer a variety of activities, according to the nature of the area. National parks are a good example.

* **Unique natural areas of outstanding natural beauty or scenic grandeur** are areas where the main activity is likely to be sightseeing, but they are increasingly being exploited by adventure travellers. An example of such an area is the Grand Canyon.

* **Primitive areas of undisturbed wilderness** are areas with no roads, where natural wild conditions can still be found. Associated ATAs include trekking in the Himalayas and exploring Amazonia.

* **Historic and cultural sites** may be local, regional, national or international in scale (e.g. the Inca Trail). They are a significant attraction for the adventure traveller.

Theory into practice

The following task will help you to appreciate the effects of adventure tourism. Complete Table 13.5 by placing the impacts listed below in their most appropriate contexts:

* conservation of heritage sites
* regeneration and redevelopment of derelict sites
* pollution controls
* traffic management schemes
* decline in traditional employment
* population migration
* seasonal underemployment
* exposure to alternative lifestyle(s)
* increased crime
* decline in importance of traditional ways of life
* increasing local or regional income
* greater employment
* greater hotel occupancy

- more visitors
- visitor spend
- infrastructure improvements
- new projects
- multiplier effect
- more part-time and seasonal employment
- preservation of traditional activities
- better recreational facilities
- urban sprawl

- traffic congestion
- 'honey-pot' sites
- footpath erosion
- loss of open space
- water supply issues
- wildlife habitat disruption
- loss of biodiversity
- water and air pollution

IMPACT	POSITIVE EFFECTS	NEGATIVE EFFECTS
Economic		
Environmental		
Socio-cultural		

TABLE 13.5. *Possible impacts associated with the growth of adventure tourism in particular destinations*

CASE STUDY

Sustainable adventure tourism in the Andes

We end this section with an example of one way in which adventure tourism can be managed sustainably for the long-term benefit of both the environment and the local population. The Inca Trail & Quechua Community Trek in Peru has been pioneered by a local tour operator, Andina Travel. Local communities have been closely involved with the opening up of this region for tourism from the very beginning. In collaboration with national and international protection agencies and a handful of trekking companies, a plan was put together with these local communities to promote tourism in the area following the guidelines of sustainable tourism. This recent introduction of tourism to the region has brought some very valuable economic development to the local communities.

The local population are remote Andean farming communities with traditions dating back to the Incas. They are primarily Quechua-speaking, with some Spanish, and they have very little contact with the general population of Peru. Their daily lives consist of potato cultivation, weaving, and the herding of llamas, alpacas and sheep. In order to minimise disruption to local traditions and culture, the following tourism development strategies have been adopted:

- the establishment of campsites to avoid the contamination of existing local community areas

* the use of local community animals and personnel on organised treks

* the training of local community members through workshops on camp maintenance, hygiene and client services to enhance their economic viability

* environmental conservation

* the introduction of fixed payments for local products.

In this way the impact of tourism causes little disruption and will allow the local communities to develop hand in hand with future visitor growth.

* **What is meant by the term 'sustainable development'?**

* **The negative impacts have been minimised for the local community, but what ones might remain?**

* there has been some growth in the over-50s market

* the majority of adventure holidays are booked and taken independently

* participants tend to come either as individuals or with a small group of friends (usually males)

* couples and families are also a strong market, but for particular kinds of activity

* overall, adventure seekers are more likely to use self-catering accommodation and camping than general holidaymakers.

Benefits of ATAs

Range of participants

The market for ATAs is quite wide: they attract business management teams, groups of students, individuals, couples, families and different types of competitor participating in or preparing for particular events. There are different reasons for wanting to take part in an adventure tourism trip (see below) and this produces the cross-section of participants indicated in Table 13.6.

In the UK, leisure travellers taking part in adventure activities tend to have the following characteristics:

* a younger population than for holidays as a whole – the 16–34-year age group accounts for 55–60 per cent of adventure holidays

* the 35–55-year age group participates in these types of activities as well

Reasons for participation

Some adventure travellers will want to participate in an activity for its own sake, some will be attracted by the element of danger or risk and others will want to impress their friends with tales of their personal exploits. The specific benefits of participation in an adventure activity include:

* personal enjoyment

* improved communication, teamwork and leadership

* social interaction

* fitness and health (depending on the type of activity, this could include improved balance, rhythm and coordination)

* personal development in terms of assertiveness and motivation

* improved skill and further qualification.

MARKET SEGMENT	CHARACTERISTICS OF PEOPLE IN THAT MARKET SEGMENT
Those wishing to sample an activity for the first time	Participate on impulse Activity was not a factor in destination choice Not likely to make repeat visit(s)
Those wishing to learn a particular activity or develop their level of skill	Serious participants and sports competitors Likely to become independent and revisit Sport/activity governing body will direct these individuals to particular providers/destinations A constant stream of new participants
Those who are keen enthusiasts	Very serious and experienced participants Undertake activity regularly Often compete in events at destinations High levels of repeat visits Very skilled and knowledgeable about their chosen activity
Those who are only occasional participants	The largest market segment Have reached a certain standard of performance Do not participate regularly Most will participate on an independent basis
Business users – corporate groups and incentives	Organisations buy into activity packages from providers Comparatively high spend Focus on team-building exercises, management training and provision of incentive packages
Groups of young people such as schools, colleges and youth groups	Residential and day trips Field study visits Strong repeat visit – same slots each year Use local education authority outdoor education centres and/or commercial activity centres
Those buying activities for special occasions	Interested in a package Use commercial providers Specialised themes (e.g. stag and hen parties)
Activity clubs	Very important as clubs arrange trips for their members Many repeats to popular destinations Experienced and much knowledge about options that are available Likely to make independent arrangements

TABLE 13.6. *Adventure tourism market segments*

Participating in an ATA

Assessment Objective 4 asks you, as part of a team, to plan and participate in an ATA, and to evaluate your performance. A good understanding of the above will help you when you come to consider the benefits to be had from it. Remember that different users will have different values and attitudes relating to participation in particular ATAs, and that your own values and attitudes could change as a result of your participation.

Summary: two example destination reports

To help you to prepare for your investigations of your three destinations and your activity to try, and to help you fully meet the requirements of

Assessment Objectives 1 and 2, we will now have a look in some detail at two destinations: the Lake District and Dubai (these were also featured in unit 3 of the AS textbook). The following should guide you in the writing of your own report about the growth in ATAs at your chosen destinations, by illustrating the assessment of the development of adventure tourism, and its impacts and benefits, and how they can be managed.

Adventure tourism in the Lake District

Lake District tourism began in the late 18th century. The first guidebooks to the area had been published by then and the writings of authors like Wordsworth, Coleridge and Southey advertised the beauty and splendour of the Lake District to the nation. By the end of the 19th century the numbers of visitors to the Lake District had caused many changes to be made. The railway reached Windermere in 1847 and the age of the leisure visitor began.

The Lake District was established as a National Park in 1951. The Lake District National Park Authority (LDNPA) is the local government body appointed to look after the Lake District National Park. It has two main purposes (under the Environment Act 1995 – see above): to conserve and enhance the park, and to promote the understanding and enjoyment of it. Furthermore, the LDNPA has a duty to foster the economic and social well-being of local communities within the park.

With the growth in popularity of outdoor activities there is now an urgent need to protect the area, not only for future generations but also to maintain the area's intrinsic values. Adventure brings freedom but also a responsibility to respect and conserve the environment. With over 14 million visitors each year, there is the danger that several areas will suffer overuse and it is vital that the area is managed properly.

Types of activity available

Having looked briefly at the development of the area, we can now look at the main ATAs that take place within the Lake District National Park.

Walking

As shown on Figure 13.6, the Lake District is hard to beat as a hill walking destination. There

FIGURE 13.6. *Walking in the Lake District*

are many types of walk: hikers and ramblers can choose from lower-level routes around the lakes themselves to the challenges presented by famous routes like Striding Edge, Jack's Rake and Sharp Edge, all within a comparatively small area. Walks are currently offered by around 100 providers/activity centres in and around the local region.

Climbing

The Lake District is generally accepted to be the birthplace of modern rock climbing, with the ascent of Nape's Needle on Great Gable in 1886. The area provides an ideal environment for the sport; there is a variety of easy-access roadside crags in Borrowdale as well as more remote cliffs flanking the higher peaks of Scafell and Pillar. The heavily glaciated rock lends itself to a wide variety of climbing styles. Visitors interested in undertaking an organised climbing session have a choice of some 79 local providers, such as the one shown in Figure 13.7.

Scrambling

The Lake District provides excellent locations for scrambling; this includes such options as ghyll scrambling, canyoning and aquaseiling (descents of waterfalls). Mountain scrambling gives access to challenging routes to summits via little-used places. Ghyll scrambling and canyoning allow exploration of gorges and chasms. Such activities are operated by 25 licensed providers and are offered within a comprehensive safety framework. The providers have highly motivated staff and their main interest is to give the customer an experience to remember.

Paragliding

From Skiddaw and the hills around Keswick to Coniston Old Man and Jenkin Hill, the Lake District offers a wide diversity of sites for paragliding. Steep ridges and deep bowls produce the thermal air currents that paragliders use. The Lake District has a multitude of easy launching and landing areas, and in many cases convenient access by road. Three local providers offer this activity.

Mountain biking

Although a relatively new sport, mountain biking has very much taken the Lake District by storm.

KESWICK INDOOR CLIMBING WALL

TEL. 017687 72000
www.keswickclimbingwall.co.uk

CLIMBING LESSONS

- Lessons available all year round for individuals, families and groups
- Open daily 10 am - 9 pm
- Suitable for complete beginners
- Ideal for families with kids
- No minimum (or maximum) age limit
- Excellent all-weather activity
- Stay all day after your lesson

We teach you the basics of knot tying and ropework, then once we are happy that you have mastered them safely, you can stay and climb unsupervised for as long as you like.

Every person climbing needs someone to hold their ropes, which makes it ideal for people who are not keen on leaving the ground! **Please note** that small children cannot hold the ropes for adults; climbers need to be belayed by someone of a similar or greater weight.

OTHER OUTDOOR ACTIVITIES AVAILABLE See details and prices overleaf

Booking is essential for lessons, although at quieter times we can take bookings at short notice.

Please call any time between 10am and 9pm for further information or to book.

We are located only a couple of minutes' walk from the centre of town, just behind the Pencil Museum.

FIGURE 13.7. *To cater for the local demand for climbing, indoor facilities have been developed and climbing schools established*

Come rain or shine, you will find mountain bikers enjoying themselves out on the hills, often covering surprising distances. Keswick, Windermere and Ambleside are the main locations and also offer bike hire and equipment, as Figure 13.8 indicates. Sixty-seven local providers offer this activity. For all sorts of cyclist, from beginner

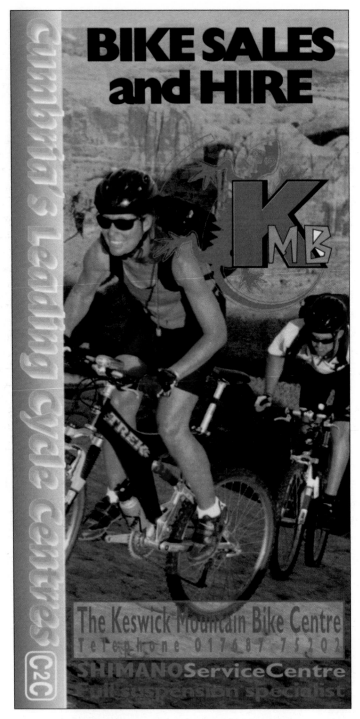

FIGURE 13.8. *Promotional leaflet from the Keswick Mountain Bike Centre*

to expert, there is an amazing choice of options, with routes ranging from woodland tracks in Grizedale and Whinlatter Forests to challenging climbs and descents, with the summit of Skiddaw being the longest.

Skiing

Private ski clubs run several lifts on mountains near Glenridding (20 miles south-west of Penrith) and Alston, which operate when there is sufficient snow cover. The Lake District Ski Club runs a button lift in Raise, near Glenridding. Yad Moss, near Alston, whose lift is operated by the Carlisle Ski Club, boasts the longest ski lift in England.

Water sports

The Lake District is an excellent venue for canoeing, as well as white-water kayaking and slaloming. Lakes Windermere, Coniston, Derwent Water, Ullswater and Bassenthwaite are regularly used by all types of canoeists of all abilities. The Lake District offers something for everyone – from the five-foot drop at Eamont Bridge to the River Rothay, meandering through Wordsworth territory. Challenging white waters abound, such as on the Eden between Lazonby and Armathwaite, where the rapids cut through a sandstone gorge. Sixty-five providers offer kayaking and canoeing.

Windsurfing is offered by 12 providers in the Lake District. The most popular lake is Coniston Water but the coastline of Cumbria also offers many opportunities for the sport. There are several windsurfing schools in Cumbria – principally on Windermere, Coniston, Ullswater and Derwent Water.

Sailing is a popular activity in the Lake District and 15 providers offer a range of opportunities for visitors. There are venues such as the Low Wood Watersports Centre, which will provide private tuition, as well as residential certification courses run by residential establishments.

Windermere is the UK's largest remaining public access lake. The fact that it has over 5,000 registered ski and wakeboard boats shows how popular this location is for recreational and professional athletes alike. There are three local activity providers offering tuition to visitors.

Other ATAs

There are many other types of ATA available for visitors. Table 13.7 illustrates the range of options available.

Many of the providers offer a wide range of activities in order to maximise their potential appeal to different market segments. Figure 13.9 shows two examples of this multiple provision. This wide provision of ATAs can

ACTIVITY	NUMBER OF LOCAL PROVIDERS
Quad biking	6
4×4 off-road driving	6
Paint-balling	5
Horse riding	7
Hot air ballooning	2
Skydiving	1
Clay pigeon shooting	4
High wire and ropes	2

TABLE 13.7. *Some more specialist activities available in the Lake District*

FIGURE 13.9. *Two examples of providers offering multiple activities*

be partly explained by the increasing number of Cumbrian farms now entering the tourism market. Many of the farmers in Cumbria who offer tourist facilities make more money than through farming. It's said an average farmer yielded between £300 and £400 a year from each 10 acres of land, but revenue from tourism could generate the same profit in just a few days. On average, a farmer earns around £15,000 a year, but those farmers who offer tourist activities or accommodation make an average annual gross profit of £20,853. This involvement in tourism is moving far beyond the traditional concept of bed-and-breakfast farmhouses or self-catering accommodation. An increasing number of farmers, especially among the younger generation in the industry, are looking to provide activities and adventures to attract visitors in the 21st century and maximise potential revenues by providing a greater variety of products and a higher quality of both accommodation and attractions.

Impacts and issues

The large number of tourists puts the environment under great pressure. One of the main problems is footpath erosion, which can create huge scars on the landscape (now so large that they can be seen on satellite pictures). To give an idea of the scale of the problem within the LDNPA area, a recent survey found that some 41,690 person-days of work were required, at an estimated total cost of £4,656,512, to repair the damage along 180 footpath routes. This topic often attracts students to locations in the Lake District to investigate the environmental impact of visitor activities such as hill walking and climbing. At selected sites, such as that shown in Figure 13.10, data can be collected to identify:

* width of path and its associated trampled zone

* gradient of path

* vegetation cover

* evidence of existing management

* appraisal of existing management (safety, appearance, ease of walking, etc.)

* facilities around site (car park, etc.).

Environmental problems can be prevented by a combination of good design, regular

FIGURE 13.10. *Evaluating footpath erosion in the Lake District*

maintenance and managing the impact of visitors to the area. Measures which can be taken include:

* the construction of hard-wearing, user-friendly paths

* ensuring effective water drainage, which is fundamental to successful path management

* carrying out regular maintenance tasks, such as clearing water gullies, removing gravel and repairing minor damage

* reducing grazing pressures

* 'resting' routes, for example by temporarily changing the line of the path, particularly in the early stages of erosion

* fertilising and reseeding, which may be used on their own or in conjunction with the resting of routes

* fencing, which can be used on its own or in conjunction with other methods to allow vegetation to recover, although fencing is an extremely sensitive issue because of the access issue

* directing people along a preferred route using physical and psychological barriers such as walls, plants, stones and water

* routing people away from areas prone to erosion, although this may be difficult if the path has very rigid boundaries or has been designated as a right of way

* educating mountain users through leaflets, talks and notices

* managing visitor numbers through the limiting of car parking or directing publicity at areas less likely to suffer damage.

Managing the Lake District is a balancing act involving the weighing up of various interests of the environment, the visitors and the local residents and then arriving at decisions which are in the best long-term interests of the National Park. This is not easy, because the various stakeholders will have contrasting values and attitudes. The potential for conflict is present not only between the different users but within particular user groups as well.

CASE STUDY
Values and attitudes

In 2005, Lake District National Park chiefs wanted to stop, partly for cost-saving reasons, free guided walking tours because they drew mainly middle-aged, middle-class, white people. The LDNPA provides around 400 free walks each year for some of the area's 14 million visitors. When a public meeting was held, members of the LDNPA were told there was massive opposition to the plan. The locally based clothing company Hawkshead pledged £38,000, enough to save the walks for that year. These events were widely reported in the media.

* **In what ways does this controversy illustrate the extent to which different types of organisation operating within the National Park can display very different values and attitudes to those expected.**

The LDNPA runs the Lake District Visitor Centre at Brockhole and this facility attracts over 160,000 visitors each year. Figure 13.11 shows the range of services provided. A key function of the centre is to provide an education service about the National Park. The central theme of the centre's displays is an introduction the National Park's history, geology, wildlife and people. In line with its statutory purpose, the LDNPA here attempts to explain the reasons for the establishment of National Parks and the role of the National Park Authority in maintaining the

FIGURE 13.11. *The range of services provided by the LDNPA's Lake District Visitor Centre at Brockhole*

balance between the environment, visitors and local people. The education service is provided by the Field Studies Council (FSC) and this partnership between the public and voluntary sectors is very appropriate considering that the FSC's motto is 'Environmental Understanding for All'.

Activity

Research two private sector adventure activity providers operating in the Lake District and describe the ways in which their operations are influenced by the LDNPA, government legislation and the codes of practice of the governing body for the activity.

Assessment Objective 1 requires you to produce a report that examines the growth of ATAs in your chosen destinations. Which of the following descriptions best fits the above example report on the Lake District?

FEATURES OF MARK BAND 1	FEATURES OF MARK BAND 2	FEATURES OF MARK BAND 3
Brief report Only some understanding of reasons for the growth of ATAs Limited reference to organisations involved in ATA development Little reference to organisation values and attitudes	It is a descriptive report which shows only basic knowledge and understanding of the reasons for the growth of ATAs in the Lake District. There are links between the reasons for the development and the specific destination. There are omissions in the range of organisations involved in the development of ATAs, but some values and attitudes are explained briefly.	Detailed report Thorough knowledge and understanding of reasons for the growth of ATAs Organisations and ATA growth and development are clearly linked Clear illustration of organisations' values and attitudes

Assessment Objective 2 requires you to provide an assessment of the impacts and benefits of adventure tourism and how they can be managed in your chosen destinations. Which of the following descriptions best fits the example report for the Lake District?

FEATURES OF MARK BAND 1	FEATURES OF MARK BAND 2	FEATURES OF MARK BAND 3
The impacts of adventure tourism are identified, but there is nothing on the benefits, hence an imbalance between the positive and negative impacts.	Clear understanding of both positive and negative impacts and benefits of ATA development Discussion of ways to manage impacts Few omissions Appropriate use of terminology	Thorough understanding of all impacts and benefits of ATAs Full discussion of impact management Realistic recommendations where no management strategy in place Accurate use of all terminology

Think it over...

What additions would you make to the Lake District report in order to improve its coverage of Assessment Objectives 1 and 2?

Adventure tourism in Dubai

Dubai continues to attract increasing numbers of UK visitors. Table 13.8 indicates the scale of recent growth. Long-haul specialist Kuoni ranked Dubai as its top luxury destination for the 12-month period ending in June 2005.

	1998	1999	2000	2001	2002	2003	2004
Total UK visitors	197,571	251,895	301,461	348,477	447,006	458,451	605,240
Percentage change	73.4%	27.5%	19.7%	15.6%	28.3%	2.6%	32%
Number of UK tour operators	64	81	91	91	110	113	190

TABLE 13.8. *Recent growth in visitor numbers to Dubai and numbers of tour operators offering Dubai as a destination*

This south-eastern part of the Arabian Peninsula enjoys a sub-tropical climate with average temperatures of 18°C in January, 33°C in July and less than 150 mm of precipitation. Visitors can count on sunshine and comfortable water temperatures all year round, as well as a choice of well-established clubs and leisure companies specialising in a range of activities. The provision of ATAs is increasing within Dubai and we can now have a look at the range of options that are available.

Types of activity available

Water sports

Dubai's geographical location on the southern shore of the Arabian Gulf makes it an ideal holiday destination for water sports. As shown in Figure 13.12, the government of Dubai's Department of Tourism and Commerce Marketing (DTCM) actually produces a promotional leaflet to emphasise this aspect of the destination's potential appeal.

Diving

The local waters contain a variety of submerged wrecks which, as well as attracting a variety of tropical fish species, also make for fascinating diving. The nearby sheltered waters of the Gulf of Oman enjoy a global reputation for their coral reefs, and sea temperatures are warm enough between May and October for wetsuits not to be needed. The main scuba providers run courses and tuition can be found in the following languages – English, Arabic, French, German, Italian, Russian, Japanese, Swedish, Farsi, Hindi and Urdu. Tuition approved by the Professional Association of Diving Instructors (PADI) and by the British Sub Aqua Club is available from a variety of providers in Dubai. This is an indication of Dubai's appeal to

FIGURE 13.12. *Promotional leaflet from Dubai's Department of Tourism and Commerce Marketing (DTCM)*

a global market of scuba enthusiasts.

By 2007, the Palm Jumeirah (an artificial island development) will feature a unique 'Dive Experience', including four key themed zones:

＊ Snorkeller's Cove

＊ The Lost City

* Dives of the World
* Spearfishing area.

Furthermore, on the trunk of the Palm will be 'Atlantis, the Palm' (the 2000-room sister resort to its Bahamas namesake), which will boast one of the world's largest marine habitats, including a snorkel trail and a dolphin encounter programme. There will also be a diving challenge whereby divers will have the opportunity to search for and keep a 1 kg bar of gold!

Deep sea fishing
The warmth and shelter of the Gulf attracts a large variety of fish. It is common for local operators to offer half-day or full-day trips to the best fishing waters some 12 miles offshore. There are at least ten leading providers of such services in Dubai.

Water-skiing
Dubai's reputation for water-skiing is well established. The Dubai Water Sports Association stages an annual week-long competition and festival. Local facilities are such that Dubai can now attract advanced skiers as well as beginners. There are nine major providers in Dubai.

Sailing
Sailing is one of the most popular leisure activities in Dubai and it is a pastime enjoyed by both residents and visitors. The interest in sailing is part of Dubai's maritime heritage. Conditions are near perfect with minimal tides and currents in the Gulf. Winds are usually predictable and reassuring for the beginner but strong enough to challenge the experienced sailor. The Dubai International Marine Club at Mina Seyahi hosts a number of racing events for vessels ranging from traditional dhows to modern yachts. There is an extensive list of providers in Dubai as well as two private sailing clubs primarily for members with their own boats or boards (the Dubai Offshore Sailing Club and the Jebel Ali Sailing Club).

Kite surfing
Kite surfing is a popular choice for those in search of an adrenalin rush. The kites used are up to 80 feet across and can take you across the surf at 60 mph. Dubai's coastline offers excellent conditions, with long, flat beaches and calm waters. On any given day, local enthusiasts can be seen around Jebel Ali and other stretches of beach. The activity is best attempted under expert supervision because handling the kites takes both balance and upper-body strength. Indeed, catching the wrong cross-wind can leave an individual dumped on the sand from 20 feet in the air. The Dubai Kite Club (www.dubaikiteclub.com) lists qualified local instructors, who charge around £30 per hour with kite hire included. The Kitepeople store (www.kitepeople.net) sells and hires equipment.

Wadi-bashing
This type of off-road activity involves bouncing a four-wheel-drive (4WD) vehicle along and

FIGURE 13.13. *On the route to the Hajar Mountains in a four-wheel-drive vehicle*

through dried-up creeks. Several operators run safaris to Wadi Hatta or the Hajar Mountains and Figure 13.13 shows part of this route. The region also offers chances for exploring independently and camping. For those willing to make the four-hour journey, Muscat offers spectacular scenery. Jebel Shams lays claim to the title 'Grand Canyon of the Middle East', climbing up to nearly 1.5 miles above sea level. The eastern emirates also have plenty to offer the adventurous off-road driver. Ras Al Kaimah to Dibba is a classic route, climbing from sea level to over 6,000 feet and back again. It is always advisable to take a second car and tow rope on such ventures in case you get stuck. Most major car-hire firms are represented in Dubai, though 4WDs need to be booked in advance and British visitors can expect to pay between £310 and £370 for one week's hire.

Dune-bashing

For those keen to explore the dunes for themselves, 'Big Red' (also know as Al Hamar) is a useful starting point. The site is 25 minutes along the Hatta road, heading south from Dubai. This is also a suitable location for quad biking. The dune

tops 300 feet and can become crowded, with local riders making charges to the top, usually in the late afternoon, when it is cooler. There are several fenced-off areas nearby and local providers hire bikes for around £20 per half hour. Many visitors to the dunes try their hand at sand-boarding. This activity is often included in packages with dune-bashing and most of the operators listed in unit 11 run these adventures. You can expect to pay around £40 per person.

Indoor skiing

Ski Dubai has five slopes, which vary in difficulty, height and steepness, the longest run being 400 metres with a fall of over 60 metres. Visitors can test their skills on the world's first indoor 'black' run or practise their turns on the gentle beginner slopes. Snowboarders can also practise their stunts on the 90-metre quarter pipe. For the non-skiers, there is an interactive Snow Park, which, at 3,000 m^2, is the largest indoor snow park in the world.

Team-building activities

The Hatta Fort Hotel offers a variety of activities for business groups, including field and target archery, which can be practised under the supervision of trained instructors in a specially equipped area on the landscaped grounds, shown in Figure 13.14. The facilities for clay shooting are fitted with the latest equipment for two main clay-shooting disciplines, skeet and trap. Lessons and practice sessions are available under the guidance and supervision of qualified instructors. There is also a small adventure training course, which has been established in the grounds of the property to help meet local business demand for such team-building activities.

FIGURE 13.14. *Archery range at the Hatta Fort Hotel*

Provision in the future

Dubailand will contain 45 'mega-projects' and over 200 tourism, leisure and entertainment sub-projects, making it the most ambitious tourist destination ever created. Dubailand is being created to appeal to the widest audience of tourists, covering all age groups, nationalities and activities. On completion, Dubailand theme park will be twice the size of Walt Disney World Resort in Florida. Phase 1 of the Dubailand project will extend from 2007 to 2010 and the final phase of the Dubailand will be completed between 2015 and 2018.

Dubailand's Sports and Outdoor World will cover approximately 19 million m², with an investment of AED2.5 billion and will contain a total of five projects (Extreme Sports World, Dubai Sports City, Racing World, Polo World, Golf World). We end this look at adventure tourism in Dubai with a review of what is planned for this 'Sports and Outdoor World' theme. The activities will include the following by 2008:

* flying and soaring – fly by wire and ballooning

* shooting and training – cross-country running, Commando training, paint-balling, archery and skeet/trap clay shooting

* falconry

* driving academy – bikes, go-karts, motocross, quad bikes and 4×4 off-road course

* water – white-water kayaking, wakeboarding, wave riding and surfing, extreme body slide

* skateboarding, BMX and in-line skating

* rock climbing

* waterfall climbing

* bungee jumping

* caving

* cliff jumping.

There will also be a hotel and chalets providing 200 rooms as well as various retail and entertainment facilities.

Impacts and issues

We can see that Dubai is actively preparing to cater for a range of different tourism market segments and that the opportunities available for ATAs are slowly increasing. However, the rapid growth of the destination will produce stresses and strains on both the environment and the existing infrastructure without careful management. Already there is conflict with the Palm development and existing water sport providers along Jumeirah beach. Hotel guests notice beach erosion due to altering tides and the continuing development work causes a variety of impacts, including congestion.

Dubailand's expansion over the coming years will pose some threats to the environment but there are quite extensive controls imposed by the government. In terms of adventure tourism, the rapid expansion of tourist attractions and facilities within the destination may prove to be a disincentive – adventure travellers may be more likely to seek out destinations that pay closer attention to the principles of ecotourism in their development plans (see unit 12).

Assessment Objective 1 requires you to produce a report that examines the growth of ATAs in chosen regions. Which of the following descriptions best fits the above report on Dubai?

FEATURES OF MARK BAND 1	FEATURES OF MARK BAND 2	FEATURES OF MARK BAND 3
Brief report Only some understanding of reasons for the growth of ATAs Limited reference to organisations involved in ATA development Little reference to organisation values and attitudes	Descriptive report Knowledge and understanding of reasons for the growth of ATAs Clear links made with destination Range of organisations identified Some explanation of their values and attitudes	Detailed report Thorough knowledge and understanding of reasons for the growth of ATAs Organisations and ATA growth and development are clearly linked Clear illustration of organisations' values and attitudes

Assessment Objective 2 requires you to provide an assessment of the impacts and benefits of adventure tourism and how they can be managed in your chosen regions. Which of the following descriptions best fits the above report on Dubai?

FEATURES OF MARK BAND 1	FEATURES OF MARK BAND 2	FEATURES OF MARK BAND 3
Some impacts and benefits identified Imbalance between positive and negative effects Some unrealistic impact management recommendations Inaccurate use of terminology	Clear understanding of both positive and negative impacts and benefits of ATA development Discussion of ways to manage impacts Few omissions Appropriate use of terminology	Thorough understanding of all impacts and benefits of ATAs Full discussion of impact management Realistic recommendations where no management strategy in place Accurate use of all terminology

Think it over...

What additions would you make to the example report on Dubai in order to improve its coverage of Assessment Objectives 1 and 2?

Choosing a feasible and safe ATA

This unit requires you to research, plan and participate in one group ATA. Before this activity actually takes place, you need to consider whether or not it is suitable for your group. In order to do this, both you and your group must follow a logical planning process, in which the following issues need to be considered. Decide on the purpose of the task and its objectives. This unit requires your group to consider at least three or four possible activities and to produce evidence of your research in the form of a feasibility study. Note that one or more of these could be an urban location, in the interests of access and costs – adventure activities are not necessarily located in rural areas, or even outdoors.

It is on the basis of this study that you will select your chosen activity. It is more than likely that your group will contain young people (under the age of 18) and that you will be participating in the activity to help you generate evidence to meet the assessment requirements of this unit. Therefore, the activities that you initially consider will need to be assessed in terms of their fitness for purpose.

> **Think it over...**
>
> When you start planning your ATA, you must give some thought to its later evaluation (see below). What kind of feedback will you require, and from whom? If you plan this well in advance, it will be much easier to gather the information as the project proceeds.

What are your group's requirements?

* Does the activity under consideration require specialised equipment?
* Who will provide it and at what cost?
* Is this affordable?
* Have you the expertise to participate?
* Will you need tuition or supervision?
* Is this included in the price?
* Where will the activity take place?
* How can you get there?
* Is transport provided?
* Is the activity suitable for all members of the group?
* Are there physical ability and fitness constraints?
* Is the size and gender composition of the group an issue?

* Have you any particular reasons for undertaking this activity?
* If you are a school group, are there particular health and safety and child protection issues?

Your answers to these questions will help you to assess the suitability of potential providers. You need to give consideration to their facilities, programmes on offer and whether or not the overall costs represent value for money. Remember that many facilities will offer group discounts and fees may be negotiable.

What are your reasons for participation?

Any adventure activity trip is a learning experience which develops personal values and concepts, generates skills for lifelong learning, encourages group cooperation, and enhances knowledge and appreciation of the natural environment. Good planning will ensure a successful experience for all concerned. You and your group, under the careful guidance and direction of your teacher or tutor, should determine the goals and objectives of the trip and identify ways to accomplish them. You and your group should then be committed from the outset to making the trip a success.

You may decide on a particular activity on the basis that it offers:

* skills development
* team-building
* enjoyment
* a proficiency award.

Other factors to consider

Among the factors to be considered in deciding on the type of trip to be undertaken on a group basis are the following:

* size of the group – the numbers involved
* characteristics of group members, such as age, special needs and special skills
* purpose for which the trip is to be made
* length of time the trip will last (including travelling time)

* distance to be travelled, transportation and destination

* activities to be undertaken

* season of the year

* support tasks to be performed.

The most common type of group activity trips, and probably the easiest to plan for, are single-day visits and visits undertaken during a residential trip. The main advantage of the latter is that the group can use their residential centre like a base camp and take individual activity trips from there. There are numerous locations for an adventure trip and your research into your local region will have highlighted some possibilities. The trip leader should visit the site(s) before the trip to determine the exact facilities available.

A ratio of one adult to 8–12 students should be maintained, with a minimum of two adults for small groups. The total number of students should be no more than can be handled safely and effectively for that particular age group. Consideration must be given to the activities planned as well as to transport and accommodation, if appropriate. It is imperative that duties and responsibilities be assigned in advance. If all the students have been involved with the planning, the many duties necessary to run a successful trip will be evident. The supervising adults should assist the students with various details and this may include the provision of both guidance and positive reinforcement of task management in the light of local authority directives.

Risk assessment

As suggested above, there is nearly always an element of danger in many ATAs. The hazards need to be identified and prepared for. For this, you should apply the principles of risk assessment to your three or four potential activities. This assessment should be applied to *all* the component parts required by the activity trip overall, that is:

* transport

* accommodation

* all aspects of the activity itself.

Indeed, many local education authorities will now insist on a risk assessment before any adventurous pursuit can be undertaken from school.

Principles of risk assessment

A useful form of risk assessment involves you having to rate, on a scale of 1–5, the chances of a particular risk or hazard occurring:

1   almost never – highly unlikely to ever occur (e.g. a meteorite landing on or close to your party)

2   highly unlikely – may occur but very rarely (e.g. the chance of someone walking over a cliff)

3   happening every so often but only rarely (e.g. a *serious* change in the weather)

4   likely, if not probable, but does occur from time to time (e.g. a pebble falling off the top of an abseil pitch or a child tripping on rough ground)

5   certain or very likely to happen (e.g. someone in your party getting tired on a long walk).

You then have to consider the severity of outcome and rate the worst probable consequence due to that risk or hazard on a scale of 1–5:

1   cause for minor concern, a slight inconvenience (e.g. a small graze, helmet rash, a small bruise)

2   minor injuries treatable with first aid but which would not normally require the attention of a medical officer (e.g. cuts, sprains, twists)

3   injuries and ailments which require evacuation and the attention of a medical officer (e.g. mild hypothermia, animal bites, an asthma attack treatable with an inhaler)

4   a major injury leading to hospital treatment (e.g. trauma, epileptic seizure, head injury, broken bones)

5   fatal or serious injury leading to disability.

Very simply, the risk level is obtained by multiplying the likelihood of occurrence by the severity of outcome. A value of 6 is acceptable in outdoor activities, although this value might easily be reduced with appropriate instruction, warning and advice. A risk value of 8 would require detailed warnings and the close monitoring of all instruction given. Risk values above 8 must be reduced or the activity terminated.

For all the risks and hazards that you identify, calculate a value and offer solutions to help you minimise the level of risk. You can then justify your choice of activity in terms of risk management.

To help you appreciate the principles of risk assessment, try applying the above formula to the locations and activities shown in Figures 13.2 (page 161) and 13.13 (page 187).

Final selection

Your final selection from the three or four activities under consideration should be justified in terms of:

* the location of the activity and the prevailing environmental conditions (including time of year and likely weather conditions)

* the number of participants involved

* the type of activity and equipment required

* its suitability for the group's needs

* the level and quality of supervision required

* the level of risk and overall group safety.

Much of this information will be available from the providers directly; however, you will need to validate this with the national governing body of your chosen activity, where appropriate (on which, see below).

Role of national governing bodies and regulatory bodies in ATAs

Most sports and activities have a national governing body. For example, the British Mountaineering Council (BMC) is the representative body that exists to protect the freedoms and promote the interests of climbers, hill walkers and mountaineers, including ski mountaineers. Governing bodies set safety standards and this is very important, bearing in mind that we have just been looking at risk assessment. Indeed, the BMC's website even has the following statement on its homepage (www.thebmc.co.uk):

The BMC recognises that climbing, hill walking and mountaineering are activities with a danger of personal injury or death. Participants in these activities should be aware of and accept these risks and be responsible for their own actions and involvement.

Information about participation in an adventure activity will be available from various providers.

Assessment guidance

This unit requires your group to consider at least three possible activities and to produce evidence of your research in the form of a feasibility study. You should be able to provide details of your own suggestions about all the above issues as well as providing full details of the group's final decision. You should be able to offer advantages and disadvantages for each of the activities considered.

Research, analysis and planning are very important for each possible activity if you are to gain the higher mark bands for Assessment Objective 3. It is on the basis of this study that you will select your chosen activity.

Mark band 3 for Assessment Objective 3 is quite specific: each individual should 'undertake comprehensive research from a broad range of sources when assessing the feasibility of your selected activity, and you produce a detailed analysis of the benefits of the activity to individuals, the group and other participants in the chosen activity'. Furthermore, to meet the requirements for mark band 3, your research must be relevant and you must use your findings to inform the running of the activity, including your participation at all stages of the event.

However, you should always check and validate this information with the national governing body of your chosen activity, where appropriate. Many groups will choose to go canoeing as an activity and the case study for this section relates to this. Whatever activity you choose, you will need to find out:

* the national governing body involved
* its safety standards and codes of practice
* how it promotes the activity you have chosen
* the proficiency and leadership awards available.

CASE STUDY

The British Canoe Union (BCU)

The BCU is the governing body for the sport and recreation of canoeing in the UK. It represents the interests of canoeists at local, national and international level, and is a member of the International Canoe Federation. The BCU sets a variety of safety standards and its training and qualification standards emphasise these. Staff supervision ratios are clearly indicated and their coaches and instructors are expected to follow the BCU's code of conduct, reproduced below:

On the river bank, beach or lakeside:
Obtain permission to use restricted water
Avoid overcrowding one site
Park cars sensibly and pay parking fees
Keep the peace – reduce noise
Do not upset others
Pick up litter, close gates, take care with fires, avoid damage to land and crops
Obey instructions such as National Trust rules, local by-laws and camping/caravan regulations.

On the water:
Avoid banks from which anglers are fishing
Avoid anglers' tackle, do not loiter in fishing pools, cause little disturbance
Comply with fishermen's requests, alert them to your approach

Be careful not to touch anglers' lines
Give way to larger boats that are less manoeuvrable
Keep clear of rowing craft and organised events.

General:
Avoid damaging banks and shoreline vegetation
Avoid areas important to wildlife
Whenever possible come ashore only at recognised sites
Do not trespass on private banks/moorings
Avoid pollution
Obey general rules of navigation
Show due regard to beginners
Know signs of underwater swimmers/divers
Keep well clear of wading fishermen.

In 'sheltered water', the person leading the activity would be expected to be at least of BCU level 2 coach standard. The instructor should ensure that participants have a knowledge and practical experience of placid water canoeing. There are additional requirements to be followed in this context, including:

* buoyancy aids must be worn by participants at all times

* the instructor must work with a maximum of eight boats

* the instructor must carry basic repair equipment

* leaders should carry a first aid kit, tow and throw lines, map and compass, spare paddles and equipment to make a hot drink

leaders to make sure group members stay within signalling distance and monitor the group for signs of exposure and so on.

BCU Coaching UK is designed to ensure that coaches and participants are fully and properly prepared to take part in the sport and that coaches are qualified to instruct participants in all aspects of technique, safety and understanding. Tests and qualifications are structured to take account of the type of craft being used and the type of canoeing environment. The BCU Coaching UK coach education and training programmes are available at a geographically balanced network of centres. Details of availability are promoted nationally and regionally via a range of both in-house and external publications, a regional and local coaching organiser network, and an extensive network of clubs and paddle-sport organisations.

The BCU, as the governing body, has an established range of discipline committees to help promote and inform on aspects of associated specialisms. It also promote a large network of competitive events, offers you the chance to take part in 'taster events' and, perhaps, even the real chance to represent your country.

* **What does the BCU's code of conduct suggest about its values and attitudes as an organisation?**

* **How does the BCU promote and encourage participation in the sport?**

* **What are the main proficiency and leadership awards made available by the BCU?**

Regulatory bodies influencing ATA provision and participation

Regardless of the adventure activity being planned, day or residential visits involving young people still in full-time school education are subject to additional controls. The Department of Education and Skills (DfES) produces a good practice guide, *Health and Safety of Pupils on Educational Visits*, and supplements provide the main source of guidance on competence in connection with adventure activities and for educational visits.

Another body with an important role in relation to educational trips is the Health and Safety Executive. In this regard, the Executive emphasises the following ten points (see www.hse.gov.uk/schooltrips/tenquestions.htm):

1   What are the main objectives of the visit?

2   What is 'Plan B' if the main objectives can't be achieved?

3   What could go wrong? Does the risk assessment cover:

* the main activity

* 'Plan B'

* travel arrangements

* emergency procedures

* staff numbers, gender and skill mixes

* generic and site-specific hazards and risks (including for 'Plan B')

* variable hazards (including environmental and participants' personal abilities and the 'cut-off' points).

4   What information will be provided for parents?

5   What consents will be sought?

6   What opportunities will parents have to ask questions (including any arrangements for a parents' meeting)?

7   What assurances are there of the leader(s)' competencies?

8   What are the communication arrangements?

CLIMBING	WATER SPORTS	TREKKING	CAVING
Rock climbing	Canoeing	Hill walking	Caving
Abseiling	Kayaking	Mountaineering	Pot-holing
Ice climbing	Dragon boating	Fell running	Mine exploration
Gorge walking	Wave skiing	Orienteering	
Ghyll scrambling	White-water rafting	Pony trekking	
Sea-level traversing	Improvised rafting	Off-road cycling	
	Sailing	Off-piste skiing	
	Sail-boarding		
	Windsurfing		

TABLE 13.9. *Activities for which the AALA can help you identify a suitable provider*

Source: www.aala.org

9 What are the arrangements for supervision, both during activities and 'free time' – is there a code of conduct?

10 What are the arrangements for monitoring and reviewing the visit?

The Adventure Activities Licensing Authority (AALA) inspects activity centres and other activity providers on behalf of the DfES. If the Authority is satisfied that the provider complies with nationally accepted standards of good practice, it issues a licence. If your planned activities involve any of those shown in Table 13.9, the AALA can help you identify a suitable provider.

The Activity Centres (Young Persons' Safety) Act 1995 aims to give assurance that good safety management practice is being followed. This guarantees that providers have been inspected and that they can demonstrate compliance with all appropriate health and safety legislation. This Adventure Activities Licensing Regulation, operated by the AALA:

* applies to anyone who provides, in return for payment, adventure activities to young people under the age of 18

* is aimed at those who sell adventure activities to schools and the public

* does not cover activities offered by voluntary associations to their members, schools to their pupils or young people accompanied by their parents or guardians.

Finally, all maintained schools in England will have to comply with the policy of their local education authority. Schools are expected to have educational visits coordinators and it is their initial responsibility to make sure that the authority's agreed policy for the organisation and arrangement of educational visits is being followed.

For your purposes, the designated person in charge of school visits will have to agree with the overall aim(s) of the trip, approve the risk assessment, consider the emergency arrangements, ensure that all staff are properly qualified, monitor contractors and undertake an evaluation of the exercise. These responsibilities will have a direct bearing on your chosen activity if you are currently a student in a maintained school.

Effective planning of and participation in your chosen ATA

You may like to consider the type of planning that is expected to be undertaken by a local authority youth worker who is organising an adventure activity trip. Local authority employees will have to show that they have given proper consideration to all the factors and issues shown in Table 13.10. This is a very important framework for any activity trip because, if done properly, it will satisfy the requirements highlighted in the Health and Safety Executive's ten-point guide (presented in the previous section).

PLANNING	DETAILED PROPOSALS
Contact venue (provider) and make sure that it is suitable for the trip	Risk assessment and hazard control measures Emergency procedures and home contacts
Decide on transport	Transport arrangements
Decide on group leader/supervisor	Staffing details – qualifications and experience
Decide on budget and funding arrangements	Costs
Undertake a risk assessment	Insurance arrangements
Undertake an exploratory visit, if required	Contingency plans for bad weather, etc.

TABLE 13.10. *Issues to be covered in planning and proposals for an adventure activity trip*

Your final selection of an activity also needs to consider the legal requirements, such as:

* all health, safety and security arrangements

* consumer protection legislation

* industry codes of practice and how these can affect the planning of your activity.

Individual providers such as activity centres will frequently emphasise to potential customers the ways in which they meet prescribed standards and codes of conduct. Such undertakings are usually made to provide evidence of the safeguards that are now required by most customers in the youth groups market.

Finally, you should make sure that your final report (for Assessment Objective 4) covers in appropriate explanatory detail the points itemised in the adventure activity checklist shown in Figure 13.15. You may find such a checklist of use in reaching your final decision about which adventure activity your group eventually undertakes.

✓ Requirements of the ATA (equipment, transport, etc.)

✓ Reasons for doing the ATA (benefits for participants, etc.)

✓ Objectives for your ATA

✓ How the ATA can be evaluated in terms of the objectives

✓ Resources needed (physical, including equipment, human)

✓ Date, times and duration

✓ Features of the group (numbers, fitness, level of skill, etc.)

✓ Provider location and facilities offered

✓ Range and choice of ATAs available

✓ Booking arrangements

✓ Transport requirements and arrangements

✓ Costs, value for money, payment terms and conditions

✓ Full risk assessment

✓ Safety equipment needed

✓ Accident and first aid procedures

✓ Instructor support available and safety equipment supplied

✓ How the group will function during the activity

✓ How you will monitor each other's performance and participation

FIGURE 13.15. *Adventure activity checklist*

Assessment guidance

Make sure that you have established procedures that minimise the risk of any hazard occurring and that you have put in place measures that can minimise the damage should a hazard occur, such as:

* accident and first aid procedures

* principles of group safety (e.g. how to recognise personal difficulties such as hypothermia and low motivation)

* the range of safety equipment to be taken

* teamwork and methods of communication.

Evaluation of your chosen ATA

All details of your trip should be evaluated by each member of the group, using an evaluation sheet such as the one shown in Table 13.11.

Further evidence for evaluation purposes can come from witness statements supplied by any or all of the following:

* the instructor or activity provider
* your tutor, if you are taking part in a field study residential trip
* the teacher or lecturer accompanying your adventure trip
* your peers taking part in the activity.

The precise form that a witness statement may take can vary from centre to centre but the format

	RATING: 1 = THE WORST; 5 = THE BEST
Locations used	
Duration of journey	
Ease of travel	
Scenic beauty	
Activities offered	
Activity conditions	
Meeting expectations	
Instructor	
Local knowledge	
Professionalism	
Friendliness	
Safety	
Availability	
Fun	
Provider	
Availability	
Professionalism	
Promptness	
Overall knowledge	
Specific knowledge	
Degree of preparation	
Overall customer service	

TABLE 13.11. *Adventure tourism activity evaluation*

indicated in Figure 13.16 will help you generate evidence for Assessment Objective 4.

In order to produce a good evaluation of your chosen ATA, it is important that your report:

✳ comments on your own contribution to the activity and highlights the role that you played within the group

✳ appraises the group's performance during the activity and comments about such matters as group behaviour and learning

✳ makes reference to your teacher's assessment of your role in the planning of the group's chosen activity

✳ considers what the activity provider/instructor has said about your development of skills and your interaction with others

✳ examines the relationship between the group's objectives and the actual outcomes

✳ assesses the benefits that both you and the group as a whole gained from participation, such as personal development, increased fitness or the achievement of a proficiency award

✳ comments on the effectiveness of planning and the extent to which plans were actually adhered to, especially in relation to unforeseen circumstances

✳ makes appropriate recommendations and suggestions for future adventure activities

✳ summarises what you have learnt about the importance of thorough planning.

Finally, remember that it is important when you start planning your ATA to think about your evaluation, so that you can gather feedback from varied sources at different times.

In order to clarify what is expected, we can now look at an evaluation produced by a student after participating in a group adventure activity in the Lake District (Figure 13.17). What follows is an example of the kind of report you should produce.

A student's account of ghyll scrambling in the Lake District

My contribution

My contribution to this activity was that I helped the rest of the group to plan it and to produce a risk assessment on the ghyll site. Once we started the activity we made our way along the ghyll in single file. I was the last one of the students in our group in the line. However, behind me was our teacher. Throughout the scramble I gave encouragement to people in front of me by telling them how well they were doing and warning our teacher behind me if there were any rocks under the water that he should be aware of.

I followed the safety instructions that the instructor had given us at the start of the scramble. We were told to walk as low to the water as possible, to avoid slipping on rocks, and to keep looking under the water to check if there were any rocks coming up. If any of the people around me were not walking low or didn't look for the

---

ADVENTURE TOURISM WITNESS STATEMENT

Name of candidate: ....

Adventure activity: ....

Name of provider: ....

Date of activity: .... Group size: ....

Individual's contribution to the group activity:

....

....

Demonstration of listening skills:

....

....

Interaction with others:

....

....

Skills development:

....

....

Initiative shown/problem solving:

....

....

....

Signed: .... Date: ....

Name and job title: ....

FIGURE 13.16. *Pro forma for an ATA witness statement*

rocks then I told them to. Although I did give some verbal encouragement to other people in the group who were around me, I didn't give as much as I could have done. This was because I was concentrating on the rocks in the water and my own performance.

Overall I feel my contribution was successful in that I achieved what I had set out to in this ATA.

Performance of the group

The overall performance of the group was very good. Throughout the scramble everyone stayed close together and nobody tried to go off ahead of everyone else. There was lots of verbal encouragement from everybody in our group and there was also verbal help from people when someone wasn't very confident when walking over the rocks under water or walking under overhanging branches. There wasn't one who led the group really but individual support was given by all ten students in the group to help everyone get through the scramble.

All the members of the group followed the safety instructions that were given at the start by the instructor. However, when we did the final jump there is a tree above it with branches hanging over the ghyll and we were told not grab hold of the branch as we jumped off the rock. Nonetheless, one member of our group did grab hold of the branch as they jumped, but the instructor pushed their hand off the branch. Everyone in the group enjoyed taking part in the ghyll scramble and would take part in this ATA again. There wasn't one member of our group who didn't enjoy this activity and wouldn't try it again. The group's performance was successful: overall, we achieved what we had set out to.

ATA provider's assessment

Our instructor for the ghyll scramble said the following about our group.

> *All-round excellent team effort. Everyone achieved all of the challenges that they faced. One of the best groups that we have had because of the verbal encouragement that was given by the members of the group.*

FIGURE 13.17. *Ghyll scrambling in the Lake District*

This is relevant to our group's performance because it shows that we all took part in the ATA and we all did our best on the day. This comment also shows that our planning was successful as well because we had no problems during the scramble.

Teacher's comments and assessment

Our teacher said he was very impressed by the team performance and how well our objectives were met. The objectives that we set ourselves as a group for the ATA were met, as we all aimed to complete the scramble and have a go at all the slides and jumps that we came across. We encouraged team-building with physical and verbal encouragement for each other. Overall the whole group met the set objectives well.

Benefits gained from doing the ATA

There were many benefits that as a group we gained from doing this adventure tourism activity:

* completed the scramble with very few problems
* team-building by encouraging each other
* improved communication skills
* basis to start our unit coursework
* enjoyment
* fitness and health
* improved confidence

How well were plans stuck to?

We stuck to the plan that the instructors had agreed with us. We did, however, finish the scramble 50 metres short; this was because of the cold waters due to some overnight rain in the Lake District. The group would have liked to have carried on the extra 50 metres.

Final evaluation

The group activity that we undertook was very successful. All the planning we did before we had a go at the activity paid off, as everyone in the group enjoyed the day and took part in all jumps and slides. However, it was disappointing that we could not finish the whole of the scramble (with the extra 50 metres). The event was a very good one for us to do, as none of the group had ever taken part in an ATA like this before, so none of us really knew what to expect from the activity, apart from seeing pictures from the previous year's group and also from our teacher telling us about it.

The instructors who took us on the scramble were very competent; they were always there to help if you needed them. One of them would go at the front of the group and direct them where to go and the other stayed at the back of the group to help the rest. At the start they told us about all the safety measures that we should take; they warned us of the dangers (e.g. the sharp and slippery rocks in the water, the overhanging branches). They were also trained in first aid, which makes you feel more confident undertaking an ATA like this. They were always giving us instructions along the way as well, so we knew what was coming up; they stayed along the bank so they could have a good overview of the group.

There was nothing really that anyone would have changed about the scramble. However, the place where we got out of the ghyll was not safe enough to do so, as our teacher hit his leg against a tree root and had to have treatment on it. We were only 50 metres away from the end of the ghyll and we only stopped early because the water was very cold; however, we would have been better carrying on the extra 50 metres and all getting out safely.

Recommendations

For anybody who is going to take part in this ATA it would be better doing it for the first time in warmer weather, as the water then wouldn't be as cold as it was when we took part. This wasn't a problem for the group as we quickly got used to the temperature but we couldn't finish off the ghyll scramble because the water was too cold. Before getting out of the ghyll, if you haven't got to the end, you would need to be careful and check that you can get out there because our teacher ended up needing medical attention after hitting his leg on a tree root.

1   Identify six types of adventure tourism activity in each of the following categories and provide details of a UK destination where each type is found:

 * land-based

 * water-based

 * air-based.

2   People who participate in adventure tourism activities can be classified into various categories or market segments. Describe the characteristics of each type of group.

3   Describe the main effects of the development of adventure tourism activities and give examples of destinations where they have occurred.

4   What are the main benefits of taking part in adventure tourism activities?

5   Explain why the Lake District is a good location for adventure tourism activities.

6   With reference to Figure 13.10, explain why this site is at risk from footpath erosion. How might this problem be managed?

7   With reference to Figure 13.13, explain the appeal of wadi-bashing. What hazards are associated with this adventure tourism activity? How can the risks associated with these hazards be reduced?

8   Using Figure 13.17 as a guide, propose and justify a code of conduct for ghyll scrambling.

9   Apply the content of the Health and Safety Executive's ten points to an activity trip of your choice.

10 Evaluate your chosen trip using Figure 13.16 and Table 13.11 as a guide.

References and further reading

Books, journals, magazines

Blackman, H., Rowe, A. and Smith, J. (2005) *GCE AS Level Single Award. Travel and Tourism*. Chapter 3. Oxford: Heinemann Educational.

Blackman, H., Rowe, A., Smith, J. and Stewart, S. (2005) *GCE AS Level Double Award. Travel and Tourism*. Oxford: Heinemann Educational.

Department for Education and Science (1998) *Health and Safety of Pupils on Educational Visits*. Available at www.teachernet.gov.uk/wholeschool/healthandsafety/visits/

Websites

www.lake-district.gov.uk
www.lakedistrictoutdoors.co.uk
www.cumbria.gov.uk
www.rookinhouse.co.uk
www.activity-centre.com
www.keswickclimbingwall.co.uk
www.field-studies-council.org/blencathra/
www.nettoursdubai.com
www.jebelali-international.com
www.dubailand.ae
www.dubaitourism.ae
www.skidxb.com
www.dubaikiteclub.com
www.kitepeople.net
www.hse.gov.uk

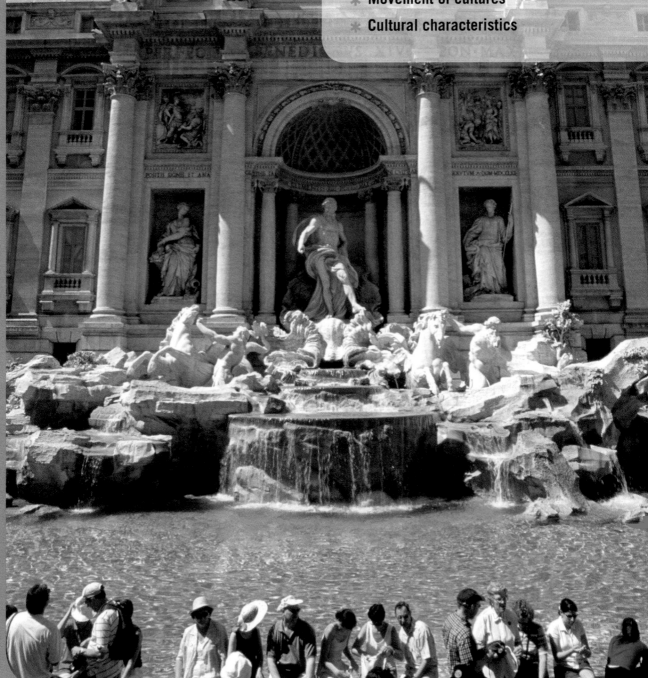

Cultural tourism

This unit covers the following sections:

* Travel motivators
* Movement of cultures
* Cultural characteristics

This unit explores the exciting and dynamic role of culture within tourism. Culture is important to tourism and is the reason why many tourists are drawn to visit people and places. Every country attaches cultural importance to places, buildings and artefacts which give meaning to that country's heritage and achievements.

Global statistics from 2002 compiled by the World Tourist Organization (WTO) showed that tourism in the niche areas was growing faster than traditional (mass) tourism. In fact, cultural tourism, ecotourism (unit 12) and adventure tourism (unit 13) showed trends which would indicate continued growth for the next few years – more growth than any other forms of tourism.

This unit gives you the opportunity to study tourist behaviour and shows that cultural characteristics affect the experience for both the visitor and the host. You will learn about the variety of reasons why tourists search for new experiences. In particular you will investigate:

* travel motivators and the movement of cultures

* cultural characteristics through religion, traditions and customs

* the issues of culture and heritage

* how tourism can influence lifestyles.

You will learn what is meant by culture and how culture is at the heart of tourist motivation. You will come to appreciate the significance of cultural backgrounds and see that visitors demonstrate a variety of complex motivations that affect their choice of destination.

How you will be assessed

For your assessment you will need to produce evidence of an investigation which examines the reasons for cultural tourism in two diverse international destinations. Your evidence should include:

* the results of an investigation into the reasons for the travel experience and evidence of the movement of cultures at your two chosen diverse international destinations, including internal and external features and motivational appeal (Assessment Objective 1)

- an explanation and comparison of how religion, traditions and customs have helped define the culture at your two chosen diverse destinations (Assessment Objective 2)

- relevant research and analysis informing your assessment of the importance of cultural heritage at your two chosen destinations (Assessment Objective 3)

- an evaluation of tourism's cultural impacts on traditional ways of life at your two chosen destinations (Assessment Objective 4).

Assessment is explained in more detail at relevant points later in this unit.

Travel motivators

As you can imagine, there are many reasons why people wish to travel (see Figure 14.1). Naturally, motivations vary from person to person. The reasons for making a 'travel and tourism' trip are often summarised by the following distinct categories:

- leisure

- business

- visiting friends and relatives.

These categories can of course be refined, to give categories such as the following:

- **Educational trips**. These can be for all levels and types of learner. Popular educational trips include those for studying languages, history, geography, art and, of course, travel and tourism.

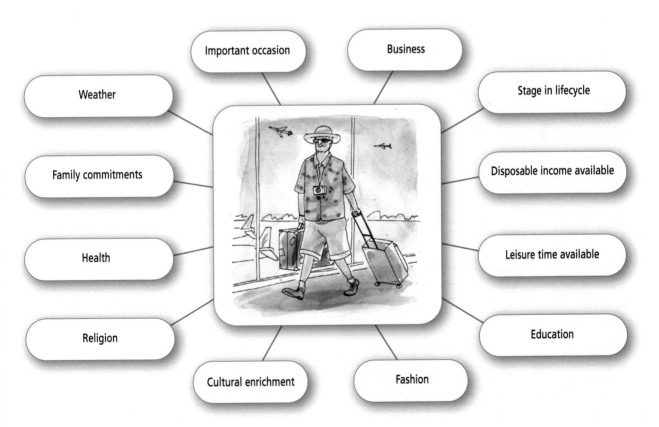

FIGURE 14.1. *Some motivations for travel*

* **Holidays and excursions**. These can be shorter and longer breaks to a variety of destinations and resorts.

* **Attending an event**. There are numerous cultural and sporting events regionally (e.g. the Cumberland Wrestling Competition held in Cumbria each year, see Figure 14.2; the Sani Festival of Music, Dance and Visual Arts in Halkidiki, Greece; Mardi Gras in Rio de Janeiro, Brazil, and elsewhere; the Notting Hill Carnival in London), nationally (e.g. the Last Night of the Proms in the Albert Hall, London; the Edinburgh Festival) and internationally (e.g. the Olympic Games).

* **Religious pilgrimages**. Popular destinations include Lourdes, Jerusalem, Mecca, Amritsar and Knock.

* **Attending conferences, meetings and exhibitions**. Harrogate, Brussels, Paris and Brighton have made the hosting of such conferences an important part of their local economies.

* **Staying with friends and family**.

FIGURE 14.2. *Cumberland wrestling is a good example of a regional sporting event*

CASE STUDY
Pilgrimage to Knock

Ireland's National Marian Shrine is located in Knock, a town in Mayo on the west coast of Ireland. On 21 August 1879, 15 people reported seeing St Mary, St Joseph and St John the Evangelist at Knock parish church. Since that time, Knock has become an internationally recognised Marian shrine (Marian means 'of or relating to or venerating the Virgin Mary'). In 1979, Pope John Paul II made the pilgrimage to Knock, to commemorate the centenary of the visitation. This served to increase the popularity of the shrine. Then, in June 1993, Mother Teresa of Calcutta visited Knock. Now one and a half million pilgrims visit the shrine annually.

* **Visit the web pages of some other famous pilgrimage sites. Find out why they are so important to different cultures.**

* **For two of your examples, describe the reasons why these pilgrimage sites are so important for the visitor.**

* **Assess the importance that these pilgrimage sites have on their destinations. Try to find annual visitor numbers.**

Personal preferences for travel

Naturally, our decisions regarding the trips we make are largely influenced by our personal preferences. A sightseeing tour of historic monuments may attract some people, while for others this would be the least desirable choice. What might make a visit to Venice more appealing than visiting Las Vegas, or indeed staying at home and watching a travel programme? Personal preferences along with our own needs and wants help us to form a picture of travel motivation. At the same time, you should remember that any tourism experience is not one which can be easily standardised: every individual will have a unique experience at any particular destination.

FIGURE 14.3 *The souvenir trade builds on people's wish to take home a bit of the local culture*

Many people travel to experience culture, while others travel for different reasons but may become interested in that culture. Essentially, the people, places and objects attached to each destination help visitors to gain a greater understanding of that culture. In many instances, elements of culture are brought back by travellers to enrich their everyday lives at home, as in Figure 14.3. The souvenir trade is huge and well established in most popular tourist destinations.

Theory into practice

Conduct a short survey of your classmates. Find out who brought back souvenirs from their last holiday.

Features of a destination

Our choices to visit certain destinations are influenced by a variety of factors. Two key ones will be the amount of time we have to spare and the amount of money we can afford. Policy makers and marketing teams will also affect our decision making. They will try to entice us with exciting advertisements and destination brochures to visit particular destinations. There will, though, be many factors relating to the destination itself, other than personal choice or clever marketing, that will sway our choice of destination. Some of these are considered here.

Climate

The climate is a very important factor influencing a decision to visit a destination. Depending upon the type of trip, we may require hot sunshine, wild winds or deep snow. Most of us would choose hot sunshine for a relaxing beach holiday. This may lead us to travel overseas, where sunshine is virtually guaranteed. Blustery or windy conditions may be required for windsurfing in Croyde Bay in Devon or land yachting on the Pembrokeshire coast. Similarly, snow is essential for a ski holiday.

Attractions and festivals

Visitor attractions generally make up one of the most important factors in deciding to go to a particular destination. Many people travel to well known landmarks; these attractions are categorised as either 'natural', such as Niagara Falls and the Grand Canyon, or purpose-built, such as the Taj Mahal, the Parthenon, the Pyramids and the Coliseum. Other attractions include festivals and traditional events, which can provide colourful spectacles that entice us to visit (e.g. the carnivals in Rio and Notting Hill).

Seasonality

Some tourists enjoy visiting destinations during 'off-peak' times, when the region is less busy. This has the advantage of making access easier to attractions and making it possible to walk along a quiet beach, for example. There is a downside to this, as many visitor attractions and amenities such as toilets and car parks close during the off-peak times (in the UK, for example, they may close completely for winter or have a winter opening policy with reduced opening times). Some tourist destinations are making an effort to extend the season and to encourage more visitors to attend during the quieter periods. This often leads to the provision of 'wet weather' attractions, creating an all-year-round experience for the visitors.

Key term

Seasonality describes whether an attraction or amenity is open all year round or only at particular times of the year.

Accommodation types

There is, of course, a wide variety of types of accommodation, from self-catering to serviced. Accommodation standards will differ depending on where we go and how much we are prepared to pay. In the UK we have classification and grading schemes that allow us to benefit from hotel inspections. We can often, therefore, make a considered choice based on the facilities provided and the level of service we can expect to receive. While some destinations will offer a wide range of accommodation, others may offer a very narrow range (perhaps a single expensive hotel, or a basic lodge) – or none!

Restaurants, cafés and bars

Once at a destination, visits to local bars, restaurants and cafés – trying out local foods

Seasonality affects some resorts more than others!

and delicacies – are frequently an integral part of enjoying the local culture. Food is readily linked to many famous areas, such as snails and frogs' legs in France, and haggis and whisky in Scotland.

Transport to and around the destination

Choosing a destination is often linked to how far away it is and how easy it is to reach. (This of course is also linked to the cost of a trip.) The importance of distance is often influenced by the number of people travelling and their ages. Small children are likely to become bored and tired if they are made to wait for long hours in airports with flight delays. Generally, the waiting areas in stations and airports are not the most comfortable. Nevertheless, we can also experience delays while travelling by road (driving cars or taking buses or coaches).

Most of us just wish to get to our destinations as quickly as possible. However, some groups of tourists take great interest in and enjoy the mode of transport they take: indeed, the transport they have chosen is a very important part of their trip. They may not be bothered or restricted by time factors. Examples of the trips taken include cruise holidays and travelling on the Orient Express or other scenic rail routes.

In order to indulge fully in the delights of a new destination, some visitors will find it essential to experience the local transport. Naturally some destinations are far busier than others: compare the roads of Shanghai to those of Jersey! Local transport is often the cheapest form of travel and gives a visitor chance to sample at first hand the lifestyle of the hosts. These modes of transport vary according to the destination. They may not be familiar to our British roads and consequently provide an interesting link to the local culture as well as providing an essential service. Consider the *tuk-tuks* in Thailand – a motorised bicycle with passenger seats at the back; a trip in one may seem fun to the visitor but is a serious business for the driver. Everyone will have an image of the busy throng of rickshaws in China; however, there are also the more sophisticated forms of travel, such as the bullet train in Japan. Transport mechanisms have been adapted to each destination, such as the snow mobile in Greenland, the *jeepneys* in the Philippines and the gondola in Italy.

Destination security

Many of us would not necessarily wish to visit war zones or areas where our safety and security cannot be guaranteed. The Foreign and Commonwealth Office has a detailed website that can easily be accessed to assess the dangers of visiting any country in the world. Travel advice is given by country on issues such as:

* climatic issues and natural disasters, such as typhoons, tsunamis, hurricanes and tornados

* terrorism, for example in Indonesia (Bali) and Iraq

* health concerns, such as SARS (severe acute respiratory syndrome, an outbreak of which severely affected travel and tourism in 2003) and (more recently) bird flu.

It has launched a campaign entitled 'Know before you go' that gives detailed information on local laws and customs in each country. This is linked to insurance and health information sites. See www.fco.gov.uk/travel.

Exchange rates

Exchange rates have a big influence on whether we get good value for money when we travel abroad. Political issues around the globe will often influence the exchange rate. If we do not get a good rate of exchange, our trip will become more expensive, as we cannot buy as much for our money. We may therefore decide to visit a destination with a favourable exchange rate, where goods can be purchased much more cheaply – this often creates the impression of having had a really good time.

Needs and wants of the individual

During our lives we have differing *needs* according to our circumstances; these needs, in turn, make us *want* something. Traveller and tourist motivation can often be viewed as a need or a want – essentially, tourists take a holiday in order that it will satisfy various needs or wants.

During the late 1940s in the USA, Abraham Maslow developed his 'hierarchy of needs' model in order to understand human motivation.

Maslow's model proposed that certain lower needs must be satisfied before higher needs can be satisfied, as shown in Figure 14.4.

The model could be applied to travel and tourism in the following way:

* physiological needs – relaxation, gain relief away from stresses and strains of day-to-day living

* safety needs – health, recreation, staying healthy and active on holiday

* belonging needs – family closeness, companionship, social interaction, tracing roots or family trees

* esteem needs – prestige and status (achieved by travelling to the 'right' locations)

CASE STUDY
Travel advice

The following is cultural advice provided by the Foreign and Commonwealth Office for visiting foreign countries.

Top tips

1. Get a good guidebook. This will tell you about the country you are visiting. Find out about local laws, customs and culture.

2. Take a phrase book and try speaking the local language.

3. Respect local customs and dress codes. Think about what you wear and how you fit in. Ask your tour operator or guide if you are unsure.

4. Be discreet about your views on cultural differences and behave and dress appropriately, particularly when visiting religious sites, markets and rural communities.

5. Particular care should be taken not to offend Islamic codes of dress and behaviour with regard to sexual relations, alcohol and drugs.

6. Always ask an individual's permission before you take a photograph and respect their reply. In some cultures you should not attempt to photograph women.

7. Don't haggle too aggressively. In most countries where haggling is the norm, it is done with good humour and not for too long. Although prices are usually inflated for tourists, it's also important to remember that the discount you are haggling over could be a few pence for you but a significant means of income for a seller.

8. It is always best to err on the side of caution. Behaviour that would be regarded as innocuous elsewhere can lead to serious trouble.

* Choose two diverse international destinations. Briefly compare these two destinations in terms of customs, language, dress codes, alcohol, photography and haggling.

* Create a poster which shows how religions, traditions and customs have helped to define the culture of two destinations. Use as many photographs, signs and symbols as possible to help create a clear comparison of your two destinations.

* Draw up a list of 'top tips' which could be incorporated on a website for potential travellers to your two destinations. The information should be detailed and help the reader to understand how religions, traditions and customs are important for defining that particular culture.

FIGURE 14.4. *Maslow's hierarchy of needs*

✳ self-actualisation needs – cultural or educational aspects of a holiday, such as learning a new language or trying a new hobby while away.

Different types of holiday might fulfil different types of need. For instance, people who enjoy taking holidays to 'exotic' or unusual destinations may thereby be meeting some esteem and self-actualisation needs, although the more demanding aspects of the travel involved may not meet a physiological need for relaxation, say. Esteem needs might be specifically targeted by a visit to a fashionable resort or by being the first to visit an up-and-coming destination. A package holiday is likely primarily to meet physiological and safety needs, as it will be to a 'safe' destination (free from terror alerts) and the traveller will be looked after in getting to the destination and while there, so making the break more relaxing. What sort of trip do you think might meet 'belonging needs'?

Theory into practice

With a partner, draw up a list of all your personal needs and wants for a holiday trip to France. Are you a sunlust or wanderlust traveller?

Key terms

A sunlust tourist is one who searches for the sun.

A wanderlust tourist is one who wishes to explore and experience different cultures and places.

CASE STUDY
Responsible Travel

The Responsible Travel company offers a large number of different activity-styled holidays. Visit its website, www.responsibletravel.com, and locate the 'Cultural holidays' section. Make a study of the trips on offer.

✳ **Make a list of all the cultural holidays available. Provide a brief description of the reasons why travellers would choose each.**

✳ **Describe in detail how motivational theory can be applied to two examples.**

✳ **Find out what campaigns Responsible Travel is involved with. Provide a comprehensive assessment of the travel motivation for visiting two of their travel destinations. Detail how this is affected by the culture which is represented in the different countries advertised.**

✳ **Conduct research into other companies that run cultural and educational tours. Make a list of the ones you find and share them with the rest of your class.**

✳ **Choose a holiday which best suits you.**

Many tourists are becoming very demanding; their levels of expectations are high. (Everyone now expects good customer service; we like to have en suite facilities and to feel as if we have made a good choice at a good price.) Some tourists take the satisfaction of basic needs (food and comfortable accommodation) for granted. They automatically move onwards to the higher levels, craving social needs and contact with other people that ultimately lead to self-actualisation through the seeking out of creative activities. Tourism needs have changed and the motivation for higher things has led to the rebirth of a new travel culture, one that incorporates ecotourism and adventure tourism, as well as cultural tourism.

Movement of cultures

Cultures travel as well as people. The movement of culture can be demonstrated by the migration of objects as well as people. As people travel around the globe they collect objects or souvenirs as mementos of their visit and they may also leave objects.

Cultures move in time as well as in place. Many attractions will offer activities such as re-enactments of famous battles (e.g. from the American Civil War, or in Britain from the War of the Roses). In some instances you can be transported back in time – good examples are the Jorvik Viking centre in York and the Beamish North of England Open Air Museum.

There are many examples of cultures expanding into different countries or destinations. If you have visited popular mainland European resorts for a holiday, how many times did you come across an 'English bar' or 'English restaurant' or see signs advertising 'British food available'?

In many places, a British tourist can feel not too far from home!

The following case study is a review by a holidaymaker who has visited Spain; the British influences here are obvious. The way some destinations have become anglicised appears to draw both positive and negative comments from the reviewer. Nevertheless, for many visitors to overseas destinations, the security and familiarity of finding similar products and services to those from home can make a visit seem more secure and less daunting – remember Maslow?

Reinvention of culture

Culture becomes reinvented as resorts and destinations use replicas of famous cultural sites to help entice visitors. Las Vegas is famous for its replica of Venice's Grand Canal. Luxor has been recreated in Las Vegas, where a pyramid is home to over 2,000 hotel rooms with 236 spa suites. One of the rooms in the Luxor Hotel, aptly Egyptian themed, is known as the Royal Chambers. It is a lavish suite which is decorated in the style of the Egyptian royalty bedchambers in homage to Queen Nefertiti, who is believed to have been pampered and spoiled all her life. Here guests are enticed to a sumptuous package of extras: total indulgence is the order of the day! Room service is, naturally, available 24 hours a day, as is the use of a valet and other staff to answer your every need. The suite has impressive views of Las Vegas. The Egyptian theme is carried through to other products and services. Souvenirs are available following a Cleopatra theme – body lotions, bathing products and perfume bottles. More conventional objects are also available – including the obligatory T-shirt and baseball cap (there is

CASE STUDY

Review of Hotel Roja Verde, Lloret de Mar, Spain, made by a British holidaymaker

Imagine that the Hotel Roja Verde is now owned by a local Spanish family (they have renamed the hotel La Casa Roja Verde). The family are keen to demonstrate the importance of their Spanish culture.

✳ **Rewrite the review, making as many changes as possible.**

✳ **Compare the two reviews and explain why some people would prefer to stay at the Spanish-owned hotel rather than the one owned by the English family.**

✳ **Research Spain as a destination. Draw up as many examples as possible to demonstrate the influence of other cultures.**

Good points
✓ Excellent food and a wide variety of English food is available.
✓ The hotel proprietor is from England and is happy to serve English food and drink.
✓ Each evening there is a schedule of entertainment, from English pub quiz to karaoke.
✓ There is also live TV in the bar which shows English and Scottish premiership football games, cricket and rugby. You can also keep up with all the British soaps – *EastEnders*, *Coronation Street* and *Emmerdale* are all shown each day.
✓ The fact that English food, drink and TV programmes are available is advertised on a large board as you enter the hotel.

Bad points
✗ No escape from England.

even a selection available for children entitled 'Tiny Tuts').

In Las Vegas, other hotel rooms can be hired with themes, ranging from Bedouin tents to a Caribbean island (see Figure 14.5). Tourism here is big business and Las Vegas proudly promotes facilities for weddings, meetings, shows and, of course, its casinos.

and explorers have been bringing back new tastes from all over the world. In 1585 Sir Francis Drake returned from the West Indies. He is credited with introducing the potato and tobacco to Britain. Many other British ships travelling to and from the spice routes, and later India, brought exciting tastes and unusual flavours to us. Today, it is virtually impossible to walk along a British high

Activity

In the UK today there are many hotels, shops, restaurants and bars that have contributed to the reinvention of culture. With a partner, research the web to find information on the products and services of one of the following:

* Past Times (shops)

* Sports (Irish bars)

* hotels situated in theme parks.

Food and cooking techniques

Food and cooking techniques have, for some time, travelled around the globe. For years, travellers

Activity

What would you say was Britain's favourite food? Love or hate it, it now appears that curry is top of the food league for Britons. Today, there are more than 8,000 curry restaurants in Britain, and they are visited by 2 million people each week. Marks & Spencer claims to sell 18 tonnes of chicken tikka masala weekly.

Conduct a survey of your classmates to find out their favourite food and ask them to guess what Britain's favourite dish is. You may have a few surprise results from your class survey. Do people still enjoy roast beef and Yorkshire pudding? What *is* jam roly-poly?

FIGURE 14.5 *The Luxor Hotel in Las Vegas*

street and not be dazzled by the sights, sounds and smells of restaurants and bars from overseas destinations. Many of the larger towns and cities have well established Chinatowns, but you will also be able to enjoy Italian, Japanese, American, Indian and French restaurants, to name but a few.

There are always many opportunities for tourists to sample the delights of a culture before they visit the real thing. The following case study shows the extent to which culture really does travel.

The arts

There are numerous touring companies and exhibitions that present music, opera, art, theatre and dance, for example. These bring a taste of the culture to different regions. For example, at the time of writing Britain had recently been exposed to an array of east European culture by hosting the Moscow City Ballet, the Russian State Ballet of Siberia, the Chisinau National Ballet, the Ukrainian National Opera and the Latvian

---

CASE STUDY

Beijing – changing tastes in food

The following is an article written by an American living and working in China. It is an interesting insight into the changing face of food and restaurants. Twenty years ago it would have been unheard of to have a McDonald's restaurant in China. As you will read, McDonald's is not the only western restaurant to stake a claim in the east.

FAST FOOD IN BEIJING

The first thing you need to know about fast food in China is that it's an upscale event, a fashionable way to spend the evening, and, depending where you go, a good deal more expensive than 'real' restaurants – quite different in this regard from fast food in America, where it was invented for the express purpose of being casual, convenient, and cheap. McDonald's is the oldest and most widely established west-ern fast-food franchise in China and you will see Beijing families by the score eating exotic hamburgers and taking photographs of each other in front of that red-headed clown, Ronald. The second most popular franchise in Beijing is KFC. Pizza Hut has seven locations in Beijing, and this is the most upscale of all the local fast food outlets. It is far beyond the budget of most Chinese families. Fast food outlets seem to be opening as quickly as you can blink in Beijing. If you feel like listening to country music, you can have BBQ ribs and rotisserie chicken at one of the several Kenny Rogers about town. Dunkin' Do-nuts has four locations at the mo-ment, but there are plans for several more. There are also two Subway franchises where you can have a 6 inch or 12 inch sub, on wheat or white, just like you would at home.

Source: www.expatsinchina.com

* With a partner, try to find examples of other foreign foods which have been adapted to become an accepted part of British culture. Can you think of British dishes which have become popular in at least two other countries?

* Do the cultures that move enhance the travel experience? Explain your answer using examples from two international destinations.

* Are there any negative aspects to the movement of culture? What might be the implications for the host country?

FIGURE 14.6 *The English National Opera performing at Glastonbury*

National Ballet. These companies do not just limit themselves to London and the larger cities – audiences outside the larger cities are able to enjoy seeing international performers. At the same time, British companies tour both Britain and overseas destinations, for example the English National Opera (Figure 14.6).

Other aspects of the arts include poets, playwrights, staged performances and books (written and illustrated). A visit to the English Lake District allows visitors to enjoy an area which has become a major inspiration for sculptors, authors and painters. One author who lived, wrote and painted in the Lakes was Beatrix Potter (1866–1943). She is famous for her stories of Peter Rabbit, Jeremy Fisher, Mrs Tiggy-Winkle and many others. She wrote her now classic children's stories nearly 100 years ago, and yet they still remain as popular today as ever. The Lakeland towns where she lived now have popular visitor attractions depicting important influences in her life. Should you visit any of these attractions, you will probably find yourself standing next to or near to a Japanese

visitor. There are an astonishing number of Japanese visitors to this region, who come to see where Beatrix Potter lived and worked. The reason why they are so interested may surprise you: in Japan, the books of Beatrix Potter are used to help students learn English. Many of these students in turn save up and visit the Lake District and visit the land which was the inspiration for Beatrix (see Figure 14.7).

Activity

When you look around your own town or city you will come across a vast array of other cultural influences. There have been many architectural styles which have influenced different designers in Britain; these include Romanesque, French gothic, Greek, Venetian and many more.

With a partner, visit the web pages covering your own town or city. Assess the kind of images which are used to attract visitors. Which of these relate to cultural issues?

Souvenirs and objects of culture

There are so many cultural influences all around us that we often take them for granted. The shops in the UK are full of clothing, material and jewellery from many different countries; these will have their own specific cultural contexts. Some of these objects are similar to those you would buy while on holiday in these countries, such as Guatemalan worry dolls, African wooden carved tables and animals, Chinese masks, stone Buddhas and Russian dolls. However, there are many other objects which have become an integral part of British daily life; in fact, they are so common that we forget that they have important connections to other places, such as Italian shoes, Egyptian cotton, Irish linen, Italian marble, Asian tea, Japanese sushi and wines from all over the world.

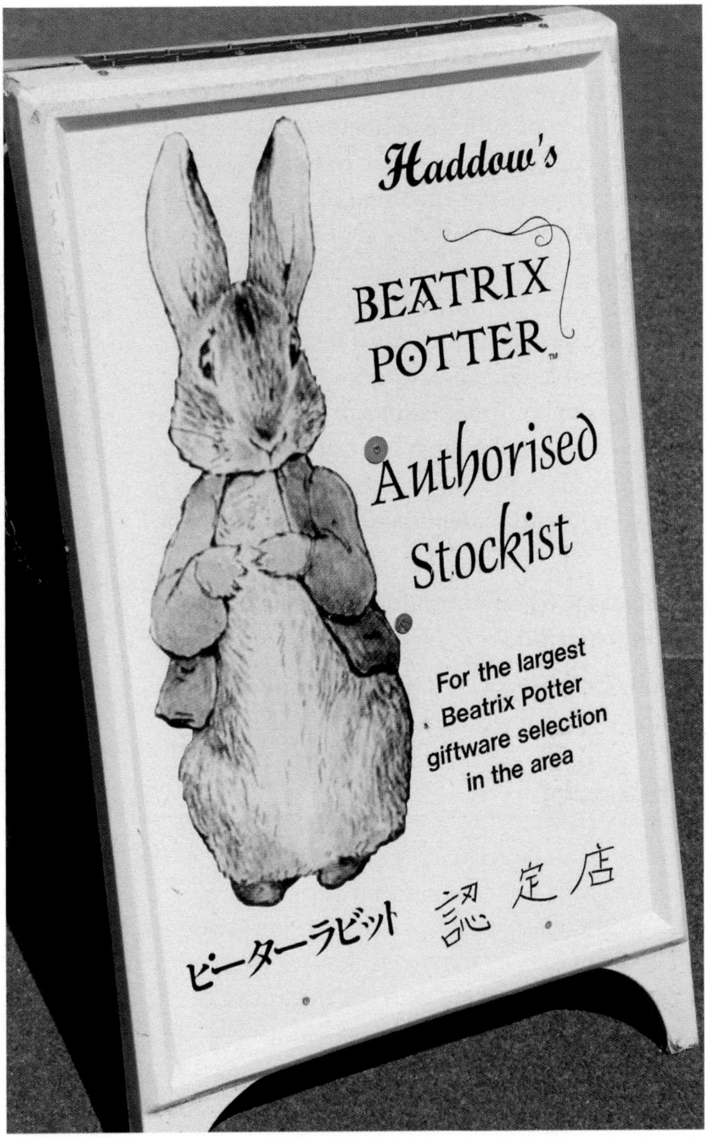

FIGURE 14.7 *This advert board shows the souvenir industry that has built around Beatrix Potter*

Cultural characteristics

As you can imagine, different peoples have a variety of different cultural characteristics. As culture is made up of all the things which we have learnt and the attitudes we share with the people from our same background, there will be common characteristics within any particular region. Understanding and appreciating another person's cultural differences will help us to gain greater empathy with each other and avoid

Think it over...

You may sleep on a futon (Japanese bed), you may eat a French croissant for breakfast, you may wear a pair of Spanish espadrilles and you may listen to reggae music on your radio. What cultural influences affect you?

Assessment guidance

To complete Assessment Objective 1, you must investigate the reasons for the travel experience and show evidence of the movement of cultures at your two chosen diverse international destinations, including internal and external features and motivational appeal. The destinations should be contrasting and may be at different stages of tourism development. To gain higher marks, you will need to give a detailed and logical account of cultural movements.

insulting or upsetting others. This is especially relevant within the travel and tourism industry, and when interacting with tourists generally.

The 'rules' of cultural etiquette while visiting a country are sometimes given to tourists by travel agents; this information can also be gleaned from travel guides. It is very easy to offend host countries by behaving in culturally inappropriate ways.

Clearly, as tourists, we must be aware of the different languages, attitudes, values and behaviour of host populations. If we do not make ourselves aware, then this can cause frustration and stress for both visitors and hosts.

The most easily identifiable aspects of culture are:

* language (communication) – verbal and non-verbal methods

* religion – practices, important festivals, days and places of worship.

Communication

As individuals, we communicate in both verbal and non-verbal ways. We give out signals through our body language, the pitch and tone of our voice, and the use of pauses and silences.

We often take our cultural background for granted and assume that everyone will express themselves in the same way as us. In fact, there are large differences between regions in a country, let alone between countries. In Britain we have a range of regional accents and colloquialisms. There are many different 'affectionate' names that we use: in different parts of the country you may be called 'love', 'lovey', 'dear', 'chuck', 'me duck', 'hen', 'pal' or 'mate'. Sometimes how you are spoken to will depend on how old you are and what sex you are.

There are many subtle differences that affect our ability to understand people from different

COUNTRY	MAIN RELIGIONS	MAIN LANGUAGES
Spain	Christian – Roman Catholic	Spanish, Catalan, Basque, Galician
Australia		
Belgium		
France		
India		
Republic of Ireland		
Japan		
Egypt		
Iceland		
Brazil		

TABLE 14.1. *Languages and religions as prominent aspects of national culture*

Personal hygiene

Dress

Behaviour

Personality

Culture

Attitude

FIGURE 14.8. *Things that can affect how our messages are given and received*

cultures (Figure 14.8). In China, for example, young people tend not to display close male-to-female contact in public – they do not hold hands, do not kiss and so on.

Culture determines how close we stand to another person while talking, whether or not we avoid eye contact and how much we willingly show emotions.

Think it over...

In India it is insulting to show the sole of your shoe to someone.

In Morocco the thumbs-up sign is an obscenity.

In Hong Kong it is thought to be good luck to touch a person on the head who has red hair.

Find out five more examples from different countries.

the majority of religious buildings are open to the public. For many travellers, religious buildings such as St Paul's Cathedral, Whitby Abbey and Canterbury Cathedral are the main reason for their visit. This can also be the case in other countries (e.g. the Duomo in Florence, the Vatican in Rome, the temple at Amritsar and the Taj Mahal in India).

It is important to remember that there are always certain standards that apply to visits to religious buildings and as visitors it is imperative to pay attention to these rules in order not to offend the host country. In Morocco, all mosques, except for the Grand Mosque in Casablanca and the Old Tin Mal Mosque, are closed to non-Muslims. When visiting mosques, shoes must be removed. Visitors must never insist on being admitted to a mosque and must not try to see inside it by peeping through the door. Behaviour such as this is considered sacrilegious.

Religion

The different types of religions around the world provide an interesting insight into the people and their lives. It is very important that all tourists are respectful of these different beliefs and how they are practised. In the UK,

Theory into practice

Conduct research into two religious festivals or celebrations and create a list of accepted behaviour at each of these.

In every country around the world, important festivals or significant days are celebrated. Some religions also call for a curbing of behaviour or impose certain rules over particular periods. The following is a selection of different days celebrated:

* Yuan Tan
* Al-Hijra
* Palm Sunday
* Easter Day
* Ascension
* Trinity Sunday
* Corpus Christi
* Baisakhi
* Rosh Hashana
* Eid al-Fitr
* Diwali
* Remembrance Sunday.

Other important cultural characteristics

There are also other important cultural characteristics which need to be considered:

* social customs (greetings, ceremonies)
* food and drink (permitted and excluded food/ drinks, fasting)
* dress (covering the body in religious buildings, costumes, formal dress for functions – such as the wearing of a black tie and evening suit in the UK)
* arts and crafts
* music and dance
* superstitions.

Social customs

Social customs include how we greet people. In the UK it is customary to shake hands. In many countries people greet each other by kissing on both sides of the face.

Social customs will also determine:

* how people use eye contact
* people's postures
* their aromas
* how assertive people are
* the gestures they use
* whether they smoke, and if so where and when
* the noises they make (e.g. whether or not it is polite to burp or slurp food)
* what is eaten, when and how.

Activity

Design a leaflet which could be used by travel agents to give to prospective visitors to the UK entitled 'What are Britain's social customs?' You should include information on:

* punctuality
* accepting invitations
* appropriate dress
* greetings and introductions
* dining etiquette.

Think it over...

Imagine you are advising a visitor to come to your town or city. What accepted customs and standards of behaviour would you ask them to abide by?

Table 14.2 gives examples of acceptable behaviour from around the world. Try to find similar information for two other countries, such that you could fill in two more rows on the table.

CASE STUDY

Social customs in Thailand and Japan

Thailand

Putting on a smile

In Thailand, almost everything in life involves a smile, even blunders and mishaps. Westerners often mistake this for being laughed at. For example, if a waitress forgets an order and laughs, she is not showing contempt, just making the best of a bad situation. If you complain, do so as gracefully as you can.

Dressing for the occasion

Cleanliness and neatness are important. In tropical Thailand, never put off showering or doing your laundry. Most Thais keep themselves scrupulously clean and dress respectably. T-shirts, sandals and knee-length shorts are suitable for most occasions, but visits to palaces, government offices and some temples usually require something more formal. Nudity is forbidden, and topless bathing can offend, even though it is tolerated on some tourist beaches.

Showing respect

The head is high and the feet are low, both physically and spiritually. Never touch anyone's head and avoid gesturing (especially towards a Buddha image), moving things and touching people with your feet, even if you do see people doing it to their friends. Before entering a temple or a person's home, you should remove your shoes.

Good table manners

Shared meals are served in separate dishes with serving spoons. If someone invites you to eat, use the serving spoons to put food on your plate, not your personal spoon. Take small amounts of all the food instead of keeping one kind for yourself. Using a toothpick after the meal is acceptable if you cover your mouth with one hand.

Japan

Japanese people tend to be somewhat more relaxed about the behaviour of foreigners than they would be about the behaviour of other natives. Below is selection of social customs.

Signs of affection

It is considered a shameful act to kiss in public. Hugging is considered impolite, as is any other sort of physical contact. You will not see young boys and girls holding hands unless they are really in love.

Chewing, smoking, eating

Chewing gum in front of someone is not accepted, but smoking in front of someone is. It is also considered rude to be the only person eating something.

Visiting

When entering a Japanese house or restaurant you should always take off your shoes (you will most often be supplied with slippers). Also (and of all of the points, this may seem the strangest to foreigners) it is considered rude to look into the kitchen of a house that you are visiting.

Legal proceedings

(This point may be the most pleasant to foreigners.) Civil court proceedings are avoided, as Japanese people emphasise relationships based on trust rather than contracts. Therefore most problems of a civil nature are resolved through third-party mediation. The only time you go to court is when there is no hope of maintaining a relationship between two parties. It is interesting to note that the number of lawyers in Japan is one-fiftieth of that in the USA.

* **Design *two* newspaper advertisements to encourage holidaymakers to visit Thailand and Japan.**

* **Using both the information presented above and your own research, create a newspaper article intended for the British press which gives details on the traditions and social customs in both Thailand and Japan.**

COUNTRY	POINTS OF BEHAVIOUR
Australia	Australians generally do not like to talk business during leisure hours and avoid making class distinctions. When riding alone in a taxi, it is considered polite to sit in the front seat with the driver
China	When dealing with business associates in China, remember that the Chinese people place a great deal of emphasis on trust and mutual connections. Always use a person's proper title and expect a slight bow or handshake upon an introduction
England	In general, the English are a reserved people for whom manners are important. A handshake is the most common form of greeting. When visiting, guests often bring a gift such as chocolate or flowers. Sending a thank-you note is also considered appropriate
France	The French are very proud of their culture, heritage and way of life. As such, they expect visitors to have some knowledge and appreciation of the French culture; therefore, foreign visitors should not bring wine as a gift unless they are certain it is of high quality
Hong Kong	When doing business in Hong Kong, showing respect is paramount. You must show respect to gain respect. Trustworthiness is a point of pride; therefore, it is common to apologise when asking for a written contract, even though written contracts are recognised as standard practice. Also, avoid using the colours blue and white in presentation material, as they represent death and mourning
Russia	Russians shake hands firmly when they meet. While it is frequently done, pointing with the index finger is considered impolite. Russians enjoy giving and receiving gifts. Guests usually bring the host a gift of flowers, food or vodka, although this is not expected

TABLE 14.2. *Examples of acceptable behaviour from around the world*

Food and drink

Food and drink are important not only for sustenance but also for supporting traditions, and reinforcing cultural traits and sometimes important ceremonies. There are also great cultural variations in what is eaten, when and how. In the UK it is uncommon for people to eat horse meat and in China chicken feet are a delicacy. In many countries, especially Islamic ones, alcohol is not permitted. Religion often underpins cultural variations in diet, and many religions stipulate times of fasting, for example.

One of the most famous food-related ceremonies is the tea ceremony that takes place in Japan. The ceremony, or *sado*, is a ritual way of preparing and drinking tea. The custom has been strongly influenced by Zen Buddhism. Today, many Japanese who are interested in their own culture take tea ceremony lessons with a teacher.

Tea ceremonies are held in traditional Japanese rooms in cultural community centres, special tea rooms or private houses. The ceremony itself consists of many rituals that have to be learned by

> ### Key terms
>
> Buddhism originated in India in the 6th century BCE. It consists of the teachings of the Buddha, Gautama Siddhartha. Buddhism found its way to Japan via China and Korea. It was then welcomed by the ruling nobles as Japan's new state religion. There were a few initial conflicts with Shinto, Japan's native religion, but the two were soon able to coexist harmoniously and even complemented each other.
>
> Zen is the Japanese term for a particular school of Buddhism.

heart. Almost each hand movement is prescribed. Basically, the tea is first prepared by the host and then drunk by the guests. The tea used is a 'green tea' which tastes quite bitter and is made of powdered tea leaves.

Britain has its own food-related culture (think of the Christmas dinner). A famous food ceremony takes place annually on 25 January in Scotland, known as the Burns supper. Burns suppers have been part of Scottish culture for over 200 years. It is celebrated to commemorate the life of Robbie Burns, a Scottish poet famous for writing 'Auld Lang Syne' in 1788 and much more. The haggis ritual began a few years after the death of Burns in 1796. It began as a tribute to his memory by his friends. Today, the Burns supper is a very important part of life in Scotland and the format for the evening has practically remained unchanged since the 18th century. Burns wrote 'The Address to the Haggis', now a world-renowned poem that is recited at every Burns supper.

Activity

For the following list of well-known foods and drinks, try to give the country of origin. The first one is done for you.

* Sushi – Japan
* Whisky
* Sake
* Earl Grey tea
* Pizza
* Sauerkraut
* Fajitas
* Guinness

Can you think of other foods and drinks to add to this list?

Arts and crafts

Arts and crafts often provide the tangible link to a destination's past. This is demonstrated by local designers and artists using skills which have been passed down to them from previous generations. They also will use local resources to create their work; for example, coconut fibres are used extensively in the Cook Islands – they are a rich resource which can be turned into furniture and clothing. Similarly, the Maori in New Zealand perpetuate their important carving and weaving skills; the young are taught by the older members of the community to create beautiful wooden artefacts. This not only provides good souvenirs for tourists but also helps to retain vital links to traditions and techniques from old.

Music and dance

There are many famous cultural music and dance festivals. Tourists are drawn to different parts of

CASE STUDY
The WOMAD festival

In the UK a music festival growing in popularity is WOMAD (the initials stand for World of Music, Arts and Dance). The central aim of the WOMAD festival is to celebrate many forms of music, arts and dance, drawn from countries and cultures all over the world. The festivals try to bring together an international audience and through music and the arts, to encourage a deeper insight into other cultures. As an organisation, WOMAD now works on many levels at festivals, performance events, through recorded releases and through educational projects. The result is to entertain, inform, and to create awareness of the worth and potential of a multicultural society. The festivals are weekend-long, family-oriented, active and diverse musical events, featuring simultaneous performances on two or three stages, including participatory workshops and special events for children, as well as music and dance sessions hosted by many of the visiting artists.

Visit the WOMAD website (www.womad.org) and find out:

* **How long has the WOMAD festival been running?**
* **What kind of people attend WOMAD?**
* **What else does WOMAD do?**

the world to see particular styles of music and dance and visit festivals.

Examples of regional musical culture include:

* blues in the Mississippi delta in the USA

* the Glastonbury Festival in England

* Mozart's Salzburg in Austria

* *dangdut* in Indonesia

* the Maori *haka* in New Zealand

* reggae in Jamaica.

Music is certainly one aspect of culture which transfers with ease around the globe. Consider the rhythmic chanting of Buddhist monks or the melodic sound of pan pipes in Peru. The sounds and meanings are as diverse as their origin. Music is often incorporated into other cultures and sometimes changed or adapted in some way in order to give it a new meaning or to make it more relevant to that particular culture. The origins of different types of music are often entwined in cultural practices and beliefs. Music is often present at important ceremonies and significant occasions such as weddings, funerals and bar mitzvahs.

Superstitions

In the UK we have many superstitions. Think of the number 13 and Friday the 13th, which is considered an unlucky day in much of western Europe, North America and Australia. Many people avoid travelling and avoid signing contracts on this day. In some tall buildings the floors skip from 12 to 14. The origins of this superstition appear to be based in Christian culture: many Christians have long believed that Friday was unlucky because it was the day of the week when Jesus was crucified; the number 13 was believed to bring bad luck because there were 13 people at the Last Supper. The origins of other superstitions may be difficult to trace.

Each country has its own superstitions:

* A crane is lucky in Japan (it is believed to live to 1,000 years!).

* If your nose itches it is thought to be good luck in Holland.

CASE STUDY

Origins of reggae music

Reggae music originated in Jamaica during the 1950s and 1960s, at the time of the country's independence from British rule. It was the Jamaican people's own music at a time of political campaigning and civil disorder. It developed around the same time that rhythm and blues was popular in America and Britain. It is thought that its influences were from Africa and associations with the slave revolts.

Reggae became popular and then commercial through the international recognition of music artists such as Ken Boothe, Toots Hibbert and perhaps most famously by Bob Marley. It has influenced musicians such as Ms Dynamite, Roni Size, So Solid Crew, Massive Attack, Madness and the Clash. Jamaican musicians in Britain have also been influenced by reggae music.

It is not clear where the name 'reggae' comes from. Various suggestions as to the literal meaning of the term give further clues as to the origins of the music itself: from the words in the song 'Do the regga' by Toots and the Maytals; from the Bantu-speaking Regga tribe on Lake Tanganyika; a corruption of the term 'streggae', which is Kingston street slang for prostitute; from Spanish origins meaning the king's music; from the description of the beat itself.

* **Think of *two* other major musical influences on British culture.**

* **Provide evidence of research from a variety of sources showing the musical influences at two destinations.**

* **Analyse the importance of music to your two destinations.**

Can good luck cancel out bad luck?

* If you see a chimney sweep it is thought to be good luck in Germany and Switzerland.
* In the UK it is considered bad luck to walk under a ladder.
* It is good luck to find a four-leafed clover in Europe.
* It is lucky to see spiders at night in France.

It is interesting to note that something which may be good luck in the UK may be considered bad luck elsewhere.

Activity

Find out other superstitions for the two destinations you have chosen to study.

The growth of cultural and heritage tourism

During the past decade, tourism has matured and the public have become much more demanding. Tourists are increasingly searching for more rewarding and inspiring trips, and very often culture and heritage fulfil that role. Indeed, such is the interest in cultural and heritage tourism that an abundance of trips and tours have emerged. These include links to poetry, painting, music, cookery and wine, to name but a few. The following is a list (and not a comprehensive one) of tour operators that promote popular 'culture tours' in one specific area, Spain and Portugal:

* ACE Study Tours. These are designed both to educate and to entertain, with expert guides and itineraries. Eight itineraries are offered, including a September trip to High Aragón.
* British Museum Traveller. Three tours are offered: the pilgrims' route to Santiago, Islamic Andalusia, and a new exploration of the Kingdom of Navarre.
* Martin Randall Travel. These tours feature expert lecturers, four-star hotels and small groups; 17 different trips are offered, focusing on history, art and architecture, and some also on gastronomy.
* Arblaster & Clarke. This company runs wine tours, led by an expert, to Rioja and Oporto.
* Holts Tours. These are tours of battlefields, including Peninsular War tours in both Spain and Portugal.
* Cesa. These are essentially for learning a language, with classes and intensive courses for all abilities, in resorts and cities.
* Cox & Kings. This company offers expert-led tours and botany trips to La Gomera, the Algarve, Majorca and the Pyrenees.

Assessment guidance

To achieve Assessment Objective 2, you must provide an explanation and comparison of how religions, traditions and customs have helped define the culture at your two diverse destinations. To obtain higher marks you must provide a detailed explanation and present your work logically and clearly, and relate local culture to your own values and attitudes.

Many tourists now search for the 'authentic', and cultural and heritage tourism cater to this segment of the market. The importance of heritage attractions and their cultural significance on a national and international scale should not be underestimated – and neither should the growth in their popularity.

It should be remembered that this type of tourism can be operated and owned by the public, private or voluntary sectors. Indeed, there are often very good partnerships between the sectors, where they work together for sustainable development. Generally they aim to improve three things:

* the local, regional and national economy
* visitor satisfaction
* quality of life for the local community.

There can be a strong community interest in any development proposals. Local people are often proud of their heritage and enjoy having an input into protecting and promoting it. Today, tourism planners have an understanding that both established and new cultural and heritage sites need to develop in a sustainable way in order to protect and enhance the environment.

Cultural and heritage events which are supported by tourists

There are many cultural and heritage events which are supported and rely heavily on the tourist to ensure their continuation. Consider the battle re-enactments at Bosworth, Worcester and Hastings, for example: these spectacles are enjoyed not only by history enthusiasts but also by local people and overseas tourists. In the USA there is an annual Gettysburg Civil War battle re-enactment, which includes:

* exciting battles each day
* live mortar fire competition
* living history activities tents
* tours of the military camps and a chance to chat to the participants.

Another notable type of cultural event that is used by many towns and cities across the world to attract a wide variety of visitors is the film festival. Some of the largest are those held in Cannes, New York, Berlin and Toronto. Each year these popular film festivals attract film actors, directors, producers and, of course, the media. Cannes held its first film festival in 1946; it is still the most influential of film festivals, where producers launch their new films and try to sell their work to an array of international movie distributors. Each year the famous Palme d'Or or Golden Palm is awarded to the best film.

Think it over...

There are many arts, film and music festivals across the UK each year. Under the different headings of Art, Music and Film, make a list of all the festivals you can think of. Compare your list with those of other class members.

As you may know, the main motivation for many overseas people to visit the UK is our royal family. There are many important visitor attractions associated with the royals and their lifestyles. These include not only the palaces – Buckingham, Kensington and Balmoral – but also the many traditional events associated with the royal family, such as Trooping the Colour in June, when the Queen celebrates her official birthday. The display takes place on Horse Guards Parade in Whitehall, London, and is watched by both other members of the royal family and thousands of tourists each year (see Figure 14.9).

Activity

Research two other countries where there is currently a royal family. What events are held in their country? Do these events attract tourists as well as local people?

FIGURE 14.9 *Trooping the Colour at Horse Guards Parade*

Bizarre events

There are many very unusual and at times eccentric cultural events which attract visitors. Each country will have its own selection. Consider the following examples.

Bog Snorkelling World Championship

This takes place annually on August Bank Holiday Monday in Llanwrtyd Wells, in Powys, mid-Wales. This unusual race involves competitors (wearing snorkels and flippers) making their way through a 60-yard trench filled with muddy water. Conventional swimming strokes are not permitted, which makes the task even more demanding! Competitors come from all over the British Isles and many from Europe, Australia and America.

La Tomatina

On the last Wednesday of August each year an estimated 10,000 people converge on the small Spanish town of Buñol, near Valencia, to take part in a massive tomato food fight! It all started in 1944 when a simple tomato fight began between a group of friends in the town's main square – the Plaza del Pueblo. La Tomatina begins with a week of celebration of the town's patron saint. There are fireworks and street parties.

Oktoberfest

The Oktoberfest (which, strangely, begins in September) is a beer festival in Munich, Germany. The breweries prepare for millions of foreign visitors, mostly French, Italians and Americans. The beer halls fill with gallons of beer and it is estimated that 500,000 sausages and 600,000 chickens are consumed! Outside the beer halls there are fairground rides and attractions.

Wife carrying

This unusual event, held in Finland, has its origins in a local 19th-century practice of wife stealing! To enter the modern championships, a wife is not a necessity – any female over the age of 17 is acceptable. Thousands of spectators attend to see the men carry the women over a 253.5-metre

Religious tourism, pilgrimages

Their faith often leads people to visit sites of great religious importance. Visits to religious sites or pilgrimages account for millions of trips each year. The following are examples of significant sites.

Jerusalem

The two most sacred places in Jerusalem are the Dome of the Rock and the Western Wall. The Dome stands on the legendary site of Muhammad's journey to heaven and is the third holiest place of Islam after Mecca and Medina. The Western Wall is the only remaining part of the original temple of King Solomon, and is the holiest place of pilgrimage and prayer for Jews.

Lourdes

The French town of Lourdes, in the Pyrenees, receives more than 5 million pilgrims every year. It was just a small market town but in the 1850s Bernadette Soubirous (now St Bernadette) saw visions of the Virgin Mary. Spring water from Lourdes is believed by pilgrims to have miraculous healing properties. Today, Lourdes has the second greatest number of hotels in France – 270 establishments. Its geographical position, at the foot of the mountains makes it an ideal starting-point for excursions to the Pyrenees.

Haridwar

Here, the world's largest number of pilgrims converge to dip into the River Ganges. Hindus believe that the river will wash away their sins. Visitor numbers can get dangerously high – up to 10 million. The Kumbh Mela festival is when the river is believed to turn into purifying nectar and allows the faithful to cleanse their souls.

Amritsar

Amritsar, literally 'Pool of Nectar', derives its name from Amrit Sarovar, the holy tank that surrounds the fabulous Golden Temple. The temple complex is surrounded by a maze of narrow lanes, or *katras*, that house one of the busiest markets in India. The *gurudwara*, as Sikh temples are called, is the holiest of Sikh shrines, but it is not just Sikhs who travel to the Golden Temple to pay homage: it is equally revered by Hindus and people of other faiths, who also make the pilgrimage to offer prayers.

The success of cultural and heritage sites

Many tourists go to a particular region specifically to visit a cultural or heritage site. Cultural heritage contributes greatly to the attractiveness of a country or destination to tourists. All countries attach cultural importance to places, buildings and objects which they see as representing an important stage in their history or their country's achievements. When the heritage of a country is demonstrated by beautiful visual imagery and exciting historic stories, the attraction for tourists is even greater.

Stonehenge, for example, is much visited and photographed; it is one of Britain's most enduring symbols. It is thought to have originated between 3000 and 1600 BCE. However, its origin is unclear: some say it was designed as a temple, while others believe it helped mark significant celestial events. The stones themselves are surrounded by more than 300 burial mounds. Today, even though many of the original stones have fallen or been removed, it is still regarded as a site of high historical importance. It was designated a World Heritage Site in 1986.

Theory into practice

Visit the World Heritage website, http://whc.unesco.org, and find out more about what it means to be a World Heritage Site. Draw together a list of all the UK sites.

Many sites of cultural and historic significance have now been redefined and have been given new titles or names. For example, the use of the word 'museum' in the name of an attraction has often been dropped in favour of 'heritage centre'. Many other sites have been redeveloped, such as the Eden Project and Jorvik. Some of these sites are renamed in order to create greater interest in a project. The names often have strong links to a site and this will help educate and publicise a redevelopment.

Activity

In Britain, many visitor attractions are now situated within land that was previously used for industry. Wigan Pier Heritage Centre is situated in two restored 18th-century warehouses. The Leeds–Liverpool Canal passed through the pier area and the warehouses belonged to the British Waterways Board. Visit the websites for the Eden Project and Jorvik. Find out what the sites were used for originally.

Key term

Star UK presents national statistics on tourism, and www.staruk.org.uk is the official website of the UK Research Liaison Group. The group is made up of representatives of the national tourist boards for England, Scotland, Northern Ireland, Wales, Britain and the Department for Culture, Media and Sport.

Activity

With a partner, find out as much as you can about the following important heritage and cultural attractions:

* Westminster Abbey
* The Coliseum
* The Parthenon
* The Leaning Tower of Pisa.

Culture is constantly evolving and as such we have seen that parts of our everyday lives can become reasons why tourists may wish to visit certain places. Many towns and cities have realised that they can use their culture and heritage to attract visitors on city or short breaks. Notable examples are Prague, Paris, Athens and Dublin. Within the UK, some towns and cities similarly rely heavily on their culture and heritage in order to attract visitors, such as Bradford, Chester, York, Durham and Nottingham.

As you can imagine, it is not just buildings that have significance for culture and heritage. Tourists will often visit sites which are linked to famous people. Sometimes it will be the birthplace of a famous person, such as Winston Churchill at Blenheim Palace. Other links can be equally important, such as the place where someone famous once visited, such as Charles II.

In the UK the birthplaces of famous people are marked by plaques displayed on the houses; these sites include the house where Shakespeare was born and lived in Stratford-upon-Avon. In the south of Wales you can find the birthplaces of many famous singers, actors and poets, such as Tom Jones, Anthony Hopkins and Dylan Thomas. In London and other big cities in England you can often see plaques on the wall of buildings stating that a famous person was born there.

Some destinations have become known for the wide range of cultural and heritage attractions they are able to offer. Large capital cities such as London and Paris are obvious examples, but some smaller cities and towns have also been able to meet the desires and expectations of a multitude of visitors, such as Buxton in the Derbyshire Peak

CASE STUDY
Major English visitor attractions

Table 14.4 is taken from the Star UK website (www.staruk.org.uk). It shows the most popular visitor attractions in the UK.

ATTRACTION	LOCATION	2001	2000	% CHANGE
British Airways London Eye	London	3,850,000	3,300,000	16.7
Tower of London	London	2,019,210	2,303,167	−12.3
Eden Project (2)	St Austell	1,700,000	498,000	na
Natural History Museum	London	1,696,176	1,576,048	7.6
Legoland Windsor	Windsor	1,632,000	1,490,000	9.5
Victoria & Albert Museum	London	1,446,344	1,344,113	7.6
Science Museum	London	1,352,649	1,337,432	1.1
Flamingo Land Theme Park & Zoo	Kirby Misperton	1,322,000	1,301,000	1.6
Windermere Lake Cruises	Ambleside	1,241,918	1,172,219	5.9
Canterbury Cathedral	Canterbury	1,151,099	1,263,140	−8.9
Chester Zoo	Chester	1,060,433	1,118,000	−5.1
Kew Gardens	Richmond	989,352	860,340	15.0
Westminster Abbey	London	986,354	1,241,876	−20.6
Royal Academy of Arts	London	910,276	760,800	19.6
London Zoo	London	906,923	930,000	−2.5
Windsor Castle	Windsor	904,164	1,126,508	−19.7
Roman Baths	Bath	864,989	932,566	−7.2
St Paul's Cathedral	London	837,894	937,025	−10.6

TABLE 14.4. *Major English visitor attractions with paid admission*

* Indicate which of the above attractions have cultural and heritage links.

* Visit the Star UK website and assess the visitor attractions which are free to enter.

How many of these sites are linked to culture and heritage?

District with its Georgian architecture and Opera House, and Edinburgh, which has year-round appeal for its architecture and buildings, as well as associations with writers, combined with its summer festival of culture and famous 'fringe' events.

Other cultural activities

There are also many cultural events which are particularly important for sustaining destinations. Consider just two examples:

✱ Llangollen in Denbighshire, Wales, hosts the annual week-long International Musical Eisteddfod. Each day, top artists from around the world compete in a variety of competitions, from folk dance to male choirs, classical soloists and barbershop quartets. In the evenings, professional performers gather together. In the past, the stage has seen famous names such as Placido Domingo, Luciano Pavarotti, Lesley Garrett and Montserrat Caballe.

✱ A famous Passion Play is performed in the Bavarian German town of Oberammergau. The Passion Play is a form of mystery play that depicts the suffering, death and resurrection of Jesus Christ. The play originated in 1634, and today the day-long performances are attended by thousands of visitors.

These cultural activities help to draw attention to destinations by their extensive advertising, marketing and promotional work. They also often help to bring many visitors during the quieter months. Such cultural activities allow the preservation of many traditional and important festivals/celebrations that can be shared with current and future generations. Can you find other examples of cultural activities which help to support destinations?

To complete Assessment Objective 3, you must

How tourism can influence established lifestyles

Culture and tourism are intrinsically linked. Inevitably, tourism will affect most cultures and populations in either a positive or negative way, or often in both ways. In some instances, tourism has forced a host population to adapt to it. Some customs may be lost while new lifestyles and behaviour may be introduced. Some cultural and heritage sites have been lost, and some areas have been redeveloped in order to meet a new and evolving market.

Key terms

The host country or host population is the country or population that is receiving visitors.

Redevelopment/restaging of traditional cultural/heritage sites

The redevelopment or restaging of traditional events is associated with keeping the tourist happy. Many significant historic events are re-enacted to provide a show and to entertain visitors (e.g. the battle re-enactments considered above). At Warwick Castle and Stafford Castle fighting knights joust in colourful re-enactments. The restaging may not always be to true to life and on many occasions is altered specifically for the tourist (for example being shortened to fit in with tourist schedules). Similarly, many types of cultural 'shows' do not necessarily depict real life within the host country.

Industrial heritage sites have long been altered to become more appealing to tourists. Buildings are adapted to give them a new lease of life, and these sites use new marketing and promotional techniques to encourage visitors to attend. One

Assessment guidance

provide relevant research and analysis into the importance of cultural heritage at your two chosen diverse destinations. For higher grades you should carry out a detailed and comprehensive study from as many sources

as possible and show critical analysis while assessing the importance of cultural heritage at your two chosen destinations.

example is Wigan Pier. Situated on the banks of the Leeds–Liverpool Canal, it is a collection of canal-side warehouses and wharves that have been restored and preserved to partly re-create life of the people of Wigan and Lancashire during the 1900s. Today, Wigan Pier is one of the north-west's favourite visitor attractions. You can see what life was like for the Victorians, from schooldays through to work and play. There is also an opportunity to experience life below ground at the coalface, to see how the famous Lancashire 'pit brow lasses' lived and to feel the horrors of the Maypole colliery disaster.

Altering the tourism product

As we have seen, each destination will, in some way, be altered in order to accommodate the needs of certain types of tourist. In some instances tourists create changes by their continuous demands. Consider the Spanish costas during the 1960s. What were once tranquil villages are now large resorts. Employment is now found in the high-rise hotels and the countless restaurants, bars and nightclubs that replaced the traditional fishing and agricultural jobs of old. Many of these catering outlets have been taken over by British people who have seen that there is a market to provide specific 'British' products direct to the tourist trade. Similarly, the bars and nightclubs in resorts such as Ayia Napa in Cyprus have music adapted to the youth clubbing market.

Think it over...

As with many forms of development, tourism can cause its share of problems. Consider the following statement: 'The club scene in Ayia Napa has erupted over the last five years. It has transformed the remote sleepy fishing village into the dance capital of Europe. There are now 17 clubs spread over less than a 2 km^2.'

✳ In small groups discuss this statement.

✳ With a partner, think of other tourism examples where the local products and services have been altered in order to accommodate foreign tourists.

Tourism operators often create images based on the physical appearance of a destination. However, they also help to create a perception of an area by using images of what they think certain visitors or consumers will want. In Thailand, which is visited by 10 million overseas tourists each year, operators will use images of rainforests, islands, beaches as well as the cultural heritage and the way of life of the Thai people. In some instances these images do not always portray an accurate picture of what life is really like. It will give an illusion constructed specifically for the western tourist. In this way, tourists are being misled and the people of Thailand are being misrepresented.

Positive cultural impacts

Travelling brings contact and therefore educational benefits. This will help with understanding between different cultures (which in turn is said to help to reduce world tension).

Tourists produce economic benefits for local people, through the creation of jobs by bringing their money to an area. They may allow the development of new facilities (e.g. in health care) and the upgrading of infrastructure (e.g. for transport), for the benefit of tourists and locals alike. With an increase in tourism the opportunity may arise to develop or redevelop leisure facilities, restaurants, arts and crafts and amenities such as toilets and car parking.

Tourism may also benefit the local people by the introduction of better-quality food and general commodities.

Tourism can strengthen communities by sustaining traditional festivals, customs and traditions, and may even make it possible to introduce new cultural events of various kinds. Tourists may help to preserve local natural resources, encourage the protection of the local heritage, reinvigorate local cultures and help to sustain arts and crafts.

Some tour operators are actively complementing conservation efforts not only by providing direct financial assistance, but also by providing indirect support, such as tourism development aid. An example of this is in the remote mountain destination in the Karakorum region of South Asia. The aid has helped revive local music and traditional activities like sword dancing.

Tourism can also help raise *local* awareness of the culture and heritage of certain sites. This in turn will often give local people a feeling of pride and pleasure as they gain greater involvement, for example in town planning by offering their comments on planning applications and by offering support or showing an interest in sustainable or community development.

Negative cultural impacts

Tourism can cause a site to become changed through the impact of visitors. This can also create a loss of local values and, indeed, local identity. This happens as visitors search for a predetermined vision of an area. Local people can change their religious rituals and festivals in order to fit in with changing tourism tastes. Sacred sites and religious objects may not be respected. Replicas are sold for the benefit of the tourist and may deform or alter completely the meaning of the object.

Tourist sites may lose their originality and become a sanitised and standardised product. There are many hotel and restaurant chains which have infiltrated certain destinations. It is possible to visit Thailand and then move to France but to stay in the same chain of hotel and eat a burger from the same type of restaurant. Local communities may find that they cannot stage their authentic rituals as tourists prefer a 'watered down' version.

As more tourists move around the globe there can be obvious culture clashes between ethnic and religious groups, values and lifestyles, languages and levels of prosperity. Offence may be taken in the host country if there is a lack of understanding on the part of the visitor. There is even an obvious anti-tourist feel to particular destinations. This is likely to be heightened where there is a huge gap between the wealth of visitors and that of the host population.

In some instances, host populations attempt to imitate the behaviour of their visitors. This can be particularly difficult in less well-developed countries such as Indonesia or Brazil.

Tourists can often fail to respect local customs and may insult the moral values of their hosts. It is always important to research local customs and to investigate what behaviour may be acceptable or unacceptable before visiting a country. For

example, it would greatly offend local people in a Muslim country should a tourist be seen drinking large quantities of alcohol. This kind of behaviour could also tempt the younger generation to copy it. There are also very strict dress standards for when Muslim women appear in public. Once again, thoughtless behaviour by tourists could greatly offend the host community should they disregard or be unaware of these standards, and wear very short skirts or indeed sunbathe topless. The same types of culture clashes happen in conservative Christian communities in Polynesia, the Caribbean and the Mediterranean.

There is also a danger that tourists will simply stereotype their hosts, which will serve only to widen the gap between cultures.

> ### CASE STUDY
> ## Kuna blouses
> Tourists sometimes create a demand for certain products and services in a way that conflicts with those products and services available. Traditions, habits and ways of life are lost in consequence. One example is the blouses made and worn by the Kuna women in Colombia and Panama. The blouses have been made for years to a design with important symbolic and spiritual meanings. Today, because of tourism, the designs of these blouses are gradually changing to appease new commercial markets generated by the demands of tourists. The Kuna women are gradually losing their knowledge of the old designs and their significance. These losses will continue and are likely to result in the complete alteration of the product when the younger generation of women come to make their blouses.
>
> * **Do research and find *one* positive effect of tourism for the Kuna people.**
>
> * **Identify *another* negative effect.**

Key term

A stereotype is a simplified, standard image or idea held by someone.

Poorly behaved tourists can also upset their hosts. This may involve anything from simply touching objects that should not be touched, or being loud and obnoxious, through to crime (e.g. well-documented drinking and clubbing behaviour of tourists in the resort of Falaraki in Rhodes). In some instances tourists can damage cultural artefacts, for example by collecting stones from the pyramids in Egypt.

Unfortunately, tourism can also encourage a growth in serious conflicting ethical issues. This is demonstrated by the growth of both sex tourism and the use of child labour for the production of goods to be sold to tourists.

Competition for resources may also irritate local communities. Tourists will require commodities such as fuel and water, and these resources can be channelled away from local communities. Consider the amount of water required to keep a golf course green.

Acceptable behaviour

An understanding of appropriate cultural behaviour is required. This is made more difficult by the fact that in some countries there is not only one language but a large variety of different customs, dialects and forms of etiquette; it is necessary nonetheless. It is important to respect the local customs and the dignity and rights of the local people. You should never take photographs without asking permission to do so. It is also not appropriate to enter someone's living space without invitation. Modest behaviour with dress sense may be required in some destinations. In some communities it is inappropriate for a woman to show her shoulders or even her thighs when swimming. In some Greek Orthodox churches people should not show too much naked skin. In monasteries women have to cover their shoulders and wear long skirts, and men must wear long trousers. In Thailand, it is also unacceptable for swimwear to be worn away from a beach. A man not wearing a shirt or a woman in shorts and skimpy clothing would be frowned upon in restaurants and public areas, and particularly while visiting religious shrines.

Good tourist behaviour – 'the responsible tourist'

Key term

Good tourist behaviour means acting in an appropriate way while visiting other countries.

Being a responsible tourist is, today, high on the agenda for many tourism policy makers. Essentially, anyone who visits another country should be respectful of the traditions, cultures and environment in which they find themselves. There are many organisations that focus their business interests on the principles of responsible tourism. Generally, doing a small amount of research about your intended destination will help you abide by social and cultural customs. Many destination managers try to ensure the protection of their destinations by outlining a code of conduct for tourists. These can cover:

* behaving in an environmentally sensitive way (e.g. not dropping litter)
* appropriate dress
* religious adherence
* traditional ways of life and customs
* issues of gender.

Tourists can make a big difference by supporting only the type of tourism that is not harmful to the environment, recycling where necessary and by not abusing the land and its fruits.

Theory into practice

Design a code of conduct that is appropriate for tourists visiting your two chosen destinations. You should cover issues on the environment, religion, traditions, customs, dress and gender where appropriate.

Good tourist behaviour is closely related to the issue of sustainable tourism. Sustainable tourism seeks to provide people with an exciting and educational holiday that is also of benefit to the people of the host country. This may be in terms of their culture and heritage, as well as their physical environment and economic development.

Activity

Look up the website of the International Council on Monuments and Sites (ICOMOS), www.international.icomos.org, which is an international non-governmental organisation that is dedicated to the conservation of historic monuments and sites. ICOMOS provides a forum for professional dialogue and a vehicle for the collection, evaluation and dissemination of information on conservation principles, techniques and policies.

Assessment guidance

To achieve Assessment Objective 4 you need to provide an evaluation of tourism's cultural impacts on traditional ways of life at your two chosen diverse destinations. To gain a higher grade you should provide a critical and comprehensive evaluation using accurate data to indicate clear cultural impacts on the traditional ways of life in your two chosen destinations.

Knowledge check

1 Give a definition of culture.

2 List five travel motivations.

3 Explain the relevance of Maslow.

4 Explain the terms 'sunlust' and 'wanderlust'.

5 Give three examples of the movement of cultures.

6 Explain the term 'anglicising'.

7 What is meant by a social custom?

8 List four traditional ceremonies held in the UK.

9 Name three sites where cultural/heritage attractions have been redeveloped.

10 Name one cultural event which is held on each of the world's continents.

11 List five positive effects of cultural tourism.

12 List five negative effects of cultural tourism.

References and further reading

Books, journals, magazines

Krippendorf, J. (1991) *The Holiday Makers: Understanding the Impact of and Leisure and Travel.* Oxford: Butterworth Heinemann.

Travel Trade Gazette

The series of guidebooks published by Lonely Planet Publications, Fodor's Travel Publications and Rough Guides

Websites

http://travel.excite.com
www.fodors.com
www.geographia.com
www.lonelyplanet.com
www.odci.gov/cia/publications

General

National tourist boards
Embassies
Regional tourist boards
World Tourism Organization
British Heritage Tours

Marketing in travel and tourism

This unit covers the following sections:

* Marketing of travel and tourism
* The marketing mix
* Market research
* Marketing communications

Introduction

The study of this unit is mandatory for candidates on the double award programme. Marketing of tourism products and services is an essential business activity for all travel and tourism providers within a highly competitive industry. This unit will allow you to investigate the marketing process, to understand its importance within the industry and to recognise how different organisations use a wide range of marketing approaches to raise customer awareness.

Travel and tourism is a customer-driven industry and, as such, tourism providers must reflect the expectations and needs of their customers. The study of this unit will enable you to understand the processes which allow organisations to identify and meet these expectations and needs within the ever-changing tourism environment. Marketing is much more than the obvious advertising and selling of a product or service. Within this unit, you will investigate a range of techniques employed by travel and tourism providers to ensure that the right product gets to the right people at the right place and price, using the right promotion.

How you will be assessed

This unit is externally assessed. Candidates will receive a pre-released case study before the examination. Questions in the examination paper will be based on the case study material and will examine your understanding of the marketing process in relation to particular travel and tourism organisations. Candidates are required to undertake a detailed investigation into the marketing efforts of *at least one* travel or tourism organisation for this unit.

Marketing of travel and tourism

The marketing concept

The Chartered Institute of Marketing defines marketing as:

> *the management function which organises and directs all business activities involved in assessing customer needs and converting customer purchasing power into effective demand for a specific product or service, so as to achieve the profit target or other objective set by the organisation.* *(Holloway and Robinson, 1995, p. 4)*

The travel and tourism industry is customer driven, and marketing therefore focuses on the needs of the customer and involves finding out what the customer wants and expects first, before any attempt is made to provide a product or a service to meet those needs.

Key terms

An organisation is described as being market oriented if it focuses on the needs of its customers. This is different from product orientation, which is when an organisation develops a product and then tries to find a market for it.

Travel and tourism products and services rely on being described to customers, rather than demonstrated, and usually have to be purchased in advance of them being used. The industry is characterised by fierce competition and ever-changing customer needs and expectations. Marketing plays a significant role in attracting the attention of the consumer. It ensures that the right product gets to the right customer at the right place and price, using the right promotion. Whatever travel and tourism product or service is being offered, the basic principles underpinning the marketing concept are the same.

Deciding how to market a specific travel or tourism product or service requires a carefully calculated and coordinated approach. This is known as marketing planning. Marketing planning allows an organisation to make best use of its resources to achieve its goals within the existing marketing environment. The marketing plan establishes how much of a product or service needs to be sold over a given timespan, and at what price, in order to exceed the organisation's operating costs.

Travel and tourism products and services are difficult to separate out – a customer evaluates the contribution made by the staff who deliver the product as much as the product itself (see Figure 15.1). For example, customer service in a restaurant is as important as the food. Similarly, the assistance given by staff during the booking of a holiday through a travel agent is as important as the booking confirmation and so on. Therefore it is essential that all staff involved in the delivery of a product or service within the travel and tourism industry understand the essential role they play. This is why most travel and tourism organisations invest heavily in the training of employees in customer service and marketing techniques.

Getting marketing right is crucial to the success of travel and tourism organisations. The consequences of getting marketing wrong could be disastrous – having the right facilities

FIGURE 15.1. *The customer can evaluate the person who serves them as much as the product*

and a perfect location are important factors for a holiday resort, but if the resort does not market itself correctly then it may not gain the level of occupancy it needs to make a profit. This explains why large-scale tourism providers employ specialist marketing personnel to ensure that the marketing function for the organisation is carried out effectively.

The marketing plan

For a travel and tourism organisation, the marketing plan is used to set both short- and long-term objectives for volume and value of sales. It takes into consideration the nature of competition within the market. A range of marketing tools will be used to analyse the organisation's position within the market. The ultimate purpose of the marketing plan is to enable an organisation to improve its performance, which is particularly important within a fast-changing environment.

Most travel and tourism organisations will produce a marketing plan which spans, on average, three to five years. The plan will include:

* the organisation's mission statement
* a list of its aims and objectives
* a situation analysis/marketing audit
* a proposed marketing strategy (including setting the marketing budget)
* a statement on the organisation's intended marketing mix (which is considered in the next section).

Mission statement

A mission statement is used to communicate the central purpose and objectives of the organisation to its stakeholders. It is also used to guide employees in their role in achieving these objectives.

Key term

A stakeholder is any person or group of people with an interest in the business. It includes the owners, employees, customers, suppliers and the wider community.

Different types of travel and tourism organisation will have very different mission statements. For example, the mission statement for the budget airline easyJet is as follows:

To provide our customers with safe, good value, point-to-point air services. To offer a consistent and reliable product and fares appealing to leisure and business markets on a range of European routes. To achieve this we will develop our people and establish lasting relationships with our suppliers.

The mission statement for a tour operator specialising in Disney holidays, Mouseketrips, is given below:

1 *We want you to have a Disney experience before you even arrive at the parks.* We love our Disney vacations and know how special and unforgettable they can be. We also know how confusing and overwhelming it can be to plan a trip to the Happiest Place on Earth. Our first priority is to make sure the superior service and individualized attention delivered by the friendly Mouseketrips staff has you feeling Disney magic before you even leave.

2 *We believe in a personal approach.* There are no automated prices or reservations on Mouseketrips. All of our pricing and packages are carefully constructed by one of our travel experts to fit your exact needs. Your personal Mouseketrips consultant will help you design your dream Disney vacation.

3 *We want to get you the best price possible.* We have access to all of the current discounts, specials, and deals available. We look at all options to find you the most cost effective solution possible. We will carefully monitor your reservation prior to your arrival, and if a better deal becomes available we will automatically rebook for you and contact you with the good news.

4 *We want you to have the best Disney vacation possible.* We want you to enjoy your vacation more than any vacation you have ever taken. Our staff of travel experts possess

a passion for all things Disney and want nothing more than to help you enjoy your Disney experience as much as they enjoy theirs. We will provide you with all necessary maps, guides, and paperwork.

Mouseketrips – DISNEY DONE RIGHT!'

Think it over...

Study the mission statements for easyJet and Mouseketrips carefully. Identify which stakeholder groups are targeted by each organisation through the wording of their mission statement. Decide which mission statement is most effective and explain why. Make at least *two* recommendations for improving the mission statement you consider the less effective.

Aims and objectives

The organisation's aims and objectives should reflect and make direct reference to the organisation's mission statement. *Aims* tend to be broad general statements of intent, which could be difficult to measure but which are nevertheless important to the organisation. *Objectives* are usually more specific statements of an expected outcome, which are often more precise than an aim and can therefore be used to evaluate performance over a given time frame. Travel and tourism organisations use aims and objectives in the same way as any other form of business: to set performance targets and to review progess against these targets at regular intervals.

'SMART' objectives

Many travel and tourism organisations use 'SMART' criteria in setting their business

CASE STUDY

Royal Forest of Dean Tourism Association

The Forest of Dean Tourism Association has existed for over 25 years, to promote accommodation and attractions in the area.

The *short-term* objectives of the Association are:

❁ to promote and to increase the membership of the Royal Forest of Dean Tourism Association

❁ to increase the funds available to the Royal Forest of Dean Tourism Association.

Its *long-term* objectives include:

❁ to increase the number of tourists who visit the Forest

❁ to ensure that an increase in tourist numbers is also accompanied by an increase in average visitor spend

❁ to ensure tourist information, of every description, is more widely available

❁ to ensure that the Forest, as a tourist destination, is more widely publicised

❁ to improve communication from and between tourist providers and tourists

❁ to become a recognised source of information on the tourism market in the area, for use by members and by the media.

✳ **Give *two* examples of types of travel and tourism organisation that are likely to be members of the Association.**

✳ **Identify at least *three* stakeholder groups for the Royal Forest of Dean Tourism Association.**

✳ **Explain why you think organisations use short-term and long-term objectives.**

✳ **Choose three of the objectives from the above list. Suggest why these have been set for the Association.**

✳ **Summarise the general aim of this Association and evaluate the significance of this aim for its members.**

objectives. Each business objective should meet all of the 'SMART' criteria.

An example of this can be seen in the way in which South Staffordshire Council has set its tourism objectives. Three initial aims were identified – namely, to establish high-quality facilities, to achieve 'best value' and to maximise awareness of tourism opportunities across South Staffordshire.

The next stage was to identify key performance indicators, by starting to apply the 'SMART' criteria. This resulted in the following statements:

* Attract external funding into the area from network partners.

* Specify the percentage of users who feel visitor services are good to excellent.

* Achieve 60 per cent satisfaction rates from tourists.

Once these statements had been analysed, the final tourism objectives could be set:

* Over the next five years, we shall work with tourism partners to develop high-quality leisure and cultural activities.

* By March 2006, we will have increased awareness of South Staffordshire through tourism opportunities by 60 per cent of evaluated feedback.

* By 2006 we will have implemented a district-wide tourism strategy that maximises the district's profile.

CASE STUDY

Leeds City Council's approach to tourism

Leeds City Council plays a central role in the provision of tourism services in the City. The mission is to manage and promote tourism in order to optimise the industry's contribution to the prosperity and quality of life in the district. General aims are:

* to create and sustain additional employment and business opportunities

* to maintain and improve the quality and variety of visitor attractions, amenities and services, for the benefit of both residents and visitors

* to attract visitors with whom the resident population feels comfortable.

Currently Leeds does not publish a tourism strategy. There are, however, three agreed objectives for promoting Leeds:

* to increase the number of visitors to the city

* to develop the city as a tourist destination by investment

* to offer a quality service to visitors and residents.

Study the above information about tourism in Leeds. Imagine that you have recently been appointed Tourism Officer within the Leeds City Council Tourism Division and have been asked to review the goals set.

* **Rewrite the promotional objectives for Leeds to make each one 'SMART'.**

* **Explain the general aims for tourism within Leeds.**

* **Assess the suitability of the Tourism Division's mission.**

These final objectives are much more specific than in their original format; moreover, they are time-framed and realistic. However, only the second of these objectives is measurable in its current form. The Council would need to state a target number of tourism partners in the first objective and introduce a surveying mechanism to allow the success rate of the third objective to be measured in order for these objectives to be truly 'SMART'.

Situation analysis/marketing audit: the internal and external influences on the travel and tourism industry

An important part of the marketing planning process for travel and tourism providers is to conduct an analysis of the business environment in which they currently operate. The process involved in carrying out this analysis is often referred to as a 'situation analysis' or a 'marketing audit'. The results are the same: the organisation is able to identify the positive and negative influences on its business activity. The analysis covers its own internal resource capabilities (budgetary constraints, expertise of staff, experience in the market, etc.) as well as those influences outside its control (government regulation, competitor activities, demographic changes, etc).

Commonly, a SWOT analysis is used by the travel and tourism industry as the first stage of the marketing audit process.

Key term

A SWOT analysis is a marketing tool used in many business contexts. SWOT is an acronym that stands for: Strengths, Weaknesses, Opportunities and Threats. These are assessed in relation to the product, organisation or (in tourism terms) a destination, to assess market position. Strengths and weaknesses are internal factors (i.e. within the control of the organisation) while opportunities and threats are external factors (i.e. beyond the control of the organisation).

CASE STUDY

Destination Lancashire

The following SWOT analysis was conducted to investigate the potential of Lancashire as a tourism destination and to examine the contribution that tourism makes to the county's economy. Lancashire includes a number of closely spaced towns and cities, such as Burnley, Lancaster, Preston, Blackburn and Blackpool.

Strengths
Transport and accessibility

✴ Excellent road communications infrastructure, including the M6, M55, M58, M61 and M65 motorways.

✴ Preston and Lancaster railway stations are important stops on the London–Glasgow electrified West Coast Main Line.

✴ Blackpool Airport provides daily fights to London (Stansted), Dublin and Barcelona (Girona) via low-cost airline Ryanair. Other regular services operate to Belfast and the Isle of Man and there is also charter traffic to European holiday destinations.

Culture and tourism

✴ Blackpool is the most visited resort in the UK and a major conference centre. Tourism in Lancashire is reckoned to support more than 51,000 jobs (8.6 per cent of all local jobs) and to generate £1.75 billion of visitor expenditure – more than half of the total volume of tourism spend across the north-west of England.

✴ Lancashire offers a wealth of attractions, including cultural and built heritage as well as many natural features.

✴ In 2001 the county's bathing water quality results were the best ever, with all

11 Lancashire beaches complying with the European standard.

Weaknesses
Culture and tourism

※ The image of the county's seaside resorts needs updating – they retain the traditional family holiday image of the 1960s and 1970s. In particular, Blackpool has a low-quality, 'cheap and cheerful' image that is unattractive to higher-spending market segments, overseas visitors and the important conference trade.

※ There are few National Trust, English Heritage or other historic properties and gardens open to the public in the area, which would appeal to identified growth market segments.

Opportunities
Transport and accessibility

※ Manchester International Airport is within 45 minutes travelling time of Preston by motorway and is accessible by direct train services from Blackpool and Preston. With two runways it offers scheduled and charter services to a wide range of destinations and operates with low-cost carriers such as BMI Baby and Jet2.com.

※ Leeds/Bradford Airport continues to grow and is easily accessible by road from north-east Lancashire.

Culture and tourism

※ Blackpool is securing investment to transform the main resort area, including casino-based development.

※ An extensive built heritage, much of it based upon Lancashire's industrial past, has considerable potential for economic reuse and tourism benefit.

※ Lancashire offers easy access to three national parks: the Peak District, the Yorkshire Dales and the internationally renowned Lake District.

Threats
Transport and accessibility

※ Blackpool Airport, although recording record passenger numbers, is small and struggles in the shadows of Manchester International and Liverpool airports.

Culture and tourism

※ The area is dependent on Manchester and Liverpool (future European capital of culture) for many social, cultural, business and financial services.

※ There is a lack of foreign visitors to the county.

※ Continued growth in air travel for business and leisure purposes and continued growth of overseas holidays may have a further effect on the long-term decline in the number of overnight stays in Lancashire resorts.

✳ **Choose *one* weakness and *one* opportunity from the above SWOT analysis. State why these are important for tourism in Lancashire.**

✳ **Explain how these could be used to develop tourism to Lancashire.**

✳ **Prepare a five-minute presentation for the Marketing Manager of Lancashire Tourism in which you evaluate ways in which the area could be made more appealing to a wider customer base.**

Source: Adapted from the website: www.lancashire.gov.uk/ environment/lancashireprofile/monitors/swot.asp

SWOT analysis

A SWOT analysis looks at both the internal and the external influences on the market – the internal strengths and weaknesses of an organisation's current operation and the external factors that present opportunities and threats to market proposals for the future. Tourism development relies heavily on the outcomes of such analysis – tour operators may decide not to promote certain destinations if the weaknesses and the threats from a SWOT analysis outweigh the strengths and opportunities.

As the travel and tourism industry is always changing, there are many forces affecting trends in the marketplace that could affect the popularity of specific tourism products and destinations. These forces include the political arena: civil unrest, military coups and acts of international

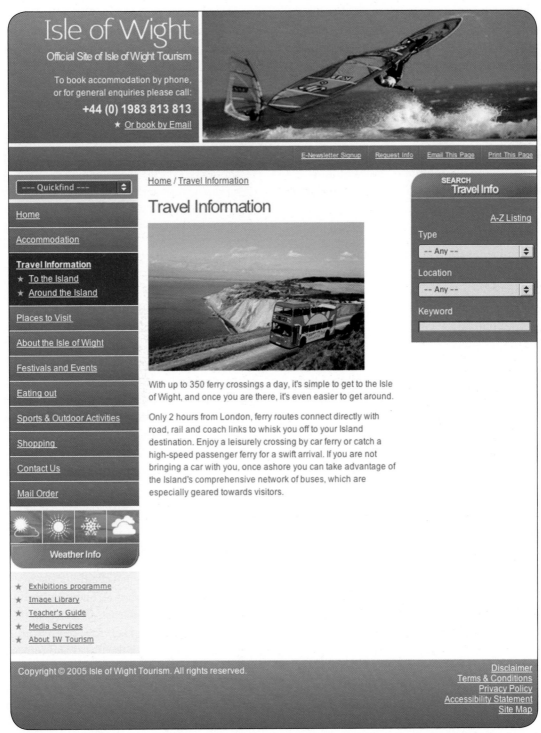

FIGURE 15.2. *An example of a tourism website offering a wide range of tourism services*

Source: www.islandbreaks.co.uk

terrorism are detrimental to tourism development. Economic conditions can have both positive and negative effects on tourism – foreign exchange rate fluctuations, for example, make the dollar, the euro or the pound stronger or weaker, offering better or worse value for money for the tourist. The social and cultural environment is also an important market force for travellers and tourists – how often have you heard friends explain that they enjoyed experiencing a different culture as the main motivation for travelling to their latest holiday destination?

Modern technology also plays a significant role in marketing travel and tourism products – you cannot have escaped noticing that the Internet provides a seemingly unlimited choice of tour operators, travel companies and the like directly to our homes, 24 hours a day.

PEST analysis

A PEST analysis enables an organisation to investigate all of those forces outside its control, to determine how great a threat they pose to the business. Imagine you are the chief executive of an airline company, trying to plan future business immediately after the tragic events of 11 September 2001. The PEST analysis of your company and of the tourism industry at that time would provide essential information about how to market your products and services to a reluctant market. The influences identified through PEST analysis remain outside your control, but this does not mean that their impact on your business cannot be minimised.

Key term

PEST analysis is another marketing tool used to assess the external influences on business, known by its acronym – Political, Economic, Social and Technological.

The travel and tourism industry, like all other forms of business activity, is subjected to laws and regulations imposed by governments and other regulatory bodies to protect customers, suppliers and the environment. Unlike most other external influences, legislation is difficult to

bypass. Compliance is essential for continuation within the marketplace, and travel and tourism providers must take into account the implications of a wide range of laws governing their business activities. You will need to recognise some of the most important pieces of legislation relating to the travel and tourism industry in preparation for the external assessment for this unit and you will have an opportunity to study key details of these later within this chapter.

Think it over...

Discuss with your classmates the likely results of the PEST analysis for an airline company after 11 September 2001. You should try to identify at least one statement under each heading. Once you have listed these, compose a short report to issue to the airline's shareholders about its future. You should make direct reference to the PEST analysis within your report.

Competitor analysis

Another important piece of marketing situation analysis that is carried out by businesses in the travel and tourism industry is known as competitor analysis. As its name suggests, this tool is used by organisations within a competitive market not only to identify who the main business rivals are, but also to estimate the probable extent of competition that each rival organisation poses. Competitors are divided into direct and indirect competition.

Direct competition exists between organisations that offer an identical or similar product, resulting in customers having a choice. Thus, a museum would consider other museums and art galleries in the area (or perhaps nationally or even internationally) to be in direct competition with it.

Indirect competition exists in the form of substitute products and services, often from different components of the travel and tourism industry. Returning to the example of a museum, indirect competition comes from theme parks, natural attractions and shopping arcades within the locality. Recognising who your competitors are and being aware of their marketing activities allows you to seek competitive advantage over them.

CASE STUDY

Competitor analysis

There are five travel agents within the high street area of a small market town. One agency puts up an eye-catching window display about 0 per cent commission on foreign currency exchange. Two doors down, another agency keeps up its old poster advertising competitive rates on foreign exchange, including a minimum charge of £3 commission, while the remaining three agencies remove from their windows any mention of foreign exchange.

* **As a customer, which agency would you choose when you needed to exchange some money?**
* **Which would you definitely not use?**
* **As the manager of one of the other agencies, how would you respond?**

CASE STUDY

Visitor analysis

Below are the results of a visitor analysis carried out by an independent bed-and-breakfast establishment, the Enchanted Vineyard, in Oregon, USA.

Geographical

* Approximately 10 per cent of visitors are from countries outside the USA.

Demographics

* male and female
* ages 35–55
* an income over $50,000
* college or graduate education.

Behavioural factors

* makes bookings independently using telephone or Internet
* tends to use bed-and-breakfast accommodation when travelling, instead of hotels
* enjoys weekly meals at restaurants.

* **What is the expected total volume of visitors to Oregon over this three-year period?**
* **Give two characteristics of the visitor profile.**
* **Describe how you would use the information given as behavioural factors to help market the Enchanted Vineyard.**

VISITOR TYPES	2004 (ACTUAL, 1,000s)	2005 (ACTUAL, 1,000s)	2006 (FORECAST, 1,000s)
Weekend getaway customers	12	13	15
Travellers	18	20	22
University of Oregon visitors	12	14	16
Total	42	47	53

Visitor analysis

Many travel and tourism organisations also carry out a detailed visitor analysis as part of their marketing audit. This type of analysis enables providers to understand the scale and characteristics of their customer base, and often informs the wider marketing research function, which allows different types of customer to be enticed towards differentiated tourism products or services. You will study marketing research, different types of customer and differentiated products further on in this chapter.

Proposed marketing strategy

There are three main directions an organisation can strategically take, once a company has evaluated its marketing position using the variety of analytical tools described above:

* competitive pricing
* product differentiation
* market focus.

The marketing mix

This section examines in detail each of the four components of the marketing mix – *product*, *place*, *price* and *promotion*. These components are interlinked, and each affects consumer choice.

FIGURE 15.4. *You need to be able to understand the way in which each component of the marketing mix affects consumer choice and to recognise that the four components are interlinked*

Product as part of the marketing mix

According to the *Oxford Dictionary of Business*, a product is:

> *Anything that can be offered to a market for attention, acquisition, use or consumption that might satisfy a need. It includes physical objects and services.*

This definition gives you an idea of the scale of coverage of the term 'product', but it doesn't help you distinguish the differences between a product, a service or a brand, all of which are essential to the product component of the marketing mix.

The tourism product is difficult to define, because:

> *the product covers the complete experience from the time the tourist leaves home to the time he returns to it.*

(Medlik and Middleton, 1973, p. 85)

In general terms, products may be defined by the fact that they are:

* tangible – you can see and physically hold a product (e.g. a meal in a restaurant)

* separable – you can distinguish between one product and another

* homogeneous – 'like' products are all standardised (e.g. one Travelodge room is the same as another)

* storable – a product will last and is not perishable.

For travel and tourism products, these distinctions are not always clear. Defining a tourism 'product' is very difficult because what is sold has the qualities of a product and a service simultaneously. Let us take a typical package holiday as our product. This comprises three main elements – transportation, accommodation and excursions. These are all intangible at the time of purchase. You do not usually get a sample or demonstration of the product before purchase and must rely on its description in a brochure. It is impossible to separate out each element of a package holiday because they are marketed and sold exactly as that – a package. There is no homogeneity about package holidays – no two packages are the same and no two holidaymakers who have booked identical packages will experience exactly the same holiday because of additional influencing factors (e.g. the weather, differences in the events calendar). Finally, package holidays are perishable – if the tour operator has not sold the same number of packages it has booked with the travel and accommodation principals for a given period, these packages and their associated costs and revenue are lost. They cannot be transferred to a different time slot or to a different location.

Because of these qualities, tourism products are described as sharing many of the characteristics of services. Services form an invisible and integral part of a customer's expectation. Insurance, banking facilities, being waited on in a restaurant are some services with which you will be familiar (see Figure 15.5).

Most tourism products have inseparable services associated with them – staying in a hotel requires the services of the reception staff, the cleaning and concierge staff, chefs, waiters and so on. Flying from one airport to another involves

FIGURE 15.5. *An example of a tourism-related service*

the services of the airline – check-in, baggage handling, flight deck staff, outside caterers – a seamless amalgamation of products and services to bring you the 'total tourism product'.

Product differentiation

The ultimate goal of marketing a travel and tourism product or service lies in attracting customers to buy or use your product rather than one offered by your competitors. Therefore it is necessary to ensure that your product is clearly differentiated from others in the market. There are several methods used by travel and tourism providers in product differentiation, the two most common methods being the use of branding and of 'unique selling propositions' (or 'unique sales points', both abbreviated to USPs).

Branding

> **Key term**
>
> Branding is giving a name, sign, symbol or design or a combination of these features to identify the products of an organisation and distinguish them from those of competitors.

Branding is an important marketing tool which helps attract customers to a particular product or provider. Even service providers are able to benefit from branding. Think of the logos and colours used by airline companies on their fleets of planes or consider the associated features of a Hilton hotel – these are all connections that the organisations want customers to make with their product. Brands are often registered as a trademark, which prevents other organisations copying the brand too closely. Figure 15.6 shows an example of a brand.

Branding is especially useful in gaining customer loyalty – if you have been happy with a previous purchase or have enjoyed using a particular travel or tourism product, you are likely to return to the same company for future purchases or experiences. This is known as repeat business for the organisation, based on brand loyalty on the part of the customer.

Unique selling propositions (USPs)

In an ideal world, every product would have a USP to distinguish it from any other product already available on the market. However, given the highly competitive nature of the travel and tourism industry, very few products or services nowadays can honestly be described as having a USP. Package holidays, for example, are very similar in their composition. Tour operators try to persuade their customers that their package does, in fact, differ from those offered by rival companies, using a variety of means to entice us. You probably already know about Club 18–30, which sells its packages on its 'sexy' image. Thomson emphasises the rigorous checks made on resorts and hotels as its USP in its television advertisements.

Core values

If you read general marketing books, you will find a section on the three 'levels' of a product (see Table 15.1). These levels provide a fuller understanding of how a customer makes a purchasing decision.

Core values can be applied to any travel or tourism product. Let us apply this to a hospitality product with which you are familiar. You need

LEVEL		CHARACTERISTICS
1	Core product	The real or perceived benefit to be gained from the product
2	Actual product	An amalgamation of the features of the product and the brand characteristics
3	Augmented product	The level of customer service needed to achieve customer satisfaction

TABLE 15.1. *The core values of a product*

easyJet.com
Come on, let's fly!

FIGURE 15.6. *Examples of the copyright logos associated with the easyJet brand image*

to stay overnight in an unfamiliar town. The first level is the core product, which here is an accommodation booking before your trip. This gives you peace of mind before you travel. The second level is the actual product – the amalgamation of the features and brand characteristics of the type of accommodation selected. The brand image of the chosen hotel will influence your purchasing decision. You are likely to book with a hotel chain you have previously heard of, in order to match expectations of the product with the actual product you experience. The final level is the augmented product (customer service/satisfaction). You may not have gone ahead with the booking if you were dissatisfied with the quality of service you initially received from the booking clerk. Customer satisfaction will also depend on the actual performance of the product on use. In this instance, if the hotel accommodation did not live up to expectation, then you are unlikely to leave feeling happy with your purchasing decision.

Product analysis

As with all other aspects of the marketing process, organisations need regularly to evaluate the range of products they offer and the positioning of these products in the market. Product analysis enables organisations to gain competitive advantage over their rivals and can increase profitability in the long term.

Most of the travel and tourism organisations you can probably name are large businesses: most operate on a national scale and have a large number of branches across the UK (e.g. Thomas Cook), because they have assumed national significance in the number of customers they receive annually (e.g. the Beatles Story in Liverpool) or because they are part of a larger organisation, offering more than one product (e.g. Alton Towers as part of the Tussaud Group). Large organisations are involved in constantly reviewing the portfolio of products they offer at any one time. A tour operator may have at least four main types of package within its portfolio – summer sun, winter sun, skiing and long haul, for example. It is important for the organisation to understand exactly how each of these products is performing in the marketplace. This type of

analysis is commonly conducted using one of three frameworks:

* the product life cycle model
* the Ansoff model
* the Boston matrix.

The Ansoff and Boston product analysis tools are commonly used by business organisations with several products within their portfolio to analyse the exact market position of their products.

Product life cycle model

This model allows an organisation to identify the stage of growth or decline for an individual product from within its portfolio at any given time. It will come as no surprise to you to learn that some products will be earning large amounts of profit and will grow in popularity while others are struggling to maintain a hold in the market and are making little revenue for the organisation. A graph like the one shown in Figure 15.7 is used to plot the sales volume and profitability of a product, service or destination in the travel and tourism industry.

There are six distinct stages in any product life cycle, and these are shown in Table 15.2. Any product at the same stage will display similar market characteristics, in terms of the volume of sales and the level of profitability within that stage.

FIGURE 15.7. *The product life cycle model*

STAGE	CHARACTERISTICS
1 Research and development	There are no sales during this stage, as the product is still being tried and tested before being launched on the market. This stage is expensive for the organisation
2 Introduction and launch	It is at this point that the product is launched onto the market. This will be signified by a period of intense marketing to raise awareness and to gain customer confidence in the product. There will be a limited number of sales compared with the high cost of marketing during this stage, but there is no competition
3 Growth	Demand continues for the newly launched product, but some competitors will begin working on substitute products. The growth period is critical to the success of the product. Sales volume is increasing together with levels of profitability
4 Maturity	It is towards the end of this stage that the sales curve peaks and begins to decline. The company will continue to make a profit during maturity but competition from other products will be strong, with many similar brands entering the market. Marketing efforts are needed to extend the appeal of the product, through special offers, etc.
5 Saturation	Almost all potential customers have now been exploited and the product is losing its appeal. The market cannot be expanded further and sales are starting to drop off
6 Decline	The number of sales falls rapidly and the organisation must make a decision about the viability of the product for the future. Some products are relaunched and others are scrapped completely

TABLE 15.2. *The product life cycle model*

Theory into practice

Tourist destinations go through a life cycle in much the same way as other products. Place each of the following destinations on the life cycle model and give a reason for its position:

1 Mexico

2 Bali

3 Goa

4 Egypt

5 Costa Brava

6 Cyprus

7 Prague

8 Florida

9 Dubai

10 Paris

FIGURE 15.8 *The tourist resort at Dubai*

The Ansoff model

The Ansoff model is also commonly used to analyse a product's position in the market. It is based upon a fourfold classification of a product (often shown in a quadrant) according to whether it is a new or an existing one and whether the market is a new one or an existing one. An example of the Ansoff quadrant is shown in Figure 15.9.

Think it over...

Explain the advantages and disadvantages of using the Ansoff model to analyse your market position. Give at least one example of tourism products or services for each section of the quadrant. Which category of product would be most expensive to market? Explain your answer.

Market penetration	Product development
Existing product in an existing market e.g. Frequent-flyer programmes	New product in an existing market e.g. Leisure centres in hotels
Market development	**Diversification**
Existing product in a new market e.g. Wedding packages	New product in a new market e.g. Special events such as the Scottish International Storytelling Festival

FIGURE 15.9. *Characteristics of the Ansoff model, including reference to a tourism example*

The Boston matrix

The Boston matrix approach is named after the Boston Consulting Group, which devised a model for assessing market growth rates and relative market share. Products are categorised according to their current level of performance in the market. The results are then analysed to consider the most appropriate marketing strategy for each product within the portfolio. This allows an organisation to prioritise its marketing efforts in terms of 'best return'. The categorisation is shown in Table 15.3.

CATEGORY	CHARACTERISTICS	RELATIVE MARKET SHARE	MARKET GROWTH
Star	Market leader Fast growing High profitability	High	High
Cash cow	Profitable Generates more cash than needed to maintain market share Operates in mature market	High	Low
Problem child	Rapid growth Poor profit margins Needs huge input of cash	Low	High
Dog	High failure rate No market growth	Low	Low

TABLE 15.3. *The Boston matrix*

Place as part of the marketing mix

'Place' is used in relation to two different aspects of the marketing mix for tourism products and services: the physical location of destinations or tourist facilities and the chain of distribution used by tourism providers to get their products to their customers.

Physical location

Organisations must take into consideration a range of different factors when choosing to site a new facility or attraction. These are known as locational factors. Typically, these include:

* cost and availability of suitable land

* character of the local area – crime rates, general cost and standard of living

* natural features – proximity of beaches, mountains and so on

* access to local population – to act as both a workforce and a potential customer base

* access and transport links – if the local infrastructure is poor, customers will choose alternative facilities

* closeness of competition – depending on the type of organisation (e.g. you often find several travel agents on the high street)

* closeness of linked tourism facilities – cafés near to tourist attractions, bars and restaurants close to hotels and so on.

The chain of distribution

Choice of distribution channel

There are many different ways in which travel and tourism organisations get their products and services to their customers. Some chains of distribution remain small and simple, involving only the provider and the customer. Others have many links to their chains, as intermediaries such as travel agents become involved. The decision about which channel to use lies with the organisation itself. The choice is likely to be influenced by:

* **cost factors** – costs arise because the involvement of intermediaries brings with it commission charges, but direct selling also requires a high capital investment in promotion to ensure that customers are made fully aware of the existence of products and services

* **control of the product** – control can become an issue if a provider believes that an agent is underselling a particular product or that the level of service being offered to customers is below standard.

Figure 15.10 illustrates the most commonly used distribution channels in the travel and tourism industry. Model 1 shows the process through which customers gain travel and tourism products and services straight from the provider. The provider assumes sole responsibility for getting its products to its customers through the process of *direct selling*. This means that no intermediaries are used, thus saving the provider from having to pay commission. This channel is frequently used

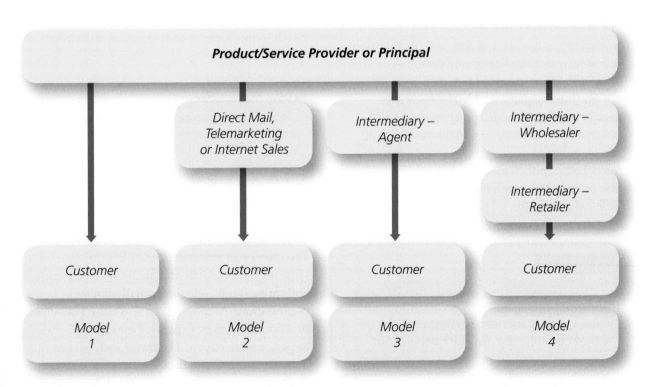

FIGURE 15.10. *Channels of distribution commonly used in the travel and tourism industry*

within the private sector by, for example, guest house owners.

Model 2 illustrates how *direct response* marketing communication tools are used to reinforce the direct selling model. Direct response distribution channels are often used by hotel chains and time-share operators. The concept will be covered in greater detail towards the end of this unit, so do not be put off by this term – it just covers any communication method which provokes a reaction from customers which can be measured. As you can see from Figure 15.10, three commonly used methods of direct response are direct mail, telemarketing and Internet sales. Direct mail involves an organisation sending promotional material to existing or potential customers whose details they have on their customer database. The promotional material may contain special offers, discounts and so on, and can be coded to enable the organisation to track the response rate. Telemarketing is, as its name implies, the use of telephone calls to target customers. You will already be aware of the huge impact that the Internet has had on the travel and tourism industry. Customers are able to access information and make reservations via their home computers at any time of day, and organisations are able to monitor how many customers access their website in order to track their promotions.

The intermediary in model 3 is known as a retailer or agent. In travel and tourism this role is commonly undertaken by a travel agent, either an agency acting independently on behalf of principals or an agency owned by the principal (through the process of 'forward vertical integration'). The use of intermediaries enables tourism providers to extend the access

Key terms

Vertical integration occurs where a company obtains control of its suppliers or its distributors/ sales agents. Backward vertical integration would occur if a tour operator bought into the transport principal or the accommodation suppliers. Forward vertical integration exists in cases where tour operators take control of their own retail travel agencies.

that customers have to products and services. It also provides customers with a face-to-face point of contact and allows them to make advanced bookings. Transport providers, tour operators and hotels all regularly use this form of distribution.

The final model, model 4, shows a two-layered intermediary role within the chain of distribution. This involves the use of wholesalers (tour operators) as well as retailers (travel agencies) in getting the product from the provider to the customer. Wholesalers buy products in bulk, to benefit from economies of scale, before selling them on to retailers.

Key term

Economies of scale – the larger the scale of operation, the more discount is offered, because the actual costs of putting together the package are reduced.

Tour operators act as wholesalers in the way in which they buy in bulk from airline companies and accommodation providers at discounted prices, before they put together the components of the holiday package to sell on to the retailer. Having two intermediaries within the chain of distribution further extends access to products for customers.

Think it over...

Choose one public sector tourism provider and one private sector tourism organisation. Identify the distribution channel/s each company operates. Consider how important the distribution channel is to the success of each business.

Cooperative distribution systems: consortia

The travel and tourism industry comprises a very large number of small and medium-sized business enterprises and a relatively small number of large organisations. Marketing is a specialised business function and can be expensive for small businesses to perform effectively. The travel and tourism industry has found that cooperative or joint marketing efforts are a useful way of overcoming some of the difficulties that small businesses face in trying to market themselves to a wide audience.

One method of cooperative marketing exists through the establishment of a consortium. A consortium is usually made up of similar types of businesses across several regions or of contrasting businesses within a given locality. The businesses combine forces to produce a joint marketing leaflet or brochure. These publicity materials are then distributed on a much wider scale than individual promotional materials for each organisation could be, thereby reaching a larger number of customers via hotels, libraries, tourist information centres and so on. Joint ventures such as these often keep costs down for members of the consortium as well as allowing for marketing expertise to be shared by consortium members.

Consortia are common among hotels and, as the case study on the Royal Forest of Dean Tourism Association earlier in this chapter shows, are especially effective for groups of local tourist attractions.

Franchises

Franchising is a formal business arrangement between a brand name owner (the *franchisor*) and a dealer (the *franchisee*) that allows the franchisee the right to distribute products under the brand name. The franchisor will receive a percentage of the franchisee's turnover, as well as the opportunity to expand its business operations in exchange for key business support in the marketing and promotion of the branded product.

Franchising is used extensively in the travel and tourism industry. The Holiday Inn hotel chain demonstrates the international success that can be achieved through franchising. As the industry continues to expand, more franchising opportunities are becoming available, as illustrated in the following case study on 'Eurodrive', a car rental franchise operation.

CASE STUDY

'Eurodrive' – the vehicle rental franchise

Eurodrive is Europe's only truly franchised vehicle rental system. It currently operates in over 80 locations throughout the UK and is looking to expand its network to 160 locations in the next decade.

The Eurodrive system offers a total support package to its franchise network. This package includes the following:

* recognised brand name
* fully integrated training programme covering all aspects of the rental industry, including operation, business development and sales
* comprehensive rental insurance programme
* national, discounted fleet supply from eight vehicle manufacturers
* supported by global rental computer system ('Eurores')
* centralised retail, leisure and corporate reservations
* full local and national marketing support
* system dedicated to the success and profitability of each individual franchise.

Finance requirements

Franchise fee	£17,500
Working capital	£35,000 to £55,000

Available areas

Franchise opportunities available in most areas of the UK and Ireland.

* **What are the advantages of running the Eurodrive business as a franchise for both the franchisor and the franchisee?**
* **Why is having a global rental computer system beneficial for the franchisee?**
* **Using information from the case study, identify *two* ways in which the corporate brand image of the Eurodrive organisation can be upheld.**
* **From your knowledge of the concept of franchising, explain how you would expect the marketing of Eurodrive to be undertaken. Assess the impact of this process for the franchisee.**

Computer reservation systems (CRS)

Given that we know the majority of travel and tourism products are intangible and perishable, advanced booking and reservation of these products plays an important role in the distribution process for the industry.

Accessibility and availability are essential elements of the distribution process. Advanced developments within computer information technology have assisted with the creation of computer reservation systems (CRS) to support both the principals and their customers in the coordination of reservations.

A broad range of computer systems have been developed and operated by many leading tourism principals via their business intermediaries. Travel agents can therefore access the computer systems of airline companies and accommodation providers to check 'live' on flight availability and room occupancy on a specified date to a preferred destination.

The inter-connectivity of these CRS has led to the creation of global distribution systems or GDS, which means that the total tourism product can be managed at the touch of a few buttons.

Key term

The total tourism product refers to all elements of the tourist's experience from leaving home to the time of return. It includes transport and transfer arrangements, accommodation and meal plans as well as ancillary services such as car rental and optional excursions.

There are several internationally recognised CRS, including AMADEUS (mainly European), APOLLO (USA), GALILEO (European), SABRE (USA) and WORLDSPAN (USA and the Far East).

Information technology plays a crucial role in distributing the travel and tourism product and is likely to contribute more significantly to the distribution process as technological advances continue.

CASE STUDY

E-ticketing

An e-ticket (electronic ticket) is a paperless electronic document used for ticketing passengers, particularly in the commercial airline industry. Virtually all major airlines now use this method of ticketing. When a customer books a flight by telephone or on the Internet, the details of the reservation are stored in a computer. The customer can request that a paper copy by way of confirmation is sent by post, but it is not needed at the check-in desk. A confirmation number is assigned to the passenger, along with the flight number(s), date(s), departure location(s) and destination location(s). When checking in at the airport, the passenger simply presents some identification. Then necessary boarding passes are issued, and the passenger can check in luggage and proceed through security to the gate area.

* **Describe how the check-in process for an e-ticketed passenger differs from that for a passenger with printed documentation.**

* **Give *two* advantages of e-tickets for both the customer and the transport provider.**

* **Draw a diagram to illustrate the distribution channel used by principals in e-ticketing.**

* **Analyse the likely impact of technology on the distribution process for the travel and tourism industry of the future.**

Price as part of the marketing mix

There are a great number of factors which determine the final price a customer pays for a travel and tourism product or service. Obviously the actual cost of putting together the product or service will play an important role in setting the end price, as will the business orientation of the company. Profit-seeking organisations will adopt a very different approach to pricing their products than an organisation that is financed through public sources.

Other influences on price include:

* **The price–quality relationship and customers' expectations**. This includes customers' perception of value for money. An organisation should charge only what a customer is willing to pay.

* **The uniqueness of the product and the level of competition in the market**. If no substitutes are available, a higher price can be set than if a large number of substitute products are available. This is a simple case of supply and demand. The greater the supply and the less the demand, then the lower the price has to be. This also links into peak and off-season charges, whereby higher prices are set during popular periods.

* **Positioning of the organisation and the product in the market**. Companies with greater market share can set the price for a product. Those with less market share follow the price set by the market leaders.

* **Government influence**. The level of taxation or levels of subsidy available will influence price.

* **General economic factors**. General levels of prosperity, standards of living and interest rates, for example, will influence the price that can be charged.

The tourism market is described as being 'price sensitive'. Because there are a huge number of very similar products and packages available for customers to choose from, the actual price being charged may exert the greatest influence over the final choice of package.

Travel and tourism organisations make conscious marketing decisions about the type of pricing strategy they will adopt for each product they offer to the market. You will find a brief outline of the most common strategies used in the travel and tourism industry below.

* **Market skimming**. This is often used for products which are new and do not have any real competition. A high price is charged and often attracts those who do not mind paying for the privilege of being first to try the product. These customers are known as 'innovators'. Once they have adopted the product, the market is described as having been 'skimmed' and the price will gradually be reduced until it becomes affordable for a wider range of consumers.

* **The going rate**. Where there is a high degree of similarity between products offered by several organisations, the pricing policy may be based on 'the going rate'. This is also sometimes referred to as *competitor-based pricing*. An example would be in a town with two museums which had similar ticket prices. Tour operators often offer to 'price match' their competitors.

* **Penetration pricing**. When launching a new product into a highly competitive market, artificially low prices are set initially, to entice the consumer to try the product. The aim is to win a large market share and earn more revenue from high sales. Customer loyalty is also hoped for, even if the price later increases. Penetration pricing is often used with fast-moving consumer goods (e.g. food) but in recent years tour operators have successfully used penetration pricing strategies. This results in price wars between rival companies and can lead to bankruptcy.

* **Promotional pricing**. Examples of this include special offers, such as two for the price of one, money-off coupons, reductions for bulk buying and so on, as well as free tickets for a series of concerts, or a free towel with membership of a hotel leisure centre.

* **Discount pricing**. Prices may be marked down if the product fails to sell sufficiently or when it comes close to expiry (e.g. half-price theatre tickets on the day of performance, heavily discounted stand-by tickets hours before departure).

* **Prestige pricing** (sometimes known as *premium pricing*). Where products are of high quality or have an exclusive appeal, high prices can be set, based on the assumption that people associate high prices with high quality (e.g. health club memberships or holidays to upmarket resorts).

* **Variable pricing** (also known as *price discrimination*). This is based on the principle that demand for a product varies. Examples would be different telephone rates at different times of the day, peak-time rail travel and off-peak holidays. Lower prices are set to encourage higher sales during less busy periods. Prices can also vary according to customer type (e.g. different prices being set for children, students, the unemployed and the elderly).

* **Loss leader pricing**. Prices can be lowered from time to time to promote a specific product. A loss leader is a product that is sold at little or no profit or even at a loss. It gives the impression of goods being cheap, and entices the customer to spend on other, more profitable items in addition to purchasing the loss leader items. This pricing policy is rarely used in the travel and tourism industry.

Think it over...

An established hotel chain is considering expanding to open a tourist hotel on Rannoch Moor in the Scottish Highlands. The hotel would be situated just a few hundred metres from the well used West Highland Way long-distance footpath.

What pricing policy would you recommend for the hotel when it first opens? Explain how the pricing policy for the hotel might be linked to market opportunities after the first couple of years.

CASE STUDY
Great London Deals

'Great London Deals' is a tourism campaign designed to boost last-minute bookings from the rest of the country for the Easter break and beyond, following recent acts of terrorism. It is part of the biggest ever marketing drive to get people to the capital. Short-break operators and air, rail and coach companies are combining to offer 'Great London Deals', to attract more visitors. A new website details offers worth more than £10 million in total, including:

❉ *Hotel offers*. London's major hotel groups have come up with a range of offers, including 50 per cent off room prices and three nights for the price of two.

❉ *Short-break offers*. These include theatre packages, luxury breaks and all-inclusive packages with reduced-price entrance to attractions.

❉ *Kids-go-free with BA*. British Airways are offering kids-go-free on their domestic routes to London.

❉ *National Express two-for-the-price-of-one*. A special deal on all coach routes into London allows two people to travel for the price of one.

❉ *Two-for-one visitor attractions*. Buy a day-return rail ticket and get two for the price of one to many of London's top attractions, including the Tower of London and Madame Tussaud's.

The promotion will be supported by a two-week nationwide poster campaign and national and regional press advertising promoting the new website.

* **Which pricing policies are being adopted by the 'Great London Deals' marketing campaign?**

* **Describe *three* factors influencing the cost of tourism products in London.**

* **Identify *two* benefits of the campaign for the organisations involved.**

Promotion as part of the marketing mix

> **Key term**
>
> Promotion is any activity designed to boost the sales of a product or service.

The concept of promotion is often confused with advertising – the two terms are often used interchangeably. However, promotion involves a much wider range of activities than just advertising, although we should not underestimate the power of advertising, especially in promoting intangible products such as package holidays. Now that so many different forms of media offer advertising, it has become an indispensable part of promotion.

Promotion occurs for four interconnected reasons:

* to raise and maintain customer awareness of the product or service

* to inform customers of the product's features and to highlight its benefits

* to create demand

* to entice customers to buy.

There are a number of different techniques commonly used to achieve these aims. Some of these will be covered briefly here; however, you will find more detail about many of these techniques later in the unit, under 'Marketing communications'.

Advertising

Advertising is one of the most expensive forms of promotion and takes up a large chunk of most organisations' marketing budget. Small travel and tourism businesses often have to compete for advertising space in their local press, while the multinational chains can invest huge amounts of money in national media campaigns and usually employ the expertise of a specialist advertising agency to run these campaigns.

Advertising generally occurs through three different media:

* **broadcast** – television, cinema, radio

* **print** – newspapers, magazines, leaflets

* **display** – billboards, posters and signs.

The impact advertising has on a target audience is difficult to measure – it permeates our everyday life and yet we are often barely aware of the messages it is trying to convey.

Direct marketing

As its name implies, direct marketing is a promotional technique used by organisations to sell directly to customers. *Direct mail* enables organisations to target specific customers through the normal postal system. Hotel chains often send out promotional letters combined with other promotions (special offers, competitions, etc.) to try to stimulate demand. *Telemarketing* involves organisations (often time-share consortia) using the telephone to try to create interest in a product. They obtain potential customers' details from a database. Most forms of direct marketing rely heavily on the use of database information in targeting potential customers with details of products and sevices.

Public relations (PR)

This promotional technique involves any activity which enables an organisation to project itself in a favourable light to its public. Public relations concerns presenting a positive image of the organisation and its products and services. It hinges on the reputation of an organisation. Examples of PR include:

* press releases

* features – on television, in a magazine or a newspaper

* trade fairs (see Figure 15.11)

* familiarisation trips for trade representatives

* press conferences

* lobbying – campaigning to influence government and legislation (e.g. lobbying of the Association of British Travel Agents for consumer protection issues).

PR is also considered below, as a form of marketing communication.

FIGURE 15.11 *A trade fair for the travel and tourism industry*

Personal selling

This term is used to describe a face-to-face interaction aimed at gaining the sale. As travel and tourism is a people-focused industry, face-to-face contact is an essential element of the business activity. Personal selling is an important promotional technique used by visitor attractions at the entry gate to promote sales of the visitor guide, for example, or by hotels promoting the use of their leisure facilities.

Sales promotion

This is one of the most important tools used by organisations to raise awareness and to get customers to make a purchase. It is widely used in the travel and tourism industry and takes many different forms. Some of the most common are given below, but see if you can think of any other examples.

✳ coupons – money-off next purchase (e.g. free entry vouchers for theme parks, if one adult purchase is made) but usually time-bound

✳ competitions – win a holiday by entering a competition in your local newspaper, for example

✳ special offers – buy one, get one free, free children's places, etc.

✳ loyalty incentives – frequent-flyer programmes, Airmiles, etc.

✳ trade incentives – discounted products, free gifts, familiarisation trips.

Sponsorship

Organisations offer financial or other support to community events or commercial activities in order to gain greater recognition for their own products or services. Travel and tourism organisations have become more readily involved in sponsorship in recent years. This can take several forms, such as donating a prize for a particular fundraising event, or television sponsorship – the airline BMI Baby has sponsored local weather forecasts on ITV for several years and you may remember the travel agency Going Places sponsoring the television show *Blind Date*, which sent couples on a variety of matchmaking holidays.

CASE STUDY
Promoting SeaBritain 2005

SeaBritain was a national tourism campaign led by VisitBritain, the chief body promoting tourism nationally. SeaBritain lasted throughout 2005 and celebrated Britain's relationship with the sea. It took as its inspiration the 200th anniversary of the Battle of Trafalgar. One of the major events that took place during this campaign was the annual Mersey River Festival.

The following examples of web resources (some no longer active) indicate the extent to which the city of Liverpool was promoted as a result of the festival programme:

Mersey River Festival –
http://visitliverpool.com
2005: Sea Liverpool –
from the City of Culture 2008 website,
www.liverpool08.com/Events/ThemedYears/
2005SeaLiverpool/index.asp

SeaBritain was sponsored by the following organisations:
wherecanwego.com (online 'what's on' event guide)
Hotelpacc (online reservations)
GNER (Great North Eastern Railway)

Tom Wright, chief executive of VisitBritain, said of the event:

VisitBritain is very pleased to be supporting SeaBritain 2005. The wide variety of planned activities throughout Britain provides enormous opportunities for tourism, both internationally and domestically – encouraging the British to take part in water-based recreation and sport. Britain provides tremendous scope for water-based tourism, whether actually on the sea itself, enjoying our many miles of coastal paths, or venturing inland and enjoying our rivers, inland waterways and lakes for which Britain is famous. With SeaBritain 2005, we are set for an exciting year.

✴ Other than using websites, suggest *two* alternative forms of promotion that the SeaBritain campaign would have used.

✴ What benefits would the three named sponsors have gained from sponsoring the event?

✴ Design a poster to promote the event.

✴ Give *two* reasons why VisitBritain would support an event such as SeaBritain.

✴ Tom Wright (chief executive of VisitBritain) promotes more than just the SeaBritain event. Suggest some reasons for this.

✴ Imagine you witnessed some of the SeaBritain event yourself. Produce a 150-word press release about your experiences, ensuring that you avoid author bias within your press release.

Main-stay touring campaigns play a key role in much of VisitBritain's marketing. In 2002 touring holidays accounted for 20 per cent of the overall UK holiday market. International *and* domestic tourists engage in this type of holiday activity.

Campaign message
Key offer: Britain's unique touring product – town, country and city easily accessible; living history and landscapes.

Key product: Historic cities, bustling market towns and sleepy villages. Open spaces and National Parks. Built heritage and attractions. Regional food and drink. Events and spectator sports. Unique mix of accommodation providers.

Campaign components
Market-specific coverage on visitbritain.com website. Brochure. Direct mail. Exhibitions. Press. PR.

The above information, adapted from the VisitBritain website (http://www.visitbritain.com), provides an overview of the marketing mix for the main-stay touring holiday campaign.

1 Take each of the four 'P's of the marketing mix individually and explain their importance for this tourism offering.

2 List the range of travel and tourism providers who would benefit from joining this campaign.

3 Discuss how VisitBritain might use the product life cycle model and other tools of marketing analysis to benefit UK tourism.

You will be examined on the marketing mix in travel and tourism. You need to be able to apply the marketing mix to a range of different travel and tourism organisations and evaluate how the components interact. You should demonstrate the ability to analyse marketing mixes in travel and tourism and how effectively an organisation's marketing mix meets its customers' needs and expectations. You should make recommendations as to how an organisation could improve its marketing mix.

Market research

We keep reminding ourselves that the travel and tourism industry is founded on the provision of products and services that meet the needs of the customer. If we refer back to the definition that the Chartered Institute of Marketing gives us, we know that assessing customers' needs provides a mechanism for achieving customer satisfaction. If you do not know what it is that the customer wants, how can you provide it? Market research enables these needs to be identified and in turn catered for.

Knowing how to conduct research, and even where to start and whom to consult, is a skilled process. Many of the larger travel and tourism organisations employ the services of specialist market research agencies to carry out research on their behalf, while the smaller, independent firms have to try to conduct their own market research.

There are five key stages in the market research process. These are shown in Figure 15.12.

1 *Identifying the problem*. This sets the aim, scope and objectives of the research. This is usually in the form of a hypothesis, which has to be proved or disproved. An example of such a hypothesis might be 'Most British families take beach holidays.'

2 *Devising a research strategy*. This involves setting a plan of action, including time and resources required, and so on. During this stage, appropriate primary and secondary data sources are identified.

3 *Data collection*. A range of data collection techniques will have been identified during the first two stages. These are then put into action. This could involve conducting a survey, using a questionnaire, monitoring the discussions of a focus group or conducting face-to-face interviews. It could also involve gathering data from customer records, databases, government statistics and so on.

4 *Analysis of data*. This will depend on the nature of the data collected. Statistical analysis can be done where quantitative data have been collected, whereas more detailed written interpretation will result from the collection of attitudinal statements as qualitative data.

5 *Reporting of findings*. The results will be summarised and wherever possible should be visually presented. The original aims and objectives of the research should be addressed and conclusions drawn about the initial hypothesis. Necessary actions and recommendations should also be included.

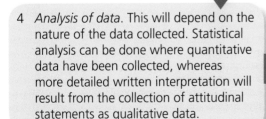

FIGURE 15.12. *The five key stages in the market research process*

Primary research methods

Primary research is often called 'field research', as it is obtained first hand from customers in the market. This type of research can be carried out by asking customers questions or by observing consumer behaviour. There are many commercial market research organisations which will carry out primary research on behalf of another organisation, but this is very costly. Questionnaires and surveys are the main methods used in primary research, although in-depth interviews, focus groups and participant observation are also used.

Questionnaires

Questionnaires must be carefully designed to ensure that respondents can easily understand what they are being asked. The language needs to be simple and should avoid the use of jargon. Closed questions (i.e. those with a Yes/No response) or multiple-choice questions are used to guide respondents towards a uniform answer, and so make data analysis more straightforward. Scaled-response questions are also useful in gauging customers' opinions (e.g. 'Rate the service you received on a scale of 1 to10', 1 being poor, 10 being exceptional). Open questions, where respondents are left to answer in any way they choose, make analysis more difficult. Questions should start by being quite general and gradually become more specific. Around 10–15 questions is the recommended number for most questionnaires.

> **Key term**
>
> A **respondent** is a person filling in a questionnaire or taking part in a survey (i.e. the person responding to the questions).

CASE STUDY
A visitor questionnaire

Thank you for participating in our visitor survey. Your answers will be held in confidence; however, summary statistics will be used to improve services for you and other visitors.

1 How many times, including today, have you visited our area during the past 12 months?

   _____

2 Other than today, when did you last visit our area?

   ☐ spring
   ☐ summer
   ☐ fall
   ☐ winter

3 What was the main purpose of your visit?

   _____

4 Which of the following activities have you participated in during the past year in this area?

   ☐ outdoor recreation
   ☐ cultural events
   ☐ museums/historical sites
   ☐ other tourism attractions
   ☐ other (specify activity)

5 Usually, what is your main mode of transportation in this area?

   ☐ commercial airline
   ☐ personal car
   ☐ other (please specify)

6 How many days and nights did you stay in our area during the last year?

   _____

   If you stayed overnight, how many overnights did you stay?

   ☐ in a motel or similar lodging facility?
   ☐ with friends/relatives?
   ☐ at a bed and breakfast?
   ☐ other (please specify)

7 Approximately how much money did you spend during your longest visit to our area? $ ___.

8 Indicate an approximate breakdown ($) of your total spending:

   ☐ Lodging
   ☐ Restaurants/meals
   ☐ Entertainment
   ☐ Retail stores
   ☐ Gas and auto service
   ☐ Local transportation/taxis/car rental
   ☐ Other (please specify)

   _____

   _____

9 The expenses in the last two questions were for how many persons?

_____adults plus _____children (less than 18 years old) for _____ days.

10 What three things do you like most about visiting here?

1. _____

2. _____

3. _____

11 What three things do you not like about visiting here?

1. _____

2. _____

3. _____

For classification purposes, your answers to the following questions would also be much appreciated.

Thanks again for your cooperation!

12 Your approximate yearly income (before taxes):

☐ less than $10,000
☐ between $10,000 and $20,000
☐ between $20,000 and $30,000
☐ between $30,000 and $50,000
☐ over $50,000

13 Your age:

☐ less than 25 years
☐ between 25 and 35 years
☐ between 35 and 45 years
☐ between 45 and 55 years
☐ between 55 and 65 years
☐ over 65 years

14 In which city and state do you currently reside? (please include zip code):

City_____

State_____ Zip_____

Source: www.montana.edu/wwwwrdc/attach2-e.html

✳ **Give _one_ example of a multiple-choice question from this questionnaire.**

✳ **Give _one_ example of an open question from this questionnaire.**

✳ **Why do you think the questionnaire has an introduction, explaining what will happen with individual customer responses?**

✳ **Why might respondents find questions 7 and 8 difficult to answer?**

✳ **Explain the importance of collecting data specifically about the respondent, as in question 13.**

✳ **Critically evaluate the design of the questionnaire and make recommendations for improving it from the perspective of both the organisation and the respondent.**

Surveys

A survey is often referred to as a contact method for market research. There are various types of survey:

✳ **Postal surveys** are quite common, where a respondent is sent a copy of the questionnaire and a reply-paid return envelope. While this survey method is commonly used, its major disadvantage is a generally poor response rate. To try to overcome this problem, many organisations link responses to an entry into a free prize draw, but even with this encouragement the average response rate for postal surveys is less than 10 per cent.

✳ **Exit surveys** are often used by tourist attractions and hotels. Users are invited to provide customer feedback on the level of service they have received during their visit. These often use a scale of response in order for companies to assess levels of customer satisfaction.

✳ **Telephone surveys** allow an organisation to input responses as the respondent speaks, thus saving administration time and costs. However, these are relatively uncommon in the travel and tourism industry.

In-depth interviews

In-depth interviews tend to be conducted face to face. These allow for detailed opinions and attitudes to be sought but are expensive and time-consuming.

Focus groups

Focus groups usually consist of 8–12 respondents, led by a moderator, who discuss in detail a product design or similar issue. Discussions are usually recorded and observed to allow the organisation to analyse respondents' behaviour during the discussions. These discussions are also costly to set up and take a long time to organise.

Participant observation

Participant observation is difficult to manage – if respondents know they are being filmed or secretly watched their behaviour may be unnatural. This type of research on its own is rarely used in travel and tourism, although some travel agents monitor how long a customer spends looking at brochures before requesting assistance through this method.

Think it over...

Imagine you work for a small, independent hotel in your town. Occupancy rates are decreasing and you believe the competition from a large hotel chain is taking away some of your custom. You decide to conduct some primary research into the matter.

Explain what method of primary research you would select. Give reasons for your answer. Describe the advantages and disadvantages of the methods you rejected.

Sampling techniques

Knowing how many respondents to target through primary research is often difficult. In the ideal world, you would want to get to know what all of your existing customers thought of your product or service, but this would usually be impossible. Therefore, organisations have to choose a sample of respondents to target for research purposes.

Key term

A **sample** is a small cross-section of people specifically selected to represent the whole population or target market.

Sample sizes are difficult to determine. The larger the sample, the more the results will reflect the opinions of the total population. However, market research experts recommend that a sample should represent approximately 10 per cent of the total target population in order to be effective in predicting future sales trends. For many organisations, surveying 10 per cent of the population would be too time consuming and too costly, and so sample sizes more often reflect the resources available to the organisation.

The way in which a sample is selected will differ from organisation to organisation. There are many different techniques used to choose whom to survey.

* **Random sampling** gives all members of the target population an equal chance of being chosen. This is also known as basic probability sampling. Each member of the target population will have a number assigned. These numbers are then selected by sequence (e.g. all people with a 7 reference, i.e. 7, 17, 27, etc.).

* **Stratified sampling** divides the population by common characteristics (e.g by sex, age or ethnicity) and then a random sample is conducted within each group.

* **Cluster sampling** divides the target population geographically and the sample is then chosen within these areas. Sometimes researchers will use the nth house in a street, or sometimes random sampling is used within a cluster sample.

* **Quota sampling** is different from the sampling techniques described above. This is because it allows researchers to use their own judgement in choosing respondents, as long as respondents are representative of the target population. Some control measures are imposed to provide a balance between age

and gender. This is by far the most common sampling technique adopted, especially within the travel and tourism industry.

Secondary research

This is also commonly known as 'desk research', as it involves researching information that has already been collected for another purpose. As much of this is in printed or electronic format, the researcher can sit at a desk to carry out the research. An incredible amount of data already exists in a variety of government and trade reports (though these are not always easily accessible by the general public). Companies also have a considerable amount of internal data from their own sales records with existing customers. In the UK travel and tourism industry, external secondary data sources include:

* the World Tourism Organization (online statistics service)
* government publications (e.g. *Social Trends, Overseas Visitor Survey, International Passenger Survey*)
* the Star UK website (http://www.staruk.org.uk/)
* intelligence-gathering agencies and market reports (e.g. Mintel, Euromonitor, Keynote)
* the trade press (e.g. *Travel Trade Gazette*)
* supplements in the weekend newspapers (e.g. in *The Sunday Times* and *The Observer*)
* academic journals (e.g. *Journal of Travel Research*)
* Tourism Society reports, etc.

When conducting secondary research, it is important to remember that much of the available data may be irrelevant to your own research objectives. You therefore have to be very selective in what you use. Data sources should be checked for validity and authenticity – this is especially important when using the Internet as a research tool. You should also check for author bias – this occurs where an author expresses a subjective (personal) point of view. Data could be outdated. Quoting market

size and value from two decades ago will not be helpful unless you are plotting patterns and trends over that particular time span.

Market segmentation

You will have noticed that much of this section makes reference to the target market. It is important that you understand this phrase because all of an organisation's marketing efforts centre around its target market.

In order to establish an effective marketing strategy for your product or service, it is important to choose the correct target market. This is done through a process known as 'market segmentation'. This means that customers are classified according to pre-set characteristics. The total market is then divided into a series of subsections or 'segments' based on these characteristics.

There are seven clearly identifiable types of market segmentation that are commonly used by the travel and tourism industry to 'target' its customers. These are set out in Table 15.4.

Market segmentation allows an organisation to focus its marketing efforts only on those customers who are likely to buy or use the product offering. It also benefits customers as they need receive only

TYPE OF SEGMENTATION	CHARACTERISATION OF CUSTOMERS
Demographic	By age, gender, ethnicity, levels of disposable income, etc.
Geographical	By locality, area, region, etc. This includes domestic versus overseas visitors
Geodemographic	This is an enhanced version of geographic segmentation, which breaks the target group down further into type of residential area – based on postcodes and housing types. It is known in the UK as 'ACORN': A Classification Of Residential Neighbourhoods. Data from the census are used
Psychographic	By the type of lifestyle. This can be based on socio-economic factors as well as general levels of interest and attitudes. Risk takers versus risk avoiders fall into this category
Buyer motivations	This can also include 'benefit' segmentation. Customers have different wants and needs from their tourism purchases – some desire relaxation while others seek adventure and challenge
Purpose of travel	The reason for a trip automatically segments customers (e.g. leisure tourism, business tourism)
Price	As the industry is described as being price sensitive, customers could be grouped together as a result of their attitude to the price charged. Examples could include first-class versus economy-class passengers

TABLE 15.4. *Seven types of market segmentation*

STAGE ON LIFE CYCLE	DISPOSABLE INCOME LEVEL	TYPE OF HOLIDAY
'Young single'	Reasonable	Short-haul package or independent
'Young couple'	High	Exotic, romantic
'Full nest 1' (young couple with baby)	Decreasing	Self-catering
'Full nest 2' (couple with young children)	Low	Self-catering or family package
'Full nest 3' (couple with older children)	Low	Domestic
'Empty nest 1' (couple whose children have left home)	Increasing	Overseas, short breaks
'Empty nest 2' (older couple, chief breadwinner retired)	Restricted	Low-season packages
'Solitary survivor 1' (single or widowed but still in work)	Restricted	Low-season packages
'Solitary survivor 2' (retired single person)	Low	Coach tours

TABLE 15.5. *Model of age, disposable income and likely type of holiday, as used in travel and tourism industry*

the marketing information about products that are likely to interest to them.

The travel and tourism industry has worked at refining specific market segments. There are several models that segment by age and lifestyle. The relationship between age and levels of disposable income forms the basis of the model outlined in Table 15.5.

Some travel and tourism providers use market segmentation to build a customer profile, which sets out for you the characteristics of a typical customer or product user.

HOLIDAY TYPE	GEOGRAPHIC SOURCE	DEMOGRAPHIC CHARACTERISTICS	LENGTH OF STAY	TRAVEL PARTY	TYPE OF TRANSPORT	SPECIAL INTEREST
Corporate Traveller	SEQ SYD/MEL/BNE	Income >45k	Daytrip, 1–2 nights	Singles	Fly Self-drive	Business
VFR	SEQ Regional QLD SYD Regional NSW	Income >35k	1 week (average)	Couples Families Singles	Self-drive Fly Coach Rail	Visiting friends or relatives
Big Tour	SEQ Northern NSW	Aged over 45 Income >35k Mid-life and older households	2 nights	Couples	Self-drive	Part of a 2-week drive holiday, Seeking to broaden knowledge/ experience
Grand Tour	SEQ Regional QLD Regional NSW SYD/MEL	Aged over 50 Income >50k Mid-life and older households	2 nights	Couples	Self-drive	'Trip of a lifetime', Part of an extended drive holiday
Short Break	Regional QLD	Income 35–60k	1–3 nights	Families Couples	Self-drive	Rest and relaxation, Seeking beach or nature escape, eg. Carnarvon Gorge, Sapphire Gemfields
Beach Holiday	Regional QLD SEQ	Income >35k Mid-life and older households, Mid-life families, Young parents	3 nights +	Couples Families	Self-drive Fly Coach Rail	Beach and island, Rest and relaxation, Family activities
Fly & Stay – Island Holidays (Great Keppel Is, Heron Is)	Regional QLD SEQ Regional Interstate SYD/MEL/BNE	Income >35k	3–5 nights	Singles Couples Families	Fly Self-drive	Party holiday – Contiki, Family holiday. Diving, Island/nature experiences

Source: Tourism Queensland (www.tq.com.au/tq_com/index.cfm?D50839EB-04B9-94BF-4B78-00F677C4FA17)

TABLE 15.6. *Market segmentation table for Central Queensland, Australia*

Study the segmentation table for Central Queensland, Australia (Table 15.6). Imagine you work for a domestic tour operator based in Queensland wishing to attract new market segments.

1 Choose *one* market research technique that will allow you to collect appropriate market research data. Explain your choice in terms of:

  * cost
  * time
  * accessibility
  * validity and reliability
  * fitness for purpose.

2 Select *two* of the customer profiles that the segmentation table provides and explain how this information could be used to provide a total tourism product which caters for the specific needs of each of your selected customer types.

Using information and communication technology to analyse findings

It is beyond the scope of this unit to cover the software used to analyse the results of market research. Professionally, some very sophisticated statistical and presentation packages will be employed. You should appreciate how this could be done using spreadsheets and databases to produce graphical interpretations of the results.

CASE STUDY

British Conference Venues Survey

The objective of the British Conference Venues Survey is to measure the key characteristics of the UK conference and meetings market. A variety of methods is used. A sample of around 3,000 venues is initially contacted by email and invited to access an online survey questionnaire. After two weeks all non-respondents are contacted again with a 'reminder' email. A paper version of the questionnaire is sent to a further 1,000 venues together with a reply-paid envelope. A total of 358 venues responded to the most recent questionnaire. Of these, only 196 were complete.

The key information collected is:

* volume of conferences
* conference duration
* type of conference
* size of conference
* month of conference
* average duration
* revenues
* venue type
* regional analysis.

* **Study the above information and use your knowledge of the market research process to prepare a five-minute presentation for a representative from the Meetings Industry Association to explain the purpose of the British Conference Venues Survey and the research process that it entailed. Outline the pros and cons of the approach taken and evaluate the importance of the research in influencing the marketing mix for the conference market.**

Marketing communications

The term 'marketing communications' is used to describe the many ways in which an organisation can make the market aware of its products and services. It relates specifically to the promotion aspect of the marketing mix and there is some overlap with the material presented in that section above.

Travel and tourism providers rely heavily on marketing communications to rouse the interest of potential consumers in intangible products and services. They employ a wide range of techniques to achieve this, which you will be able to study in more detail in this section. Advances in technology enable more interactive communication methods to be employed.

Advertising

Advertising is a powerful way of allowing travel and tourism providers to communicate with potential customers away from the point of sale – in the customer's own home, on billboards while travelling, and so on. The messages that advertisements carry are intended to influence customers' buying behaviours and to stimulate demand. Alluring images of idyllic holiday settings are often used to assist in the process.

Advertising is known as a 'mass media' approach and is not personalised in any way. In travel and tourism, the majority of advertisements are very product-focused. Brand images and logos are often prominent within an advertisement, to enhance the corporate image of the organisation.

The main objectives of advertising include:

* creating awareness

* acting as a reminder

* projecting positive images

* stimulating desire

* encouraging a response.

There are six stages to the advertising process.

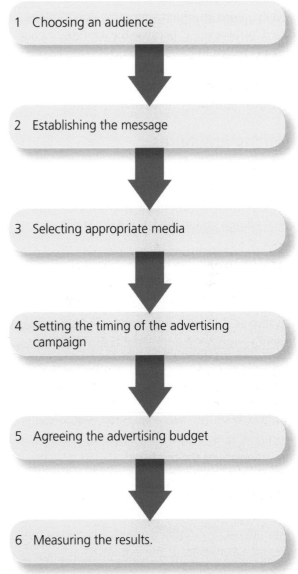

1 Choosing an audience

2 Establishing the message

3 Selecting appropriate media

4 Setting the timing of the advertising campaign

5 Agreeing the advertising budget

6 Measuring the results.

FIGURE 15.13. *The six stages in the advertising process*

As already discussed earlier in this unit, advertising itself can take on a variety of formats. The Internet is widely used by both large-scale and small, independent operators in the travel and tourism industry. The press provides wide-scale coverage of tourism products and services through the advertisements it runs. Television advertisements are particularly expensive, which limits the type of organisation that can afford them. Commercial radio is also sometimes used, where the cost of television coverage is prohibitive. Advertisements in magazines, leaflets, point-of-sale material, posters and so on are commonly used in the travel and tourism industry.

Many of the larger organisations within the industry will employ the services of an advertising agency to run an advertising campaign. (This is called 'out-sourcing' because the advertisements are not created in-house.) Agencies often have more resources available to them, as well as specialist knowledge and skills in producing objective (unbiased) views of the product.

Holiday brochures

A holiday brochure is almost unique as a piece of marketing communication. It provides documented evidence of the product or service being offered and in the UK it has a statutory (legal) requirement to provide detailed, accurate information about the exact nature of the product being offered. (More detail will be given about these legal requirements below.)

When you enter a travel agent's outlet, the number of holiday brochures on display can be quite daunting – row upon row, shelf upon shelf of them, often filling two walls of the shop. Therefore, it is hardly surprising that tour operators, hoteliers and others all attempt to produce an attractive, attention-grabbing brochure in order to ensure that potential customers choose to investigate their products and services further. Travel agents also use airline timetables (now mainly through CRS) and resort area guides to assist in communicating product knowledge to customers.

Direct marketing

We have previously looked at direct mail, telemarketing and direct response marketing communication methods. Another example of direct marketing which utilises advanced computer technology is through email – organisations use their database of 'subscribers' to deliver promotional emails, often giving hyperlinks to related web pages. The aim, as with all other marketing communication techniques,

---

Theory into practice

Visit at least *two* different travel agents in your local area. Collect holiday brochures from each outlet. Share these with the rest of the class. Compare and contrast each of the brochures in terms of the following:

* attractiveness of the front cover
* quality of the cover – glossiness versus sturdiness
* thickness of the brochure
* use of photographs and other illustrations
* size of print
* clarity of information.

Produce a checklist of the features of a successful holiday brochure in your opinion, and cut out and collate examples of good practice from the brochures you have collected.

Now use the Internet and view the website pages of a tour operator. How does this example of a piece of marketing communication match up to your checklist? Some tour operators allow you to build your own brochure through their websites, to incorporate only those destinations that interest you. A printer-friendly version of your tailor-made brochure is then emailed to you.

Some resorts will even issue their own brochure on CD-Rom. What are the advantages and disadvantages of this form of marketing communication?

is to entice the potential customer to make a purchase.

Public relations

A brief outline has already been given of the way in which PR operates in the travel and tourism industry. Here we shall look at four specific aspects of PR: press releases, media inclusions, community relations and corporate communications.

Press releases

Press releases can generate coverage of and therefore interest in a product without the organisation having to pay for it. An example of a press release published by the tourism division of Gloucester City Council is given in Figure 15.14.

GLOUCESTER.GOV.UK

Press Release

Putting some fizz into a romantic weekend break

Gloucester is offering visitors to the city the choice of six specially themed weekend packages – including a 'Luxury & Romance' package. Hatton Court Hotel's 'Champagne Getaway' is priced at £334 for two people on a two-night break. The Bear at Rodborough offers dinner, bed and breakfast for £150 per couple per night. Both packages are available throughout the year for anyone looking to celebrate a special anniversary, birthday, or to simply enjoy a romantic weekend away in a historic city.

These breaks are all featured in Gloucester's Visitor Guide produced by Gloucester City Council which can be obtained either by telephoning 01452-396572, or by e-mailing tourism@gloucester.gov.uk.

Source: Gloucester City Council

FIGURE 15.14. *Example of a press release*

Media inclusions

Many travel and tourism organisations benefit from media inclusions. A media inclusion is when the organisation gets a mention in a newspaper or magazine article, or on a radio or television programme. It is a cost-effective means of getting media attention and raising public awareness.

Community relations

Community relations refer to any instances when a travel and tourism organisation is involved with events or activities involving local community groups or charitable causes. It is a means of gaining positive recognition. A travel agency offering discount vouchers as a prize for a raffle or a newspaper competition is an example of it developing its community relations.

Corporate communications

This is probably the most important form of PR that any organisation undertakes. It is a subtle but powerful way of influencing public awareness. It entails the projection of the company's image in all print and broadcast media, through the use of logos, brand identity and so on.

Sales promotion

It is important to be able to distinguish between the sales promotions that are aimed specifically at customers and those aimed at the trade (i.e. people working within the industry as agents or intermediaries).

Sales promotion aimed at customers

Special offers, discounts and loyalty incentives are commonly used with customers. These include price reductions, free gifts or 'buy one, get one free' offers. Competitions are also used to generate sales and to increase customer recognition of the organisation. An example is the flyer shown in Figure 15.15.

Sales promotion aimed at the trade

Trade shows allow travel and tourism principals to demonstrate their products and services and to entice tour operators and tourism boards to endorse these products and services for tourism customers.

FIGURE 15.15. *Example of a competition used as a means of sales promotion*

Familiarisation trips have previously been mentioned as an incentive for those working in the travel and tourism industry. These are offered to representatives so that they can experience at first hand new destinations or facilities in order to enhance their product knowledge in sales situations. Other incentives for those employed in the industry include bonus payments, commission and trade passes, which give employees direct access to exhibitions and so on.

The media used in marketing communications

There are many different media now commonly used by the travel and tourism industry to communicate with potential customers. Some are mass media, which allow an organisation to target a widespread audience using television or billboard campaigns, whereas other formats target individual customers using interactive technology. The most commonly used types of media are listed below:

* television – national or regional campaigns (e.g. Alton Towers advertise within a set radius of two hours' travelling time) as well as satellite/digital channels (e.g. Sky Travel)

* radio – local campaigns promoting discounts

* teletext – holiday sales pages

* national press – daily and Sunday newspapers and especially the travel supplements

* local press (e.g. coaching holiday advertisements)

* consumer magazines (e.g. *Holiday Which?*)
* trade press (e.g. *Travel News, Travel Weekly*, including online versions)
* Internet – travel websites (e.g. www.expedia.co.uk)
* cinema advertising
* DVD/CD/video (e.g. regional tourist boards produce promotional videos)
* tourist board brochures and guides
* point-of-sale materials (e.g. brochures, information leaflets, merchandising at reception desks, ticket offices, etc.)
* posters (e.g. in travel agents' windows)
* displays (e.g. at trade shows).

The main decision influencing the final choice of media to use within any given promotional campaign is the funds available within the marketing budget. Media costs are high – printed advertising space is charged per page, half page or per column centimetre. Costs for printed documentation are also affected by the use of colour. Television advertisements are charged per second and are affected by the time of day to which the slot is allocated.

Organisations have to be able to justify the high expenditure of running a promotional campaign. This is usually accomplished through a 'cost per response' analysis – this is where organisations are able to monitor the response rate to a specific campaign and to calculate the cost of bookings taken to offset the costs of the outlay to media providers.

Above and below the line

'Above the line' marketing is the term used to describe the five major media:

* the press
* television
* radio
* cinema
* outdoors.

These are all 'purchased' forms of advertising media, where traditionally the advertising agency received commission payments from the media in return for generating business on the behalf of the media. Costs here are all directly related to a promotional campaign.

'Below the line' marketing relates to non-media-based advertising or promotion. It includes direct mail, point-of-purchase displays, sales promotion and sponsorship. Costs here are not generally considered as advertising costs but supplementary to the marketing budget.

The AIDA principle

Any piece of marketing communication or promotional material has to be carefully planned, designed and presented in order to maximise the effect it has on potential customers in terms of generating sales. In order to analyse how effective any promotional material is in its general aim of raising awareness, the AIDA principle is used.

Key term

AIDA is an acronym taken from the following: Attention, Interest, Desire, Action. An advertising campaign must bring the product to the *attention* of the customer, stimulate the *interest* of the target market, provoke a *desire* within the customer for the product and to whet the customers' appetite sufficiently to motivate them to take *action* towards acquiring the product.

Theory into practice

Collect as many examples of marketing communications media for travel and tourism products as you can. If possible, try to borrow a promotional video or CD from the library, collect press releases, magazine articles and advertisements. Retain examples of direct marketing, if possible, and search the Internet for promotional websites.

Choose *three* different types of media from the examples collected and apply the AIDA principle to each. Identify specific features of each piece of marketing communication that gain customers' *attention*, stimulate *interest*, provoke a *desire* and allow the customer to take *action*.

Factors contributing to effective promotional materials

There are a number of important factors to consider when planning a marketing campaign.

✳ **Costs**. Advertising is an enormous drain on an organisation's limited budget. The travel and tourism industry traditionally operates with low profit margins, so many organisations rely on PR as their main form of marketing and promotion. This often results in a high level of interest being created by journalists.

✳ **Timing**. Marketing campaigns for the peak summer season traditionally begin in January, although many organisations start in December to try to gain a competitive advantage. Customers need sufficient notice to access products as they become available, but not too much notice or the customers will lose interest before it becomes available. If the organisation gets the timing of a promotion wrong, it may not meet its marketing objectives, irrespective of how attractive the product or price of its offering is.

✳ **Appropriateness of media for target market segment**. Potential customers must actually see the advertisements or other promotional material in order for them to be effective.

✳ **Brand image**. The right tone and atmosphere are required.

Legislation

We have already mentioned the fact that the content of a holiday brochure is governed by the legal requirements placed upon an organisation to protect the consumer. General legislation relating to the content and style of advertisements also applies to the travel and tourism industry. There are a number of pieces of legislation that you should be familiar with.

Trade Descriptions Act 1968

The Trade Descriptions Act 1968 makes it an offence for a trader to make, by any means, false or misleading statements about goods or services, knowingly or recklessly. The Act carries criminal penalties and is enforced by local authorities' trading standards officers.

Most goods and services are sold with a description of some sort, and any description given in the course of business must be accurate and not misleading. Descriptions can relate to most characteristics of goods, including:

✳ age or history

✳ quantity or size

✳ fitness for purpose

✳ method and place of manufacture

✳ composition

✳ approval or recommendation.

A description of services, for the purpose of this legislation, can relate to any of the following:

✳ the nature of any services, accommodation or facilities provided

✳ the time at which, manner in which or persons by whom any services, accommodation or facilities are provided

✳ the examination, approval or evaluation by any person of any services, accommodation or facilities

✳ the location or amenities of any accommodation.

A description can be given verbally, in writing, in advertisements, by illustration or by implication.

Consumer Protection Act 1987

As its name implies, the main focus of this piece of legislation is on protecting customers, especially from the sale of faulty goods. As travel and tourism goods tend to be intangible in nature, many aspects of this law do not often apply. However, there is one important clause within this legislation that has a significant impact on the travel and tourism industry – namely, where it states that businesses may not give misleading information about prices. This includes false price reductions or overcharging.

European Directive on Package Travel, Package Holidays and Package Tours 1990

This Directive applies to all businesses that organise package tours or sell them to consumers. It sets out the responsibilities that travel businesses have to their customers, which include:

* how information is provided
* contract issues
* the handling of price changes
* cancellations
* insolvency protection.

It also covers other aspects of the package holiday business, such as advertising, brochures, contracts, surcharge limitations and compensation responsibilities.

The Directive defines a 'package' as follows:

* The holiday must cover a period of at least 24 hours, or involve overnight accommodation.
* The holiday must consist of a pre-arranged combination of at least two of the following components: transport; accommodation; other tourist services that form a significant proportion of the package (e.g. excursions, entertainment).
* The holiday must be sold at an inclusive price.

Data Protection Act 1998

This applies to businesses that keep records about their clients and suppliers. For example, a tour operator might keep a database of existing clients' details so that it can send them new marketing information as it becomes available. If the business holds information about its customers and suppliers on paper or in electronic form it must comply with rules on data protection. If the organisation processes information about its customers, then it must comply with the regulations under this Act. 'Processing information' means obtaining, recording, using, holding, retrieving, disclosing, erasing or destroying personal data. Personal data are any information on an identifiable living individual.

The main principles of the Act are:

* personal data should be obtained and processed fairly and legally
* data should be held only for a specified purpose and not be unlawfully disclosed to other companies
* data should be up to date and accurate
* personal data should be accessed only by authorised personnel via passwords and user identification.

Regulatory bodies

There are several organisations with responsibility for overseeing how marketing communications are applied and to ensure that relevant legislation is observed in the UK. These organisations monitor the marketing activities of all industries, including the travel and tourism industry.

> **Key term**
>
> A **regulator** is an official organisation with authority to control a specific area of business or industry by imposing the relevant rules, restrictions or pieces of legislation.

Office of Communications (Ofcom)

This independent regulator was established in December 2003 to take overall control for the UK communications industry. It has responsibilty for television, radio and telecommunications and has taken over control from the Broadcasting Standards Commission and the Independent Television Commission in dealing with complaints about all forms of broadcast – programmes and advertisements.

It has a comprehensive website (http://www.ofcom.org.uk) which provides detailed information about its role in regulating all forms of communication between suppliers and customers and offers a complaints service in relation to the broadcast media.

Advertising Standards Authority (ASA)

This is another independent body set up specifically to control all forms of advertising in the UK wherever it appears. The ASA maintains close links with central government, consumer associations and trade unions. It enforces legislation concerning the decency, honesty and legality of all advertisements. It produces codes of practice for broadcast and non-broadcast advertising, and guidelines to assist in the preparation of promotional materials and advertisements. It closely monitors the content of advertisements in the printed media and deals with complaints from members of the public.

Office of Fair Trading (OFT)

This organisation has direct links with the Department for Trade and Industry and is hugely influential in the enforcement of consumer protection rules in the UK. Each local authority operates a branch of the Office of Fair Trading and employs trading standards officers to investigate how markets are working and to investigate complaints of unlawful or unfair business practice.

Think it over...

A new tour operator, 'Dreams Come True', has recently set up in the luxury market, offering all-inclusive package holidays to exotic destinations. The marketing manager is collating information to include in a promotional leaflet to issue to every customer; it will include a section entitled 'Booking Information – Terms and Conditions'.

List five pieces of marketing information you think this leaflet should contain. Explain why each of these is important.

Assessment guidance

You will be examined on the purpose of marketing communications in travel and tourism. You need to be able to explain fully the purpose of different methods of marketing communications and analyse their suitability based on examples from selected case studies. You will need to evaluate the effectiveness of specific marketing communications.

Assessment guidance

A few examples are given here of questions taken from the specimen examination paper which is available online. The section also contains some sample answers to show how marks would be awarded for specific responses.

A pre-release case study on the National Museum of Photography, Film and Television is provided as part of the specimen paper. It would be useful for you to obtain a copy of the pre-release materials and the question paper to use with the following guidance materials.

Question 1 (c) (ii) Explain *three* ways in which an organisation such as the National Museum of Photography, Film and Television can reinforce its brand identity. [6 marks]

Answer: Brand identity can be reinforced by using a brand name, by having an easily recognisable logo and by using the same colour in all marketing and promotional materials.

Marks and comments: This response would score 4 out of a possible 6 marks. The

candidate has identified three appropriate ways (name, logo and colour) but offered only one explanation across all three ways (use in all marketing materials). To score maximum marks, the candidate needed to include two other explanations, such as emphasising all three elements of its name, using house style in all corporate communications or ensuring its brand is unique and easily distinguishable from its competitors.

Question 1 (d) Evaluate the external influences on the marketing environment of the National Museum of Photography, Film and Television. [12 marks]

Answer: External influences are often identified using a PEST analysis. The Museum will conduct its own research to see what political, economic, social and technological influences are impacting on the market at the time. Political influences might include the government promoting tourism activities associated with English culture, heritage and the arts. This would be a positive influence. An example of a negative economic influence might be a drop in levels of disposable income as a result of increased inflation rates. Social impacts might include local residents and tourists mixing together in the city. The introduction of IMAX cinemas is an example of a technological impact on this museum of film.

Marks and comments: This type of question uses a three-level response range of marks:

Level 1. Candidates demonstrate knowledge and understanding of external factors and may carry out very simple PEST analysis. [1–4 marks]

Level 2. Candidates analyse the external marketing environment of the Museum using PEST. [5–8 marks]

Level 3. Candidates evaluate the external influences on the marketing environment of the Museum; reference is made to other factors, such as environmental, legislative, cultural factors, etc.; evaluation is appropriate and accurately stated; comments about the external environment are in-depth and relevant, substantiated conclusions are drawn. [9–12 marks]

In this response, the candidate is able to evaluate the external influences on the marketing environment of the Museum using PEST but the evaluation is brief and does not go beyond the basic PEST categories. Level 2 = 6 marks awarded.

To score maximum marks, the candidate must incorporate a detailed analysis of the wider range of external influences on the marketing environment – i.e. cultural or legislative influences. The response would need to be analytical rather than descriptive. Specific conclusions need to be included.

Question 3 (c) With reference to a travel and tourism organisation with which you are familiar, recommend and justify how it could improve its pricing policies. You should name your chosen organisation in your answer. [9 marks]

Answer: Alton Towers is my example. Discount pricing would gain lots of customers because groups would be attracted by 10 per cent off a ticket, so would OAPs and students. Special offers could be used – people like to get something for nothing, such as free pens or an extra ride for the price of two.

Marks and comments: This is another example of a level of response question.

The marking criteria for Level 1 state:

'Candidates apply some knowledge and understanding, e.g. what pricing policy is, at the lower end; at the upper end, there is greater evidence of knowledge and understanding, e.g. the different pricing policies; may only look at the more general pricing policies, e.g. discount. [1–3 marks]'

This time, the candidate's response is very limited. It describes two of the more simple pricing policies but shows no understanding of what a pricing policy is and little evidence of a tourism organisation having been studied in depth. Level 1 = 2 marks awarded. To achieve maximum marks here, candidates need to explain a wider range of appropriate pricing policies for their chosen organisation and explore at least one policy in depth. The response should also include other factors which influence how the price is determined for specific products. There should also be at least one suggestion for improvements based on realistic pricing changes (e.g. seasonal discounts).

Knowledge check

1 Why do tourism organisations produce a marketing plan?

2 What is the purpose of a mission statement?

3 Explain why organisations use SWOT and PEST analyses.

4 Give an example of a USP for a tour operator.

5 Describe the six stages of the product life cycle model and explain why the model is useful in analysing the popularity of tourist destinations.

6   Explain how the Boston matrix and the Ansoff model can be used to assess market performance in the travel and tourism industry.

7   Explain the distribution channel for a package holiday booked through a high street travel agent.

8   Describe three pricing policies used in the travel industry.

9   Explain the difference between direct marketing and personal selling.

10 Explain what a quota sample is.

11 Give five examples of market segmentation used in the tourism industry.

12 Explain the difference between primary and secondary research.

13 Give one advantage of qualitative and one advantage of quantitative data.

14 What is the difference between 'above the line' and 'below the line' marketing?

15 Explain the role of Ofcom in dealing with a complaint against a tour operator's advertisement in breach of the Consumer Protection Act 1987.

References and further reading

Books, journals, magazines

Holloway, C. and Robinson, C. (1995) *Marketing for Tourism*, 3rd edition. Harlow: Longman.

Lumsdon, L. (1997) *Tourism Marketing*. Oxford: Thomson Learning.

Medlik, S. and Middleton, V.T.C. (1973) 'Product formulation in tourism'. *Tourism and Marketing*, Vol. 13, p. 85.

Middleton, V. (1995) *Marketing in Travel and Tourism*, 2nd edition. Oxford: Butterworth Heinemann.

Human resources in travel and tourism

This unit covers the following sections:

* Human resource management
* Human resource planning
* Recruitment and selection
* Induction, training and development
* Staff motivation
* Performance management
* Appraisal and termination of employment

Introduction

Introduction

The study of this unit is mandatory for candidates on the Double Award programme. The travel and tourism industry is one of the largest globally, employing millions of people both directly and indirectly. The World Tourism Council estimates that one in every 15 workers worldwide has links with the tourism industry. It is therefore not surprising to learn that people are the most important resource a travel and tourism organisation has, and enormous amounts of money are invested in recruiting, training and retaining staff within the industry.

The study of this unit will enable you to understand the processes involved in recruiting, training and managing employees within the travel and tourism industry. It will provide you with an opportunity to explore the complex issue of human resource planning within a tourism organisation, and to carry out a needs analysis of the kind used in the industry to ensure that the correct number of staff with the right qualifications for the job and with appropriate training are employed to achieve the organisation's objectives. You will find elements of this unit that link specifically with the content of unit 2, on customer service, which you studied in the early stages of your course. This unit also links to unit 10 (on event management).

How you will be assessed

This unit is internally assessed through your portfolio work, which will comprise four pieces of evidence in total.

* a report comparing and contrasting the management and planning of human resources within **two** travel and tourist organisations (Assessment Objective 1)

* your recommendation for a selection process and production of a needs analysis, job advertisement, job description and person specification for a job role in **one** of your chosen organisations (Assessment Objective 2)

* evidence of your participation *as a candidate* for an interview for a travel and tourism related job role, with an analysis of your performance (Assessment Objective 3)

* an evaluation of how **one** of your chosen organisations manages the training, motivation, performance and discipline of its staff, with reference to relevant legislation (Assessment objective 4)

Assessment is explained in more detail at relevant points later in this unit.

Human resource management

Definitions of human resource management

All members of staff represent not only the company they work for but also the industry as a whole. The impression they create will influence customers' perceptions of the organisation and its ability to satisfy their needs. Ensuring that staff are able to work efficiently and that they can commit fully to the objectives of the organisation is a management function. As you will have gathered from the introduction to this unit, most travel and tourism organisations consider their staff to be their most valuable asset. Human resource management is an essential business function within this predominantly service-based industry, and if done well it enables an organisation to maximise its competitive advantage.

Textbooks on the subject sometimes differentiate between *human resources* and *personnel*, but in fact the two terms are used virtually interchangeably – there are many similarities and few discernible differences. *Personnel management* implies a more bureaucratic concept of people management, often linked to staff welfare and administrative record keeping, for example holiday entitlement and employment contracts, whereas *human resource management* more closely mirrors other key management functions within an organisation, for example financial resource management, by closely

tracking the large investments associated with staff, such as salaries, training budgets and so on.

Human resource management is 'resource centred' and focuses on the planning, monitoring and control of the human resources (the staff) available within the organisation. It is concerned with the provision and deployment of human resources – in other words, making sure that sufficient staff are employed to deal with the various job roles that the organisation requires at any given time to fulfil its aims and objectives. Furthermore, human resource management centres upon the management of employee performance. This involves specialist human resource professionals as well as the specific line managers for individual members of staff.

The Chartered Institute of Personnel and Development (CIPD) defines human resource management as a 'management process to enhance individual and collective contributions to the long and short term success of the organisation'.

HUMAN RESOURCE MANAGEMENT AREA	HUMAN RESOURCE TASKS*	INDUSTRY EXAMPLES
Organisation		
Resourcing		
Employee relations		
Performance management		
Human resource development		
Reward development		

*Match the following tasks to each area of management:

* Job role and design
* Pay systems
* Career management
* Recruitment and selection
* Target setting and monitoring
* Industrial relations

TABLE 16.1. *Human resource management areas*

Organisational resources

Many medium- and large-scale businesses divide the management of resources into three distinct areas:

* physical resources (premises, capital equipment, etc.)
* financial resources (profit, loans, investments, revenue, subsidies, etc.)
* human/intellectual resources (employees and the specific skills and expertise they bring to the organisation).

Resource distribution and the inter-relationship between these three functional areas are important to the success of the business.

The resources of travel and tourism organisations are often limited; this means, for example, that office space may be cramped and that different departments therefore have to fight for workspace. Lack of finance may constrain the range and type of activities each department can carry out – for instance, the marketing department may have to run smaller promotional campaigns than were initially planned if their budget

allocation has had to decrease as a direct result of unexpected additional staffing costs.

How resources are allocated within an organisation can lead to conflict between managers in these three different areas. However, it is essential that all employees continually focus on the overall goals and objectives of the organisation, in order to be able to resolve any

FIGURE 16.1 *Harmonious working relationships are essential within the travel and tourism industry, and this is one aspect of human resources management*

such conflicts in resource allocation, without affecting the smooth running of the business.

The cost of human resources within the travel and tourism industry

Given the scale and nature of the travel and tourism industry globally, and the vast number of staff employed either directly or indirectly in providing services for travellers and tourists, it is impossible to calculate the exact cost of human resources to the industry. It is, however, a valuable exercise to consider the likely economic impact that human resources have within the travel and tourism industry, by drawing comparisons with other economic factors.

According to the World Tourism Organization, tourism generates a higher contribution of GDP (gross domestic product), jobs and investment than most other economic activities. In many developing countries and in particular in emerging tourism destinations, tourism is the principal service sector activity and source of employment for young people.

Key term

The term cost is used for the overall economic impact of a business activity within a cost–benefit analysis, in which the negative economic impacts are weighed up against the positive.

However, the hotel, catering and tourism sector pays its workers on average at least 20 per cent less than other economic sectors, as it employs a higher proportion of unskilled workers. Within the sector itself, wages and salaries are often less attractive in small enterprises, whereas larger organisations usually pay their core staff better.

Staff turnover in the travel and tourism industry is costly to employers, as they will have to find and train new staff. It is tempting to assume that there is a link between unattractive working conditions and high staff turnover but there are, in fact, a variety of reasons for staff leaving. Poor career prospects, low pay, unsocial working hours and physical stress all appear to play a part.

Think it over...

The most obvious costs to a travel and tourism organisation associated with human resources are the salaries or wages paid to employees. However, there are many more 'hidden costs'. Make a list of as many of these as you can think of.

Current theories and trends in human resources

Human resource management is a field of academic study as well as a business function. There are therefore many theories that describe how it can be done. There are many highly regarded, established models, some of which are considered below, under 'Staff motivation', but new theories and ways of working emerge all the time. Some of these may come to influence the way in which human resource staff work.

Human resource management, especially within travel and tourism organisations, faces continuous change. The contemporary issues within human resource management include:

* responding to greater competition
* managing international operations
* implementing technological innovation
* meeting the requirements of the law
* dealing with ethical issues.

Outsourcing is another example, which is dealt with under 'Contract labour', below.

Competition

Intense competition between airline companies and tour operators, for example, leads the human resource department of such organisations to look at cost-cutting exercises. This may be as extreme as cutting jobs, which will require renegotiation of remaining job roles to ensure that the organisation can still operate effectively. It may result in keeping pay levels low, but this in turn will make it more difficult to recruit and retain staff – especially if competitors are offering better rates of pay.

Cost-cutting, however, is not the only way in which travel and tourism organisations can attempt to remain competitive. They may decide instead to offer enhanced goods and services, for example. This will still involve the human resources department, as it is likely to demand high-quality customer service performance by all front-line staff. This has significant training implications for the organisation as a whole, and specifically for the human resource manager with overall responsibility for staff development.

> **Key term**
>
> **Front-line staff** are all those who come into direct contact with customers.

International operations

As many travel and tourism organisations have links with foreign destinations, global providers of products and services, and overseas customers, the need for the human resources department to be able to manage international operations is great. Any large multinational organisation needs to be able to standardise the way in which its staff work in all divisions around the world so as to be able to create and maintain its corporate culture.

> **Key term**
>
> **Corporate culture** refers to the overall identity an organisation creates through the values and beliefs that influence the behaviour of all its staff members.

Technology

Developments in the field of technology can both provide opportunities and pose problems. The human resources function is directly affected by the use of new technology, such as using email and intranet systems as an internal communication tool, creating web-based training materials, and using management information systems to conduct tasks such as human resource planning and payroll administration. Technological change often also enforces organisational change – where computer technologies take over certain tasks, former job roles and work allocations may have to change.

Legislation

The number and rigour of statutory regulations affecting the way in which employer–employee relations operate are increasing. Later within this unit you will have the opportunity to study specific aspects of employment legislation which affect the work of the human resources department. However, the following list gives you some idea of the areas in which employment law has recently changed in ways that affect the travel and tourism industry (needless to say, this list is not exhaustive):

* equality of opportunity laws, including disability discrimination laws
* working time regulations
* national minimum wage
* maternity and paternity regulations.

Ethical issues

There are some ethical issues that human resource managers have always had to face, such as a conflict between what is right for the organisation and what they feel to be right on a personal level. This could involve something as simple as withholding crucial information about a job role to potential recruits, in order to secure their services, or having to dismiss a senior manager on the grounds of misconduct, when you, as human resource manager, are not convinced of that person's guilt. However, in recent years ethical tourism and ethical business practices have come to the fore, which may involve not exploiting local workers.

> **Theory into practice**
>
> Look back over the list of current issues that affect the work of the human resource department in all business organisations. Imagine that you work in the human resource department of a national transport provider such as the Eurolines coach company. Describe how each issue might affect your work and what you could do to minimise the negative impacts these influences could have on the way staff work within the organisation.

Human resource planning

Larger organisations often have a discrete human resource planning function within their human resources department, particularly where they plan to expand their scale of operation by opening new outlets. For the majority of small travel and tourism organisations, however, human resource planning very much falls into the day-to-day job role of the line managers, in identifying how many staff they need to perform a particular function over the short term. This may in its simplest sense involve the planning of staff rotas against the available budget, to make best use of the money available in the light of customer demands.

Human resource planning is not just simply about the number of staff needed but also has to take into consideration the types of skills and experience required, as well as the types of roles staff would be expected to fulfil. This is done through needs analysis.

> ### Key term
>
> Needs analysis is a management tool used to identify the staff required by an organisation at any given time. It identifies not only the number of employees required, but also enables the human resource department to distinguish the type and skills of the employee best suited to each job role.

Needs analysis

The seasonality of travel demands – the peaks and troughs in visitor numbers to tourist attractions and destinations – makes it vital for any travel and tourism organisation to ensure that it will have the right number of suitably qualified and experienced employees in the right place at the right time. Making a formal plan of staffing needs is sometimes referred to as *human resource needs analysis*. You may also sometimes see it referred to as 'manpower planning'.

CASE STUDY
Disneyland Hong Kong

The fifth international theme park within the Disneyland brand officially opened in Lantau Island in Hong Kong in September 2005. Before it opened, the human resource function within the Disneyland Corporation carried out a detailed needs analysis to identify all the various job roles that would be created. The needs analysis also identified the specific skills and personal qualities that staff recruited to these job roles would need to have. Job roles were classified under two main headings – cast members and operations team. Cast member roles include character performers, dancers and musicians, while the operations team includes staff employed in the following areas: food and beverages, hotel, merchandise, park maintenance, and security.

* **Produce a short statement to describe the typical duties that the following types of employee would be expected to carry out within the Hong Kong theme park: character performer; hotel receptionist; merchandise seller; security guard.**

* **List the general skills that all Disneyland employees would be expected to possess.**

* **Explain how the skill levels might differ between the job roles and consider how previous experience might enhance the skill levels of individual applicants for each post.**

* **Assess the importance of specific personal qualities required for each of these job roles.**

* **Identify a range of other factors relating to each of these job roles that might have occurred as part of the needs analysis.**

The labour market

Employers offer jobs or work. Employees offer skills. Together they work for one another's benefit. Along with economic conditions and other factors, they determine the nature of the labour market.

The human resource departments of large travel and tourism organisations, or the staff member with responsibility for human resource management within smaller organisations, must keep well informed of the changes which affect the labour market, as these will affect recruitment and retention of staff within the organisation. They will therefore have an important bearing on the human resource planning function.

Many factors can affect the labour market. These can be broadly classified as *external influences* and *internal influences*.

External influences on the labour market

External influences are those that are beyond the control of the organisation. They may have an impact on the operating environment of the travel and tourism business at a local or a national level. External influences will affect all the companies within a sector or region. They include the following.

The economy

The state of the global and national economy will have a profound effect on the labour market. For example, high rates of inflation and high interest rates would mean that employees would want higher rates of pay and regular pay rises, or to be able to work longer hours (earning overtime payments), in order to increase their level of disposable income.

Employment levels

The number of economically active members of the population is generally increasing. This means there are currently more people actually in work or seeking work than has previously been the case. However, as more people are living longer, the proportion of the population in employment in the future may decrease, as there will be more retired workers. This will affect the labour market, in that employers will have to compete to recruit and retain employees from a smaller pool of available staff.

Employment trends

The types of careers available in travel and tourism change over time. Consider the declining role of travel agents given the significant growth of online reservations. Fewer people may therefore choose to train in travel agency work, which will make it difficult to recruit while agents still operate in the high street. Other trends involve the number of part-time workers compared with full-time workers within the travel and tourism industry and the availability of permanent versus temporary contracts.

Skills shortages and surpluses

We have already mentioned that a large proportion of staff employed in certain sectors of the travel and tourism industry are unskilled. However, this is not always necessarily the choice of employers. Many positions actually require a high level of technical knowledge, or practical skill, which many recruits into the industry do not possess. For example, it is generally reported that there are too few people with the high-level information and communication technology (ICT) skills required to keep abreast of technological developments within travel organisations. Employers also complain that too many school leavers lack the required level of numeracy and literacy skills with which to carry out their basic job roles. In the UK, only a small proportion of the overall population is able to speak another language fluently, and this represents another skills shortage.

Employers have to compensate for such so-called skills gaps or skills shortages either by 'recruiting harder' or by providing specific training as part of the induction programme for new recruits.

Skills surpluses can also occur, where large numbers of potential recruits possess a certain skill but one which is not sought by employers at the current time. These people are likely to face unemployment or low wages, even if they are highly qualified.

Competition for job seekers

This occurs where experienced or highly qualified staff are required to fill a particular type of vacancy in a part of the industry where employers report a skills gap. Here, competing businesses will have a small number of applicants to choose from, and will be in direct competition with one another to recruit and retain the most experienced and best-qualified staff. Competitive salaries, personalised training and development programmes and a range of other benefits will be used to appeal to prospective applicants.

Market demand

The demand for particular types of product or service can influence the labour market and hence the human resource planning of travel and tourism organisations. For example, the recent global growth in ticket sales from low-cost, 'no-frills' airlines, leading to the expansion of services of companies such as Ryanair, has necessitated a broadening of the recruitment campaign by such organisations to secure sufficient staff to operate these new services. As Ryanair and other low-cost airlines have grown, the market demand has had a big influence on the labour market.

Location issues

Most jobs in the travel and tourism industry appeal to a local labour market, largely because the pay rates and career opportunities are not so great as to attract people from outside the area in which the job is based. This has significance for the target market in recruitment campaigns, which will aim at people living within the 'travel to work area' (i.e. within a reasonable commuting distance).

Seasonality, tangibility, perishability

The labour market on which an organisation draws will be influenced by the seasonality, tangibility or perishability of the product it offers (and so these factors are closely linked with market demand). For example, visitor attractions tend to open only between March and October, although some may put on a special Christmas or New Year event, for which additional staff may have to be sought.

Current issues affecting the travel and tourism industry

Human resources staff must be fully aware of any current issues affecting the industry within which their organisation operates. At present two of the main ones are the growth of online operations and the emergence of home-based working (which we will study in greater depth further on in this unit).

CASE STUDY
Hotel labour market

The human resource department of the Best Western chain of hotels has to carry out a needs analysis for the Best Western Lodge Hotel in Richmond, situated 2.5 km from the Wimbledon tennis ground. This will involve planning staffing levels for the coming summer for this 64-bedroom hotel.

* Identify the range of external influences that may affect the labour market for this hotel.

* Explain how market demand for this product might affect the staffing levels at different times of the year.

* Assess the personal qualities and skills essential to the job role for front-line staff working in this hotel.

Internal influences on the labour market
Internal influences are those that are within the control of the organisation. Examples are shown in Figure 16.2.

FIGURE 16.2. *Examples of internal influences on the labour market for travel and tourism organisations*

The organisational structure of a travel and tourism company will affect the way in which potential employees view the business. Some are based on an obvious hierarchy, in which clear lines of management and supervision (and thus responsibility and accountability) are set out. Others arrange themselves more democratically, with fewer levels of management and with a larger proportion of the workforce sharing responsibility for the direction in which the business is heading. Potential applicants to an organisation are customarily sent detailed information about the business's structure. They may then choose whether to apply for an advertised position or not, based on the view they formulate about how the company operates.

The way an organisation responds to customer trends forms an important aspect of human resource planning. Within the context of travel and tourism, customer trends are ever changing, and this demands from staff a high degree of flexibility. High-quality communication and interpersonal skills are required, and these are often gained through intense customer services training. Consumer trends may also influence how and where products and services are made available, and this will affect how staff are deployed within the selected chain of distribution. For example,

most people nowadays visit out-of-town retail parks, and multinational travel agencies have changed their distribution channels to include holiday hypermarket outlets within their chain as a direct response to this consumer trend. These outlets operate different opening hours from a traditional high street travel agency, and staffing levels must reflect the late-night, all-week opening times.

Other internal influences on human resource planning, relating to levels of motivation, staff turnover and general absenteeism, are examined below, under the heading 'Staff motivation'.

Recruitment and selection

The changing needs of the organisation

The results from regular needs analyses will inform a company's decision to take on more staff at any given time, in response to the changing needs of the organisation. There are three main justifications for recruitment in the travel and tourism industry:

* growth of the organisation
* changing job roles within the organisation
* natural wastage.

Growth

Successful businesses grow. They gain more customers and therefore often require more staff to deal with the larger customer base. Small, local businesses may expand by opening another branch in a neighbouring town, thus gaining regional recognition. This new branch needs staffing and the most obvious way of obtaining the necessary staff is through recruitment.

Changing job roles

Competition within the travel and tourism industry is fierce, especially among the larger tour operators and travel principals. In order to remain competitive, these organisations often change the job role of employees, and ask them to take on a more diverse workload. New roles may also be created to compensate for any gaps created by the changing focus of individual roles. This then necessitates a recruitment campaign to ensure that a sufficient workforce is in place to fulfil the needs of the organisation.

Natural wastage

This term is used to describe the staff turnover that occurs as a result of resignation, retirement, internal promotion or disciplinary dismissal (as distinct from redundancy). Once employees are no longer in post as a result of such natural wastage, the organisation can decide whether or not to fill the vacancies.

Documentation used in the recruitment and selection process

Once an organisation determines that a job vacancy exists, it is usual for the human resource department to produce a range of supporting documentation to identify what the job consists of and the key attributes that the selected post holder will possess.

Job descriptions

A job description is a written document that sets out:

* the overall objectives of the job
* the main activities or duties it entails
* the span of control and reporting relationships involved (i.e. the lines of responsibility and accountability for the post holder).

The version of a job description which is sent out to potential applicants for the post also often includes information relating to the training and professional development opportunities associated with the post, together with the terms and conditions of the job, such as pay and other benefits. The purpose of the job description is to provide a framework of specific tasks and duties that the job will involve. Examples are shown in Figures 16.3 and 16.4.

TOUR GUIDE

JOB DESCRIPTION

A tour guide escorts people on sightseeing, educational or other tours and describes points of interest.

MAIN TASKS

- taking people along a route prescribed in their travel itinerary
- pointing out areas of interest and providing commentary or handing out written information
- answering questions
- arranging entry to places such as amusement parks, museums, etc.
- arranging hotel check-ins, meals and entertainment
- in some cases, acting as an interpreter.

PREFERRED PERSONAL TRAITS AND SKILLS

Tour guides should be cheerful, good at planning and excellent at solving problems. They should enjoy interacting with people and looking after their needs. A clear voice is important, as is confidence in presenting information publicly. Tour guides need to know about the culture and history of the areas they are covering. Sound knowledge of current affairs in these areas is also important. Tour guides should have a smart appearance and generally be comfortable speaking and operating in at least two different cultures/societies.

QUALIFICATIONS REQUIRED

There are no specific entry requirements for tourist guides. Some colleges offer a certificate or diploma in tourism studies but many employers will train you on the job. Generally speaking, employers will value prior experience in the travel and tourism industry or any work requiring public interaction. Experience working abroad will also be useful.

Source: www.career.edu.

FIGURE 16.3. *An example of a generic job description for a tour guide*

RESORT ADMINISTRATOR

Olympic Holidays is the leading, independent, tour operator to Greece and Cyprus. We pride ourselves on our commitment to quality, service and value. This role is mostly office based and deals with all administration relating to arriving and departing passengers by means of computer (mainly on excel/word), providing support for resort representatives and liaising between the UK and Cyprus administration teams. There will also be some representative duties such as airport transfer runs.

Administrative duties also include writing up any in-resort incidents and assuming responsibility for updating systems, ensuring that correct information is available for resort staff at all times.

Specialist administration roles include:

Customer Service Administrator – dealing with telephone enquiries from customers, co-ordinating customer service paperwork, and trouble-shooting difficult situations.

Weddings Administrator – all co-ordination and organisation of customers' weddings within resort.

Clinic and Airport Administrator – dealing with clinic cases, liaising with insurance companies and doctors, visiting hospitals, co-ordinating staff at the airport.

*Qualifications required.

Good administration skills essential with a minimum of 1 year of work experience in a busy office. Minimum age 22 on 1 April 2006. GCSE Grade C (or above) in English and Mathematics. Please note that applicants must be UK/EU passport holders or have valid work permits for the resort locations.

Source: www.traveljobsearch.com

FIGURE 16.4. *Job advertisements usually contain most of the elements of a job description, as with this example for an Olympic Holidays resort administrator*

Think it over...

Study the job descriptions shown in Figures 16.3 and 16.4 and compare the information provided. Why do you think Olympic Holidays includes an introduction to the company as part of the job description? Why do job descriptions include information about qualification requirements when this information belongs on the person specification (see below)?

A person or job specification

This is a document that stipulates the educational background, training, qualifications, experience and competencies the post holder will require in order to be able to do the job. A person or job specification is often set out as a table, or as a list of essential characteristics and a list of additional desirable qualities. An example is shown in Figure 16.5.

Key Skills, knowledge, experience and competencies essential to fulfil role:

- Relevant catering and management experience
- Ability to co-ordinate and manage large, remote teams effectively.
- Analytical & summary reporting skills at a strategic level
- Ability to produce, present and ensure delivery of varied and interesting costed menu plans
- Trained and suitably qualified Chef
- Experience in organising and running residential cookery courses to a budget
- CIEH Food Hygiene Qualifications (Advanced)
- Experience in the recruitment of chalet and hotel staff and chefs
- Experience in the set-up & running of training courses and residential cookery courses
- Very good organisational skills & self motivator
- Excellent communication and influencing skills
- Staff management skills

Desirable:

- Overseas work experience in hotels or chalets
- Charismatic character with a strong profile in order to credibly act as 'the face' of the Ski, Lakes and Active division's catering operations
- Language skills in French, Italian or German
- Knowledge of the alpine geographical area and associated logistic issues

Source: www.shgjobs.co.uk/search_results.asp?season=Winter&overseas=1.)

FIGURE 16.5. *Example of a person specification*

A person specification has two main purposes:

✳ to allow prospective applicants to ascertain whether they possess the necessary experience, qualifications and skills essential to the post

✳ to provide interviewers with a set of selection criteria.

Job advertisements

Having identified the need to recruit staff externally, the human resource department would usually then prepare a job advertisement, in order to attract applicants to the post.

The decision about where to advertise is an important one. The local press, trade magazines and the Internet are the most common places in which to advertise job vacancies within the travel and tourism industry. Sometimes employment agencies will also be notified. These forms of advertising are considered most cost-effective in attracting as many people as possible with the appropriate skills and experience for the post. Figure 16.6 shows a range of examples.

Most job advertisements include five key pieces of information:

1 **Name and brief details of the employer**. The smaller the organisation, the more important it is to include a brief synopsis of what the organisation actually does.

2 **Job and duties**. The job title will provide some indication of what the job entails but most candidates will want to know more before contemplating applying for the position.

3 **Competency profile (essential qualities)**. If certain skills, experience or training are requirements for the post, these are detailed in this section. (For example, in the travel industry fluency in a foreign language would be an advantage.)

4 **Salary details**. Many employers are reluctant to declare the actual salary for an advertised post, but many potential applicants will not consider applying for a post if they do not know the expected salary range. You often find vague phrases promising 'competitive' or 'attractive'

Activity

Collect a range of local and national newspapers and try to obtain a copy of a trade publication such as *Travel Trade Gazette* or *Travel Weekly*. Search through the recruitment advertisements for examples relating to travel and tourism. At a local level, these may include bar staff or catering assistants. Nationally, there may be a range of managerial or executive posts. Decide which advertisements are the most effective in attracting your attention and make a list of the things that captured your interest.

Take Off with Austrian

DISTRIBUTION / MARKET ANALYST

Please send your CV to:
Personnel Department,
Austrian,
DISTRIBUTION
/ MARKET ANALYST
7th Floor,
St. Vincent House,
30 Orange St, London
WC2H 7HH

Application closes
11 November 2005
No agencies.
No phone calls please.

Austrian Airlines is seeking an experienced person to fill an immediate vacancy in our Distribution Department. From our modern & central London office the successful applicant will join a highly motivated team working in a competitive market environment. Knowledge & experience of fare distribution will be essential. The role will ideally suit a highly self motivated individual with proven abilities in the following areas:

- ATPCO & FareManager
- Profitline Pricing
- Sound knowledge of fares & ticketing
- Understanding of capacity & revenue management
- Excellent analytical skills
- Complete fluency for all Microsoft office application, specifically Excel
- Can work completely independently and is self-motivated

This position offers a competitive salary package with attractive career prospects and travel benefits that a prestigious national carrier can offer. A combination of enthusiasm, flexibility and self-dependency will be your key to success.

Austrian

Friendly inbound tour operator requires an

SOVEREIGN TOURISM LTD

OPERATIONS EXECUTIVE

To join our busy group operations department handling special & general interest programmes from the US & markets worldwide. Experience in inbound operations to the UK & continent essential. Fluent English & excellent German required however other European languages are an advantage. Must enjoy client contact & be a team player with a sense of humour.

Competitive salary & attractive package for the right person

Please apply by email to :
Valda Kampf valda@sovereigntourism.co.uk
No agencies

NATURAL HISTORY MUSEUM

Naturally Inspired

HR Learning & Development Manager

Permanent full-time contract
Salary up to £40,000 p.a.

If you are interested in making a significant impact in an organisation, enjoy having a high profile and like a challenge, then this role is for you.

The NHM is establishing a small but crucial Learning & Development Team led by the Learning & Development Manager, which will design and deliver excellent training and development opportunities for people throughout the museum as well as introducing best-of-class systems.

Operating both strategically and tactically, you will have a strong leadership ability, together with impressive analytical, evaluation and relationship-building skills. Familiarity with using pyschometrics and bundles of determination would be desirable.

For further information and details of how to apply, please send an A5 SAE (1st class) to The Natural History Museum c/o Tribal Resourcing, The Atrium, Wollaton Street, Nottingham NG1 5FW or email: NHM@tribalresourcing.com

Please quote reference: NHM/LDM/SB.

Closing date: 15th June 2005.

To confirm receipt of your application call the Museum response line on 0870 241 9031 between 11am to 2pm Monday to Friday only. No telephone requests for details will be accepted.

At the Natural History Museum we value the diversity of our employees and the unique perspectives they bring to our business.

FIGURE 16.6. *Examples of job advertisements. Note the items of information presented – and those not detailed. Natural History material taken from People Management, June 2005, © Natural History Museum, London*

salary packages, to lure people to apply for a post.

5 **Details of how to apply**. This will indicate whether candidates are to telephone the human resource department for an application pack, to apply by sending in a copy of a curriculum vitae, or to complete an application online.

Theory into practice

Use your knowledge and understanding of the recruitment process to produce a job advertisement for the position of business travel consultant to present to the rest of your group. Discuss the information you have chosen to include in the advertisement. Explain where you would place the advertisement, and why.

Psychometric testing and aptitude tests

Some job advertisements provoke applications from literally hundreds of people. Therefore, the human resource department uses a range of selection processes to narrow down the search for the right candidate to fill the vacancy. Selection tests, also known as psychometric tests, are one of these processes. They fall into four different categories:

* **Ability tests**. These test your general ability at broad skills, such as numeracy. IQ tests also fall into this category.

* **Aptitude tests**. These relate to job-specific skills such as selling or managing.

* **Personality tests**. These assess your personality type.

* **Motivation questionnaires**. These assess what drives you and what your relevant attitudes are.

Psychometric tests ascertain how you think and whether you think in the same way as the organisation to which you are applying. They give an indication of what your potential for learning new skills is and predict how you might react in certain situations, such as teamwork or problem solving.

Personality and motivation tests are very different from ability and aptitude tests in that there are no right or wrong answers. They simply aim to assess what kind of person you are. The point of this is to see how well suited you are to the type of work you would be doing within the advertised post, how well you would fit into the organisational culture and how well you would gel with the team with which you would be working. They are used to identify:

* what motivates you
* your attitude to life and work
* how you relate to other people
* how you handle emotions
* how you approach problems.

These tests are rarely used in isolation but are used to supplement other selection techniques.

It is difficult to obtain actual examples of psychometric tests used specifically in the travel and tourism industry, as these are generally classed as commercially sensitive information. However, the questions shown in Figure 16.7 are of the type used in psychometric testing.

If you are familiar with any careers software, such as Kudos created by Cascaid Ltd, similar psychological testing techniques are used to select

---

Choose the answer which most closely matches how you feel in the following scenarios:

1 *I prefer working*

a at a reception desk at a large hotel ☐

b operating a machine ☐

c in a data processing centre ☐

2 *I prefer:*

a planning social activities for a family group ☐

b making accommodation arrangements for a family group ☐

c organising travel bookings for a family group ☐

3 *I prefer:*

a working in a national park ☐

b helping plan a city break holiday ☐

c guiding a group of foreign tourists ☐

FIGURE 16.7. *The types of question that you find in psychometric tests used to screen applicants for jobs within the travel and tourism industry*

the statement you can most identify with and the statement you least identify with.

Strengths and weaknesses of different selection methods

Employers use a broad range of techniques to narrow down the field of applicants for an advertised position. The process will generally begin with an initial screening of the applications – forms, curricula vitae, letters – before there is even any personal contact with the organisation, and end with an assessment of the candidates' performance at interview or within test situations.

It is rare for one selection method to be used alone. Most travel and tourism organisations use a combination of two or more selection methods, depending on the circumstances of the vacancy.

Job applications

Application forms remain a popular method of selection. An application form contains both a record of the personal details of an applicant and an evaluation of why a candidate feels drawn to make an application for the advertised post.

The chief advantage of application forms, from an employer's perspective, is that they standardise the information that applicants can provide. In addition, the fact that all prospective candidates are sent the same form will help to ensure equality of opportunity at the initial application stage. A travel and tourism organisation can tailor the type of information requested on the application form to meet its specific needs; for example, questions relating to particular experience in the provision of customer services can be included. Handwritten completed forms allow an employer the opportunity to assess the literacy skills of applicants.

Disadvantages of the use of application forms in the selection process include the fact that many prospective applicants may be put off by the prospect of handwriting their responses, if an electronic version is not made available, or by the length or presentation of the form, or by the questions asked. If so, some excellent candidates for the post may not even apply. Such an outcome is made more likely by the fact that many organisations use the same form for every vacancy, irrespective of the level of the job, as a cost-saving exercise. This means that some sections of the form may be irrelevant for some jobs. Figure 16.8 shows extracts from a five-page application form used by Qatar Airways.

Curriculum vitae (CV)

Another written document that employers may use in the selection process is an applicant's curriculum vitae, or CV. This document provides a two- or three-page overview of the standard type of information commonly found on application forms. It provides key data about qualifications, previous employment and so on.

The advantage of a CV from an employer's perspective is that the content is selected by the applicant – which provides a useful insight into the professional capacity of the applicant. However, there could be a great deal of variation in the information included, which can make it difficult to compare one candidate with another.

With the increase in computer technology, many organisations can now utilise electronic versions of CVs. This speeds up the application and selection process and allows for greater uniformity in the submission of information via a CV. CVs can be scanned and read using optical character recognition software, which can score candidates' qualifications and experience and rank their match to the job vacancy criteria, thus short-cutting the manual selection process even further.

Letters of application

Whether candidates apply by application form or by traditional CV, the expectation is that an accompanying letter of application will be sent, which can be used further in the selection process. These are usually word-processed. They will generally state where the job vacancy was seen and give a synopsis of why the applicant thinks he or she is suitable for the position.

This document provides employers with both an additional means of assessing a candidate's ability to communicate on a professional level, and more detail about the motives for applying for the position.

Personal Details

Date of Birth							Place of Birth	City	
	D	D	M	M	Y	Y		Country	

Nationality at Birth		Height	
Nationality at Present		[In Cms.]	

Do you hold Dual Nationality? ☐ Yes ☐ No

Weight	

If Yes, please specify _____

[In Kgs.]

Marital Status ☐ Single ☐ Married ☐ Divorced ☐ Separated ☐ Widowed

Gender ☐ Male ☐ Female

Religion	

Passport Number	Place of Issue	Date of Issue	Date of Expiry

Have you ever been convicted of a criminal offence?	☐ Yes ☐ No
Have you ever required medical treatment or counseling for drug or alcohol abuse?	☐ Yes ☐ No
If Yes, please give details	

Have you any pre-existing medical condition / illness?	☐ Yes ☐ No
Do you suffer from any physical defect or partial disability?	☐ Yes ☐ No
If Yes, please give details	

FIGURE 16.8. *Extracts from the Qatar Airways application form*

The quality of letters of application varies significantly between candidates. Some applicants do not include one. This provides the employer with a means of discarding some applications if the response to an advertisement has been particularly large.

Performance at interview

An individual interview is the most commonly used selection method for short-listed applicants, especially in the service industries. It will normally involve a face-to-face discussion between the applicant and an interviewer or an interview panel. It is customary to use more than one person to interview candidates, in the interests of fairness, and in order to remove the potential for interviewer bias towards or against a particular candidate.

The advantages of an interview are that:

* they allow the employer to ask probing questions linked to candidates' experiences
* they allow the candidate to find out more about the organisation and the position itself
* both parties can assess, at first hand, the likelihood of the applicant fitting in with the organisation.

The disadvantages of interviews include the following:

* they are subjective, as interviewers make assumptions about a candidate's ability to perform
* they rely on the skill of the interviewer
* they can put undue stress on both parties.

Performance in tests

Tests are often used to supplement the interview process in helping employers make a selection decision. They provide a wider perspective of a candidate's aptitude for the job. Like interviews, though, tests are useful only when they are conducted effectively. This requires competency in administering the tests. The results of the tests must be measurable and comparable.

FIGURE 16.9. *The crew of an airline need a wide range of different skills*

Skills and personal qualities associated with working in the travel and tourism industry

Because travel and tourism is a service industry and therefore very much people based, interpersonal skills are essential to most of the job roles. In addition, many job roles require excellent written and spoken English, fluency in another language and ICT competence, together with excellent customer service and sales skills. The type of personal qualities you would need to possess include a sense of humour, flexibility, good stamina, the ability to work under pressure, a smart personal appearance and an ability to communicate with a variety of people on different levels.

Think it over...

Critically evaluate the effectiveness of your own travel and tourism skills and knowledge. Identify the range of desired personal qualities for a business travel consultant and assess how well you would match the person specification for this role.

The criteria used to select the best candidate for the job

Choosing the right person for the job is not always easy. As previously stated, most travel and tourism organisations will use two or more selection methods to help inform the decision-making process. Candidates' qualifications, work experience, skill levels and personal attributes will all contribute to the overall impression they make on the selection panel.

Many organisations use a matrix to score individual candidates against each of the selection criteria. This enables the candidates to be measured against the person specification as well as against one another. The candidate who scores the highest across the breadth of selection criteria is usually the one who is offered the job.

Equal opportunities and the legal and ethical responsibilities of employers

All staff with responsibility for human resources within a travel and tourism organisation must keep up to date with the requirements of general employment legislation. In relation to recruitment and selection, the human resource department carries responsibility for ensuring the organisation's compliance with all aspects of employment law. There are five main pieces of legislation which affect recruitment practice, each of which is concerned with equality of opportunity. These are:

* the Race Relations Act 1976
* the Equal Pay Act 1970
* the Sex Discrimination Act 1975
* the Disability Discrimination Act 1995 and the associated 2004 provisions
* the Working Time Regulations 1998.

Race Relations Act 1976

There are two main areas in which this law operates: direct and indirect discrimination. Direct discrimination is where an employer treats someone unfavourably because of his or her ethnic background or nationality; an example under this law would be using the equal opportunities questionnaire section of the application form to reject candidates from other ethnic groups.

Indirect discrimination often occurs unintentionally. For example, stipulating a UK-based qualification as a condition of employment unnecessarily disadvantages candidates from other ethnic backgrounds.

Positive discrimination is allowed in advertising when recruiting someone to provide personal services to members of a particular racial community. Thus, employers are allowed to stipulate 'must be Welsh-speaker', for example.

Equal Pay Act 1970

This Act promotes equality of opportunity between men and women and tries to eliminate unfair discrimination in pay and other conditions of service. Factors such as length of service, educational background and regional allowances (e.g. a London weighting) have to be taken into consideration when comparing pay.

Sex Discrimination Act 1975

This complements the Equal Pay Act, by looking at the equality of opportunity between men and women in selection, training, promotion and so on. Some degree of positive discrimination is again allowed here by favouring women in occupational groups in which they are significantly under-represented.

Disability Discrimination Act 1995 (amended 2004)

As its name implies, this Act protects those with disabilities from discrimination. However, it remains legal to list 'good record of health' as a job requirement. The main emphasis of this law is on the ability of people with a disability to carry out the day-to-day activities of the job.

Working Time Regulations 1998

The European Working Time Directive 1993 was implemented in the UK by the Working Time Regulations 1998. These restrict the number of hours for which an employee can be contracted to work, to a maximum of 48 hours within each seven-day period, including overtime. Employers must take reasonable steps to ensure employees take adequate rest breaks and are given an appropriate annual leave entitlement.

Current developments in recruitment

Employment rights

A contract of employment must be provided to all employees and it must detail the number of hours the employee is expected to work, together with details of the annual leave entitlement. It should also include specific information about periods of notice, should either the employer or the employee wish to terminate the contract. By setting out such details in writing, both parties (i.e. the employer and the employee) have a formal record of the conditions of service, which can be referred to in the future.

Key term

A contract of employment is issued to set out the rights and responsibilities of employers and employees at the start of a period of employment.

CASE STUDY
Recruitment

There are usually strict entry requirements for airline cabin crew staff. Imagine that you work in the human resource division of an airline. You have been asked to produce the recruitment documentation for new cabin crew, which must include the following details: minimum age 20; excellent health and good eyesight; height between 1.60 m and 1.90 m; passport that can be validated for travel to all countries covered by airline's routes. In addition, the following issues are important to this company: it is not practical to employ people whose mobility is constrained; staff will need to speak clearly and have a good command of English; the company would like more male recruits as the majority of its cabin crew staff are female. Which of the following requirements should *not* appear in the job advertisement?

✳ full English passport

✳ good command of English

✳ good health and unrestricted mobility

✳ male

✳ age over 20 years.

Produce an appropriate job advertisement for the cabin crew staff.

Employees should also be given details of the organisation's disciplinary and grievance procedures. Many employers use a system of verbal and written warnings to discipline poorly performing workers. If these do not work, dismissal from the post could follow. A formal record of how these warnings and subsequent dismissal operate should be given to all staff, along with details of how to make a complaint against the employer.

In a competitive market such as the travel and tourism industry, it is unfortunately common for people to be laid off (made redundant) and even for companies to go out of business. Clear guidelines about job loss and redundancy procedures under such circumstances must be set out in writing. These should follow national guidelines to ensure equality of opportunity for all employees.

A staff handbook is often provided for employees that outlines all of these processes, together with information relating to health and safety rights and the responsibilities of the employer and employees. This is guided by the Health and Safety at Work Act 1974, which seeks to protect the health, safety and welfare of those at work and the public from risks arising from workplace activities.

The government also sets out maternity, paternity and sickness entitlements for employees, which need to be conveyed to all staff upon appointment. Statutory sick pay and maternity pay may be supplemented by an organisation's own benefits, details of which are usually given within the contract of employment.

Effective recruitment techniques

Human resource staff must ensure they keep up to date with any current developments in recruitment and selection. Examples could include the increasing use of online advertising of vacancies or text alerts on job seekers' mobile phones. By registering with the British Psychological Society, organisations can keep informed of updated psychometric tests and their interpreted results.

A flexible workforce

The travel and tourism industry is one which continually evolves. Patterns of demand change not only over the course of the year but also with the availability of the product; additionally, the market is influenced by a huge number of political, economic and social factors. In order to operate successfully within this fluctuating business environment, travel and tourism organisations must adopt a flexible approach to the workforce – this is sometimes referred to as 'flexible employee resourcing'.

> **Key term**
>
> **Flexible employee resourcing** denotes a type of staffing that enables an organisation to reduce or expand the workforce quickly and cheaply in response to market forces (rather than employing a static number of full-time permanent workers).

Figure 16.10 shows what a modern workforce is likely to comprise, and the different kinds of worker are considered below.

Core employees

These form the main body of an organisation and are sometimes referred to as the primary labour market. They tend to be employed as traditional full-time, permanent staff and their job roles are

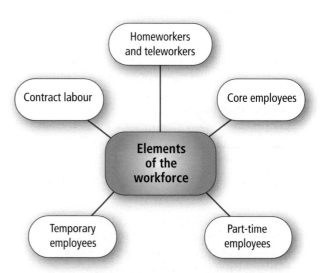

FIGURE 16.10. *An organisation operating within the travel and tourism industry is likely to draw upon all these kinds of worker*

central to the core purpose of the organisation. These employees generally have good career prospects within the industry.

Part-time employees

Part-time workers are permanent rather than temporary (see below) staff but work only for a few hours each day or for a few days each week. The travel and tourism industry is made up of a large proportion of part-time workers, mainly in the hospitality and catering sector; they are predominantly female.

Employers find that part-time workers give greater flexibility to the workforce, in covering difficult shift patterns and provide extra staffing at peak times. Part-time workers must now legally receive the same conditions of service as full-time employees, on a pro rata basis.

Temporary workers

Temporary workers are staff who are employed for a limited period of time only. A good example is seasonal labour. The employer is expected to give an indication of the likely duration of employment at the time of appointment. Many travel and tourism providers use an employment agency to provide temporary staff to cover peak seasons or special events.

Contract labour

The use of contract labour is also known as subcontracting or outsourcing. This occurs when an organisation makes a contract with another company to provide services that might otherwise be performed by in-house employees. The advantages of this include allowing core employees to concentrate on the key aspects of the business, and a reduction in employment costs. The main disadvantage is the lack of control the organisation has over the quality of the work undertaken by subcontracted staff. An example of outsourcing in the tourism industry is when a hotel uses an outside laundry firm rather than employing staff specifically to carry out laundry duties.

Homeworkers and teleworkers

Both of these terms are used to describe home-based staff who are employed as consultants, analysts or administrators. Teleworking often requires a computer at home which is networked to the main company. These forms of employment reduce company overheads as less business space is required. Many homeworkers are self-employed.

There has been a significant growth in homeworking in the travel industry as a direct result of online computer reservations. The role of the traditional high street travel agency has changed significantly, leaving a pathway for organisations such as Travel Counsellors, the UK's leading independent home-based travel agency.

Think it over...

Around 0.7 million people in the UK described themselves as homeworkers in the 2001 census. Some 0.5 million of these were women. Homeworking was most common within the service industries, including travel service provision.

Why do you think homeworking appeals to a large number of women? Evaluate the impact that homeworking has on more traditional employee resourcing methods.

Think it over...

Alton Towers belongs to the Tussaud Group, which manages a range of visitor attractions in the UK and abroad. Working with a partner, identify a range of different job roles required by a visitor attraction such as Alton Towers. Decide which job roles should be filled by core employees, which could be carried out by part-timers, which might be temporary roles and whether the organisation could use subcontracting successfully. Give reasons for all of your answers.

Managing the workforce

Managing the workforce within any given organisation is an important task. Balancing the needs of the organisation and the needs of the individuals carrying out specific job roles can be difficult. However, to be effective in managing the human resource element, human resource staff require professional and personal integrity. This means being open and honest in their dealings with prospective and actual employees. Another important quality is that of discretion; this ties in with the need for confidentiality when working in human resources. Records containing personal details of employees are held within the organisation; the contents of these records should not be divulged to other employees or external agencies.

The consequences of poor recruitment and selection processes

Recruitment and selection cost an organisation both time and money. Advertising in the trade press and local and national newspapers is expensive. Selecting an appropriate venue for the interview process may also cost the organisation money. Also, candidates who are invited from different geographical areas to attend interview are customarily offered travelling expenses. All of these are in addition to the number of staff hours spent developing the job description, the person specification and the job advertisement.

These costs are fully justified if the selected candidate performs well in post. However, if the newly appointed post holder performs badly, these high recruitment costs are unwarranted.

Induction, training and development

It is important that staff are motivated to work to the best of their ability towards achieving the organisation's goals. In order to create a working environment which best supports staff in achieving these goals, travel and tourism organisations can use a range of staff development tools. These include:

* induction training
* mentoring
* coaching
* apprenticeships (including modern apprenticeships)
* in-house and on-the-job training
* external and off-the-job training
* transferable versus non-transferable skills arising from training programmes.

Assessment guidance

Assessment Objective 2 asks you to focus on one of the two organisations you are studying in this unit.

1 Carry out some research into the type of job roles that people working for this organisation perform and conduct a needs analysis for the organisation. From the needs analysis, identify one specific job role that is essential to the business.

2 List the stages of the recruitment and selection process and explain why each is important.

3 Put together a job advertisement for this post and explain where the post will be advertised.

4 Compile an appropriate job description and a person specification for the post.

Assessment guidance

For Assessment Objective 3, your teacher will arrange for you to take part in an interview for a specified job role in travel and tourism. This should be a different organisation than the one you studied in A01. You will be provided with full details of the job (i.e. a copy of the job description and the person specification). You need to prepare for this interview by trying to anticipate some of the interview questions you may be asked and devising some questions of your own to ask the interview panel. Your teacher will organise for you to receive feedback on how well you performed during the interview. However, you should also produce a written evaluation of your performance based on self-evaluation and the feedback you received. Evidence of research is also essential.

Induction training

Induction is the process of introducing newly appointed personnel to the organisation – its systems and expectations. Its purpose is to provide new staff with an opportunity to understand the working environment, to know whom they may ask if they are unsure about what to do and to gain information about general organisational policies, including health and safety regulations. There is no set duration for induction training; some organisations have an informal approach to induction, whereas others put together a formal programme. Organisational induction may last two to three days with video and training manual inputs, but job-based induction usually lasts longer and involves the post holder's direct line manager.

Mentoring

Mentoring is an arrangement whereby one of the more senior members of staff assumes responsibility for developing the talent of a less experienced post holder. It often involves setting specific learning goals within the context of further education or vocational training. The mentor provides a role model for the mentee and mentoring can lead to career enhancement.

Key terms

Mentor is the term used to describe the person who does the mentoring of the less experienced member of staff.

Mentee and protégé are both terms used to denote the post holder on the receiving end of the mentoring process.

Coaching

Coaching is a less formal approach to individual development than mentoring. It generally involves a close relationship with a direct line manager. The manager or 'coach' encourages the trainee to perform an increasing range of tasks and to learn from these experiences. The coaching relationship is based on raising the individual's self-awareness through reflective processes. Initial coaching sessions tend to be directed by the coach but, over

CASE STUDY

Induction at Novotel

The Novotel induction programme for new staff lasts for three weeks. This is very unusual within the customer-focused hotel industry. Induction involves work shadowing, classroom-based training activities about each of the hotel's main services, role-plays and games. Since introducing this extended induction process, staff retention rates have increased by 12 per cent.

✴ **Define the term 'work shadowing'.**

✴ **Explain how new staff may benefit more from work shadowing than from actually performing their own job role in the first three weeks of their employment with Novotel.**

✴ **Suggest why lengthy induction programmes are not commonly used within the hotel industry.**

✴ **Discuss how a planned induction programme can lead to more staff remaining in post longer.**

time, the trainee will dictate the agenda and set his or her own development goals.

Coaching and mentoring both result in the employee experiencing a sense of being valued by an employer. This often leads to increased self-confidence and self-esteem, both of which may improve motivation and performance.

Apprenticeships

An apprenticeship is a means of offering vocationally specific training and a route to gaining formal qualifications in a particular career area. Apprenticeships are common in travel agency work. Employees start as junior travel consultants and receive on-the-job training from their employers, usually starting with an induction course lasting one week. They may then be sent on further specialist training courses and educational visits.

The Travel Training Programme, which provides the travel industry's apprenticeship scheme, includes work placements within the industry alongside structured training, working towards NVQ levels 2 and 3 in travel and tourism. There may also be the opportunity to gain qualifications in customer service or administration. Apprenticeships are usually available for those under the age of 24.

The benefits of apprenticeships are the focus on personal development and the achievement of recognisable qualifications in a vocationally specific area, as well as the fact that you can earn a wage while studying.

In-house and on-the-job training

This type of training is provided to meet an organisation's own specialist needs. It is often considered more cost-effective than other types of training or development. The benefits are its immediacy, as the individual works, learns and develops expertise simultaneously. The major drawbacks are that experiences can be shared only with other employees within the organisation and that the people who deliver the training may lack breadth of expertise.

External and off-the-job training

For this type of training the specialist services of training consultants are bought in by the organisation. Such training tends to have a broader scope than in-house training and may be offered to employees from a variety of organisations simultaneously. However, external training is generally expensive and so smaller organisations may find it difficult to provide it.

Transferable and non-transferable skills

Skill development is at the core of all training, and there are two categories of skill that employers seek to develop:

* **Transferable skills**. These are the non-job-specific skills that encompass the way in which an individual approaches work. They are vast in scope and include generic skills such as communication (speaking, listening, reading and writing, presentation skills, negotiation, etc.), research and planning (identifying and solving problems, setting targets, prediction, synthesis and analysis) and interpersonal skills (cooperation, delegation, leadership, conflict management).

* **Non-transferable skills**. These are job-specific and represent a staff member's vocational expertise (ticketing, silver service waiting, etc.).

Approaches to development and national recognition for training initiatives

The culture of an organisation will influence the approach it adopts to staff training and development. Its organisational objectives will also influence its staff development programmes. Travel and tourism organisations focus on the development of interpersonal skills, as they have a strong customer emphasis.

Supporting staff in their pursuit of vocational qualifications such as NVQs is common within the travel and tourism industry. Customer service training and accreditation is also important in

INVESTORS IN PEOPLE

FIGURE 16.11. *The Investors in People standard denotes that an organisation is committed to the personal and professional development of all its staff*

benchmarking organisations within a competitive market. The Investors in People standard (Figure 16.9) is a national benchmark which many organisations strive to achieve. It is recognised by customers as a mark of high quality.

Staff motivation

Much training is used as a motivational tool by travel and tourism organisations to get the best out of their staff. You will already be aware that this has benefits for the organisation as well as the individual staff member. The main purposes of motivating staff are to reduce staff turnover and to minimise staff absenteeism, both of which can cost an organisation a lot of money. Retaining good employees helps an organisation to achieve its corporate objectives.

Theories of motivation

The concept of staff motivation has been analysed in detail and there are four main theories with which you should be familiar:

* Maslow's hierarchy of needs
* Taylor's scientific management
* McGregor's theory X and theory Y
* Herzberg's two-factor theory.

Maslow's hierarchy of needs

This is the most famous motivational theory, formulated in 1954 by Maslow. It is based on a pyramid principle (see Figure 16.12).

The five stages start with the basic physiological needs of humankind – the need for food, water, oxygen, warmth and so on. Once these needs are met, the second stage leads on to a need for safety, that is, protection from danger. This then leads on to the third stage, the social need or the need for love, affection and acceptance by a social group. Beyond this, the fourth stage is that of esteem – the development of self-awareness and the need for self-esteem as well as respect from others. This leads on to the final stage – that of self-actualisation or self-fulfilment.

The pyramid shape is important in denoting how we strive for the less attainable. The need for self-fulfilment acts as the greatest motivator. Generally, the jobs people do provide opportunities for self-fulfilment and thus lead to the greatest satisfaction of needs. Employers use this theory in recognising that staff have a desire to develop their potential and so will seek more responsibility and accept challenge within their job roles.

Taylor's scientific management

Taylor is known for his 'time and motion' study, an idea from the Industrial Revolution and the desire to find the 'one best way' of achieving a task.

FIGURE 16.12. *Maslow's pyramid hierarchy of needs*

Scientific research and analysis of work processes are used. Scientific management relies on job specialisation, with clear lines of responsibility and authority, and staff are trained to do a specific job. This leads to monotony and a lack of autonomy. It also relies on the concept that incentive schemes are the greatest motivator – essentially that workers are satisfied by money alone. This theory is useful for employers wanting to examine the concept that pay is the greatest motivator.

McGregor's theory X and theory Y

These theories tie in with the development of a positive management style born out of the assumption that most employees avoid work and therefore, in order for them to complete their specified tasks, they need directing and threatening with punishment.

Theory X is an authoritarian approach to management, with staff being repressed and tightly controlled.

Theory Y does allow employees an opportunity to grow. This management style is enabling, empowering and gives direct responsibility to staff. It attains better results.

Herzberg's two-factor theory

This is sometimes known as the hygiene/motivator theory or the satisfier/dissatisfier theory. It is used to disprove the claim that money is the greatest form of motivation for a member of staff. Herzberg claims that we are not really motivated by the things we think we are – usually such things as working conditions, salary, benefits, job role status and relationships with colleagues (called the 'hygiene' factors). Instead, the greatest motivators are a sense of achievement, recognition, the work itself, responsibility and personal development. The validity of this theory was shown in the results of a survey carried out by *The Times* newspaper in 2004 – the main reasons cited by staff for job dissatisfaction were lack of promotion opportunities, the need for greater challenge and lack of variety in the work itself. Pay was not cited by many as a factor causing dissatisfaction.

Employers can again use the results of this research to encourage greater motivation on the part of their workforce, by providing employees with opportunities for career development, responsibility and greater variety of tasks, and so on.

Management styles

The theories of motivation considered above are not unique to the travel and tourism industry: they are used by many different organisations to help inform the management style used.

There are four main styles of management:

1 **Exploitive authoritative management**. The manager imposes decisions on staff, motivation is based on threats, there is little or no team spirit and communication tends to be one way.

2 **Benevolent authoritative management**. Motivation is based on a reward system but there is still limited teamwork and communication.

3 **Consultative management**. Staff are trusted and motivation is through rewards and involvement; teamwork is strong, communication is two-way. There is more widespread responsibility throughout the organisation.

4 **Participative management**. Leadership involves confidence and trust in team members, motivation is based on rewards for achievement of agreed goals, team members are fully involved in decisions, and responsibility is spread throughout the organisation.

Financial and non-financial rewards

Financial reward for meeting sales targets in the travel industry is frequently used to motivate staff. It is common knowledge that travel agents are able to earn commission from individual tour operators on the sales they make. However, less is known about other financial rewards, in the form of free or discounted travel options, company cars, profit sharing and so on. Despite the results of *The Times* survey in 2004 mentioned above, pay does remain a major motivating factor for many employees.

Non-financial rewards refer to the opportunities that staff benefit from; career development opportunities, professional/personal growth and recognition feature here. Many

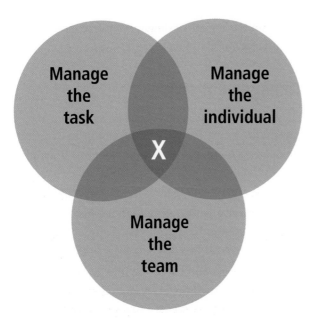

FIGURE 16.13. *The Adair model of the 'action-centred leader'*

CASE STUDY

Staff rewards and incentives

Money makes the world go round, but does it keep staff happy? Andrea Wren goes in search of the golden carrot.

It's a fact of life that the high point of most people's working month comes with the arrival of the pay packet, the little slip of paper that makes the last 30 days' grind all worthwhile.

Alex Haslam, a work psychologist at Exeter University, explains: 'If you give someone a lot of money, such as a bonus, for doing something that they actually enjoy and would do without it, they are less likely to do it in the future.'

An example of a bold staff reward system is Richard Branson's island, a very public display of generosity towards his Virgin employees. Branson bought Necker Island, off the south coast of Australia, a couple of years ago, and has invested significant sums to build an ecotourism retreat there for staff, with the added bonus that for two weeks a year it becomes a haven for the

lucky Virgin employee who wins the chance to stay there with family or friends.

Of course such schemes sound great, but do they actually help companies meet their management objectives? Only if, according to Haslam, they have been developed with staff collaboration. By involving staff in the rewards process, employers stand a better chance of offering their employees things that motivate them internally – such as commitment to their work – rather than externally – such as cash.

* **Give two examples of rewards mentioned in the above article and describe the appeal of each to employees.**

* **Evaluate the advantages and disadvantages of Branson's reward scheme for Virgin employees.**

* **Suggest an appropriate reward system for employees of a national airline company such as British Airways. Give reasons for your choice of rewards.**

Source: easyJet

companies adopt the approach of having an 'Employee of the Month' to recognise individual excellence. Some include a picture or article in the corporate newsletter. Other typical rewards are certificates, plaques, tickets for sports or cultural events, or even time off.

Job enlargement, job rotation and job enrichment

There are several techniques linked to job design that employers can adopt to encourage staff to perform their job roles more effectively. These are job enlargement, job rotation and job enrichment.

* **Job enlargement** involves combining a variety of fragmented tasks into one job, to offer the employee greater variety within work.
* **Job rotation** is where staff are moved from one task to another to reduce monotony.
* **Job enrichment** aims to maximise the interest and challenge of work by adding more autonomy and responsibility to a job role.

All three approaches have their use in developing skills and relieving monotony, but it is questionable whether they really help to motivate staff.

Think it over...

Imagine that you are in charge of staffing within the kitchen of a large restaurant. Over the past two months three of your employees have resigned, claiming that the work was too boring. You have recruited replacements and wish to avoid losing them. Explain how you would use job enrichment, job enlargement and/or job rotation to help ease the problem. Other strategies would probably also be necessary to help retain staff in the kitchen. Suggest what these might be.

Other approaches to staff motivation and retention

* **Team-based working** is often used because it is believed to improve organisational commitment and performance. This is linked to increased levels of ownership of the task among team members and a sense of commitment to team goals.
* **Multi-skilling** is a process whereby employees gain the capacity to undertake a variety of tasks by gaining a broad range of skills. This provides the organisation with a much more flexible approach and takes away the need for specialist staff. Employees benefit, as they can assume a range of different tasks, keeping the interest level in the work high.
* **'Quality circles'** comprise small groups of employees who meet regularly to generate ideas aimed at improving the quality of the product or service offered. They are also used as problem-solving groups and a way of communicating grievances to senior management. Employees generally feel more valued if they are given the opportunity to share opinions with other colleagues in this way.
* **Empowerment** occurs when organisations encourage all employees to participate in the decision-making processes of the organisation. An example of empowerment may be when a hotel receptionist can decide whether to offer a reduced room rate, or to upgrade a reservation to a superior room at no additional cost, in order to keep customers happy. The increased level of responsibility that comes from empowerment in this way may act as a motivator in the way that Maslow's theory describes.

Goal setting and management by objectives

It is claimed that motivation and employee performance are improved when staff are set specific individual goals and when feedback is given on goal achievement. Staff should be involved in setting goals and then monitored, and given advice and guidance from line managers. This process has been variously described as 'goal theory' and 'management by objectives'. It has strong links with performance management, which is covered within the next section.

In your assignment you need to consider whether these theoretical approaches to staff motivation would be appropriate in the organisations you are investigating. You also need to show you understand that some styles of management may be counterproductive.

Performance management

Within a competitive industry such as travel and tourism, it is essential that employers are able both to manage and to evaluate the performance of their staff to ensure the delivery of customer service at the highest level. There are a number of methods used by different organisations in the performance management process.

Performance reviews and appraisals

Expectations of their performance must be conveyed to employees in the travel and tourism industry, as in other fields of work. It is not enough to issue a copy of the job description upon appointment of a new staff member and to expect the individual to be able to meet all of the key accountabilities from this. There has to be a shared view of expected performance between the employee and his or her line manager. A meeting should be held during which both parties can discuss the setting of targets or objectives, with follow-up meetings for ongoing review. These review meetings work best if they are informal in nature, although a formal record of progress made and action points for the future should be made.

Appraisal formalises the review process. Line managers are required to appraise the

performance of all staff under their control, usually on an annual basis. Appraisal can be used to improve current performance, provide feedback, increase motivation, identify training needs and identify potential, as well as to solve job problems. You will learn about different methods of appraisal in greater detail within the next section.

Individual and group target setting

The principles of performance management have been defined by the Industrial Relations Service (IRS) as:

* the clarification of corporate goals

* the translation of corporate goals into individual, team, department and divisional goals

* the encouragement of self-management of individuals.

In the travel and tourism industry, target setting is important to ensure that organisations remain competitive within the market.

Self, peer and organisation evaluation

Evaluation and reflection are useful tools in monitoring performance at all levels within an organisation. Formal evaluation through appraisal is covered in more detail below, but it is worth pointing out at this stage that individual employees and groups of employees often carry out informal evaluation of performance as part of their everyday work. For example, a tour operator will regularly evaluate the volume and value of sales against targets, but not necessarily as part of the formal appraisal of an individual staff member. The results of these evaluations may, however, be carried forward into the appraisal system.

Wage and salary structures

Most large organisations within the travel and tourism industry have a grading structure in place to determine the rate of pay for each job. There will be a differential pay rate based on job evaluation: the more responsibility a post carries, the greater the rate of pay. Also used is performance-related pay, whereby salary is determined directly by the results an individual achieves against pre-set performance criteria.

Wages and salary may be affected by the number of years served. Many organisations operate an incremental system whereby for every full year served staff can progress on the pay scales by one point, until the top of the scale is reached. Each point of the pay scale has an incremental monetary value attached to it. Organisations are obliged to make staff aware of these pay scales upon appointment.

It is difficult to provide examples of pay structures from the travel and tourism industry, given the sensitive nature of this information.

Evaluation of your own knowledge, skills and experience

It would be a useful exercise to conduct a self-assessment of your current knowledge, skills and experience, in order to put together a realistic plan for developing a successful career within your field of interest. If you have access to a careers software programme such as Kudos, you will be able to audit your skills electronically. If this is not possible, you can still audit your skills by listing your strengths and areas for improvement. You could start by considering your strengths in the following areas:

* verbal communication

* written communication

* foreign language

* patience

* confidence with unfamiliar people

* ICT capability.

This list should of course be extended to match your own circumstances. An honest evaluation of your areas of weakness can also be very useful, so that these can tackled.

Appraisal and termination of employment

Different forms of appraisal

We have looked briefly at appraisal as one of the tools available in the performance management process. Appraisal is very important as it enables employers and employees to identify the training and development needs of individuals; it also supports the attainment of organisational objectives.

There are five main forms of appraisal, with which you should be familiar. We have already described performance review in the previous section. The other four are:

* supervisor appraisal
* self-appraisal
* peer appraisal
* 360-degree appraisal.

Supervisor appraisal

The direct line manager is most often instrumental in the appraisal process. He or she is the key source of feedback and assessment of individual performance. It is therefore this person who is most likely to carry out the appraisal interview. The advantage of this is that the appraisal interview then merely formalises the ongoing review process between the line manager and the employee.

Self-appraisal

Individuals can be surprisingly honest in evaluating their own strengths and areas for improvement. Travel and tourism organisations may often ask employees to carry out self-appraisal by completing a questionnaire before attending the appraisal interview. This encourages the employee to reflect on his or her own performance, and provides a useful starting point for the interview.

Peer appraisal

Colleagues may be invited by a line manager to contribute to another employee's appraisal. Other people's opinions broaden the evidence in support of the appraisal and may be useful in organisations where the line manager does not work closely with the individual. This is likely to be the case in smaller businesses, where it is more difficult to delegate the responsibility for conducting appraisal interviews.

360-degree appraisal

This is often referred to as 360-degree feedback. It denotes the whole range of sources from which feedback can be collected about the performance of any individual: line manager, peers, subordinates, senior managers, external customers and self-evaluation. A detailed picture of performance is gained in this way; another advantage is that individuals often take into account the opinions of their peers more than those of their supervisors. However, the breadth of feedback gathered makes it difficult to focus on one or two action points for future review.

> **Think it over...**
>
> Produce a list of advantages and disadvantages of each type of appraisal. Explain which method(s) you would recommend for appraising airline cabin crew.

Termination of contracts

There are a number of reasons why a contract of employment may come to an end. The most common is for the member of staff to change jobs or to gain promotion.

The travel and tourism industry is well known for the antisocial hours that employees are often expected to work and the relatively low rates of pay particular job roles attract in comparison with other industries. This goes some way in explaining why staff turnover is relatively high within the industry and why employers report problems with retention: employees may find alternative work with better hours, better pay or increased benefits. Dismissal, however, is no more common in travel and tourism than in other industries.

All employers reserve the right to terminate employment if misconduct can be proved and the necessary stages of the disciplinary policy have been adhered to. This often means that the employee has received verbal and written warnings about his or her misconduct and has been given ample opportunity to redress the situation. There is a great deal of legislation relating to unfair dismissal or constructive dismissal, and all employers must comply with this.

The travel and tourism industry often recruits staff on short-term, fixed-term or temporary contracts. Once the contract runs out, the employer is under no obligation to offer further employment to an individual. The industry therefore offers little job security to many of its employees.

Redundancy in the travel and tourism industry is, unfortunately, relatively common, given the competitive market in which many organisations operate. If an organisation cannot afford to maintain all of the job roles it has, staff are offered a redundancy package as a cost-cutting exercise.

Some staff may be forced to leave their job as a result of ill health. This occurs where the individual is incapacitated and is unlikely to return to work, even after a prolonged period of absence.

Retirement is the final reason for employment ceasing, but there is of course plenty of advanced warning of this event for both the employer and the employee. It is sometimes possible for an organisation to avoid making redundancies by offering early retirement to some of its older members of staff.

Staff turnover costs an organisation a lot of money, as we have already discussed within the section on recruitment. Therefore, many organisations invest heavily in trying to retain staff through the incentives and rewards offered.

Think it over...

Some of the reasons listed above for termination of employment can be planned for, but many cannot. Explain which ones will impact most on the work of the human resource department, and which ones can be effectively managed.

Assessment guidance

You need to conduct detailed research into human resources for one of your two chosen organisations focusing on the provision of training and the general performance management techniques used.

If you are contacting the organisation directly, please remember that much of this information is confidential, as it contributes to the way in which travel and tourism companies remain competitive. You must respect the organisation's need to withhold information from you, or the request to change some of the details.

* Evaluate the way in which training and development are managed within your chosen organisation. Provide an analysis of the advantages and disadvantages of the way in which this function operates.

* Assess the way in which members of staff are motivated by the organisation. Suggest ways of improving staff motivation using a different reward system.

* Analyse the effectiveness of the performance management systems adopted within your chosen organisation. Explain how members of staff are disciplined, if the occasion arises.

* Make recommendations for further improvement of the appraisal system(s) employed.

* Evaluate the importance of employment law, and the attitudes and values of your organisation's stakeholders in relation to human resource practice within the company.

1 Explain why travel and tourism organisations carry out human resource planning.

2 Identify two current trends in human resource management within the travel and tourism industry.

3 Define the term 'labour market'.

4 Describe the responsibilities of employers under general equal opportunities legislation.

5 What is meant by the term 'skills gap' and how can employers overcome the problems this causes?

6 State three reasons for recruitment.

7 Explain the main differences between a job description and a person specification.

8 How do most travel and tourism organisations advertise job vacancies?

9 Explain why some employers use selection tests.

10 Describe what a flexible workforce looks like.

11 Explain three motivational theories which could be used to encourage staff to achieve their potential.

12 Analyse the main reasons for job contracts to finish within the travel and tourism industry.

References and further reading

Books, journals, magazines

Reily Collins, V. (1996) *ABTA's Guide to Working in Travel*. Woking: Travel Training Company.

Reily Collins, V. (1999) *Working in Tourism*, 2nd edition. Oxford: Vacation Work Publications.

Websites

www.acas.org.uk
www.cipd-training.co.uk

Index